Second Thoughts

Second Thoughts

Second Thoughts

A Focus on Rereading

Edited by
David Galef

WAYNE STATE UNIVERSITY PRESS   **DETROIT**

Library of Congress Cataloging-in-Publication Data

Second thoughts : a focus on rereading / edited by David Galef.
    p.   cm.
   Includes bibliographical reference and index.
   ISBN 0-8143-2647-1 (pbk. : alk. paper)
   1. Reader-response criticism.   2. Literature—Appreciation.
3. Books and reading.   I. Galef, David.
PN98.R38S39   1998
801'.95—dc21   97-38386

Earlier versions of chapters 1, 3, 14, and 15 have been previously published:
David Galef's appeared as "Second Thoughts: A Prolegomenon to Re-Reading"
in *Reader* 31 (1994): 29–46; Matai Calinescu's appeared as "Orality in Literacy:
Some Historical Paradoxes of Reading" in *The Yale Journal of Criticism* 6.2
(1993): 175–90; Michael Joyce's appeared as "Nonce Upon Some Times: Rereading Hypertext Fiction" in *Modern Fiction Studies* 43.3 (Sept.–Oct. 1997): 579–97;
and Sven Birkerts's appeared in his *An Artificial Wilderness: Essays on 20th-
Century Literature* (New York: Morrow, 1987). We also wish to acknowledge the
estate of Gertrude Stein for permission to reprint work from *Bee Time Vine* and
Tender Buttons in Juliana Spahr's chapter.

Contents

Part III. Past

Part IV. Present

Part V. Musings and Beyond

Preface

A preface is by nature a bit of an oddity. It comes both before the text and at the end: though it precedes the work itself, it's usually composed after the book is completed. At one time thought indispensable to introduce a volume, it often suffers the fate of being unread, passed over in silence. Is it the same as an introduction? If the contents of the book are sufficiently self-explanatory, why does a volume require a preface? What role exactly does a preface perform?

These kinds of questions, defamiliarizing what's taken for granted, are precisely what occur during rereading. Rereading leads not just to a focus on certain kinds of detail—the shape of a man's hat, the quality of the light in the drawing room—but also to a querying of shape and purpose: why is this written in the form of a sonnet, or in this instance, as I reread my first draft of this prolegomenon, what is the proper aim and design of a preface?

To return to the matter at hand: a preface is meant to herald what's coming, which makes for what one might call prereading. On the other hand, as a subgenre of sorts, its form is already a known quantity. The stock phrases from past prefaces echo behind me: "The essays in this volume offer a wide variety of . . ." "The subject of this present volume . . ." "It is my distinct pleasure to introduce . . ." What follows is a foreshadowing or prolepsis, a brief rundown of what the reader can expect, along with some editorial pattern of chapters. This revealment enables a sort of rereading by the time the actual essays are glimpsed: the preface-reader already knows not only the outline of the contents but even the sequence of material.

Another purpose of a preface is to prepare the audience, if necessary. Wordsworth's Preface to *Lyrical Ballads,* for instance, was intended to anticipate charges and defend against them, while paving the way for an unconventional type of verse. On the other hand, those unconvinced of the importance of rereading are unlikely to pick up this volume. Writing prefaces may be preaching to the choir.

The heyday of reader-response criticism is over—in theory, if not in the classroom—and it's no longer fashionable to talk of reading per se, except to bemoan it as a dying art. Yet reading is clearly still at the heart of our education, our very lives, especially if we define reading in the broader sense, from reading a text to reading a jury: a heightened, sustained mode of perception. This is all the truer in rereading, since who can hope to take in everything the first time around? First comes the gist, later the nuances.

In any event: here is a gallimaufry of essays on rereading, from the specific to the general, from essays that discuss rereading to a few that enact it, from medieval texts to hypertext, from the repetitive nature of children's literature to the repetitive nature of postmodernism. Despite the broad spread, all the authors share a seemingly simple but in fact rather complex concern: what is gained or lost in the second reading and beyond, and how?

This book starts with a section entitled "Overviews," focusing on the idea of rereading itself. "Observations on Rereading" is my own contribution, an introduction, a map of the territory. Michael Seidel's rereading of titles comes next, suggesting the lasting importance of what's seen first. Matei Calinescu analyzes the very concept of rereading in a historically minded piece on orality, literacy, and rereading. And taking a larger cultural view, Bill Shuter argues that tradition itself is a form of rereading.

The second section, "Origins," takes the concept of rereading back to its developmental stages. Jan Susina discusses the intersection of modernism and children's literature, and Karen Odden proposes a psychoanalytically informed model to explain the rereading of popular fiction. In "Taking a Second Look," Ellen J. Esrock provides a thoughtful examination on how textual imagery is affected by rereading.

In the section simply entitled "Past," R. Barton Palmer leads off with an earlier literary tradition, finding Chaucer rereading Machaut. Peter C. Herman sees a temporal paradox in rereading the preface to *The Faerie Queene,* and David Weil Baker tackles the page/stage controversy in Shakespeare through rereading and character. The following section, "Present," incorporates three rereadings in modern literature: Elisabeth Ladenson details how gender influences rereading style in Proust, Juliana Spahr uses Gertrude Stein to show how iterative work can reread and question itself, and Gregary C. Racz provides a disquisition on the differences between modernist and postmodernist rereading.

The four final essays, in "Musings and Beyond," showcase Michael Joyce on how hypertext alters rereading, Sven Birkerts and his impressions of rereading, Alan Michael Parker on rereading poetry, and Thomas Easterling faced with rereading on a desert island. One could take numerous other angles, perhaps as many as there are rereaders. Then again, each essay here offers multiple facets, and these pieces are meant to be engaging in several senses of the term.

One other purpose of a preface is for acknowledgments. Though this may be slightly irregular, I'd like to use this space to recognize all the contributors for their help, willingness to revise, and tireless rereading.

—David Galef

Contributors

DAVID WEIL BAKER is an assistant professor of Renaissance literature at Rutgers University-Newark. His essays on Thomas More and early sixteenth-century humanism have appeared in *SEL, Studies in Philology,* and *Moreana.* His book, *Divulging Utopia: Radical Humanism in Sixteenth-Century England, 1508–96,* is forthcoming.

SVEN BIRKERTS is the author of four books of essays, most recently *The Gutenberg Elegies: The Fate of Reading in an Electronic Age.* He has edited *Tolstoy's Dictaphone: Technology and the Muse* as the first annual Graywolf Forum. He contributes regularly to the *Atlantic Monthly, Harper's,* the *New Republic,* the *New York Times Book Review,* and other publications.

MATEI CALINESCU is a professor of Comparative Literature and West European Studies at Indiana University. His publications include *Five Faces of Modernity: Modernism, Avant-Garde, Decadence, Kitsch, Postmodernism* and *Rereading.* He has also co-edited the volume *Exploring Postmodernism.*

THOMAS EASTERLING is an associate editor at the *Oxford American* and a former assistant to the director of the Freshman English program at the University of Mississippi, where he is now a doctoral candidate. His dissertation is on Robert Hass and the limits of contemporary criticism. He has also published a variety of articles covering Southern culture.

ELLEN J. ESROCK is an associate professor of literature at Rensselaer Polytechnic Institute. Her publications include *The Reader's Eye: Visual Imaging as Reader Response.* She has also translated and edited Umberto Eco's *The Aesthetics of Chaosmos: The Poetics of James Joyce.*

DAVID GALEF is an associate professor of English at the University of Mississippi. His books include *The Supporting Cast: A Study of Flat and Minor Characters, Even Monkeys Fall from Trees and Other*

Japanese Proverbs, two works for children, and the novel *Flesh.* He has also published numerous essays, reviews, short fiction, and poetry in the *New York Times, Twentieth Century Literature, Journal of Modern Literature,* the *Columbia History of the British Novel, Shenandoah,* the *Gettysburg Review,* and elsewhere.

PETER C. HERMAN is the author of *Squitter-wits and Muse-haters: Sidney, Spenser, Milton and Renaissance Antipoetic Sentiment* and the editor of *Rethinking the Henrician Era: Essays on Early Tudor Texts and Concerns.* He has published or has work forthcoming in *Texas Studies in Literature and Language, Criticism, Connotations,* and *Approaches to Teaching Shorter Elizabethan Poetry.* He teaches at San Diego State University.

MICHAEL JOYCE's hypertext fictions include the novels *afternoon* and *Twilight, A Symphony,* and shorter work including *WOE, Lucy's Sister,* and the Web fiction *Twelve Blue.* His essays on hypertext theory and pedagogy have been published as *Of Two Minds: Hypertext Pedagogy and Poetics.* He serves on the editorial boards of *Works & Days* and *Computers and Composition.* He is currently associate professor of English and director of the Center for Electronic Learning and Teaching at Vassar College.

ELISABETH LADENSON teaches French literature and gender studies at the University of Virginia. She has published essays on Proust, Colette, Joyce, and Madame de Sévigné. Her book, *Proust's Lesbianism,* is forthcoming from Cornell University Press.

KAREN ODDEN is a MacCracken Fellow at New York University, preparing a dissertation on representations of trauma in eighteenth- and nineteenth-century British novels. Previous publications include short pieces in the *New York Times* and in women's magazines. Her essay "Reading Pain and Power in *Clarissa*" is under review for an anthology on the eighteenth-century body.

R. BARTON PALMER is the Calhoun Lemon Professor of Literature at Clemson University, as well as the executive director of the South Atlantic Modern Language Association. He has published three books on film, most recently *Perspectives on Film Noir.* As a medievalist, he has been engaged with editing and translating the narrative poetry of Guillaume de Machaut, of which four volumes have already appeared.

ALAN MICHAEL PARKER'S poems have appeared in over forty magazines and anthologies, including *Grand Street,* the *New Republic,* and the *Paris Review.* He is also the author of the poetry collection *Days Like Prose,* as well as the co-editor of *The Routledge Anthology of Cross-Gendered Verse* and the North American editor for the forthcoming *Who's Who in 20th Century Poetry.* His book reviews appear regularly in the *New Yorker.* He is an assistant professor of English at Penn State Erie, The Behrend College.

GREGARY J. RACZ teaches writing and literature at Parsons School of Design and Spanish translation at Rutgers University. He has published a translation of Benito Pérez Galdós's novel *Gerona,* as well as translations of several Spanish, Peruvian, and Argentine poets. He is a frequent contributor to *Poet Lore.*

MICHAEL SEIDEL is a professor of English at Columbia University. He is author of *Epic Geography: James Joyce's* Ulysses, *Satiric Inheritance: Rabelais to Sterne, Exile and the Narrative Imagination, Robinson Crusoe: Island Myths and the Novel,* and two books on the history of baseball. He is also advisory editor for *James Joyce Studies Annual* and associate editor for the multivolume edition of *The Works of Daniel Defoe.*

BILL SHUTER is a professor of English at Eastern Michigan University, where he teaches courses in nineteenth-century British literature. His essays on Walter Pater have appeared in *PMLA, Prose Studies, Nineteenth-Century Literature,* and other journals. He also is the author of *Rereading Walter Pater.*

JULIANA SPAHR currently teaches at the University of Hawaii, Manoa. Her essay on Stein is from a manuscript on reading and twentieth-century writing. Other chapters from it have appeared in *American Literature* and *College Literature.* She also is the author of the poetry collection *Response* and co-edits the journal *Chain.*

JAN SUSINA is an associate professor of English at Illinois State University, where he teaches courses in children's and adolescent literature. He has published *Poet as Zimmer: Zimmer as Poet* and is the editor of *Logic and Tea: The Letters of Charles L. Dodgson (Lewis Carroll) to Mrs. Emily Rowell & Her Daughters Ethel and Hettie.* He has also published on Lewis Carroll, Robert Cormier, Andrew Lang, Robert McCloskey, and Christina Rossetti. He is currently the book review editor of *The Lion and the Unicorn.*

I

Overviews

1

Observations on Rereading

David Galef

One cannot step into the same river twice.
Heraclitus

In *Lectures on Literature,* Nabokov remarks, "Curiously enough, one cannot *read* a book; one can only reread it. A good reader, a major reader, an active and creative reader is a rereader. And I shall tell you why. When we read a book for the first time the very process of laboriously moving our eyes from left to right, line after line, page after page, this complicated physical work upon the book, this stands between us and artistic appreciation" (3).[1] Joyce's *Ulysses* is a famous case in point, a book for which rereading, not reading, is crucial. Over the past century, critics have devoted much attention to the act of reading, from I. A. Richards's *Practical Criticism* to Stanley Fish's *Is There a Text in This Class?,* from prescriptive methodology to interpretive communities. Curiously, almost none of the discussion has focused on what really goes on within the academy: rereading. As teachers and students, we are so involved in the study of texts that we fail to realize the fundamental peculiarity of what we do; that is, while most people simply read a document, we go over and over it, pursuing our literary analysis. Of course, rereading is necessary to catch the nuances we miss the first time. We can even define a great work of literature as one that repays continual rereading—but this only begs the question: How does our perspective change after the initial experience? What distortions emerge through repetition?

To ask this question may seem subversive, since the standard view is that rereading is an additive process, wherein we perceive more and more about a given work until we have internalized the very words. However, such continual review also dulls certain sensibilities.[2] The effects of plot, for instance, the Aristotelian cornerstone of drama, depend largely on uncertainty or the old puzzle of "What comes next?" Rereading has many joys, but suspense is not one of them. Anticipation has replaced it. Keats's sonnet "On Sitting Down to Read *King Lear* Once Again," for instance, is couched in romantic images of expectation; e.g., "once again the fierce dispute / Betwixt damnation and impassion'd clay / Must I burn through; once more humbly assay / The bitter-sweet of this Shakespearian fruit" (133).

In fact, we may argue that only after the large machinery of plot has been exposed can the reader concentrate on the subtleties of thematic motifs or image-patterns. To cite one brief example: the Bradleyan critics whom L. C. Knights famously inveighs against in "How Many Children Had Lady Macbeth?" have obviously read or seen their Shakespeare so many times that the characters have become unmoored from their surroundings. K. O. Newman's brief but acute study *Two Hundred and Fifty Times I Saw a Play* illustrates this point exactly. Inevitably, rereading has a warping effect, and, to rebut the bromide of "We gain something in every rereading," we may answer, "Yes, but what do we lose?" We can term this the gain-loss phenomenon in rereading.

Any writing likely to be reread may serve as an instance (though writing designed to be disposable presents an interesting exception, dealt with later in this essay). Take Shakespeare's sonnet 73, "That time of year thou mayst in me behold," as an example of what people reread. Crammed as the poem is with metaphysical conceits, the reader cannot attend to everything at once. What the reader notices first is probably fairly basic, if idiosyncratic: the image of the tree, the progression of the seasons, the ashy fire turned to a deathbed, or perhaps just the general mood of old age. The second time, perhaps, the reader perceives the essential paradoxes presented: the flame that has consumed itself, the love that grows stronger as the object of affection grows feebler. On rereading, the reader may begin to analyze the rhyme scheme of *abab cdcd efef g,* with such links as "fire . . . expire" and "west . . . rest."

After going through the poem enough times, the reader may fit
such rhetorical devices as personification, hypallage, and chiasmus
into a larger structural analysis. As Peter Brooks emphasizes: "To
state the matter baldly: rhyme, alliteration, assonance, meter, refrain,
all the mnemonic elements of literature and indeed most of its tropes
are in some manner repetitions that take us back in the text, that allow
the ear, the mind, to make connections, conscious or unconscious,
between different textual moments, to see past and present as related
or establishing a future that will be noticeable as some variation in the
pattern" (99). At a still later stage, the reader may relate the sonnet to
other work by Shakespeare, to a poem by Donne, or to a specific strain
of metaphysical verse. Gradually, the reader constructs an exegetical
network, as the subjects did in I. A. Richards's famous reading experiments, described in *Practical Criticism,* when presented with a
series of four unsigned poems. At some point, too, over the course of
time or through new cultural assumptions, revisionary interpretation
occurs. Rudyard Kipling's verses, for instance, represented for many
in the 1890s the might of the British empire, for those in the 1930s
the excesses of imperialism, and for more recent readers a fascination
with the alien or Other.

But even with immediate rereading comes change, at the very least
a loss of spontaneity, at the most a series of distortions that seem at
odds with the structure of the text.[3] The first losses are the surprises in
the plot. During the heyday of modernism, Virginia Woolf may have
been able to assert, "Plots don't matter" (*Woolf-Strachey Ltrs.* 19), but
as Brooks and others have shown, they are an integral element of all
literature. Many authors, such as mystery writers, deliberately inject
suspense into the structures of their novels, aware that one reading is
all they are likely to receive. In any event, suspense disappears after
the initial reading, replaced by an increase in anticipation—a trade-off
rather than an equivalency. Anyone familiar with twist-ending stories
like O. Henry's "Gifts of the Magi" or Shirley Jackson's "The Lottery"
knows how they alter on second reading.

As Wolfgang Iser notes more precisely in *The Implied Reader:*
"during the process of reading, there is an active interweaving of
anticipation and retrospection, which on a second reading may turn
into a kind of advance retrospection" (282). In essence, the entire

structure begins to appear proleptic, with interesting implications: the diachronic nature of the plot assumes a synchronicity, a conflation of events in the reader's mind. This synchronicity, as much an artistic stasis as a desired sempiternal aevum in religion, may in part account for Milton's preliminary Argument to each book in *Paradise Lost:* a plot summary that frees the reader from the suspense of unanticipated events, in a sense from chronology itself.

Modernism in its fascination with the workings of the mind applied this concept on a secular level. If memory is the key to what Joseph Frank described as the spatial form in modern literature, not a linear progression but a radial pattern linked by associations, then rereading is the best access to it. In a rereading of *Mrs. Dalloway,* for example, the very tint of the prose is colored by the foreknowledge of Septimus's death. In fact, the ending itself often pulls the work together in a way not apparent throughout the first reading. As Woolf herself remarks of Flaubert's *"Un Coeur Simple"*:

> And now the impressions begin to arrive. We accept them, but we do not use them. We lay them aside in reserve. Our attention flickers this way and that, from one to another. Still the impressions accumulate, and still, almost ignoring their individual quality, we read on, noting the pity, the irony, hastily observing certain relations and contrasts, but stressing nothing, always awaiting the final signal. Suddenly we have it. . . . A sudden intensity of phrase, something which for good reasons or for bad we feel to be emphatic, startles us into a flash of understanding. We see now why the story was written. . . . And then it is finished. All the observations which we have put aside now come out and range themselves according to the directions we have received. Some are relevant; others we can find no place for. On a second reading we are able to use our observations from the start; and they are much more precise. . . . ("Re-reading" 125)

Woolf's observations of effects are both impressionistic and exact.[4] But is the linearity of the first reading a hindrance or an aid to rhetorical effects? The point is that it is both: rereading heightens certain aspects of the text and blunts others.

One of the credos of academia is that a great work can be reread indefinitely; it seems to offer something new each time. Nonetheless, a law of diminishing returns pertains. In Iser's semantic-gap model of reading, the reader inserts him or herself in the interstices between words, phrases, and descriptions, appropriating the text or aligning it to fit his or her own mental configurations (283). On the second reading and beyond, the reader presumably accomplishes more of this alignment, made all the easier because part of the reader is now the text itself, internalized. What changes is the reader, not the invariant text. What this implies for successive rereadings is obvious: a lessening of new perceptions or change, to the point where the nth reading seems identical to the nth + 1. Anyone who has lectured on a text for the nth + 1 time is all too familiar with this state of affairs. Even a consummate rereader like Anatole Broyard confesses near the end of his life: "Anyway, how many times can you read a book—even a great book? In my own experience I have found that the fourth reading is almost always disillusioning. I don't know why this should be—it's the same book. Yet I found myself getting tired of Tietjens in 'Parade's End' and taking sides with Sylvia against him" (36). In a sense, Broyard is tiring not so much of Tietjens or of the author Ford Madox Ford, but of his usual reactions in reading *Parade's End*. Because Broyard has an inventive and polemical mind, he contrives to disagree with his earlier self in order to inject some interest into the latest rereading.

Of course, the reader may unconsciously alter over the course of a few years, by which time a rereading may again prove fruitful. As Robertson Davies remarks:

> The great sin, as I have said, is to assume that something that has been read once has been read forever. As a very simple example I mention Thackeray's *Vanity Fair*. People are expected to read it during their university years. But you are mistaken if you think you read Thackeray's book then; you read a lesser book of your own. It should be read again when you are thirty-six,

which is the age of Thackeray when he wrote it. It
should be read for a third time when you are fifty-six,
sixty-six, seventy-six, in order to see how Thackeray's
irony stands up to your own experience of life. (76)

What is true during an individual lifespan is collectively true of a
changed era of readers, providing the basis for literary hermeneutics.
On the level of criticism, as Jane Tompkins observes: "the goal of
literary criticism becomes the faithful description of the activity of
reading, an activity that is minute, complicated, strenuous, and never
the same from one reading to the next" (xvii). In fact, the degree of self-
awareness necessary to criticism makes rereading almost imperative,
requiring at the very least a circumspect first reading.

One does not have to be a reader-response critic to agree with this
model of progression and change over rereadings. Those who argue
that the burden of meaning lies entirely with the reader, as Fish does
in *Is There a Text in This Class?,* may define the act of perception as
identical to interpretation and construction, but insofar as perception
is eidetic and influenced by experience, rereading is additive, up to a
point. Those who postulate a universe of textuality, those who view all
literary works as glosses or commentaries on each other, should note
that the reread text is a nearly perfect gloss on the original, explaining,
filling in, and stressing. And if all texts contain structural cues as to
how they may be read, rereading is simpler—or more programmatic—
because the reader has already read the rulebook, so to speak. Even
critics like Terry Eagleton who postulate a Marxist determinism in the
creation (and thus re-creation or rereading) of a text must include a
model of a reader who may change ideologically over the course of
successive readings.

These effects may be seen in group responses or on the level
of the individual. A curious example of this phenomenon is in the
memorization of poetry, still practiced in many schools. This process
seems to involve three stages: first, when the reader is learning the
poem through rereading; second, when the reader knows the poem
by heart; and third, when the reader has internalized the poem to the
point of inserting other words in place of the poet's, "correcting" the
original version. This effect of rereading, almost over-reading in a

sense, may be responsible for such distortions as "Alas, poor Yorick, I knew him well" instead of "I knew him, Horatio," "The road to hell is paved with good intentions" where that road is a reconstruction, or "Play it again, Sam" with "again" silently added.

These distortions also suggest a new entry into the argument over the reader's role versus the writer's role: if the reader is the prevailing authority, can one at least be said to have overstepped that authority when altering the very words on the page? Or is this simply a natural part of even the first reading? As Newman writes about repeatedly viewing the same play: "Plays are in many ways like people one meets. After we have become well acquainted with them, we cannot remember truly, how they impressed us on the first occasion . . . the play itself—a fixed sequence of words—begins to assume an independent life and evolves and develops like an animated being, a strange mirage of the mind" (7).

Of course, views of rereading depend largely on how one views the text. Early textual models tended to emphasize the performative aspect of the material, specifically its bearing on the audience, as in the rhetoric of effects described by Aristotle's *Poetics.* Medieval and Renaissance readers concerned themselves with multiple meanings, from anagogical to allegorical, privileging the religious or moral sense. Admittedly, these two emphases were mainly tied to drama and later the Bible. For many critics, on the other hand, the standard textual model stems from the Enlightenment: a repository of data from which one can draw a variety of inferences. New Historicist, Marxist, and feminist criticism stress external contexts, whereas the deconstructive view attempts to show, as Derrida remarks, that there is nothing outside the self-contained universe of the text. But as a generation of reader-response critics have noted, reading is an experience, not merely an act of retrieval, and repetition does more than deepen experience.[5]

Applied to rereading, none of these paradigms is quite satisfactory. The additive element of rereading seems incontrovertible, but in what manner is this process accomplished? Perhaps reading is a series of grasps or gestalts, and maybe this is what Rabelais has in mind when he talks of cracking open the bone of the text to suck the substantive marrow. But what use is a gestalt on second grasp, or sucking an empty bone? Maybe reading more resembles eating per se, a view espoused by Victor Nell in his cognitive psychological study *Lost in a Book.* Amid all his scientific scales and charts, Nell includes a section entitled "Reading as Eating" (98ff.). *De gustibus non disputandum.*

Perhaps rereading is like doing a jigsaw puzzle, fitting more and more pieces together to form a complete picture. With the reader as an element in the pattern, Iser's semantic-gap model of reading applies, the rereader piecing together an ever-increasing amount of his or her psyche with the words on the page. But does one fill in more gaps on rereading, or refill differently? The reader is not in fact the same as the rereader. A model drawn from Wittgenstein's *Investigations* would show that rereading is in a sense suspect, since one cannot prove that the reader of Day One is the same as the rereader of Day Two.[6] They are, in fact, experientially different, and if one follows the logical implications of this point, one reaches an absurdity: rereading is impossible, at least in the sense of the same reader picking up the text for the second time.

In *The Reader and the Text* (4), Susan R. Suleiman and Inge Crosman revive the dramatic model as a way out of this dilemma: reading as performance, though this definition only begs the question as to what the aspects of a repeated performance are. Of course, one aspect is change. In "Writing and Rewriting Poetry" (69), Linda Jeffrey argues that repetition in both writing and recalling poetry is really a process of subtle variation, of *revision* in the etymological sense of the word. But if, as De Man has argued (9), we are all prisoners of our ideology, how do we ever alter our perspectives? David Bleich stresses this point: "if response is necessarily evaluative, deeper self-involvement brings with it more pronounced value judgments" (Tompkins 139). Yet literature can alter the reader's view, so maybe the right way to look at a piece of writing is as persuasion. One could argue that people reread only what they like and already agree with, but as a professor who has assigned Henry James's *The Wings of the Dove* to a doctoral seminar, I know this is not always true.

Perhaps the most salient example of forced rereading occurs in Evelyn Waugh's *A Handful of Dust,* in which the hapless protagonist Tony Last ends up in the African jungle rereading Dickens to old Mr. Todd for the rest of his life. Tony's discomfiture as rereader is matched only by Mr. Todd's enjoyment of the endless repetition: "The old man sat astride his hammock opposite Tony, fixing him throughout with his eyes, and following the words, soundlessly, with his lips. Often, when a new character was introduced he would say, 'Repeat the name, I have forgotten him,' or 'Yes, yes, I remember her well. She dies, poor woman' " (292–93). Given Tony's Dickensian view of the world, out of step with Britain in the 1930s, this is poetic justice of a high order.

Still, even if one is assigned to reread a work that one doesn't like, the mind's defensive strategies often rework the original appraisal. The unconscious resolution of cognitive dissonance, for instance, may cause the rereader to think the poem is good in order to avoid the position of subordinacy; i.e.: "Here I am, going over a passage I don't like, under orders from a pedagogical authority. This is not a situation pleasant to contemplate; I would rather think that I am rereading this work for my own reasons, of my own choosing. It's really not so bad, after all." In essence, individuals attempt to reconcile perceived disparities between their opinions and behavior.

Apart from external constraints, however, why do people reread texts? This is the realm of what Nell (7) terms "ludic reading," which is how most people start as readers. In *Beyond the Pleasure Principle* (18), Freud discusses the mechanism of repetition compulsion, providing an etiology based on fixation at some earlier stage of life. That is, one repeats an action to reexperience the original psychological affect. Beyond this causation, Freud claims that "repetition, the reexperiencing of something identical, is clearly in itself a source of pleasure" (36). Finally, Freud descends to the level of instinct, observing an inertia or will to return that is linked to the death drive. Repetition for Freud is thus ineluctable and not entirely explicable.

Though Freud's inferences about repetition are based on observable data, other interpretations are equally possible. On a phenomenological level, as Jacques Attali writes, "Repetition constitutes an extraordinary mutation of the relation to human production. It is a fundamental change in the relation between man and history, because it makes the stockpiling of time possible" (101). If art preserves life, rereading enables the impossible, time travel—not just an excursion to the world and era of the text, but a near repetition of the reader's experience of earlier readings. (This is not to say that rereaders as a whole reread to progress no further. Many may delight equally in continuity and change.)

One may therefore also reread for the sense of surety it provides: in a world of uncertainty, here is something that will not disappoint. If particular books are old friends, rereading allows a communion of sorts. As Nell observes: "It seems likely that rereading old favorites renders the formulaic even safer and that readers who do a great deal of rereading have especially high needs for this kind of security" (250). These preferences are particularly notable in children, who love to have their favorite books reread to them, insisting that no word be changed. In addition, one may reread to achieve a sense of mastery: to know a text well is an accomplishment that can be demonstrated, taught to others, flaunted. And since enjoyment often comes from greater appreciation, in the original sense of the word, greater discernment is intrinsically desirable. Greater discernment, as opposed to passionate engagement, also enables the reader to rise above the tyranny of the text. "It is clear that in their play children repeat everything that has made a great impression on them in real life, and that in doing so they abreact the strength of the impression and, as one might put it, make themselves master of the situation" (Freud 16–17). Regarding adult rereading, one may note Wordsworth: the child is father of the man.

As Barthes has shown in *The Pleasure of the Text,* reading—and, by extension, rereading—also has other rewards. If uncovering layers of meaning follows the text's fetishistic lure, then rereading is a kind of titillation once-removed. "I take pleasure in hearing myself tell a story *whose end I know.* I know and I don't know, I act toward myself as though I did not know . . ." (47). Barthes expands on this idea in his masterpiece of rereading, *S/Z:* "A second reading, the reading which places behind the transparency of suspense (placed on the text by the first avid and ignorant reader) the anticipated knowledge of what is to come in the story . . ." (165). Earlier in his analysis, he states: "rereading is no longer consumption, but play" (16). It provides a stimulation that the rereader has learned to count on, with anything ranging from biblical passages to pornography.

This craving may become quite intense. In *The English Common Reader: A Social History of the Mass Reading Public 1800–1900,*

Richard D. Altick reprints this confession of a Norwich clergyman's daughter who read and reread *A Merchant of Venice:* "I drank a cup of intoxication under which my brain reeled for many a year. . . . I revelled in the terrible excitement it gave rise; page after page was stereotyped upon a most retentive memory, without an effort, and during a sleepless night I feasted on the pernicious sweets thus hoarded in my brain . . ." (112–13). As in Plato's step-by-step ascension in the *Symposium,* however, what starts out as a desire for stimulation may result in genuine love for the text.

If reading influences one's personality, as it certainly can, then rereading is a less abrasive process as the text and reader become more simpatico, like a couple that has grown together. The sexual metaphor extends even to parturition: as Norman Holland notes, "all of us, as we read, use the literary work to symbolize and finally to replicate ourselves" (Tompkins 124). But not all couples are compatible, and just as all readers are not necessarily rereaders, not everyone desires to reproduce him or herself. As the character Ted exclaims in John Osborne's *Try a Little Tenderness:* "Again! I'm always amazed at people who 'go through' books again. It sounds like going through childbirth again." His wife's friend Debbie voices the standard response of the rereader: "It's great fun doing it for the second or third time. Like visiting an old friend over and over again. You both seem to change every time you visit them" (81).

But if rereading depends on the reader, it just as clearly depends on the nature of the text. To put it bluntly, not all texts repay rereading. It depends on the avowed purpose of the text: most newspapers are thrown out the day after they are read. It depends on the presumed simplicity of the text: most people do not reread the STOP sign their car is approaching. But beyond these obvious examples—and in both instances one could imagine exceptions—what are the criteria for disposable texts? In a puckish essay written for *New Library World,* "Put Down That Cornflake Packet," Mike Pearce points out that triviality is no guarantee of escaping readerly notice. On the other hand, as Valentine Cunningham observes (301), those in the 1930s who believed in poetic simplicity had somehow to justify their claim that complex poets like Auden and Herbert Read repaid a fifth reading. Cultural gatekeepers might insist that the literary value of the text determines its rereadability quotient, but this definition has two problems. First, it is teleological, since one recognizes literature as that which endures, i.e., that which can be reread. Second, it turns out to be false, as anyone knows who has seen an audience returning to *The Rocky Horror Picture Show* for the tenth time.

In the absence of any fixed rules, one may nonetheless observe some guidelines. On the simplest terms, one may reread because one has missed something the first time around. This may function as a motive even in the realm of purely ludic rereading. In this case, rereading would seem to pertain to texts of a sufficient density or ambiguity to require complex assimilation. This remark must be qualified in terms of the reader, however, since what poses an interpretational mare's nest for one reader may seem perfectly straightforward to another. Nonetheless, certain texts are arguably beyond anyone's first grasp: the Bible, *King Lear, Finnegans Wake.*

Some texts, moreover, enact rereading within themselves. Gertrude Stein's repetitive syntax, in an attempt to disrupt the linear, chronological progression of narrative, has such an effect that the reader is rereading even on first perusal. In a work such as "Patriarchal Poetry," for instance, the line "Never to be what he said" occurs four times in succession (121). The thought-provoking process of repetition here forces one to reexamine the syntax, question the meaning, and search out nuances much in the way one does when rereading. And what some see as a verbal waste is in fact an ingenious kind of conservation. As Brooks notes: "Repetition, remembering, reenactment are the ways in which we replay time, so that it may not be lost" (111). Stein's textual pattern thus accomplishes a strange effect: change through stasis.

Samuel Beckett's *The Unnamable* presents another instance of rereading's effects on first reading, though with a postmodern circularity that has become vicious, as opposed to Stein's optimistic modernism.[7] When Beckett's nameless speaker repeats "you must go on," "I can't go on," and "I'll go on," the reader traces a closed loop with no beginning and no end in a forced rereading: stasis through change. Similarly, as Italo Calvino's *If on a winter's night a traveler* passes through its seventh open-ended narrative chase, the author notes approvingly: "In short, you seem to be a Reader who Rereads"

(146). This is the kind of postmodern rereading project that John Barth pokes fun at in his brief story "Frame-Tale," with ten words meant to be cut and pasted into a Möbius strip that will forever read, "ONCE UPON A TIME THERE WAS A STORY THAT BEGAN ONCE UPON A TIME THERE WAS A STORY . . ." (1–2). In a post-structuralist world, rereading begins to resemble sheer stasis and repetition, which may be one reason that the popularity of deconstruction in the academy has begun to wane. If the humanities are to show something akin to progress in the sciences, they must focus on texts and criticism in which rereading functions by addition rather than by erasure.[8]

In fact, what the academy prescribes to reread, amid disputes over canon formation, resembles the issue of what the academy requires to be read. Peter Widdowson's *Re-reading English* from a decade and a half ago, for example, far from being any kind of an examination of rereading, is an unabashed plug for the "classics" in the English curriculum. Many scholars today tend to be, if not more eclectic than previous generations, more contemporaneous in their choice of texts, which may be taught for the first time in their classrooms. Some of the benefits are obvious, not the least of which are fresh approaches to old conundrums, formerly repressed voices speaking out, and an immediately relevant message that Spenser may be incapable of delivering. The disadvantages, apart from ruffling feathers and ignoring tradition, are less apparent, but are intimately connected with rereading. To wit, some of the texts assigned may yield little upon rereading. Their value may be polemical or based on a novel perspective, but the reader readily apprehends their message after reading the text—and then what? In classes where a teacher is fortunate if the students read even once, these texts may provoke a rousing discussion, but at more advanced levels, where does one go from there?

True, cultural overlays and dissonances invariably complicate the reading process, which may in part account for the rise of so much cultural criticism: it permits another rereading of what otherwise might be an exhausted text. Metacriticism, on the other hand, may even free one from the obligation to reread. At times, it seems as if some branches of criticism are abandoning the hermeneutic tradition in favor of disposable text, work that does not repay rereading. Or are they merely shifting the exegetical burden from the feckless comic book or cult film to the complex, rereadable society that has produced it?

Obviously, much study remains to be done, which is why this essay resembles more an introduction than a definitive analysis. The study of rereading, like rereading itself, challenges previous assumptions. Even Denis Donoghue's comfortable assertion, "Literature claims to be worth reading twice" (46), is subject to review—and, on second reading, one sees a possible hedging of bets in the verb "claims," or a question raised as to whether more than twice is too much of a good thing. And though rereading may be as basic as repetition, new technology is increasingly complicating the situation: rereading as re-viewing in film and other media, or interactive computer-and-user generated texts that are actually different each time. Will these innovations help or harm the old common reader, and what of the academy? About the only safe assertion at this point is that rereading is rethinking, and we lose this facility at our peril.

Notes

1. Though Nabokov's point about reading is well taken, rereading also involves the physical labor that he claims obstructs aesthetic appreciation. Perhaps the artistic enjoyment Nabokov is after occurs only in retrospect, like Wordsworth's pursuit of poetry: emotion recollected in tranquility.
2. As Freud notes: "If a joke is heard for a second time it produces almost no effect; a theatrical production never creates so great impression the second time as the first; indeed, it is hardly possible to persuade an adult who has very much enjoyed reading a book to re-read it immediately" (35). Borges, on the other hand, raises a contradistinctional point on the level of phenomenology: "Hume identified our habitual idea of causality with the experience of temporal succession. Thus a good film seen a second time seems even better; we tend to take repetitions for absolutes"(1136).
3. This is not the place for a full discussion of textual intentionality. Suffice it to note that W. K. Wimsatt, Jr., and Monroe C. Beardsley's "intentional fallacy" does not state that works have no intentionality, simply that the artist's intentions are irrelevant and often unavailable (3). As Roman Ingarden has written, "Works of art have a right to expect to be properly apprehended by observers who are in communion with them" (43); cf. M. H. Abrams's interpretational middle ground of

author, text, and reader in essays such as "What's the Use of Theorizing about the Arts?" or D. W. Harding's "Reader and Author." Thus, if a reader is scanning *Macbeth* solely for its imagery of blood, perhaps with an eye toward writing a paper on the subject, one can argue that this rereading is a distortion of sorts.

4. Note E. M. Forster's description of Woolf's modus operandi in reviewing: "The first time she abandoned herself to the author unreservedly. The second time she treated him severely and allowed him to get away with nothing he could not justify. After these two readings, she felt qualified to discuss the book" (8).

5. See Tompkins's "The Reader in History: The Changing Shape of Literary Response" (Tompkins 201–32) for a background of these epochal shifts.

6. The disjunction of experience is based on Wittgenstein's paradigm in *Investigations* (92–93) of a man who jots down a capital "E" every time he registers the sensation that corresponds to it—but how does he know that today's "E" means the same as yesterday's?

7. One should nonetheless keep in mind David Lodge's caveats on repetition in *Language of Fiction* (82–87): it does not have to be a conscious intent on the part of the artist, nor does it have to be consciously apprehended by the reader, nor is it a matter of statistics (i.e., the number of times the same word crops up).

8. This motive is not unique to any one school of criticism, however. As Fish notes in "Anti-Professionalism," the humanities have for years been on a level with the sciences in their pressure to come up with discoveries, even if some academics decry the practice, and rereading through new critical eyes has become a time-honored tradition. It's also worth noting that certain critical movements are best paired up with their congruent literatures. It cannot be mere historical coincidence that, despite Derrida's Platonism, deconstructionism works most satisfyingly with post-structuralist texts.

Works Cited

Abrams, M. H. "What's the Use of Theorizing about the Arts?" *In Search of Literary Theory.* Ed. Morton W. Bloomfield. Ithaca: Cornell UP, 1972. 1–54.

Altick, Richard D. *The English Common Reader: A Social History of the Mass Reading Public 1800–1900.* Chicago: U of Chicago P, 1957.

Attali, Jacques. *Noise: The Political Economy of Music.* Trans. Brian Massumi. Theory and History of Literature. Vol. 16. Minneapolis: U of Minnesota P, 1985.

Barth, John. *Lost in the Funhouse: Fiction for Print, Tape, Live Voice.* 1968. New York: Anchor-Doubleday, 1988.

Barthes, Roland. *The Pleasure of the Text.* Trans. Richard Miller. New York: Hill and Wang, 1975.

————. *S/Z.* Trans. Richard Miller. New York: Hill and Wang, 1974.

Beckett, Samuel. *The Unnamable. Three Novels.* New York: Grove, 1965. 289–414.

Borges, Jorge Luis. "Some Versions of Homer." Trans. Suzanne Jill Levine. *PMLA* 107.5 (1992): 1,136–38.

Brooks, Peter. *Reading for the Plot: Design and Intention in Narrative.* New York: Knopf, 1984.

Broyard, Anatole. "Moving Day: The Books I Left Behind." *New York Times Book Review* 18 Nov. 1989: 1, 36–37.

Calvino, Italo. *If on a winter's night a traveler.* New York: Harvest-Harcourt Brace Jovanovich, 1981.

Cunningham, Valentine. *British Writers in the Thirties.* Oxford: Oxford UP, 1988.

Davies, Robertson. "Reading and Writing." *The Tanner Lectures on Human Values.* Vol. 13. Ed. Grethe B. Peterson. Salt Lake City: U of Utah P, 1992. 59–106.

De Man, Paul. *Blindness and Insight: Essays in the Rhetoric of Contemporary Criticism.* 2nd ed. Theory and History of Literature. Vol. 7. Minneapolis: U of Minnesota P, 1983.

Donoghue, Denis. "Listening to the Saddest Story." *The Presence of Ford Madox Ford: A Memorial Volume of Essays, Poems, and Memoirs.* Ed. Sandra Stang. Philadelphia: U of Pennsylvania P, 1981. 44–54.

Fish, Stanley. "Anti-Professionalism." *New Literary History* 17.1 (1985): 89–117.

————. *Is There a Text in This Class? The Authority of Interpretive Communities.* Cambridge, MA: Harvard UP, 1980.

Forster, E. M. *Virginia Woolf.* New York: Harcourt, Brace, 1942.

Freud, Sigmund. *Beyond the Pleasure Principle. The Standard Edition of the Complete Psychological Works of Freud.* Vol. 18. Trans. and eds. James Strachey and Anna Freud. London: Hogarth Press and the Institute of Psycho-analysis, 1953–74. 1–64.

Harding, D. W. "Reader and Author." *Experience into Words.* New York: Horizon P, 1963. 163–74.

Holland, Norman. *The Dynamics of Literary Response.* New York: Oxford UP, 1968.

Ingarden, Roman. *Selected Papers in Aesthetics.* Ed. Peter J. McCormick. Washington, D.C.: Catholic U of America P, 1985.

Iser, Wolfgang. *The Act of Reading: A Theory of Aesthetic Response.* Baltimore: Johns Hopkins UP, 1978.

Jeffrey, Linda R. "Writing and Rewriting Poetry: William Wordsworth." *Creative People at Work: Twelve Cognitive Case Studies.* Eds. Doris B. Wallace and Howard E. Gruber. New York: Oxford UP, 1989. 69–89.

Keats, John. *Selected Poems and Letters.* Ed. Douglas Bush. Boston: Riverside-Houghton Mifflin, 1959.

Lodge, David. *Language of Fiction: Essays in Criticism and Verbal Analysis of the English Novel.* New York: Columbia UP, 1966.

Nabokov, Vladimir. *Lectures on Literature.* Ed. Fredson Bowers. New York: Harcourt Brace Jovanovich, 1980.

Nell, Victor. *Lost in a Book: The Psychology of Reading for Pleasure.* New Haven: Yale UP, 1988.

Newman, K. O. *Two Hundred and Fifty Times I Saw a Play, or Authors, Actors, and Audience.* Oxford: Pelagos Press, 1944.

Osborne, John. You're Not Watching Me *and* Try a Little Tenderness. London: Faber & Faber, 1978.

Pearce, Mike. "Put Down That Cornflake Packet." *New Library World* 75 (1974): 213–14.

Richards, I. A. *Practical Criticism: A Study of Literary Judgment.* London: Kegan Paul, Trench, Trubner, 1930.

Stein, Gertrude. *The Yale Gertrude Stein.* New Haven: Yale UP, 1980.

Suleiman, Susan R., and Inge Crosman, eds. *The Reader in the Text: Essays on Audience and Interpretation.* Princeton: Princeton UP, 1980.

Tompkins, Jane, ed. *Reader-Response Criticism: From Formalism to Post-Structuralism.* Baltimore: Johns Hopkins UP, 1980.

Waugh, Evelyn. *A Handful of Dust.* 1934. Boston: Little, Brown, 1988.

Widdowson, Peter, ed. *Re-reading English.* London: Methuen, 1982.

Wimsatt, W. K., Jr., and Monroe C. Beardsley. *The Verbal Icon: Studies in the Meaning of Poetry.* Kentucky: U of Kentucky P, 1954.

Wittgenstein, Ludwig. *Philosophical Investigations.* Trans. G. E. M. Anscombe. New York: Macmillan, 1953.

Woolf, Virginia. "On Re-reading Novels." Vol. 2 of *Collected Essays.* 122–30. 4 vols. New York: Harcourt, Brace & World, 1966.

———, and Lytton Strachey. *Virginia Woolf and Lytton Strachey: Letters.* Eds. Leonard Woolf and James Strachey. New York: Harcourt, Brace, 1956.

2

Running Titles

Michael Seidel

When the ambassadors from England arrive in Denmark at the end of *Hamlet,* they are eager to inform King Claudius that the English king has accomplished the mission set for him in a letter written by the Danish king: "Rosencrantz and Guildenstern are dead" (5.2.376). Of course, so is the Danish King Claudius by then, and, what is more, the original letter, altered by Hamlet aboard ship, called for Hamlet's death, not for Rosencrantz's and Guildenstern's.

In 1967 Tom Stoppard had the ingenious notion to write a play about *Hamlet* that tracks the path upon which Rosencrantz and Guildenstern meet their doom. Naturally, he titled the play *Rosencrantz and Guildenstern Are Dead.* But only by rereading *Hamlet* as it is interspersed through Stoppard's play do we come to realize how titles at once precede, predispose, dispose, and look back upon action.

Late in Stoppard's play, aboard the ship heading to England but after Hamlet has transferred to the pirate ship taking him back to Denmark, Guildenstern wonders what he and Rosencrantz can tell the English about Hamlet's disappearance. One of the players on board— Stoppard extends the action of Hamlet by assuming that the frightened traveling players stowed away after their disastrous production of *The Murder of Gonzago*—tries to calm Guildenstern: "Pirates could happen to anyone. Just deliver the letter. They'll send ambassadors from England to explain . . ." (87).

The ellipsis reproduced in this speech is intended to solace Rosencrantz and Guildenstern. In other words, not realizing that the English have been instructed by Hamlet's ruse to execute them, they will imagine the ellipsis as containing something like "Hamlet has been pirated away." Of course, that is what Stoppard has done with Shakespeare's play. It is in *Hamlet,* written 366 years before, that we first hear the line that at once fits so neatly into the ellipsis and becomes the actual title of Stoppard's play.

Here is an instance where a title, standing outside a play and literally contradicting the phrase that the characters suppose ought to serve them, names an action that determines them. Rosencrantz and Guildenstern exist for Stoppard because they are dead for Shakespeare. How they got that way is partially explained in *Hamlet;* what it means to be heading that way is the stuff and substance of *Rosencrantz and Guildenstern Are Dead.* The running title colors every action and comment in the play.

I begin with this example because my premise is that rereading is not something that occurs only after a book has been completely read. Rereading—a virtual process if not an actual one—takes place in the midst of reading all the time. Titles are merely the first instance of a phenomenon really so complex that all its intricacies can never be entirely revealed. Suffice it to say, as in *Rosencrantz and Guildenstern,* if readers do not reread the particular work they are reading while they are reading it for the first time, they are inevitably rereading or rethinking another work that they will have done well to already have read. Titles set a work within the contexts of a tradition, link it to what has been, or ought to be, assimilated by a reader even before beginning to read. This is so even for titles that appear nondescript, say, *Robinson Crusoe* or *Emma.* These markedly ordinary names tell a part of the story of post-Renaissance narrative as it shifts its focus from the higher ranks of romance and epic to the middling ranks of a professional, productive, trading, and gentry class. Readers might expect the romanticized *Oroonoko* or even *Don Quixote* (the old hidalgo's name, really, was Quejana, thus producing the same doubleness or redundancy of romance and novel that exists in the action), but to encounter a Gil Blas or Robinson Crusoe or Tom Jones or Humphry Clinker is to refocus narrative away from exotic romance material that distances action from a contemporary sense of experience, exactly what early novelists in the seventeenth and eighteenth centuries were trying to do. Ordinary names as titles become prescriptive; they modify scope, set confines, suggest the familiar, merge the narrative strategies of fiction with confessional, biographical, and autobiographical literature.

Titles may seem by their nature anticipatory, a form of advertising, but when they are reread into the design or, indeed, into the historical place of the works they name, they are also recapitulative and reflective. Titles gather material already experienced and allow reading processes to begin anew at various points inside a work, before it, or even after it. Titles are at once hypothetical and revisionary. As part of a first reading, titles are apprehensive; as part of subsequent or retroactive readings they are comprehensive.

Consider all that can be packed into a title: an invitation (Nabokov's *Invitation to a Beheading*), an epic tradition (Joyce's *Ulysses*), a local habitation and a name (Eliot's *Middlemarch,* Sinclair Lewis's *Main Street,* Dickens's *Bleak House*), a thematic partition (Austen's *Pride and Prejudice,* Dostoevsky's *Crime and Punishment*), a generic promise (Roth's *The Great American Novel*); a citation (Faulkner's *The Sound and the Fury*—a citation that by dint of its half-utterance advertises that one of the tale-tellers is an idiot), a portent (Steinbeck's *Grapes of Wrath*), a pun (Proust's *Du Côté de chez Swann*), a pun that asks a question (Beckett's *Watt*), a question that implicates the reader (Trollope's *Can You Forgive Her?*), a possessive that becomes a plural (Joyce's *Finnegans Wake*).

Titles may even tell stories beyond one text and into another. That is, one title rereads another and modifies the experience of a work that is designed to arrive as an advent, a coming attraction. Milton's title, *Paradise Lost,* for example, is a miniature or imploded version of his entire narrative poem that carries forward to its sequel, *Paradise Regained. Paradise* means enclosed garden or park and *lost* derives from Old Norse *los* (still with us in German), meaning dissolution, dispersal, a kind of relaxation. The term has a powerful specific meaning that refers to breaking the ordered ranks of an army. Milton's title allows the reader to overlap the military action of Satan's loss of the third part of heaven with Adam and Eve's loss of paradise. Someone's ranks have fallen out of order. Someone else relaxed. That Milton seems to reread his first title into his second, *Paradise Regained,* is fairly clear when the dictionary reveals that one of the meanings of the word *gain* in his second title refers to ordering the ranks of an army for direct attack. It is inescapable that the action in Milton's second poem—an embodiment of the Church militant—hinges on etymologically reversing the action of loss. The ranks that are broken in the former poem are restored to order in the latter. Gain actually is the opposite of loss. Looking up words in a dictionary is what many readers and almost all rereaders do.

Not only in fictional narration but in other forms of narration as well, titles serve as epitomes, concentrated versions of the whole whose language serves to register the thematic and figurative features of the text apprehended and, just as important, reapprehended. A famous title such as *The History of the Decline and Fall of the Roman Empire* is rich in this respect. It is not fully clear until one begins to look back upon the run of Gibbon's volumes a second or third time that the mechanism of the disintegration of the empire is built into the ordering of details from the first and that the book plays out its title in its briefest narrative moments. The themes that Gibbon collects as he chronicles the shifting values and fault lines of imperial Rome are redistributed in the minutest asides, even in the footnotes of the text, in a much more systematic way than readers might perceive upon first reading. The effect is to produce in the texture of his narrative the overlapping and often redundant threads that make up the fabric of history.

To cite but one example from the opening of Gibbon's narrative, the first sentence from the preface to the first complete edition of the history reads: "I now discharge my promise, and complete my design, of writing the History of the Decline and Fall of the Roman Empire, both in the West and the East" (1:xlv). Not only does this opening repeat the title, but it advertises the narrative's temporal and spatial scope, while employing as its first metaphor—*discharge*—a term from the nomenclature of the military, the law, and trade, all institutions heavily imbricated in the structure of the Roman Empire as Gibbon portrays it.

On first reading, the metaphor seems almost inadvertent. But on second reading, we glean through the thousands of pages we have stored in memory that for Gibbon the ethos of discipline inspired by military honor in Rome decayed at the borders of the empire to an ethic of unscrupulous trade and luxury. Decline and fall generate from policies connected to an imperial velleity, a certain relaxation, a loss of discipline that Gibbon strongly contrasts in later sections of his text to the "renown" and "valor" he sets up at the beginning. What seems a neutral description at the opening truly sets the time and place from which the title makes sense in the larger sweep of the history of imperial and Christian Rome. The metaphor of "discharge" incorporates the idea of expended energy replicated by the very writing curve of the enterprise. Discharge—of weaponry or cargo— follows the parabola of decline. As Gibbon himself puts it, tracking the moral calculus of the parabola, "war was gradually improved into an art, and degraded into a trade" (1:10).

Titles can do even more. They can refer to a program that encompasses a larger reading or rereading project. John Dryden's poem *Absalom and Achitophel* or William Faulkner's novel *Absalom, Absalom!* work this way. By virtue of a title, neither of these narratives begins at its own beginning. Instead, in both instances, a reader must grasp the story of David and his progeny already told in 2 Samuel of the Old Testament. That text is necessarily a prerequisite for the course that Dryden's and Faulkner's narratives offer. To miss this point is to thin out the texture of works that bear another story's title. In these instances, reading straight through for the first time produces a completely different experience than having read a prior work through before beginning the current one. But at what point and in what detail do the titles of these works entail a rereading of 2 Samuel? Before, during, or after a first reading of Dryden's poem or Faulkner's novel? Obviously, or onerously, the answer is before, during, and after. That is the only way to account for the programs set out by these titles, programs that, by their nature, insist on the memory of one text as a prior, ongoing, and reflective means of comprehending another. More than that, a work that bears another work's title or subject makes linear reading into contrapuntal reading.

There are even more subtle instances of a reading process in which a title becomes a syllabus of sorts. Joyce's *Ulysses* is an instance of one work becoming party to already having read another, perhaps even several others, in that Homer's Greek Odysseus appears as a latinized Ulysses first in Virgil's *Aeneid* and then in Dante's *Divine Comedy.* I will return to Joyce soon enough, but the titles of other works perform in comparable ways without even naming the work they absorb and reread. There is, for example, a way of comprehending T. S. Eliot's *The Waste Land* that identifies debris and refuse scattered through the poem as the reading list of a bright undergraduate. Or think of Henry James's *The Ambassadors*. At first, ambassadors seem to be the key and central characters who speak for their respective cultures, new and old world, America and Europe. Ambassadors refer not only to those who represent but those who negotiate, those who carry values and those who ultimately may compromise them. What James knows (indeed, what he counts on) is that readers have seen ambassadors before in the narrative tradition, most prominently in a story of the abduction of a figure from an emergent Western culture to an Eastern one, not America to Europe as in his own *The Ambassadors,* but from an emergent Greek culture to a refined Trojan one, a story in which the principal ambassadors are also the principal combatants. I am thinking, of course, of *The Iliad,* where ambassadorial missions comprise much of the poem's action. James's *The Ambassadors* is a reprise of that epic in ways perhaps less dramatic but no less substantial than Joyce's *Ulysses* is a reprise of *The Odyssey.* Clearly, James's ambassadors do not fight in open combat, but much of the action of his novel is war by another means. James plays out in his narrative an abduction—*to* Paris this time, rather than *by* Paris—in a classically updated story of cultural conflict that places entire civilizations at odds over the transferred loyalties of a key figure who has absorbed a rival set of values.

As reading challenges—that is, as tests of one's previous reading— titles can sometimes expect and demand too much. F. Scott Fitzgerald perhaps came to this realization when at first he wished to compare the roaring 1920s setting of his *The Great Gatsby* with the declining days of Rome. He suggested the title *Trimalchio of East Egg,* but Maxwell Perkins, his editor, balked. Fitzgerald wanted his own novel to evoke the wealthy and decadent parvenu host of a night-long feast depicted in a Roman satiric narrative from the first century A.D., Petronius's *Satyricon.* His point of departure and comparison would provide a reading of history that would explain his own Jay Gatsby as a figure of Western decadence.

The fruit of certain civilized orders ripen only as a prelude to their rapid decay: Trimalchio feasted in the time of the Emperor Nero, and

Petronius served as arbiter or director of entertainments. At the time of *Gatsby,* Fitzgerald had been reading Oswald Spengler's *Decline of the West,* and his original title for *Gatsby,* with its allusion to a decadent Rome, made his point dramatically, albeit in a way few of his contemporary readers would recognize unless they had the wherewithal to do a far greater amount of historical and cultural reading than first Perkins and then Fitzgerald thought likely. By choosing *The Great Gatsby* instead, Fitzgerald retained his bread and circuses theme of decadent Rome, but allowed his novel to circulate in the world of P. T. Barnum rather than that of the far too obscure Petronius Arbiter.

Another intriguing title change that entails a form of rereading or cultural absorption is the one D. H. Lawrence made for *Women in Love.* One of his rejected titles was *Dies Irae* or "day of wrath" from the requiem mass (itself absorbed from apocalyptic biblical tradition). Lawrence wanted his very modern book to represent the very end of modern things. His decision to change his title to the much more normative *Women in Love* was probably wise. Not only does it anchor his action to the here and now, but it capitalizes on the fate of women characters already introduced in an earlier novel, *The Rainbow.* For good measure, the men in the book still seem blown to the corners of the firmament and beyond (or beneath), a fit narrative fate given Lawrence's original title.

At times, titles do an entirely different sort of comprehensive work in narrative, especially fictional narrative. I have already suggested how a simple name attached to a book as a title can serve as a commentary on an evolving set of conventions within a genre. But titles can also tell other parts of the story of radical shifts in convention that mark the history of the form in which an author works. Laurence Sterne's seemingly subtle but truly crucial shift in the full title of *Tristram Shandy* from the expected *Life and Adventures* to the startling *Life and Opinions* marks a change in the narrative terrain of the novel in the eighteenth century from ostensibly objective to subjective space. And the change from presumably external narration (adventures) to internal relation (opinions) reveals Sterne's place in introducing subjectivity to the development of the genre. Of course one of Sterne's key points in *Tristram Shandy* is that those novelistic spaces once thought merely objective have been deeply subjective all the while. That is why the alteration of a traditional subtitle to *Life and Opinions* allows Sterne to alter the bearing of another word traditionally linked to fiction, "history." When lives are opinions, history always repeats itself. For Sterne, what goes on in his fiction "is a history.—A history! of who? what? where? when? Don't hurry yourself—It is a history-book, Sir, (which may possibly recommend it to the world) of what passes in a man's own mind" (70).

When Sterne titles his next book *Sentimental Journey,* he continues to challenge and alter novelistic convention. His book's place in the history of the form to which it contributes can only be understood as a function of its title. *Sentimental Journey* revises the traditional on-the-road narrative or picaresque so that the text might travel the much more complex byways of emotional life. Sterne's is a journey, as he points out to his reader, "a journey of the heart." At the same time, Sterne is very much aware that emotion has its insidious and comical aspects, and part of the interest of *Sentimental Journey* is that emotional journeys, very much like the newer forms of fiction in which Sterne represents them, sometimes go in all directions at once. His unique and quirky prose represents the movement of sentiment and its bathos.

Sterne's title is so rich that it has served the fictional tradition from its origins in picaresque travel to its full evolution as *bildungsroman* (development or education novel). Gustave Flaubert rereads some of the dimensions of Sterne's title into what he thought his best book about nineteenth-century sensibility, *L'Education sentimentale.* For Flaubert there is no education unless it assimilates emotional life (and all its ironic components) into the material and historical life of the age.

Within individual narratives—that is, considered apart from the tradition in which they might exist—titles serve the reader at different moments in different ways. It is not rereading so much as corrective reading, revisionary reading when the ramifications of titles do not become apparent until the middle or the end of a book, or when they keep accruing meaning as the book progresses. Again, rejected titles are often better indicators of this process than chosen ones. Jane Austen changed to the title *Pride and Prejudice* from *First Impressions,* though the reader learns in the course of the narrative that first impressions are exactly what foster pride and prejudice. Yet another rejected title, *The Saddest Story,* for what would become Ford Madox Ford's *Good Soldier,* provides one of the best commentaries on the revisionary processes involved in reading. There are two stories told in the book, the one the narrator thinks is happening and the even sadder one that actually happens. Upon rereading or reapprehension, the saddest story of all becomes the deception of the novel's narrator. The title finally chosen by Ford, *The Good Soldier,* gets at the same issue from another perspective. The soldier is good; the person is not. Or, in a more nuanced sense, behavior is well mannered, but the moral core of a person is not easily described by such categoric adjectives as "good," and that is what the reader and, sadly, the narrator learn ex post facto from the title.

The titles of many Dickens novels are wonderfully revisionary in this sense. They seem part of Dickens's effort to tease or coax a reader into reconsidering the substance of a changing or deepening narrative. To what, after all, does *Great Expectations* refer? Or who and what is *Our Mutual Friend*? The redundancy of "our" and "mutual" helps to set what are the intricate and formally elaborated sets of relationships that govern friendship in the novel and that allow friendship, variously construed, to govern plot. "Our mutual friend," a kind of conversational place holder in the best of circumstances, hints at the barely apprehended network of connections that determines the action of the narrative. A first reader hardly pays attention to the title—it does not seem to signify much. But upon rereading, the removed and almost casual quality of the cliché marks the degrees of connectivity and separation that plot out the book's action.

Another title whose richness grows upon multiple readings is the one Marcel Proust chose for his chronicle of *fin de siècle* and early *belle époque* France, *In Search of Lost Time* (*À la recherche du temps perdu*). A witty colleague once read the title as a report on doomed weather. A student of the French tradition notes that Proust has absorbed two Balzac novels, *Illusions perdus* and *La recherche de l'absolu.* A comparatist or a translator recalls the Shakespearean sonnet on "remembrance of things past." A reader (more assiduously, a rereader) discovers that the full implications of the title cannot be gleaned until the final magnificent pages of the book in which the narrator does not so much search for lost time as have lost time find him. The hint of the action of the whole is provided by the narrative's first word in French, *longtemps,* which picks up the title word, though it has no real equivalent in English. In context, the word means "for a long while," but within the complex arrangement of the novel it means all that time means for Proust: duration, anticipation, time filled, time wasted, time remembered, time forgotten. *Longtemps* represents the experience of the novel, the experiences in it and the experience of reading it—all that is recollected, collated, discovered, lost, reexperienced, and, one could even say finally, reread.

There are occasions—only discoverable through rereading— when a title not only performs part of the symbolic work of a novel but also, in curious ways, adds to the interpretational problems at hand. Vladimir Nabokov's *Pale Fire* is a title of this sort. As first readers we know a number of things about the title, but the key thing to know is not easily available to us unless we know what to reread in order to find out. And Nabokov does all he can to make that difficult.

Nominally, the name on Nabokov's book cover refers to a poem by an American poet, John Shade, that has been published and annotated by the novel's narrator—an academic émigré, supposedly an exiled king from a place called Zembla. During the composition of the poem, John Shade, a seeker of titles, asks Shakespeare rhetorically to help him find one for his poem, "Help me Will! *Pale Fire*" (68). What we do not know—unless we immediately begin to scurry for a Shakespearean word index—is that the phrase "pale fire" comes from a passage in *Timon of Athens* about the moon stealing the light of the sun. But we do learn from the notes that Shade's annotator has (or imagines he has) an uncle named Conmal who translates Shakespeare into Zemblan. We also know that the only work the narrator has at his disposal is Conmal's version of *Timon of Athens,* and indeed we get a passage from that play translated back into English from the supposed Zemblan that should contain the reference to pale fire. Conmal, unfortunately, is the kind of portmanteau word that, broken down into Latin derivatives, means one who knows badly. Hence his translation job is so badly botched that the phrase "pale fire" does not appear in the passage that ought to contain it when the narrator retransliterates it.

The problem posed by the missing source of the book's and the poem's title gets to the core of Nabokov's narrative. Does the annotator not know the source of the poem's title because he is Zemblan or because, much better for the passage, he represents what the passage implies? Does he, like moon to sun, steal the substance of Shade's poem for his own subjective annotations? Nabokov's novel is all about the reflected light imaged in its title. The way Nabokov works with the title indicates how he wishes the book reconstructed by its readers, possibly against the grain of the way its protagonist would wish it constructed for himself, and even counter to the faith a first-time reader might be expected to place in the form of annotated commentary.

The annotator's story in *Pale Fire* is a kind of ghost image. Ironically, the very distortion of the mechanism by which we might derive the source of Shade's title is similar to the distortion of the mechanism by which the annotator produces *his* reality from Shade's poem. Reflection is part art, part psychosis, and part theft. The word *reflection* means that which is mirrored and that which is reflected upon and quite probably altered, qualified, emended, differentiated. The title, *Pale Fire,* confirms the ambiguous status of reflection, but the substance of that confirmation can only be gleaned from an exercise involving the title that is not really available to the reader until three-quarters of the way through the book, and then only upon the exercise of some deductive and inductive detective work that most readers would not even engage until a second or third rereading.

I have held James Joyce in reserve so far because his work with titles serves almost as a *summa* of the rereading process. Not only do his titles set out a program in which Joyce formulates his own career by repositioning other titles, works, writers, and even writing careers before him, but also he employs versions of his own earlier titles in each of his subsequent books. There is indeed no writer for whom titles are more programmatic on first or on multiple readings. *Chamber Music,* the refined (and comically applicable) title for Joyce's first book of poems reappears when Leopold Bloom in *Ulysses* thinks of the sound of his wife at the chamber pot and comments on the musical implications, "Could make a kind of pun on that" (232).

Even more pointedly, Joyce retrieves his earlier titles in his later books as a way of allowing the reader insight into his own attitude toward his career. In *Ulysses,* just before Stephen Dedalus is about to construct a story about two Dublin vestals based on information he has been gleaning that very moment from those to whom he is speaking, he says, by way of introduction, "Dubliners" (119). Joyce is asking his readers to pay attention to the kind of material and its compilation that allowed—indeed inspired—him to write his earlier collection of that same name, *Dubliners.* The arrangement of scraps of Dublin experience, cites, street names, gestures, produces what Joyce called "street furniture" for the epiphanies of his *Dubliners* volume, and Joyce repeats his title in the dialogue of *Ulysses* when he is ready to show readers of a later book how he performed in an earlier one.

During a nighttime meeting of Stephen and Bloom in *Ulysses,* Stephen comments to Bloom that "Ireland must be important because it belongs to me" (527). Bloom is a bit puzzled, but Stephen's point (and Joyce's) is that his titles reinscribe the artist's country and city in forms amenable to genius. *Dubliners* is what Joyce must produce to have Dublin belong to him. The language of *Finnegans Wake* repeats the title of Joyce's first collection of short stories exactly in that guise, where the place—Dublin and the book's title, *Dubliners*—belongs to the artist because he remakes the city as his own. Resettled in *Finnegans Wake,* Joyce's first book of short stories becomes the same question of belonging that Stephen articulated to Bloom, a question that now the city asks all its exiled writers: "So This is Dyoublong?" (13).

Joyce rarely misses a chance to let his titles reread his narratives. *Portrait of the Artist as a Young Man* reappears in *Finnegans Wake* as "Poor traits of the artless" (114) precisely because a romanticized and genius-driven reading of Joyce's first novel misses much of its irony. *Portrait* contains the name of a famous Greek artist, Dedalus, but implies, on occasion, the fate of Icarus, a proto-artist who exhibits his poor traits for one great soaring (and swooning) moment. Many of the overblown qualities of a young artist are precisely those that Joyce represents. The accurate portrait of such a being is one of vision without subject, inspiration without structure, bathos without pathos. Joyce's title can be read any number of ways, and one of them is articulated in the revision of the *Portrait*'s title in the language of the *Wake.*

Ulysses, too, as a title reappears in other guises in *Finnegans Wake,* one of them in its own ironic manifestation as "usylessly." What is key here is that Joyce reads the very premise of his work the way some of his initial critics did. Who, after all, would or should bother trying to make sense of a book about Dublin called *Ulysses*? Perhaps the effort involved is too great for the subject matter and the enterprise is useless. This is not a position altogether abandoned by modern readers. But titles are also read in what Joyce calls in *Ulysses,* a "retrospective kind of arrangement" (532). They tell the reader how to grasp the gist of the fuller narrative project undertaken, a project played out in *Finnegans Wake* when the place and pattern of all history repeat in the combination and permutation of letters within words that allow everything to be something else, so that the lead character, insofar as there is one in the *Wake,* H. C. E., becomes not only a man named Henry Chippenden Earwicker, but a phenomenon named Here Comes Everybody.

Joyce begins his titling with stories about Dubliners. Dublin becomes a version of Ithaca and Ireland of the Greek Mediterranean world in *Ulysses.* What Joyce does not tell us directly about his method in *Ulysses,* he does tell us in the polyglot language of *Finnegans Wake,* which means we have to read his glosses on the title *Ulysses* in that book as a way of understanding something of what Joyce was up to. I say *reread* here deliberately because it is not likely any reader will read *Finnegans Wake* as a way of preparing to read *Dubliners* or *Portrait* or *Ulysses* for the first time. The hero of all heroes for Joyce in *Finnegans Wake* is a "greeken hearted yude" (171)— which is exactly who Ulysses is when figured as Joyce's Dublin Jew, Leopold Bloom. Joyce's earlier books are possible, we learn in *Finnegans Wake,* because he studies all the narratives of migration and wandering to write them, "All the time he kept on treasuring with condign satisfaction each and every crumb of trektalk, covetous of his neighbour's word" (172). The story of Dedalus the exiled artist in *Portrait* is as much a trektalk as that of Odysseus in *The Odyssey.* And in *Finnegans Wake,* the artist seems to participate in the spectacle of rereading his own laboriously produced *Ulysses.* The result is something quite original, shocking, bound in blue covers, faced with charges of obscenity, and reread by its sight-impeded author (as it is by many of its readers) whenever the chance at self-inflation offers itself. It would have diverted, if ever seen, the "shuddersome spectacle of this semidemented zany amid the inspissated grime of his glaucous den making believe to read his usylessly unreadable Blue Book of Eccles, *édition de ténèbres* . . ." (179).

The point is that *Ulysses* is always reread with greater or lesser degree of comprehension because any book with another book's title for its premise is going to leave the reader somewhat in the dark. Of course, that "*ténèbres*" specifically refers to the northwest territory of Odysseus's wanderings in *The Odyssey* is not a point lost on Joyce the epic amalgamator. Whether *Ulysses* or "usylessly," the title remains a guide to the reading process. It represents a match of sorts between a theater of action in the ancient world and the theater of action for one Dublin day in 1904. Joyce speaks about matches all day long in *Ulysses*. When a character waves a cigarette and asks in the newspaper office chapter, "Who has the most matches?" (107), that is what Joyce's title asks of the reader. A great part of the pleasure in reading Joyce is that matches become easier and easier to make the more often one reads his books. And the same is surely true for *Finnegans Wake*.

By *Finnegans Wake,* we should be ready to see what Joyce has been up to from the first. No one place or person is ever just one place or person in the reading experience. So that when Joyce identifies Ireland in *Finnegans Wake* with, among thousands of other places, the "Emerald Illium" (62), we know that the original epic that made Ireland Greece and Dublin Ithaca has now incorporated even the precedent Homeric epic set on the plains of Trojan Troy.

The title for Joyce's last narrative, *Finnegans Wake,* is what all titles secretly strive to be: possessive and plural at the same time. Plurality is the way the story keeps repeating itself. The title is paradoxical—Finnegan revives at his wake, which is what the ballad of "Tim Finnegan" is about. Readers of Joyce are encouraged, as were the attendees at the ballad's wake, to have "lovesoftfun at Finnegan's Wake" (607). Indeed, that one reference late in the book is the only time the title of the ballad of Tim Finnegan is mentioned with the correct possessive punctuation. Buried in the title's essential pun is the key structural principle in all of Joyce: the processes of life are revealed in plot from birth to death. Hence the title turns on the circle of all stories that enter the book: the celebration—almost the orgy—of death, a wake; and the revival that plots the course of many lives lived as one: "again awake." Of course the process never stops. For every rise there is another fall, "Timm Finn again's weak" (93). That the book plays on similar tropes on almost every one of its pages simply reinforces the principle embodied in the title. We are in the book in "mournenslaund," that is, morning land and mourning land.

Wake is one of those uncanny words that seem to contain diametrically opposed meanings. In Joyce's wake, both those who have lived and those who have died are revived to celebrate the undying ritual that is literature, where to give life is to render characters immortal. To read anything is to reread everything. The title does all that work and more. Once Joyce begins to play with his phonemes, "Funnegans Wake," "Finnegans wick," "Finnegans weak" (and that's just the start of it), things truly expand, and all components of the title become potential ways to read the action in this book and in every book ever written.

There are many moments in which Joyce uses words to retell all the adventures of the human race, from the original primal family in the garden, through all its migrations, wars, settlements, and repetitions. The "wake" that is the movement of the books starts in Eden, and the whole adamic story takes us right back to the "anastomosically assimilated and preteridentified paraidiotically, in fact, the sameold gamebold adomic structure of our Finnius the old One" (615). The possessive not marked in the title is the story of multiplicity and a story of rivalry where the possessive becomes its opposite as in the wonderfully formulated phrase that embodies the title, "his polar andthisishis" (177). To break down this portmanteau phrase is to read the same paradox that pervades all the text, the "this" which is "his" is also the antithesis, and becomes the "that" which "this" wants.

It all begins for Joyce at the egg birth of the world and its stories in the garden. Perhaps Joyce is playing on the opening joke from Sterne's *Tristram Shandy* at the expense of Horace's theory of epic narration that even to begin in the middle of things (*in medias res*) is to begin *ab ovo*. The one becomes the many and identity is rivaled:

> (for the farmer, his son and their homely codes, known
> as eggburst, eggblend, eggburial and hatch-as-hatch

> can) receives through a portal vein the dialytically
> separated elements of precedent decomposition for the
> verypetpurpose of subsequent recombination so that
> the heroticism, catastrophes and eccentricities trans-
> mitted by the ancient legacy of the past, type by tope,
> letter from litter, word at ward. . . . (614–15)

It is important to understand that story told in *Finnegans Wake,* no matter where it picks up, is always the oldest story and the newest, a story told of paradise and told of raids and riots, a parodic tale (in that all history's repeats are parodies) told at times (as is Shakespeare's and Faulkner's) by an idiot, hence "paraidiotically." That is what the plural without the possessive in the title signifies. All stories are reread into Finnegan's. But to begin identifying "Finnegans" is just the start of reading and rereading *Finnegans Wake.* When Joyce called his effort "Work in Progress" before he revealed the title *Finnegans Wake,* he was also revealing one of its modes of being. A wake, after all, is a kind of progress. So is a title; that is, when it does not turn tale and go backwards to pick up much that a first-time reader might have missed or did not originally know.

To conclude with *Finnegans Wake* is to restate the persistent point of this essay. Titles are a manual for reading and rereading, but part of that manual refuses to believe that reading can be separated from rereading in the first place. We do not come clean to any text, and in our efforts we are always reading again, just as Finnegan is living and dying again, "the ancient legacy of the past" in the title of a book that names the reading progress and process, "type by tope, letter from litter, word at ward" (615).

Works Cited

Gibbon, Edward. *The History of the Decline and Fall of the Roman Empire.* Ed. J. B. Bury. 7 vols. London: Methuen, 1909.

Joyce, James. *Finnegans Wake.* New York: Random House, 1939.

———. *Ulysses, The Corrected Text.* Ed. Hans Walter Gabler. New York: Random House, 1986.

Nabokov, Vladimir. *Pale Fire.* 1962. New York: Vintage-Random House, 1989.

Shakespeare, William. *Hamlet.* The Arden Shakespeare. Ed. Harold Jenkins. London: Methuen, 1982.

Sterne, Laurence. *The Life and Opinions of Tristram Shandy,* Gentleman. Ed.
    Ian Campbell Ross. New York: Oxford UP, 1983.
————. *A Sentimental Journey through France and Italy.* Ed. Graham Petrie.
    Harmondsworth: Penguin, 1967.
Stoppard, Tom. *Rosencrantz and Guildenstern Are Dead.* 1967. London:
    Faber, 1968.

3

Orality in Literacy: Some Historical Paradoxes of Reading and Rereading

Matei Calinescu

Reading and rereading are usually construed as private, solitary, silent activities characteristic of what some influential cultural anthropologists have called a "literate consciousness," as distinct from a more archaic "oral consciousness." Yet both reading and rereading, when examined more closely, reveal numerous potential or actual elements of live orality which, if properly taken into account, end up calling into question any rigid dichotomy between orality and literacy. Furthermore, a consideration of the dialectic between the oral and the written can add important nuances to our understanding of reading and rereading, particularly of their literary varieties.

In the following reflections on some key moments in the history of writing/reading, the acts of reading and rereading are seen as part of a larger process of cultural communication, involving different forms of attention, awareness, memory, and modes of understanding text—whether oral or written. It may be useful to note from the outset that the vast majority of literary critics or theorists do not distinguish between reading and rereading. The result is that they often use the word *reading* for what would be more precisely designated either by *rereading* (in the sense of repeated reading) or by what I would call *(re)reading,* that is, reading-*and*-rereading or reading-*cum*-rereading (in the sense of reading, even for the first time, or rereading with the kind of structural attention that can be achieved only from the vantage point of rereading).[1] The fact of the matter is that in many broad discussions, reading as a generic term subsumes both rereading proper and (re)reading. For purposes of economy, I myself will go on using reading as a shorthand for rereading and, as the case may be, (re)reading, whenever the implied distinctions can be usefully disregarded.

On the other hand, there are circumstances under which discrimination is necessary. When one speaks, for instance, of reader interest, of curiosity, of desire to know "what happens next," of surprise, or of a plot with many unexpected turns, one clearly has in mind a first linear perusal of a narrative, whether fictional or historical. There are genres (mysteries, fantastic stories) which are designed in view of a first linear reading. This doesn't mean that such works cannot become favorites and be reread many times. It doesn't even mean that such works are not reread for other qualities they may have, and that the second or third time around, curiosity and involvement are eliminated. In fact, the excitement of the first reading can to a large extent be reexperienced, since the game of make-believe that a well crafted, end-oriented narrative proposes can be replayed; and, what's more, it can be replayed *as if* for the first time. Rereading, however, will add important new dimensions: it will complement the linearity of the time of reading with the sense of a circular time and of a meaningful and gratifying repetition. In certain cases, the act of rereading may be invested with the significance of a small private ritual. Rereading may also reveal, beyond the most memorable surprises the first time around, a somewhat mysterious quality of "ideal surprisingness," which C. S. Lewis distinguishes from the "actual surprise" and associates with the Greek heroic *peripeteia* (87).

Almost unwittingly, when one describes certain features of rereading, one begins to resort to notions more readily associated with archaic (oral) cultures, than with modern (literate) ones. One may thus speak of a cyclical time, closer to myth (the myth of the eternal return) than to the ineluctably ongoing time of modernity. One may be led to attribute a higher value to repetition than a culture that idolizes the new might be willing to grant. The historical paradoxes that I propose to examine here—one of which is the strange, even if limited, propinquity between the world of rereading and that of orality—are premised on the thesis that orality and literacy are not separated by an unbridgeable gap, but that elements of orality, including the so-called "oral consciousness," continue to play a major role in the activities of writing/reading/rereading.

Cultural Anthropology and the Question of (Re)reading

No discussion of reading and rereading from a historical perspective can disregard the orality-literacy studies over the last few decades and the ways in which they approach such processes as memory, imagination, poetic composition, and interpretation in both oral and literate (manuscript, typographic, and, more recently, electronic) cultures.[2] Of particular interest to the student of literary reading and (re)reading is Walter J. Ong's book *Orality and Literacy.* In assessing some of the broader results of orality-literacy studies, Ong emphasizes their implications for theories of literary interpretation and especially for the study of narrative and plot construction (and reception, i.e., listening/reading for the plot) in oral and literate cultures.

Central to Ong's study is the question of (cultural) memory and the various forms it takes in societies before and after the introduction of writing. In a purely oral-aural world, he suggests, the "evanescent" quality of speech must have been tied to a sense of inescapable time and transitoriness, held in check only by memory. Later on, with the advent of writing, an alliance between memory and sight was forged, which lead to the great technological breakthrough of writing and ultimately of alphabetic writing. In the latter, speech is translated into visual signs that can be directly translated back into sounds.

Ong's distinction between the special temporality of sound (in the absence of writing) and the spatiality of vision is suggestive:

> Without writing, words as such . . . have no focus and no trace. . . . All sensation takes place in time, but sound has a special relationship to time. . . . Sound exists only when it is going out of existence. It is not simply perishable but essentially evanescent. . . . There is no way to stop sound. . . . If I stop the movement of sound, I have nothing—only silence. . . . No

other sensory field totally resists a holding action, stabi-
lization, in quite this way. Vision can register motion,
but it can also register immobility. Indeed, it favors
immobility. (*Orality* 34)

Knowledge in a "primary oral culture" (that is, a culture assumed
to be completely unaffected by writing), Ong believes, is so totally dependent on memory ("You know what you can recall") that the process
of thinking itself takes place "in mnemonic patterns, shaped for ready
recurrence" (34). Hence, the paramount importance of the various
oral mnemonic devices, such as rhythmical patterns, alliteration, assonance, repetition, antinomy and antithesis, formulary expressions,
and, on the level of larger units of discourse, standard settings and
thematic associations. Writing would introduce a completely new type
and standard of memory. Of course, orality in such a culture doesn't
disappear, but the primacy of writing transforms it structurally into
what Ong calls "secondary orality."

A brief parenthesis is in order here. Theorists of orality and oral
memory attribute a purely mnemonic function to the devices listed
above. But such devices may also have had an aesthetic function,
a function which has been preserved and even enhanced after the
introduction of writing, from the early times of literacy to the modern age. To use them effectively, a writer must have a fine sense
of the hidden oral possibilities of writing and a good musical ear.
Significantly, in order to perceive them and assess their more subtle
implications, the reader often must (re)read the text attentively, or
read it very slowly, quasi-orally. Consider, for instance, the musical
refinements in the prose of James Joyce, who was also an accomplished amateur singer. The aural/oral element is variously present
in his work, from his early poems of *Chamber Music* to *Finnegans
Wake*. The famous first sentence of *Ulysses* ("Stately, plump Buck
Mulligan came from the stairhead, bearing a bowl of lather on which
a mirror and a razor lay crossed" [3]) is compelling in terms of
its rhythm and sound effects—the most obvious of which are the
alliterations: Buck/bearing/bowl, stately/stairhead; and the assonance:
mirror/razor. The mirror/razor assonance also resonates symbolically:
the named objects being, among other things, a transparently ironic

reference to the cross, and thus appropriately introducing the scene of Buck Mulligan's parody of the Roman Catholic mass. The bowl facetiously stands for the chalice. Not fortuitously, the first uttered (quoted) words in *Ulysses* are intoned by Buck Mulligan: "*Introibo ad altare Dei*" (3)—"I will go up to God's altar"—and they point to the burlesque of liturgy, which is one of the themes running not only through the first chapter but through the book as a whole. To repeat, a reader must (re)read to capture the effects of the sophisticated orality written into the Joycean text; textualized orality creates the need for rereading.

Back to Ong, we may ask: were not the operations of a trained oral memory already a form of writing before writing? Was not memorization itself a way of "freezing" selected verbal messages—based on similarity of sound or rhythm—and "inscribing" them in mental space? And, similarly, could not visual shapes of things or artifacts (from tools to decorative patterns to figurative/symbolic sculptures or drawings) also serve as memory counters? Writing, then, would have a double origin. It could have used both oral patterns/formulas and visual shapes (ultimately letters) as memory props. Ong does not address these interesting questions.[3]

While Ong's discussion of orality/literacy is both insightful and insight-producing, one might doubt the validity of the theoretical polarities on which it is based (and which are also found in the writings of other prominent participants in the orality/literacy debate of the last decades, such as Jack Goody, Ian Watt, Eric Havelock, and Marshall McLuhan). Take the very dichotomy between orality and literacy. To be sure, this distinction is heuristically useful, insofar as it allows for generalizations and insight-producing speculations supported by intuitive, introspective evidence (thus reading or rereading a text, i.e., processing or reprocessing written information, is psychologically different from listening to speech, i.e., processing auditory verbal information, and the difference is certainly worth analyzing in both its immediate and its farther reaching implications). The same dichotomy, however, can lead to fallacious reasoning when it becomes the basis for deterministic evolutionary schemes—such as positing a *universal* linear progression from an "oral consciousness" to a "literate/alphabetic/typographic consciousness" to a newer "audiovisual" or (postmodern) "electronic consciousness," each with its distinctive epistemological characteristics. As Ruth Finnegan has pointed out in her careful critique of technologically deterministic theories of writing:

> In setting up grand historical oppositions we can also misunderstand our *own* experience. In this dichotomizing approach the primary mode of communication and transmission in western Europe is often taken to be writing (and more especially printing). . . . But this model glosses over many complexities. . . . In practice people switch from oral to written to electronic communication and back, and from personally generated to mass-media forms, without any sense that there is some radical change involved or that they are somehow thereby moving in different kinds of 'social space.' . . . This kind of interaction only seems strange if we start from a model which presupposes that these forms of communication are essentially antipathetic modes. (*Literacy* 143)

That a rich background of oral memory lies at the basis of at least certain types of meaningful reading (as opposed to the mechanizable task of converting visual signs into sounds) has been recognized for some time by theorists of communication wary of simple, and often simplistic, binary models of written versus oral communication. Oral-cultural memory is deeply involved in certain modes of writing/rewriting and reading/rereading. These modes may vary historically, but the essential link between orality and literacy is maintained: one is entitled to speak of orality *in* literacy, as well as literacy *in* orality. Reading, as Michel de Certeau once noted, is different from "recognizing signs and uttering them. . . . It is a cultural memory, derived from oral exchanges and related to audition, which allows the reader to approach the text with semantic strategies of questioning" (66).

Introspection validates such remarks beyond the historical context in which Certeau articulates them (the essay from which I have quoted deals with questions of "spiritual reading" or what Certeau also calls "la lecture absolue" in the Roman-Catholic tradition of the sixteenth and seventeenth centuries). But, bringing the matters at hand closer to us in time, and referring to experiences more familiar than certain kinds of contemplative-mystical reading, is not the ability to talk about what one has read—to summarize, paraphrase, rephrase, or comment orally—central to our main definitions of reading comprehension? It is also notable that in our society readers often communicate orally about what they read—they share reading impressions with friends or colleagues, they recommend books to them, they sometimes take their advice to read certain things and not to read others. Word of mouth is still very important, perhaps decisive, in determining the fate of a new literary work.

On a different level, in the process of education, the (re)readability of older works is always facilitated orally. Formal and informal modes of oral communication about what and how to read constitute an essential part in the teaching of the humanities in today's institutions of higher learning. The transmission of the written cultural record of society is the object of elaborate oral practices—from the formal lecture course to the more probing seminar to the tutoring session to various less formal types of intercourse between faculty and students and among students. All these oral practices (which include a proportion of oral reading: illustrative quotations, lecture materials, conference papers, and so on) are directed toward guiding and stimulating both students and faculty to read or reread (i.e., study) certain texts whose knowledge helps them to achieve cultural competence. The essential orality that surrounds and shapes our reading and the formation of our cultural competence—be it a "secondary orality"—is all too often forgotten or neglected by the theorists of a separate, literate form of consciousness, a form which is supposed to have displaced an older, more primitive "primary" orality.

On the other hand, one need not subscribe to technological determinism in order to recognize that writing is one of the most momentous and productive technological inventions in human history. Particularly the introduction of full alphabetic writing by the ancient Greeks (simpler and more "democratic" than the complicated and "theocratic" earlier scripts, the pictographic or ideographic in particular) may be seen as opening up a whole new range of possibilities of thought and action. The importance of the Greek achievement cannot be exaggerated: full alphabetic writing, developed on the basis of the consonantic alphabets of earlier Semitic scripts, "made widespread literacy possible" and it was in the Greek world of the seventh century B.C. that "for the first time there began to take concrete shape . . . a society that was essentially literate and that soon established many of the institutions that became characteristic of all later literate societies" (Goody and Watt, "Consequences" 67). Whatever its estimated range and depth, Greek alphabetic literacy, as Eric A. Havelock has insisted, was nothing short of a great historical turning point, a veritable revolution.

A Silent Revolution?

Havelock speaks of the advent of writing/reading as a "silent revolution," as a revolutionary introduction of silence and privacy into some essential processes of human communication. This revolution took many centuries to work out its main implications. During these centuries, it generated a variety of socio-cultural conflicts hard to identify and conceptualize from a modern perspective, but that need to be well understood for a proper history of writing and reading in their intricate dialectical relations. Havelock's own work on Greek literacy, and in particular his *Preface to Plato* (1963), provides us with striking examples of powerful but long ignored or misunderstood conflicts. The main subject of Plato's *Republic,* Havelock argues, is *not* political thought and the definition of the ideal state, as traditional scholarship has maintained, but *education* and the *theory of education,* with important practical implications for Plato's own time. Once we realize this, it becomes clear, for instance, that Plato's famous attack on the poets was by no means a rejection of poetry as we understand it today, but only of poetry as a privileged *mimetic-oral* mode of communication of social values, and as a tool of public education, which still commanded an undue prestige in Plato's literate times. Poetic memory (Havelock's famous "tribal encyclopedia") and its diffusion through repeated public *mimesis* (in the quasi-theatrical sense of "impersonation" and live oral performance by poet-actors) had become, in Plato's view, a harmful anachronism in a time when the rich educational possibilities of literacy (rationalism, analysis of experience in terms of cause and effects, true history as opposed to myth, and so on) remained insufficiently explored. Hence Plato's dramatization of his polemical stance by urging the expulsion of the poets from the Republic.[4]

As Havelock stresses from the beginning of his book, the real problem brought about by the introduction of writing was not that of "the art of writing by a few, but of fluent reading by the many" (*Preface to Plato* ix). Although alphabetic writing had been used in Greece since the eighth century B.C., the archaic oral mentality persisted through the fourth century, so that one should not be surprised that "the oral state of mind is still for Plato the main enemy" (41). In the long transitional period from pure orality to widespread literacy (the latter to be measured by the size of the reading public), poets from Hesiod on, while availing themselves of the new technology of writing, continued to address an overwhelmingly oral audience. As Havelock notes, "the poet can write for his own benefit and thereby acquire increased compositional skill, but he composes for a public he knows will not read what he is composing but will listen to it" (39). It was only by the middle of the fourth century that "the silent revolution had been accomplished and that the cultivated Greek public had become a community of readers" (41).

But how "silent" was the revolution of alphabetic writing and reading in its early stages? Of course a text is silent as it "speaks" to the eyes of the reader in silence, by contrast with the voice of a live person addressing an auditor. In a different sense, a text also has a way—when one would like to question it with regard to its contents or meaning—of remaining stubbornly or mysteriously silent. But reading was not always the predominantly silent and private activity that it is today, so silent indeed that it allows many readers to use the same quiet reading room in a public library at the same time. In Greco-Roman antiquity, silent writing and, more importantly, silent reading were all but unknown. Writing was very often the taking down of dictation—or self-dictation in the case of solitary composition or solitary copying of an existing text. The motives for oral reading in Greek and Roman antiquity were complex. They were in part aesthetic (Paul Saenger notes that the ancients "savored [oralization] aesthetically" and that they also valued the mnemonic effect of read-aloud texts), and in part social (often texts were read aloud by professional readers; the "notion that the greater part of the population should be autonomous and self-motivated readers was entirely foreign to the elitist literate mentality of the ancient world" ["Separation" 209]). Interestingly, the preference for oral reading may have led to the abandonment of word-separation in Latin, in the first century A.D. At any rate, between the first and the eighth century, texts in Latin consisted of continuous lines of up to forty or fifty unspaced letters, which were hard to grasp visually unless simultaneously pronounced. Historians of reading agree that, given the visual-perceptual difficulties created by the lack of word-separation, silent reading was, although possible, an astonishing intellectual feat.

Silent reading in late antiquity was, we may say, an achievement of nearly miraculous proportions, a saint's triumph of intellectual concentration and meditative power, if we consider the famous description of a scene of silent reading in Augustine's *Confessions,* Book Six, Chapter 3. The object of the description is Augustine's spiritual master, the Bishop of Milan, Ambrose, reading with sealed lips. Ambrose, Augustine tells us, spent most of his time with the throng of suffering people "whose infirmities he served." During

> the very little time he was not with these he was refreshing either his body with necessary food or his mind with reading. When he read his eyes travelled across the page and his heart sought out the sense, but voice and tongue were silent. No one was forbidden to approach him . . . but when we came into him we often saw him reading and always to himself; and after we had sat long in silence, unwilling to interrupt a work on which he was so intent, we would depart again. We guessed that in the small time he could find for the refreshment of his mind, he would wish to be free from the distraction of other men's affairs and not called away from what he was doing. Perhaps he was on his guard lest [if he read aloud] someone listening should be troubled and want an explanation . . . , and it might be necessary to expound or discuss some of the more

difficult questions. And if he had to spend time on this,
he would get through less reading than he wished. Or it
may be that his real reason for reading to himself was
to preserve his voice, which did in fact readily grow
tired. (108)

Several things are immediately remarkable about this passage.
First, there is an interesting connection between reading and time.
As one takes time off one's habitually strenuous activities to nourish
one's body, one is entitled to time off for purposes of nourishing
one's mind (with one's heart seeking out the meaning of the silently
perused page). The time Ambrose takes away from his charitable
work with the sick and the crippled is extremely limited (*perexiguus*)
and silent reading appears to be the most spiritually or mystically
economical way of using it. Augustine speculates on two possibilities
as to why Ambrose would do such an unusual thing as read silently:
Ambrose reads "to himself" in order to avoid possible questions that
normal oral reading might lead to (we note that Ambrose denies
himself any privacy, undoubtedly in the name of such Christian
values as accessibility to others and transparency); or he reads in
silence in order to preserve his voice. A third reason is implicit: a
desire for isolation with his own thoughts, contemplativeness, and
exemplarity (setting an infinitely discreet, silent "*exemplum* of self-
reliance within a scheme of reliance on God," as Brian Stock puts
it [*Augustine* 62]), in harmony with the self-effacing personality of
the saint. In this latter respect, Stock, in his important new study of
Augustine as a reader, offers a subtle interpretation: "This portrait
of the silent reader is inseparable from the notion that someone, in
this case, Augustine, is observing silent reading taking place. It is
the observation of another person's contemplativeness, rather than
the technique of reading itself, that makes the moment unique in the
ancient literature of interiority" (*Augustine* 62). Ambrose may have
had other reasons but, as Augustine concludes the passage, "whatever
his reason for doing it [reading silently], that man certainly had a good
reason" (ibid.).

Significantly, the notion that the speed of reading itself might have
been increased by the practice of reading silently does not seem to

have occurred to Augustine in a culture in which "saving time" (in our modern sense in which time is money and speed is a value) was not a central concern. Nor could it have practically occurred at a time (he wrote the *Confessions* in A.D. 399) when word-separation did not exist in the writing of Latin and when silent reading must have been almost as slow as oral reading. Real visual reading, rendered possible by word-separation and greatly facilitated, after the introduction of print, by the uniformity of type, was to lead to a dramatic increase in the speed of (visual) reading and thus to another, more significant, way of "saving time" than the one that was available to the Bishop of Milan.

Returning now to the question of Havelock's "silent revolution" of writing/reading, I would stress again that it was for a long time silent only exceptionally. Neither the act of writing (including copying), nor reading were silent in antiquity, as we saw. Nor could they be silent, except in rare cases, in late antiquity and the early Middle Ages, that is, before the (re)introduction of word-separation in writing could lead to quick visual reading. It was only as a result of word-separation and later print that individual written words acquired a graphic and semantic (and in a certain sense ideographic) identity that could be quickly grasped visually in an act of silent reading. As Saenger has pointed out in a learned article on the history of silent reading in the Middle Ages, the basic unit of meaning in reading in classical Roman times and later was not the word but the letter and, for all practical purposes, the syllable—hence the enormous importance of meter and rhythm not only in poetry but also in prose, i.e., "numbered prose" designed to be read orally:

> Paleographic evidence offers a partial explanation of why silent reading was an uncommon practice in classical antiquity. . . . Latin writing, which consisted of undivided rows of capital letters or their cursive equivalents, was entirely phonetic and had no ideographic value. Since in ancient books verbal constructs were not represented by recognizable images, the Romans developed no clear conception of the word as a unit of meaning. Instead, Roman grammarians considered the letter and the syllable to be basic to reading. The Roman

reader, reading aloud to others or softly to himself, approached the text syllable by syllable in order to recover the words and sentences conveying the meaning of the text. Quintilian considered it a special facility of a scribe to be able to glance ahead as he read to see the end of a phrase before articulating it. For all Romans, the proper coordination of the eye and the tongue was an indispensable part of the activity of reading. A written text was essentially a transcription which, like modern musical notation, became an intelligible message only when it was performed orally to others or to oneself (Saenger, *Silent Reading* 370–71).

The notion of a certain parallelism between writing and musical notation, I should like to add, does not lose its basis once the principle of word-separation is observed and silent visual reading becomes the rule. Even when the words on the page are perceived ideographically and processed directly into meaning by a fast visual reader, the possibility of pronouncing them, physically or at least mentally, is always there. Background orality can always be activated, brought into the foreground. When one avails oneself of that possibility (as when one reads a poem out loud), one finds oneself in a relation to the text which is analogous to the relation between a musician— say, a singer—and the score he or she is performing. There is, in consequence, a whole art of reading aloud (including various styles and modes that range from the highly formal and "theatrical" to the informally soft, whispered, and intimate), an art which is one of the major components of the larger and more complex art of acting. The art of reading aloud, which is nowadays taught in conservatories of dramatic art, is the verbal equivalent of the art of interpreting musical works from a score, the closest analogy being, obviously, singing.[5]

Facets of Orality in Writing, Reading, and Rereading

The root orality of writing and reading—and more emphatically rereading, which usually pays more attention to the "texture" of a text, to words, phrasing, repetition, alliteration, rhythm and other auditory

effects—raises interesting questions of difference in the speed and
pace of various kinds of linguistic communication. To put something
down in writing is obviously much slower than to say it. For one thing,
the physical act of writing is slower, in terms of number of words per
time unit, than the rate of normal oral speech, and this is so even in the
case of the fastest typist, not to speak of handwriting. On a conceptual
level, the act of writing or composing a text is, for different reasons,
slower and more painstaking than it would be to convey the same basic
information by speech. It is a truism that the situational context as well
as the fact of face-to-face communication (aided by facial expression,
gestures, "body language") simplifies the task of the speaker. Oral
communication of even lengthy and complex messages—such as
telling or retelling an elaborate story to a group—is in certain ways
more "natural" and therefore less difficult than would be the writing
down of basically the same story. The existence of a live audience
ensures constant feedback and, in the case of misunderstanding, the
possibility of clarification, change of emphasis or tone, and so forth.
Some of the conceptual difficulties of the act of writing have been
noted by Walter Ong, who points out that one of the most delicate
tasks of the writer is to construct or "fictionalize" the reader, which
includes defining a "role" for the latter:

> Lack of verifiable context is what makes writing nor-
> mally so much more agonizing an activity than oral
> presentation to a real audience. . . . The writer must set
> up a role in which absent and often unknown readers
> can cast themselves. Even when writing to a close
> friend I have to fictionalize a mood for him to which
> he is expected to conform. . . . The fictionalizing of
> readers is what makes writing so difficult. The process
> is complex and fraught with uncertainties. I have to
> know the tradition—the intertextuality, if you wish—
> in which I am working so that I can create for real
> readers fictional roles that they are able and willing to
> play. (*Orality* 102, 107)[6]

One might add that in creating fictional roles for readers, a writer
may create roles for specifically oral readers and/or rereaders, the latter

being more appropriately attuned to the sound effects of a literary text. Consider again the example of Joyce and the numerous puns, some of them "generative," which cannot be perceived without a careful "sounding out" of the text or an attentive (oral) rereading—thus, in *Ulysses,* the repeated and increasingly complex play on "metempsychosis"/"met-him-pike-hoses" with all its ramifications. Consider also the textual integration of some 400 songs (listed in the index of Don Gifford's Ulysses *Annotated* and including nursery and street rhymes, Irish folk songs, ballads, and arias from operas by such diverse composers as Mozart, von Flotow, Bizet, Michael Balfe, Donizetti, Bellini, Meyerbeer, Wagner, and others). Joyce, Joseph Frank once said, "cannot be read—he can only be reread" (19), because his work should be apprehended spatially and simultaneously, something that cannot be achieved on a first reading. But even if one grants Frank's point about the "spatial form" of *Ulysses,* there is another reason for which Joyce cannot be read, but only reread: the complex interplay between orality and writing.

In general, the act of writing—taken here exclusively from the standpoint of the writer—constitutes a considerable slowing down of the process of communication. This slowness and difficulty of writing—groping for "the right word" or phrase, attempting to foresee the effect of the text on the imagined (re)reader, including its "music," rhythm, and oral echoes—is in contrast with the normally more rapid and smoother process of reading. Reading is, at least in theory, more continuous and more uniform than writing, and this includes the mental writing or rewriting that occurs in the higher forms of reflective reading or rereading.

At its slowest, continuous silent reading proceeds roughly at the pace of normal speech. Both slow silent reading and oral reading may in fact be slightly ahead of the speed of ordinary speech, as they are free from its unavoidable hemmings and hawings and pauses for thought and redundancies. Studies of reading set the speed of reading aloud (a story to your child, a lecture to an audience) at approximately 9,000 words per hour, which is the rate of normal oral speech. Subvocalic reading or silent reading with mental uttering of the words can be considerably faster, and the speed of reading increases dramatically in the case of purely "visual reading," in which the eye "sweeps" batches of twenty or more words from the page in a single move and commits them to the short-term memory, where they are instantly processed straight into meaning. The time differential between the slowness of the conversion of thought and language into space—into writing—and its much quicker reconversion into language or thought seems to have reached its maximum point here.

But even in this extreme case, the oral dimension, with its subtle rhythmic and musical implications, does not vanish. It remains hidden, as it were, in the spatial representation of language, from which it can be brought back to consciousness at any moment by a live utterance, whether physically audible or merely mental. One can safely and even usefully ignore this dimension in cases of purely pragmatic reading—when one searches a textual memory for specific data in view of solving a well-defined problem (for instance, trying to answer a precise question by consulting an encyclopedia or dictionary). But such ignorance of the underlying orality of written language and such single-minded concern with speed would defeat the purposes of other, more reflective, types of reading, and primarily literary reading and rereading.

Literary reading—which is often (re)reading—involves special attention to linguistic detail and to nuances of sound and meaning which take time to figure out—and in certain cases, such as the reading of poetry or poetic texts, it gets very close to the basic orality of language, reproducing mentally, if not physically, its rhythmical patterns, humorous or poetic plays on word sounds, and deeper melodies and resonances. A purely visual reader will miss not only alliterations, rhymes, onomatopoeias and other external sound effects, but also puns, equivocations, double entendres, calculated ambiguities, and so on. A purely visual reader is a thoroughly antipoetic reader. Literary reading, it has sometimes been argued, *should* proceed (of course only when this is warranted by the poetic richness of the text) according to a rule of slowness, should be "reading in slow motion," and there is much to be said in favor of this view.

Thus, Reuben A. Brower has specifically recommended the reading of poetry (the genre that has traditionally remained closer to live orality) as the best teaching model for literary reading in general. His concept of literary reading is limited, however, to the great classics, i.e., to essentially "rereadable" texts, and does not include variously "readable" texts which must be read fast to be properly enjoyed. Actually, a good reader should be able to vary the speed of reading according not only to the "role of the reader" inscribed in the text but also according to his or her own purposes (for instance, involvement and pleasure in reading fiction, which may be hindered by excessive slowness, or the pursuit of a more cerebral type of interest, which is characteristic of absorption and which may demand a considerable slowing down of the process of reading with or without stress on oralization). Besides the demands of the inner orality of certain literary texts, there are, of course, other factors that can slow down the process of reading. One of them is the construction of mental images in response to the verbal instructions or suggestions contained in the text, such as portrayals of characters or various types of descriptions (landscapes, cities, interiors, situations, actions). Starting from some observations made by William Gass in two essays, "The Medium of Fiction" and "The Concept of Character in Fiction," included in *Fiction and the Figures of Life,* the question of imaging in the act of reading fiction has been discussed by psychologists (Victor Nell: esp. 216–21) and literary scholars (Ellen Esrock), and there is no need to elaborate on it in an essay concerned with the interaction between the oral and the written.

The speed of rereading can vary as greatly, depending on its purposes, as the speed of reading. One can reread very fast, as in textual searches for specific pieces of information, phrases or words— proper names, for instance—in order to check the accuracy of one's memory; but the same rereader will slow down considerably when focusing on the immediate context of the sought-after item. As in the case of reading for information, rereading of this kind is not in and of itself a pleasurable activity, although the discoveries it can lead to can be gratifying. The rereading of "ludic" texts (in Nell's sense) can be as fast, if not faster, than the first reading. Here the pleasure principle reigns supreme, and speed is one of its requirements. By contrast, the rereading of religious texts (texts imbued with orality that require periodic rereading, or what historians of reading call "intensive reading") proceeds in an altogether different fashion. When performed privately, it is usually surrounded by the memory of oral liturgical readings in church, synagogue, or mosque. It is slow, meditative, and involves a double attention—a literal attention to the verbal texture and an allegorical attention to the "spiritual meaning," a meaning which always also applies, however indirectly, to one's own life. Such double attention is also the hallmark of literary reflective rereading. But, like mental imaging, the question of allegorization in (re)reading is beyond the scope of this essay.

Also beyond its scope is another form of slow rereading, which in my book I discuss at some length under the heading of "rereading for the secret" (227–72) and which regards the text as a riddle, puzzle, or enigma. Perhaps the slowest form of rereading is what I would call "writerly" rereading (loosely connected to Roland Barthes's notion of "scriptible" as elaborated in *S/Z*). This is a "professionalist" type of (re)reading as mental (re)writing: a critic (re)reading a book in order write about it, a writer perusing or re-perusing a literary text with the intention of rewriting it (to produce a parody of it, for example). This kind of rereading will, among other things, pay close attention to the voice(s) in the text, to its verbal orchestration, to its tones, tonalities, vocalisms, murmurs, and silences. Textualized orality is both the most difficult and the most rewarding object of parody, pastiche, or imitation.

In many cases of literary rereading, as Brower has noted, it is quite important that we hear "the sentence in the inner ear both for interpretation and judgment of writing," a thing that is "neglected by reading experts" ("Book Reading" 25). It is much less neglected by writers, who may make it a regular practice to read out loud. One cannot but be impressed at the frequency with which Gide notes in his diary sessions of *lecture à haute voix* (reading out loud) from various writers, classic and contemporary, French or foreign. Here are just a few examples, taken from a highly selective English edition of Gide's journals: "We continue reading aloud Tolstoy's *Cossacks*" (54); "A reading aloud of Wilde's *De Profundis* . . . comforts me somewhat" (65); "Every evening I read for Dominique Drouin from eight thirty to nine o'clock [poems by Victor Hugo, Turgenev's short story 'The Dog']" (142); "Every day I read a chapter of *Marius the Epicurean* [by Walter Pater] (with great delight); aloud, for an hour, *The Merry Men* [by R. L. Stevenson]" (169). Thomas Mann, to cite another case, made it a family tradition to read out loud from his work in progress to his wife, Katia, and his children; also, from early on in his career, he gave numerous public readings which were appreciated as performances in their own right. As a recent biographer of Mann notes, the writer was an effective, mesmerizing reader, particularly after electronic sound amplification made his weak voice more audible:

> Recordings in later years of such readings illustrate vividly his virtuosity in maintaining, as he once said, "clarity and total 'speakability' " in his texts: the drawbacks of his style on the printed page—over-long sentences, and humor often obscure or contrived—seem to show to positive advantage. But it took the advent of the microphone to overcome his inaudibility. Reserved among people, he could project his personality best on the podium in front of them: spoken "direct from the manuscript, my lectures and stories are five times better and more gripping, more winning and enthralling, than when they are simply read." (Prater 47)

One might argue that Mann fictionalized his readers also as listeners (or oral readers).

Rereading, a phenomenon uniquely conditioned by the existence of writing, is related to orality in other, more indirect ways, too. For rereading can bring about experiences which are paradoxically close to an imagined world of orality. Is not the rereader of an old favorite in a situation which is, up to a point, similar to that of the hearer of a familiar mythical story in an oral culture? Both know how the action will develop and what the ending will be (unlike the first-time and the generically encoded single-time reader of a suspenseful detective story[7]), but they enjoy nonetheless the unfolding of the story, episode by episode, in the expected succession. Both also enjoy a certain experience of difference—difference in the perception of apparent sameness and repetition, which reflects the subject's changes of mood and experience over time.

Finally, both the rereader and the hearer of an already known tale gain access, through a complex interplay of memory and anticipation, to a different quality of time: a time that seems to move in a cycle or spiral and is thus opposed to the irresistibly linear flow of the time of everyday experience.[8] The parallelisms between a highly literate experience such as that of rereading a valued book and the experience of listening over again to a known story, myth, or legend confirm once more that there is no gap between the worlds of orality and literacy and that oral modes or patterns of consciousness are not abolished in acts of communication, even at the most sophisticated levels of literate composition and reception.

Notes

1. See my book *Rereading,* esp. xi, 8, 9, 15, 63, 77. (Re)reading is meant to emphasize a form of heightened attention to the text, a "structural" attention that is characteristic of the perspective of rereading, as opposed to the perspective of a first-time reading, which can embrace the whole only at the moment when the perusing of the text has reached its final point. In the reading process, however, "structural" attention can be applied to successive "provisional" wholes, either retrospectively or proleptically, and be profitably combined with the "linear" attention and involvement characteristic of reading for the first time (see 44–45). Without denying the necessary linearity of each singular act of reading, (re)reading may also account for the "essential circularity" of the time of rereading. "It is because of this circularity that I often speak of reading and rereading as a single (if double-faced) entity, and that I occasionally use what might look like an orthographic oddity or a manneristic affectation: the word *(re)reading*" (xi).

2. It may be useful to recall here the main moments of this debate. The first major impulse in the relatively new area of anthropological, historical, and cultural studies of orality and literacy came from the so-called "Toronto School," whose main early representatives were Eric A. Havelock, the more controversial, oracular, and popular Marshall McLuhan, with his best-selling *The Gutenberg Galaxy,* and Jack Goody and Ian Watt, with their seminal article about the far-reaching effects of the discovery of alphabetic writing by the ancient Greeks, "The Consequences of Literacy." The insights contained in this essay were nuanced and developed in subsequent books. The works of the "Toronto School" have renewed scholarly interest in the older, groundbreaking researches into the mechanisms of oral poetry and oral memory pursued by Milman Parry since the 1920s and continued by Albert B. Lord in *The Singer of Tales.*

   The methodological insights of the anthropology of oral/written communication have been fruitfully applied to various areas and periods, with notable results in medieval studies, as in M. T. Clanchy's

From Memory to Written Record or in Brian Stock's *The Implications of Literacy* and, more recently, *Augustine the Reader.* Broader in scope are the 1982 masterly survey by Walter J. Ong (*Orality and Literacy*) and Eric A. Havelock's overview of his life work on the orality-literacy problem in ancient Greek culture, including a reflective history of modern oral theory, in *The Muse Learns to Write.*

The "autonomous" and "technologically deterministic" model of literacy and literate/oral consciousness has been challenged on anthropological, sociological, and cultural grounds. The main arguments of such a critique are found in Ruth Finnegan ("Literacy versus Non-Literacy: The Great Divide" and *Literacy and Orality*). See also Brian V. Street's *Literacy in Theory and Practice* for an alternative, "ideological model" of orality/literacy. On the history of literacy in the West, Harvey J. Graff adopts a sociological and historical-materialist perspective.

3. The main philosophical theorist of writing before writing is, of course, Jacques Derrida, particularly in his earlier work (*Speech and Phenomena* and *Of Grammatology*). Derrida's project is deconstructive: it is directed against voice or *phoné,* which it tries to "demystify," voice having been responsible for the ontotheological construction of the subject as presence in Western metaphysics. It is noteworthy that Derrida's sophisticated (and not seldom sophistic) antiphonocentrism has exerted a strong influence on some recent attempts to rehabilitate (literary) voice by recovering the sound component of writing and by reasserting the connection between voice and person, self, or "speaking subject." The most ambitious of these attempts is *Literary Voice* by Donald Wesling and Tadeusz Slawek. One notices the frequency with which such intriguing metaphors as "visual voice," "printed voice," or "textual voice" are used throughout. But the book makes scant reference to reading, and rereading is not considered at all. Some of the recognized precursors of the Wesling/Slawek "philosophy of literary voice" are, aside from Derrida, the two "theologians of voice," Walter Ong and Michel de Certeau (both Jesuits), Mikhail Bakhtin, Henri Meschonnic, and, among American literary critics, Geoffrey Hartman and Garret Stewart. The latter is author of *Reading Voices,* a book that, despite what its title might suggest, is not concerned with either reading or rereading as conceptualized in this essay.

4. But we must not forget that the most famous critique of writing comes also from Plato, namely, from his *Phaedrus* (274c–275b), where one of the chief accusations against writing is that it brings about a weakening of memory (writing, Socrates says, is an "elixir not of memory, but of reminding" and reliance on reminders produces forgetfulness). The Platonic attitude toward writing remains essentially ambivalent even if we also see it, as I think we should, in light of Plato's own recommendation of universal literacy (writing and reading should

be taught equally to boys and girls) in *Laws* (Book 7, 810–810c), as well as of his rejection of the educational consequences of oral poetic memory (in Havelock's reading of the *Republic* in *Preface to Plato*).

5. Psychologists of reading have not failed to notice the analogy, as for instance Harry Levin, who writes in *The Eye-Voice Span:* "Reading music, playing an instrument, and singing have obvious similarities with reading text aloud" (79). The notion of the eye-voice span, i.e., the distance by which the eye is in advance of the voice in reading aloud (this distance may be, according to Levin, as long as eight or ten words), was used by turn-of-the-century psychologists and revived, after its abandonment for several decades of orthodox behaviorism, by today's cognitive psychologists.

6. In "The Writer's Audience Is Always a Fiction," Ong offers a highly interesting if brief history of ways in which readers were "fictionalized" at various times and by various kinds of texts (including fiction, scholarship, correspondence, and personal diaries).

7. In *Orality and Literacy,* Ong observes that the "linear" and climactic plot, which finds its purest expression in the detective story, is inconceivable in an oral culture. Carefully plotted narratives are made possible by writing. I would add that the detective story may also be seen as a triumph of pure "readability," in the sense that it is devised for a maximum effectiveness on a first reading. (The fact that fans may reread a favorite mystery many times over doesn't change the status of the generically encoded reader or "narratee" to whom the climactically plotted narrative is addressed.) By contrast, what I call "rereadable" texts (and I have in mind now such modern classics as Proust's *À la recherche du temps perdu* or Joyce's *Ulysses,* for example), while of course impossible to imagine as verbal performances in the absence of writing, display some of the typical narrative procedures characteristic of oral storytelling (beginnings *in medias res,* episodic structure, a certain apparent looseness of construction despite the strong but hidden internal teleology) and have some striking affinities with myth. Both Proust and Joyce revive mythical scenarios in a modern context: the search for paradise (which Marcel eventually glimpses when he decides to write about this very search) and the initiatory wanderings of the prototypical exile, Ulysses/Bloom.

8. Interestingly, a version of mythic time of archaic orality, about which religious anthropologists and phenomenologists of religion have written extensively, not only reappears in the world of writing/(re)reading, but is recognized as such. Thus, Roland Barthes, who spoke on various occasions of the basic circularity of the time of reading, specifically characterized it as a "mythic time." See, for example, the passage in *The Semiotic Challenge* in which he links the phenomenon of intertextuality to a circular time, a "mythic time without *before* or *after*" (231).

Works Cited

Augustine. *The Confessions of St. Augustine.* Trans. F. J. Sheed. New York: Sheed & Ward, 1943.

Barthes, Roland. *The Semiotic Challenge.* Trans. Richard Howard. New York: Hill and Wang, 1988.

———. *S/Z.* Trans. Richard Miller. New York: Hill and Wang, 1974.

Brower, Reuben A. "Book Reading and the Reading of Books." *The American Reading Public.* Ed. Roger H. Smith. New York: Bowker, 1963.

———. "Reading in Slow Motion." *Defense of Reading.* Eds. Reuben A. Brower and Richard Poirier. New York: Dutton, 1963. 3–21.

Calinescu, Matei. *Rereading.* New Haven: Yale UP, 1993.

Certeau, Michel de. "La lecture absolue." *Problèmes actuels de la lecture.* Eds. L. Dallenbach and J. Ricardou. Paris: Clancier-Guénaud, 1982.

Clanchy, M. T. *From Memory to Written Record: England, 1,066–1,307.* Cambridge, MA: Harvard UP, 1979.

Derrida, Jacques. *Of Grammatology.* Trans. Gayatri Chakravorty Spivak. Baltimore: Johns Hopkins UP, 1976.

———. *Speech and Phenomena, and Other Essays on Husserl's Theory of Signs.* Trans. David B. Allison. Evanston: Northwestern UP, 1973.

Esrock, Ellen J. *The Reader's Eye: Visual Imaging as Reader Response.* Baltimore: Johns Hopkins UP, 1994.

Finnegan, Ruth. *Literacy and Orality: Studies in the Technology of Communication.* London: Blackwell, 1988.

———. "Literacy versus Non-Literacy: The Great Divide." *Modes of Thought.* Eds. R. Finnegan and R. Horton. London: Faber, 1973.

Frank, Joseph. *The Widening Gyre.* Bloomington: Indiana UP, 1968.

Gass, William. *Fiction and the Figures of Life.* New York: Knopf, 1970.

Gide, André. *The Journals of André Gide, 1899–1949.* Ed. and trans. Justin O'Brian. Vol. 1. Evanston: Northwestern UP, 1987.

Gifford, Don. Ulysses *Annotated.* Berkeley: U of California P, 1988.

Goody, Jack, and Ian Watt. "The Consequences of Literacy." *Literacy in Traditional Societies.* Ed. Jack Goody. Cambridge: Cambridge UP, 1968.

Graff, Harvey J. *The Legacies of Literacy: Continuities and Contradictions in Western Culture and Society.* Bloomington: Indiana UP, 1987.

———, ed. *Literacy and Social Development in the West: A Reader.* Cambridge: Cambridge UP, 1981.

Harris, William V. *Ancient Literacy.* Cambridge, MA: Harvard UP, 1989.

Havelock, Eric A. *The Muse Learns to Write: Reflections on Orality and Literacy from Antiquity to the Present.* New Haven: Yale UP, 1986.

———. *Preface to Plato.* Cambridge, MA: Belknap-Harvard UP, 1963.

Levin, Harry. *The Eye-Voice Span.* Cambridge, MA: MIT Press, 1979.

Lewis, C. S. "On Stories." *The Cool Web: Patterns of Children's Reading.* Eds. Margaret Meek et al. New York: Atheneum, 1978. 76–90.

Lord, Albert B. *The Singer of Tales.* Cambridge, MA: Harvard UP, 1960.

McLuhan, Marshall. *The Gutenberg Galaxy: The Making of Typographic Man.* Toronto: U of Toronto P, 1962.

Nell, Victor. *Lost in a Book: The Psychology of Reading for Pleasure.* New Haven: Yale UP, 1988.

Ong, Walter J. *Orality and Literacy.* New York: Methuen, 1982.

———. "The Writer's Audience Is Always a Fiction." *PMLA* 90 (1975): 9–21.

Parry, Milman. *The Making of Homeric Verse: The Collected Papers of Milman Parry.* Ed. Adam Parry. Oxford: Clarendon Press, 1971.

Prater, Donald. *Thomas Mann: A Life.* New York: Oxford UP, 1995.

Saenger, Paul. "The Separation of Words and the Physiology of Reading." *Literacy and Orality.* Eds. David R. Olson and Nancy Torrance. New York: Cambridge UP, 1991. 198–214.

———. "Silent Reading: Its Impact on Late Medieval Script and Society." *Viator* 13 (1982): 367–414.

Stewart, Garrett. *Reading Voices: Literature and the Phonotext.* Berkeley: U of California P, 1990.

Stock, Brian. *Augustine the Reader: Meditation, Self-Knowledge, and the Ethics of Interpretation.* Cambridge, MA: Belknap-Harvard UP, 1996.

———. *The Implications of Literacy: Written Language and Models of Interpretation in the Eleventh and Twelfth Century.* Princeton: Princeton UP, 1983.

Street, Brian V. *Literacy in Theory and Practice.* Cambridge: Cambridge UP, 1984.

Wesling, Donald, and Tadeusz Slawek. *Literary Voice: The Calling of Jonah.* Albany: State U of New York P, 1995.

4

Tradition as Rereading

Bill Shuter

La tradizione son' io!
Pius IX

Although critics may seem the principal students of rereading, they are hardly its only practitioners; nor are literary texts the only texts that are reread. Indeed, rereading is so usual a practice that it might well be described as traditional. But the title of my essay introduces a further supposition: not only is rereading traditional but tradition is itself a form of rereading. Of course this supposition confronts us with a paradox. Rereading is, as we know, retrospective reading. It inverts the familiar order of priority, inviting us to read what comes after as if it preceded what came before and so to trace the origins of the earlier in the later. Tradition, on the other hand, is intelligible only as a means by which the present conserves what originated in the past. How then can tradition be represented as a mode of rereading?

I. Tradition and the Paradox of Precedence

We may begin by reflecting on the vocabulary we employ in speaking of what we call tradition. What the English word conceals other languages make explicit—that the noun designating tradition is derived from a verb (παράδοσις from παραδίδωμαι, traditio from tradere, Überlieferung from Überliefern) and that the verb is transitive. (There is in fact a rare verb "to tradition," but it is a back formation from the noun.) Tradition gets its name from an act—the act by which something is transmitted from one party to another.

Hence the distinctions we are compelled to respect in describing the phenomenon of tradition.

A distinction is often made between the *traditum* (what is transmitted) and *traditio* (the act by which it is transmitted). To which—*traditum* or *traditio*—is priority more properly assigned in the formation of tradition? Presumably to the *traditum* on the grounds that there can be no transmission without something to transmit. But initial presumptions are precisely what the student of rereading has learned to distrust. After all, there is nothing inherently traditional about the practice of carrying a mace or of exchanging rings. These practices became traditions by being preserved and repeated in the ceremonial rituals of commencement and marriage. In one sense a tradition presupposes the existence of some practice or belief that the past transmits to the present; in another sense it is the act of transmission itself that constitutes the *traditum* a *traditum,* and in this sense we can say that tradition as an agent is prior to what it transmits.

Another distinction is often made between the institution and the reception of tradition. By the institution of a tradition we mean the circumstances under which the tradition originated, and by the reception of tradition we mean the history of its subsequent observance, extending, in the case of a still living tradition, to the present. Even more explicitly than the distinction between *traditum* and *traditio,* the distinction between institution and reception prompts reflection on the paradox of precedence. It seems self-evident that the origin or institution of a tradition precedes its reception. But in fact when we describe some practice or belief as traditional, we are thinking not so much of its origin or institution as of its observance and reception. A tradition is no less a tradition because its origin is unknown or because it has changed its form or substance since the time of its institution. Moreover, the functions of institution and reception are not always readily differentiated. Because a particular usage or belief has been preserved, it does not necessarily follow that those who first practiced it or believed it designed it for preservation. The determination to preserve it is made in fact by those who receive it as a tradition, and a tradition they neglect to preserve ceases to be a tradition. As a *traditum* may be said to become a *traditum* through the act of transmission, so a tradition may be said to become a tradition by virtue of the act of reception, and in both cases the presumed order of precedence is inverted. It seems that we cannot reflect on the language of tradition without being led to reflect on the language of precedence, and that language proves to be a language of paradox.

We say that we look forward to the future and back at the past and speak of the future as before us and of the past as behind us. But the future to which we look forward we also call an aftertime or posterity, and the past at which we look back we also call a foretime or an anterior time. The Latin *porro* means "forward," "ahead," and also "hereafter." The Greek cognate is πρόσσω, a word of similar meaning. But when Achilles says of Agamemnon that he "has not wit enough to look behind [πρόσσω] and before [ὀπίσσω] him," πρόσσω must refer to the past and ὀπόσσω, which means "backwards" or "after," to the future (*Iliad* 1.343). The past lies before us presumably because, being known, it is visible to us, while the future, being still unknown, is behind us. Man, says Hamlet, was made "looking before and after," but a good deal depends on which way he is facing, and that is a matter, linguists assure us, about which the witness of language is inconclusive (Lakoff and Johnson 14–21; Traugott 369–400; Jaenecke). Prometheus was said to have a brother who never became a culture hero. He was named Epimetheus ("Afterthought"), perhaps because we live in retrospect as well as in prospect. At any rate, this double perspective leaves us with the paradox of precedence. In prospect the past seems to be behind us; only in retrospect does it seem to precede us. The same is true of words reread on a page.

Precedence describes a relation, but a relation difficult to define, partly because the vocabulary available to us is deficient. To speak of a precedent is to suppose some later circumstance of which it is the precedent. But we lack a convenient term for this second term in the relation. Consistency would require us to speak of the precedent and the precedented. We also lack a verb to describe the act that initiates the relation of precedence. The verb "to precede" is inadequate because to precede something else in time is not necessarily to function as its precedent. At one time English did have a verb "to precedent" (another back formation from the noun) of which only the past participle "precedented" remains in use. From the sense of the participle we would infer that the verb meant "to be a precedent for." And so it did. From 1614, the *OED* cites "The examples of diverse kings . . . do president [precedent] us in these carriages." But the *OED* also documents another sense. In 1630 Archbishop Williams wrote, "Now we are no longer able to president ourselves, in this kind, by the Chappell but by the Liturgie of Queen Elizabeth." In the first sense the agent of precedence is the past ("examples of diverse kings"); in the second sense it is the present ("we"). Reflection on the language of precedence again seems to compel us to adopt a double perspective. A circumstance we describe as a precedent must come from an earlier time than that of which it is the precedent. But only from the perspective of a later time can it be said to have functioned as a precedent. In this sense it seems that precedence is necessarily the product of retrospection or, we may say, of rereading.

Precedence and precedents are of particular importance to institutions that rely on tradition as the principal source of their legitimacy. The history of the English constitution, for example, is largely a history of the precedents on which it is based. Of these precedents, none is more venerable than Magna Carta. It has been called "the fountaine of all the fundamentall lawes of the realm," "the Bible of the English Constitution," a "sacred Covenant," "the edifice of the constitution," and "the palladium of English liberty" (Pallister 10, 56, 52, 96; Petit-Dutaillis and Lefebvre 130). But a precedent is, as we have seen, what is received as a precedent, and what is received may also be dismissed. Early in the twentieth century, writers began to speak of the "myth" of Magna Carta. An article with that title by Edward Jenks put the matter bluntly: "All the beliefs of past generations cannot make a conclusion true, if the evidence does not warrant it," and in the case of Magna Carta the evidence did not. The myth held that Magna Carta represented the first collective action of the English people and constituted "a landmark in constitutional progress," but in fact it represented the conservative, even reactionary, demands of the barons, who had grown jealous of the encroaching powers of the king. Magna Carta looks not forward but backward: "It consecrates the past, not the future" (Jenks 261, 271). The demythologizing of Magna Carta was most effectively accomplished by William McKechnie, whose scholarly historical study appeared in 1905. Magna Carta was "a baronial manifesto," "feudal, contractual, and (in parts, at least) reactionary in tone," and those who drafted it hardly deserve the "excessive laudation" they have received. "There is scarcely one great principle of the modern English constitution . . . which has not been read by commentators into Magna Carta," but the barons of the early thirteenth century had no notion of the constitutional liberties for which their document would be cited as a precedent (McKechnie 119, 110, 119, 133, 123). A French historian summarizing the state of opinion in his time noted the fundamental principle underlying the revisionist view of Magna Carta; "Texts have to be read . . . without preoccupying ourselves with the importance which has been attributed to them in later ages" (Petit-Dutaillis 128).

But the stone rejected by the historian serves as cornerstone to the student of historiography, if by historiography we understand the "record of what one age finds of interest in another" (Burrow 1). The historiography of Magna Carta is in effect a history of the rereadings given it at different periods and by representatives of different interests. In fact, Magna Carta has not always enjoyed the veneration it sometimes received. Its essentially feudal character, for example, was first discovered not in the twentieth century but in the Restoration (Butterfield 22–25). It was relatively neglected in the Tudor period; Shakespeare, it has often been noted, makes no mention of it in *King John.* At various times it has been cited as a precedent by defenders of the royal prerogative as well as by advocates of the rights of Parliament, by Conservatives as well as by Radicals, by Tories as well as by Whigs. But the rereading of Magna Carta that has prevailed over all others, the reading that became the "traditional" reading and that historians have in mind when they speak of the "myth" of Magna Carta, is the reading given it by the parliamentary leaders of the seventeenth century and in particular by Sir Edward Coke. This received reading has been described as "a skyscraper built out of . . . anachronisms" (Butterfield 13). The abuses of John were understood in the light of the abuses of James I and Charles I; functions were assigned to a "parliament" that did not exist in 1215; the phrase *liber homo,* which in Magna Carta meant "freeholder," was taken to include the commons; and the reference to *judicium parium* ("trial by one's peers") was interpreted in terms of seventeenth-century practice (McKechnie 178–79, 115, 178).

Manifestly unhistorical, these rereadings are nevertheless of great interest to the historiographer because they illustrate how a later age conceived its relation to an earlier age. The anachronistic readers of Magna Carta were men convinced that the rights and liberties for which they contended were not things to be granted by "grace" of the sovereign, but inherited possessions that Englishmen enjoyed by "right" of ancient precedent. Moreover, these anachronistic readings of Magna Carta had real historic consequences. Their determination to have their readings confirmed in law led, in fact, to the drafting of the Petition of Right, to which Charles was forced to give his assent in 1628 (Butterfield 16). From the historiographer's point of view, what Magna Carta meant in 1215 was ultimately of less importance than what it came to mean to those who appealed to it as a precedent (McKechnie 134).

The story of Magna Carta is a particularly striking instance not only of the power but also of the problematic character of what we understand by precedent. Was Magna Carta an authentic historical precedent of the Petition of Right? Our answer to this question will depend very much on whether we are readers of the story or rereaders of it. Readers, supposing that earlier historical events may not be interpreted by later events, will deal summarily with Magna Carta's claim to count as a precedent. An earlier event may count as the precedent of a later event only to the degree that what it meant at the time was what it was understood to mean at a later age, and what Magna Carta meant in 1215 differed so fundamentally from what it was understood to mean in 1628 that it cannot count as a precedent for the Petition of Right. Reading Magna Carta in the light of the conditions of their own time, the parliamentarians misread it and constructed what was in effect a mythical precedent.

Rereaders of the story, being more inclined to reflect on the ways the history of Magna Carta illustrates the paradoxes of precedence, will be less dismissive. While conceding that a retrospective reading of the past cannot make myths into historical facts, they will also acknowledge that it is retrospective reading, and retrospective reading alone, that makes an earlier event into the precedent of a later event. Precedence, unlike historicity, is a retrospective phenomenon, because what has never been accounted a precedent is no precedent. Magna

Carta, read, to be sure, retrospectively, was explicitly invoked by the drafters of the Petition of Right and functioned for them as a precedent. In historical fact, the constitutional liberties of Englishmen were strengthened by the accomplishments of Parliament, and it was this that a historian had in mind when he observed that there is a sense in which "the myth of Magna Carta was made to come true" (Butterfield 18). That Magna Carta looked backward rather than forward may in fact be said to make it more rather than less a precedent of the Petition of Right. The Petition of Right (not in the French or American style a Declaration) took the form it did—a demand that the King acknowledge the illegality of his actions—in large part because what the barons who had drafted Magna Carta were demanding was not something new but rather the restoration of customary usage. Magna Carta was, as Samuel Johnson observed, "born with a grey beard" (qtd. in Pallister 2). It was not innovation that the parliamentarians claimed they were demanding or supposed they were demanding but a return to immemorial custom. They thereby exhibited that precedental habit of mind that has been often noted as distinctively characteristic of English constitutional history.[1] More precisely, we may speak of a precedental tradition, a tradition of which the Petition of Right was a historically important product and within which Magna Carta functioned as an authentic historical precedent.

Coke revered precedent as he did because he was a lawyer and a jurist for whom law meant the English common law. Common law differs from other systems of law in its fundamental doctrine of *stare decisis* ("to abide, or adhere to, decided cases"), which requires that a case in common law be adjudicated in conformity with decisions of earlier courts in comparable cases. In short, precedent binds. Coke had a lawyer's reverence for precedent, but he also had a lawyer's understanding of it, and that understanding is rather different from the understanding of a historian. When Coke read a thirteenth-century legal precedent, he read it not like a modern legal historian, for what it meant in the thirteenth century, but for what it meant after a long series of decisions in the courts (Butterfield 13). To a practicing lawyer, the state of the law is what the courts have said it is. Thus, it appears that the established status of a precedent is less certain than an initial reading of the doctrine of *stare decisis* would suggest. When a court cites an earlier precedent as applicable to the case before it, it offers a reading of the terms and reach of the precedent, and its reading becomes itself precedental to later courts.

In common law, earlier cases may be said to enjoy a kind of afterlife in which their real work as precedents is done or not done. What an earlier case may serve as a precedent for and whether it may serve as a precedent at all are questions for the retrospective judgment of later courts that determine whether an earlier decision will be broadened and applied to cases not originally within its reach or so narrowed by exceptions that it is deprived of all effective force. This afterlife of precedent is, moreover, the actual life of the law, where real cases are decided by the living judges who function as the custodians of the tradition we call common law. Judges decide the cases before them, and their decisions refer to the precedents on which they rely. But the nature of precedence is such that the judicial function is necessarily paradoxical. Judges decide cases on the basis of precedent, but in so deciding they also determine what is meant by the precedents on which they rely. The paradox is most acute in those cases lawyers call "hard cases." A case is hard, or interesting, to the degree that there is no decisive precedent for deciding it either way, when, in other words, the law is silent or only mutters indistinctly. Nevertheless, a hard case must be decided. What is the judge doing when he exercises what is called judicial discretion in deciding a hard case? Is he "inventing" law, or is he in some sense "discovering" law—i.e., rereading with a new bent?

The distinction between inventing and discovering law is commonly made by observers and critics of the courts. Judges themselves, we are told, often employ a different language:

> [W]hen good judges try to explain in some general
> way how they work, they search for figures of speech
> to describe the constraints they feel even when they
> suppose that they are making new law. . . . They say,
> for example, that they find new rules immanent in the
> law as a whole, or that they are enforcing an internal
> logic of the law through some method that belongs
> more to philosophy than to politics, or that they are
> agents through which the law works itself pure, or

that the law has some life of its own even though
this belongs to experience rather than logic. (Dworkin,
Rights 112)

Ronald Dworkin, the legal philosopher I have been quoting, believes
that any adequate theory of law must respect the implications of such
metaphors. He proposes that we think of the law as a traditional
social practice and of judges as the tradition's authorized interpreters.
The authorized interpreter of a tradition practices what Dworkin calls
"constructive interpretation." He understands himself as participating
in the tradition he interprets, not as undertaking to overthrow it or to
introduce a new tradition. He understands the history of the tradition
he is interpreting not as a mere record of what has been considered
consistent with that tradition at various times in the past, but *"as if"*
that history reflected some informing intention, purpose, or meaning
that the tradition itself had never explicitly articulated (*Law's Empire*
58–59). Having determined the intention of the historical tradition, the
interpreter is in a position to decide what is or is not consistent with
that intention in the present by extending or limiting the tradition's requirements, even when his extensions and limitations modify what the
tradition had been understood to require in the past (*Law's Empire* 47).

In the case of the legal tradition, judicial interpretation is said to
"restructure" precedent (*Law's Empire* 88). To restructure a precedent is to reread it, because to find the formulation of a later time
present implicitly in an earlier text is to read what came before in the
light of what came later, which is what we understand by rereading.
Constructive interpretation is therefore another term for rereading. In
some respects "rereading" would actually seem the preferable term.
The interpreter of an activity is not normally required to participate in
the activity he interprets. We call a translator an interpreter because
interpretation often adopts a language or mode other than the language
or mode of what is interpreted. But a rereading does not belong to a
different genus of activity than the initial reading it rereads, and a
rereader becomes a rereader not by ceasing to read but by continuing
to read.

The notion of rereading proves particularly useful in connection
with Dworkin's argument that the complex character of a judicial in-

terpretation resembles that of a literary interpretation. To suggest this complexity he offers the hypothetical illustration of the composition of a chain novel. Before writing the chapter he has been assigned, the author of each chapter must study the chapters written by the authors who preceded him. Like his predecessors, he understands that his contribution must be designed to give the reader the sense that the novel is not the product of many hands, but it is in fact the work of a single author (*Law's Empire* 229). By analogy, a judge inherits a text to which he must contribute a chapter. His contribution must be seen as a continuation of the text he has received, not as the opening of a new text. It will necessarily represent his sense of the character and direction of the text he has undertaken to continue. It will represent, in other words, his reading of it. But the inherited text itself consists of a long series of chapters written by earlier judges who wrote under precisely the same constraint as the latest judge. They too had to read or construe the text they inherited. What the latest judge reads is in fact a series of earlier readings. He may therefore be described as a rereader. And so, of course, may his predecessors.

The constructive interpretation of past precedents that I have been calling rereading is required by the traditional character of common law. Periodic revision of existing law is made necessary by the nature of things. When the body of law on which the courts rely proves inconsistent or no longer applicable, revision becomes imperative. But an existing state of law can be revised in more than one way. A statute recognized as no longer adequate can be repealed entirely or partially. But because in common law precedent binds, earlier decisions are not normally overruled but interpreted. In this way a legal system originating under feudal conditions was adapted to a society whose relations are primarily commercial. When the past exercises authority over the present, the past must be reread. And lawyers must be reckoned among our most accomplished rereaders of the past.

And so must Catholic theologians, and for the same reasons.[2] Legal philosophers must address the question: Does the court in the person of the judge make new law? Catholic theologians must address a comparable question: Does the church in the person of the pope make new dogma? From one point of view, he certainly seems to. In 1854 Pius IX proclaimed the dogma of the Immaculate

Conception, that is, that the Virgin Mary was free of original sin from the moment of her conception. In 1950 Pius XII proclaimed the dogma of the Assumption, that is, that at the end of her mortal life, the Virgin Mary was assumed body and soul into heaven. If these dogmas were not in some sense new, why proclaim them? So, at any rate, the question might appear to an outside observer. From within the Catholic tradition, however, it is as unsatisfactory to speak of the pope as making new dogma as it would be for the courts to describe themselves as making new law. The papal proclamations stressed that the dogmas being defined had always been firmly and universally held by faithful Catholics. In the Apostolic Constitution defining the dogma of the Assumption, Pius XII repeated the words of the First Vatican Council: "The Holy Spirit was promised to the successors of Peter not so that by a revelation from the Spirit they might disclose some new doctrine but so that by the assistance of the Spirit they might piously keep and faithfully expound the revelation transmitted by the Apostles or the deposit of faith" (*Acta* 42: 757). When the pope defines a dogma, what he does is therefore the very opposite of innovation. What he in fact determines by the exercise of infallible authority is that the belief in question was the belief of the church from the time of the apostles.

Whether this distinction renders the papal claims more modest is uncertain, but it certainly renders them more interesting for the purposes of our study. The New Testament tells us nothing about the circumstances of Mary's conception or her death, and there is no record of a belief in her bodily assumption before the latter part of the fourth century. But if there is no documented early precedent for these beliefs, how can it be maintained that they were part of the revelation received by the apostles and faithfully transmitted to their successors? The outlines of the answer are familiar. A doctrine explicitly formulated only at a later time may be found implicitly present in the early expressions of the tradition, "instinct," as the lawyers say, in earlier precedent. To read the history of the tradition in this way is a prerogative of its official interpreters, who are thereby authorized to reread it. In Catholic theology, as in common law, an earlier authority may be invoked in regard to a question he never actually considered. Thus, Cardinal Newman acknowledged that St. Paul would scarcely have understood the words "Immaculate Conception," but he nevertheless argued that if Paul "had been asked, whether or not our Lady held the grace of the Spirit anticipating all sin whatever, including Adam's imputed sin, I think he would have answered in the affirmative" (159). In Catholic theology, as in common law, even the very language of an earlier authority may be appropriated and adapted to a new purpose. Thus in the Mass for the Vigil of the Assumption, the first reading, from 1 Chronicles 15–16, describes David honoring the Ark of the Covenant because, as the pope tells us, many theologians have understood the incorruptible wood of the Ark as an image of the "most pure body of the Virgin Mary preserved from every corruption of the tomb"; and in the Mass for the feast itself, the first reading is from Revelations 12, because theologians have associated the Virgin Mary with John's vision of a woman clothed with the sun for whom a special place had been prepared by God (*Acta* 4:763).[3]

To the student of tradition, Catholic theology offers much of interest. For example, the distinction between *traditum* (the content of tradition) and *traditio* (the act of transmission) with which I began this chapter was borrowed from the language of Catholic theology, and such language will again prove useful to our study. At this point we need only cite the declaration of the Second Vatican Council: "the Church does not draw her certainty about all revealed truths from the holy Scriptures alone. . . . [Both] Scripture and Tradition must be accepted and honored with equal feelings of devotion and reverence" (*Vatican Council* II 755)[4] Reading the word of God in any form requires hermeneutic skill, and Catholicism has had to perfect not only a hermeneutics of Scripture but what we might call a hermeneutics of tradition, illustrated, for example, by the Apostolic Constitution of Pius XII, which wove a chain of witnesses to the doctrine of the Assumption from early liturgical celebrations, doctors of the Greek church, scholastic theologians, earlier popes, and petitions from the faithful. The church reads tradition as it reads Scripture, and tradition, like Scripture, means what the church says it means. Of course, it has been objected that the church's procedure is circular: the church derives what it believes from tradition, but it derives its knowledge of tradition from what it believes (Congar 184).[5] The objection is not entirely unjust. In tradition the church traces her own history, reading what she has become in the light of what she has been and rereading what she has been in the light of what she has become.

Within a tradition so conceived, the Catholic theologian exercises his exacting office. Not unlike a judge, the Catholic theologian contributes to the progress of his discipline by proposing answers to new questions. For the most part, these questions concern matters that have not been authoritatively decided, but even settled matters occasion questions. For example, what is the meaning of a traditional dogma in a world whose intellectual or cultural conditions differ profoundly from the conditions under which the dogma was formulated? New questions seem to demand new answers, but when it comes to answering hitherto unasked questions, the Catholic theologian, like the judge, works under a special constraint. He remains a participant in the activity he interprets. He contributes to an inherited story that he may continue but not begin anew. He must read the story he has inherited as if it had an author, and a single author. The earlier and later forms of his tradition must be seen as determined and informed by a single intention. He is not free to ignore the later forms and respect only the earlier ones. He cannot know how close to the end of the story his contribution falls, but he does know that the story he has inherited is a very long one and that many possible directions have already been authoritatively excluded. His position is therefore similar to that of a judge who must determine how the law answers a question it has never been asked. Like the judge, he must proceed as if the tradition held the answer implicitly if not explicitly. In general, he must propose an answer consistent with tradition. But particularly in the case of a question to which the tradition offers no apparent answer or seems to offer conflicting answers (the equivalent of a hard case in law), he must also offer a reading of the tradition consistent with the answer he proposes. He must practice what Dworkin calls "constructive interpretation," because a Catholic reading of tradition is necessarily a rereading. Of course, theologians often disagree, and their readings of the story to which they contribute differ.[6] And of course, like judges, theologians have no certainty about the fate their opinions will meet. Some legal precedents will receive general acceptance, others will be neglected, and still others will be overruled. So some theological opinions will be accepted as orthodox formulations, others will be forgotten except by historians, and others will be formally condemned.

II. Tradition and the Paradox of Innovation

In common law and Catholic theology, the rereading of precedent permits tradition to accommodate the new without discarding the old. But is the capacity to accommodate innovation through rereading an inherent characteristic of tradition? How we answer this question will depend on how we understand the nature of tradition.

For the historian Eric Hobsbawm, the distinguishing quality of tradition is invariance; formalized repetition is what makes tradition tradition (2). And for the social sciences in general, tradition is a typical instance of what William Ogburn called "cultural lag" or of what Karl Mannheim described as the "contemporaneity of the non-contemporaneous" (Ogburn 200–80; Mannheim 41–43). When the present is conceived as a field of contention between the past and the future, tradition will inevitably appear as an impediment to change and therefore to progress. But when earlier and later are conceived less agonistically, tradition appears in a different light, as it does in the sociological study of Edward Shils. Traditions for Shils are not immutable but inherently capable of change at the hands of their adherents. Indeed, like a living organism, a tradition must change or perish. The changes it undergoes are, moreover, like the changes undergone by an organism, either internal ("endogenous")—a tradition may be reformulated or reordered by those who belong to it— or external ("exogenous")—a tradition may assimilate elements from alien traditions, fuse with them, or actively resist them. Traditions live, die, and are occasionally reborn (Shils 213, 215, 275–79, 255–56, 285–86).

How we conceive tradition will of course determine how much of life we suppose it to occupy. Conceiving it as invariant, Hobsbawm supposes that tradition represents a relatively narrow category of contemporary life. He distinguishes tradition from custom, which "does not preclude innovation and change" so long as they are perceived as consistent with precedent. Common law is therefore custom, not tradition, and a British courtroom provides a convenient illustration of the distinction: " 'Custom' is what judges do; 'tradition' . . . is the wig, robe and other forms of paraphernalia and ritualized practices surrounding their substantial action" (Hobsbawm 2, 3). Hobsbawm also distinguishes tradition from convention and routine, which resemble tradition in their invariance but differ from it in function. A convention like wearing a crash helmet when riding a motorcycle serves a practical purpose; a tradition like "wearing a particular type of hard hat in combination with hunting pink" does not (Hobsbawm 3). Shils, conceiving tradition less inflexibly, represents it as a far more capacious category. Anything created by human beings and "handed down from one generation to the next" is a tradition (12). It therefore includes not only what Hobsbawm explicitly excludes but a good deal more as well. Hobsbawm and Shils offer very different conceptions of tradition, but whether it is conceived as invariant or as undergoing changes analogous to those of a living being, tradition proves equally paradoxical, which is why both conceptions are of interest to our inquiry.

Viewed as essentially invariant, tradition appears in a rather unexpected light. If by a tradition we understand a repeated, nonfunctional practice, then a practice cannot become traditional until it ceases to be functional. Thus, the spurs of a Cavalry officer's dress uniform became traditional only after they became unnecessary, and the wigs of British lawyers became traditional only after it was no longer usual to wear wigs (Hobsbawm 4). As a tradition, neither of these practices is as old as it seems to be. In one way or another, this proves true of all the traditions studied by Hobsbawm and his fellow contributors to *The Invention of Tradition*. We learn, for example, that the Scottish kilt was invented after 1726 by an English ironmaster, that the clans were assigned their distinctive tartans in 1819 by an enterprising cloth merchant (Trevor-Roper 21–22, 30), that the medieval pageantry we associate with a British coronation dates largely from the period between the late 1870s and 1914 (Cannadine 120), and that the Welsh *eisteddfodau* artificially reconstructed customs no longer actually practiced (Morgan 56–62). Like all the traditions described in Hobsbawm's book, they arose not in a remote and obscure past but at a particular point in time, and a relatively recent point. Therefore Hobsbawm speaks not of the origin of tradition but of its invention.

That many traditions are in fact invented, he has no doubt. Whether there are also authentic traditions, he is uncertain, on occasion even skeptical.[7] In practice a tradition is an innovation that effectively conceals its novelty, but as Hobsbawm reminds us, "novelty is no less novel for being able to dress up easily as antiquity" (5).

Hobsbawm's view of tradition issues in another of the curious paradoxes of precedence (and therefore of rereading). People invent traditions when the once existing state of things has been so fundamentally altered that they need new and unprecedented ways of conceiving their relation to the past. It would therefore be more accurate to describe tradition as a response to change than to describe change as a repudiation of tradition. Moreover, most of what we now think of as public tradition was devised to meet needs that arose only in relatively recent times. It is therefore not so much that tradition precedes modernity as that modernity precedes tradition.

Invented tradition attracts the critical attention of the historian in the first place because it is an instance of historical retrojection, that is, of the assigning of an earlier date to a later occurrence. Retrojection is not an uncommon phenomenon; it can be observed in much that we have described as tradition but that Hobsbawm calls custom. Its operation in the history of law was studied in the middle of the last century by Henry Sumner Maine, who described it as a "legal fiction," broadening the usual sense of that phrase to include "any assumption which conceals, or affects to conceal, the fact that a rule of law has undergone alteration, its letter remaining unchanged, its operation being modified" (25). Although he believed the time had come to purge the English common law of residual legal fictions, Maine acknowledged their earlier necessity: Because they "do not offend the superstitious disrelish for change which is always present," they are, at "a particular stage of social progress . . . invaluable expedients for overcoming the rigidity of law" (25). A more recent historical account observes with regard to precedent in common law: "Although the old law books show the importance of case law, there is no trace until comparatively recent times of the doctrine that a precedent may itself have the force of law" (Baker 104). The formula *stare decisis,* which, following the handbooks, I described as the fundamental principle of common law, entered general usage only in the eighteenth century; in 1782 "an eminent judge said it was one of the most sacred rules in the law." Indeed, the present notion of binding precedent is supposed to have originated in the nineteenth century (Baker 105). Analogous observations have been made about the theological traditions considered earlier.[8] From the perspective of many historians, what we have been calling rereadings will look more like retrojections, even fictions or inventions. We have, it seems, two quite irreconcilable ways of reading the past. History is often read by historians (particularly by historians of technology) as the history of change. When history is read in this way, the new seems to displace or fundamentally alter the old, and tradition itself appears as an innovation, although, as Hobsbawm demonstrates, a self-concealing one. But when history is read, for example, by lawyers and theologians, as a history of continuities, what came before is taken as an earlier form of what comes later, and lawyers and theologians call the continuities they describe traditions. In the first case the past is read; in the second it is, we may say, reread.

Shils is more attentive to continuities than Hobsbawm, and therefore his treatment of tradition is more generous. It is, however, no less paradoxical. Conceived as anything handed down from the past to the present, tradition includes not only those practices transmitted by the social institutions of family, church, and school, but also the accumulated cultural store of what social scientists call "symbolic constructions," "cultural objectivations," or "*Ideengebilde*" (Shils 89). Many of the areas of cultural production described by Shils as tradition—theology, the arts, literature, humanistic scholarship, for example—we are accustomed to thinking of as traditional or as generating traditions. Others, however, because they are closely associated with innovation or with the rejection of the authority of the past, we are accustomed to thinking of as without tradition or as actively antitraditional. Thus the paradox of Shils's view is the converse of Hobsbawm's. Whereas for Hobsbawm what appears to be traditional proves under scrutiny to look more like innovation, for Shils what appears to be innovation proves under scrutiny to resemble tradition. For Hobsbawm "novelty is no less novel for being able to dress up easily as tradition"; for Shils tradition is no less tradition for being able to dress up as antiquity.

Advances in the natural sciences, for example, are not usually thought of as governed by tradition. The scientist makes headway in his discipline by distrusting the received view of things, in a sense "falsifying" it. A scientist who argued for his conclusions by appealing to the authority of tradition would not progress in the scientific community. But the existence of a scientific community is itself a fact that invites reflection. With no central organ of scientific authority, with no written scientific constitution or rules of association, practicing scientists display a degree of consensus that permits them to agree, for example, on which scientific papers should be published or which scientific projects deserve funding. John Ziman has, in fact, described science as "unique in striving for, and insisting on, a consensus" and characterized science as the "consensible discipline" (131, 13, 83). What is the source of this coherence of scientific opinion? According to Michael Polanyi, the very

> continued existence of science is an expression of the fact that scientists are agreed in accepting one tradition, and that all trust each other to be informed by this tradition. Suppose scientists were in the habit of regarding most of their fellows as cranks or charlatans. Fruitful discussion between them would become impossible and they would no more rely on each other's results nor act on each other's opinion. . . . It would then become impossible to recognize any statement as a scientific proposition or to describe anyone as a scientist. Science would become practically extinct. (38–39)

Ziman speaks of the need to "internalize" the standards, conventions, and "unconscious traditions" of science (96–97). He reminds us, for example, that the "typical" scientific paper is as conventional as "a sonnet, or a fugue, or a master game of chess." It employs the plural pronoun "we" because the scientist sees not only through "his own eyes" but "through the eyes of his predecessors and colleagues" (Ziman 79, 9). "Tradition," writes Werner Heisenberg, "exerts its full influence in deeper layers of the scientific process, where it is not so easily visible" (225). Polanyi speaks of a "community of consciences" (42), Shils of "the traditional ethos of science" (111), and Ziman of an "Invisible College" (130–31). But of course the procedural traditions of science are designed to secure its continuing advance, which explains Polanyi's paradoxical claim: "It is part of the scientific tradition to be constantly on our guard against suppressing by mistake some great discovery, the claims of which may at first appear nonsensical on account of their novelty" (38).

Practicing scientists are generally less aware of the traditionality of their discipline than are theologians, lawyers, or students of the humanities because theirs is a tradition skeptical of tradition. It is a tradition nevertheless. In this respect, it is not unique. Modern science belongs to that family of invisible traditions we may call traditions of antitraditionality (Shils 160, 324). Another instance, closely associated with the tradition of science, is what Shils calls the tradition of invention. In the last two centuries, technological invention has flourished in the West to a degree unprecedented in earlier periods or in other cultures. What discouraged invention in earlier periods was not an active resistance to innovation; it was rather that these periods were without an inherited "belief in the goodness of invention" (Shils 86). They lacked what the modern world, with its precedents, its incentives, and its rewards, possesses— a "tradition of inventiveness" (Shils 88). "Traditionality is reinforced by the perception of traditionality, the tradition of inventiveness is reinforced by the perception of inventiveness in others" (Shils 88).

Of these antitraditional traditions, the most paradoxical, and therefore for our purposes the most interesting, is probably the tradition of originality. The paradoxes of originality are, in fact, the paradoxes of tradition seen from another point of view. Nowhere, it seems, are innovation and tradition more decisively opposed than in the tradition of originality. By those who value innovation for its own sake, what is original is virtually defined as that which is not traditional, and by implication, what is traditional is defined as that which is unoriginal. But this decisive opposing of originality and tradition has always been unstable, and therefore reflection on the subject is almost universally attended with paradox. The instability is fundamental. It is not reduced by the familiar concession that even the most original work owes something to tradition. Subjected to reflection, the terms themselves seem to exchange places. What appears original often proves to be traditional, and what appears to be traditional often proves to be original. In "The Originality Paradox" (a chapter of *Originality and Imagination*), Thomas McFarland assembles a number of these reflections. He quotes Emerson's injunction "insist on yourself; never imitate," but also his observations "There never was an original writer" and "The originals are not originals" (*Complete Works* 2:83, 8:180; *Early Lectures* 284–85, qtd. in McFarland 4, 15, 17). From Harold Bloom, the tradition's belated but fervent representative, he quotes: "the precursors flood us, and our imaginations can die by drowning in them, but no imaginative life is possible if such inundation is wholly evaded" (154, qtd. in McFarland 11). From Goethe, he quotes: "People are always talking about originality; but what do they mean? . . . If I could give an account of all that I owe to great predecessors and contemporaries, there would not be much left over," but not the better known and equally appropriate lines from *Faust:*

> What you have inherited from your fathers
> Earn, so that you may possess it.
>
> (*Gedenkausgabe* 24: 158–59, qtd. in McFarland 29;
> *Faust I* I:1)

Because the tradition of originality is often thought to have been initiated by Edward Young's *Conjectures on Original Composition* in 1759, a particular interest attaches to Young's formulation: "may not this Paradox pass into a Maxim? *viz.* 'The less we copy the renowned Antients, we shall resemble them the more' "(Young 21, qtd. in McFarland 6). But as McFarland shrewdly reminds us, Johnson once told Boswell that "he was surprised to find Young receive as novelties what he thought very common maxims" (qtd. in McFarland 21).[9] McFarland pays the appropriate attention to T. S. Eliot's important and intentionally paradoxical essay "Tradition and the Individual Talent." Eliot argued not only that the "best" and "most individual" parts of a poet's work are "those in which the dead poets, his ancestors, assert their immortality most vigorously," but also that "novelty is better than repetition" and, echoing Goethe, that tradition "cannot be inherited, and if you want it you must obtain it by great labour" (4).

The paradox that traditionality is less unoriginal than it seems has inspired fewer epigrams than the paradox that originality is less original than it seems; nevertheless, the one is the obverse of the other. So potent, however, is the hold of the tradition of originality over our minds that instances elude our notice. Jaroslav Pelikan recalls the disappointment he felt when as a young man he undertook the study of a Byzantine florilegium for the first time. He read it through, looking for the author's own words and indications of his own views; they were not to be found: "there was only this seemingly random compilation of passages from various sources . . ." (73). (The word "compilation" is, we may note, derived from a verb that was once understood to mean "to pillage" but came to mean "to compose" [Rouse and Rouse 119–20].) From an older scholar, Pelikan later learned how a florilegium was to be read. Such a text must be recognized as "an explicit refusal to be 'original' and . . . its originality and creativity must therefore be sought in its repetition of the standard formulas, not apart from that repetition"—in, that is, "the selection, wording, and arrangement of the quotations it brings together." Pelikan had initially misread the florilegium because, as he later understood, he had misconceived "the relation between tradition and creativity" in assuming "that the second began where the first left off" (74). The same misconception encourages misreadings of such genres as midrash, pseudographia (both canonical and noncanonical), and medieval commentary on authoritative texts, not to mention such postmodern "playgiarisms" as Georges Perec's *Life: A User's Manual.*[10] Thinking more particularly of literature, Northrop Frye makes a point similar to Pelikan's. The search for what Frye calls "*residual* originality" makes it difficult properly to read not only Chaucer, "much of whose poetry is translated or paraphrased from others," but also Shakespeare and Milton. Frye detects an interesting family resemblance between two of our anti-traditional traditions in the supposition of copyright law that "every work of art is an invention distinctive enough to be patented" (96). We may add that the distinctions we are accustomed to draw between allusion and plagiarism or between imitation or generic convention and literary forgery obscure the paradoxical relation of originality and tradition that they all in one way or another illustrate.

Historical scholarship has been diligent in uncovering the paradoxes of the tradition of originality.[11] Coleridge complained of critics "who seem to hold that every possible thought and image is traditional;

who have no notion that there are such things as fountains in the world" (66), but scholars continue to demonstrate that what appears to be original is actually derivative, tracing precedents for the poetic innovations of *Lyrical Ballads* (Mayo) or for the language of Keats, or, in McFarland's favorite illustration (14), observing that Milton's boast "Things unattempted yet in prose and rhyme" (*Paradise Lost* 1.16) is actually a quotation from the *Orlando Furioso* (Quint 216).[12] And scholars have been equally diligent in distinguishing the strata of interpolation, verbal elaboration, and explanatory gloss in texts transmitted over long time. The history of the word itself exhibits its own paradox. Presumably there were what we now call "original" geniuses in earlier periods, but, as Shils reminds us, in its earliest occurrence in English the word "original" referred to the sin of our first parents (152). It was not until the eighteenth century that the word began to acquire its present sense, and not until the Romantic period that originality came to be associated with the active repudiation of tradition. Finally, the history of ideas indicates that at least since the nineteenth century the conception of originality as antitraditional has itself been transmitted as an important intellectual tradition. Like the traditions of inventiveness and natural science, the tradition of originality belongs to a category of unconsciously practiced traditions: they may be retrospectively traced by students of historical continuities, but they are not generally recognized as traditions by those who actually accept them.

III. Tradition and the Paradox of Discontinuity

Having distinguished a category of unconsciously practiced traditions, we must immediately acknowledge that it proves questionable in more than one respect. To those who define tradition narrowly, an unconsciously practiced tradition represents a contradiction. For Hobsbawm a practice becomes a tradition only when (as in the wearing of wigs by British lawyers) there is no reason for practicing it other than that it is traditional. On the other hand, Karl Popper argues, "Every day we do hundreds of things under the influence of traditions of which we are unaware," and he observes that precisely because we are unaware of them, we are more, not less, subject to their influence (122).[13] The student of rereading, who is also necessarily a student of paradox, is inclined to adopt the more inclusive view of tradition. Tradition is both what the past transmits to the present and the act by which it is transmitted and received. It is both what must be preserved unchanged and what cannot be preserved without change. It is both what is regarded as a tradition by those who practice it and what possesses the characteristics of a tradition even when it is not thought of as a tradition by those who practice it. What the student of rereading questions is not the possibility of unconsciously practiced tradition but the mode of its discovery. What occasions the retrospective recognition of a previously unnoticed tradition?

Apparently some unusual circumstance is required to render an invisible tradition visible. The transition from the unconscious to the conscious practice of tradition may be illustrated from our experience of language. If tradition is what the present cannot make for itself, what it must therefore receive as a legacy from the past, there would seem to be no tradition more universally familiar than the tradition of language. It is therefore the more remarkable that so much reflective effort is required to think of language as tradition. Evidently, the traditionality of language is not a matter of immediate intuition. Most native speakers are probably unaware of the history of their language, even of the history or etymology of the words they use. They speak a language that has been transmitted in long succession from generation to generation, but so immediate is their relation to the language they speak that it seems more like a possession than an inheritance from the past. To be sure, they experience their language as something "given," but "given" more in the sense of a fact of nature than of an ancestral bequest. For such speakers, the proper names of things are the names by which they are called in their own language. Of course, some speakers do acquire a sense of the traditionality of their language. But persons who had never learned of the existence of languages other than their own would have no answer to the question "Why do you speak the language you speak?"—not even "Because it is the language our fathers spoke." Of course, when questioned by early anthropologists, the members of so-called "traditional cultures" often replied that they believed and practiced what they did because that was what those who came before them believed and did. But was what the early anthropologists heard the actual voice of unreflective habit? Was it not rather a reflection prompted by the anthropologists' questioning of that habit?

The conscious sense of traditionality may well be less primitive than is usually supposed. Alasdair MacIntyre observes: "Indeed, generally only when traditions fail and disintegrate or are challenged do their adherents become aware of them as traditions and begin to theorize about them" (*Whose Justice?* 8). A customary practice comes to be thought of as a tradition only after it has been confronted with a novel circumstance that has the effect of questioning it. In the case of the antitraditional traditions we have examined, the novel circumstance takes the form of an unfamiliar perspective. Natural science, for example, begins to look like a tradition only when seen from the perspective of the historian or the sociologist or the practicing scientist like Heisenberg who, for the moment, adopts their perspective. Antitraditional traditions are not the only traditions that exhibit this characteristic. In common law, the novel circumstance takes the form of a hard case that asks the law a question about which it has hitherto been silent and thereby prompts a restructuring of the line of judicial precedent. But nowhere is this paradoxical generation of tradition from innovation more clearly articulated than in the history of theology.

The Catholic church has always had a strong sense of its traditions; what it has not always had is a formal doctrine of tradition. So long as the traditions of the church were not widely questioned, there was no need for a distinct theology of tradition. What has since come to be thought of as the characteristically Catholic doctrine of tradition was formulated in the sixteenth century by the Council of Trent. Like so much of Trent's teaching, its doctrine of tradition represented a response to the challenge of the Reformation, in this case to the rejection of church traditions as the "traditions of men," and, in general, to the principle of *"scriptura sola."* Trent's response was to declare that the revelation "received by the apostles from the mouth of Christ Himself, or from the apostles themselves, at the direction of the Holy Spirit" is contained in both "written books" and "unwritten traditions" (*sine scripto*) and has "come down even to us, transmitted as it were from hand to hand" (Denzinger 244).

When the Council of Trent formulated the Catholic doctrine of tradition as a response to Protestantism, it was following the practice of earlier councils convened to resolve definitively doctrinal questions about which controversy had arisen.[14] What these councils affirmed they represented as orthodoxy; what they condemned they represented as heresy, heresy being understood, virtually by definition, as a deviation from orthodoxy and therefore as an innovation. But historians describe the sequence somewhat differently: heterodoxy often preceded and precipitated the formulations of orthodoxy.[15] The council Fathers, of course, described themselves as doing no more than conserving or transmitting the faith they inherited from the apostles.

As the church's description of itself as apostolic indicates, continuity with the apostolic age is claimed by Catholicism as one of its distinguishing marks, but like so much in Catholic theology, the conception of an apostolic age is more paradoxical than it initially seems. When did the apostolic period end and the postapostolic period begin? The conventional answer—that the apostolic period ended with the death of the last apostle—is unsatisfactory, both because we have no information about the death of the last follower of Jesus and because the New Testament sometimes applies the term "apostle" to persons who had not known Jesus in the flesh. More persuasive is the view of Hans Conzelmann that the idea of an apostolic age belongs to a time somewhat later than the earliest period of Christianity: "It was sketched out in a time which saw itself already separated from the founding of the church by a certain distance" (17). In this period Christians "redefine their relation to the tradition, in that they sketch out the idea of the apostolic age and thereby set themselves apart from it" (Conzelmann 19).[16] Only when the church sensed that its immediate continuity with its beginnings had been disrupted did it invoke a medium for preserving that continuity. The name it gave to this mediated continuity was tradition. We may also call it rereading.

That the continuity with the past affirmed by tradition is actually prompted by an awareness of discontinuity thus represents still another of the paradoxes uncovered by our inquiry. A particularly telling instance is offered by what sociologists call the charismatic tradition. Many impressive and enduring traditions have their origin in a charismatic figure, but since—according to Max Weber, who is responsible for the conception—a charismatic figure is by definition a breaker of tradition, the phenomenon of a charismatic tradition requires explanation. The withdrawal through death or disappearance of the immediate presence of a charismatic leader is followed by the immediate emergence of a tradition that attempts to reassert the continuity ruptured by his absence. The "routinization" of the charismatic is, according to Weber, an inevitable process (363–73). Following Weber, Shils writes, "Nothing charismatic could survive without becoming a tradition. . . . If the charismatic message was to retain its charismatic force, it had to become a tradition. Becoming a tradition, it changed" (230). Tradition is the only form in which the charismatic survives. The history of religion offers ready illustrations of the process by which an iconoclast of tradition inevitably becomes a tradition if his ideas survive his death. (Lutheranism, for example, after more than four centuries, may legitimately be described as a tradition.) But I offer a contemporary secular illustration because its proximity makes it easier to observe.

My illustration, appropriate on several grounds, is the philosopher Michel Foucault. By virtue of his fundamental dismissal of tradition as a conceptual category, Foucault may be described as a nontraditional thinker:

> But there is a negative work to be carried out first: we must rid ourselves of a whole mass of notions, each of which, in its own way, diversifies the theme of continuity. . . . Take the notion of tradition: it is intended to give a special temporal status to a group of phenomena that are both successive and identical (or at least similar); it makes it possible to rethink the dispersion of history in the form of the same; it allows a reduction of the difference proper to every beginning, in order to pursue without discontinuity the endless search for the origin; tradition enables us to isolate the new against a background of permanence, and to transfer its merit to originality, to genius, to the decisions proper to individuals. (*Archaeology* 21)

And by virtue of the character and extent of the influence he has exerted there, Foucault may be described as a charismatic figure in the social sciences and the humanities. He became an intellectual presence impossible to disregard after the publication of *Les Mots et les choses* (translated as *The Order of Things*) in 1966. The sense of that presence was confirmed by his subsequent books, each signaling an important shift in the direction of his thought, and the immediacy of that presence was heightened by the innumerable interviews to which he seems to have eagerly submitted.[17] Dismissive of the supposition of a substantial relation between "the man and his work," Foucault spoke rarely and reluctantly of his personal history, but with regard to the history of his ongoing philosophical project he was much less reticent ("What Is an Author?" 115). The turns and shifts not only in the areas of his work but in his understanding of what that work was were subjects Foucault repeatedly addressed in books and interviews. The accounts, however, are not always consistent.

On occasion Foucault seemed to deny that his writings constitute a unified philosophical project in the usual sense of the word: "I certainly do not see what I do as a body of work [*oeuvre*], and I am shocked to see anyone call me a writer . . . I sell tools" ("Sur la sellette" 3, qtd. in Macey xxi). In his introduction to *The Archaeology of Knowledge,* Foucault himself assumed the role of his exasperated reader:

> "Are you going to change yet again, shift your position according to the questions that are put to you, and say that the objections are not really directed at the place from which you are speaking? . . . Are you already preparing the way out that will enable you in your next book to spring up somewhere else and declare as you're now doing: no, no, I'm not where you are lying in wait for me, but over here, laughing at you?" (17)

To which Foucault replied, "Do not ask me who I am and do not ask me to remain the same: leave it to our bureaucrats and our police to see that our papers are in order. At least spare us their morality when we write" (17).

On other occasions Foucault was more inclined to insist on the unity and coherence of his thought, although he acknowledged that it took directions he did not and could not initially foresee. The theoretical and methodological shift from archaeology (concerned with the question of knowledge) to genealogy (concerned with the question of power) and from genealogy to ethics (concerned with the question of the self) was, he argued, necessitated by the character of his philosophical project, but that necessity became apparent to him only at a later stage of the project: "When I think back now, I ask myself what else it was that I was talking about, in *Madness and Civilization* or *The Birth of the Clinic,* but power?" ("Truth and Power" 115) Foucault's last major undertaking, the multivolume *History of Sexuality,* underwent a fundamental redirection in the course of its composition, a fact he discussed at some length in the introduction to the second volume, *The Use of Pleasure.* His real concern, he was compelled to acknowledge, had never been any particular genus of problems, but rather how an area becomes problematic, how a problem becomes a problem:

> I seem to have gained a better perspective on the way
> I worked—gropingly, and by means of different or
> successive fragments—on this project, whose goal is
> a history of truth. It was a matter of analyzing, not
> behaviors or ideas nor societies and their "ideologies,"
> but the *problematizations* through which being offers
> itself to, necessarily thought—and the *practices* on the
> basis of which these problematizations are formed. (11)

But the introduction also contains the equally characteristic statement: "There are times in life when the question of knowing if one can think differently than one thinks, and perceive differently than one sees, is absolutely necessary if one is to go on looking and reflecting at all" (8). As his more attentive readers recognized, Foucault's thought continued to be "very much in a process of change and refinement" (Dreyfus and Rabinow 126). His was a philosophic work still in progress, the work, in other words, of a still-living author.[18]

But in June of 1984 Foucault died. There could be no further explanations by the author of the methodological shifts in his work and no further shifts to explain. In 1983, Herbert L. Dreyfus and Paul Rabinow, two American scholars who had engaged Foucault in a series of extended conversations, listed a number of important issues he still needed to address and questions to which he still owed his readers answers (205–07). When David Couzins Hoy conceived his *Foucault: A Critical Reader,* Foucault was still alive and had agreed to contribute his response to the criticisms of various authors, but after his death the task had to be undertaken by the editor himself. In several senses of the word, Foucault was already becoming a tradition, and becoming a tradition, he changed. We may speak of a Foucault tradition in the sense that Foucault is survived by followers dedicated to perpetuating his thought. Sociologists tell us that a tradition must be at least three generations old. It may therefore seem too early to speak of a Foucault tradition in the proper sense of the term. But a generation in graduate school is comparatively short, and the Foucault tradition is nothing if not academic.[19] It is, however, too early to write the history of that tradition except prospectively.[20] But there is an even more fundamental sense in which we may speak of Foucault as a tradition. Foucault, who sought to write the history of the present, has become part of the past whose history he did not think could be written. No longer the archivist of documents from the past, he has become himself a document, endlessly reread. No longer a discourse on other discourses, "Foucault" now names a discourse subject to the exclusive discourse of others. The subverter of conventional certitudes about the unity of the self and the substantial reality of the author, he is already the subject of three biographies.[21] An enemy of interpretation, he has himself become its object. Foucault, in short, has become a *traditum,* something handed down from the past to the present.[22]

Because it argues that Foucault's philosophical project demonstrates the importance of tradition to the practice of philosophy, the retrospective reading by MacIntyre is particularly instructive. MacIntyre concedes that "rationality itself . . . is a concept with a history," but he argues that rational inquiry is successfully prosecuted only when "embodied in a tradition": "it is an illusion to suppose that there is some neutral standing ground, some locus for rationality as such, which can afford rational resources sufficient for enquiry independent of all traditions. . . . To be outside all tradition is to be a stranger to enquiry . . ." (*Whose Justice?* 9, 7, 367). From the perspective of "tradition-constituted" inquiry, the question becomes not so much *who*

but *where* is Foucault. Like Nietzsche, an earlier genealogist, Foucault
was committed, in theory at least, to "utterance on the move," exposing
what lies behind all claims to truth-as-such, to objective value-neutral
knowledge, without adopting the mode of reasoning on which they
rely, and unmasking, through a series of "temporary and provisional
stances" or "strategies of subversion," such apparently substantial
conceptions as those of the self or the author without assuming a
substantial identity of his own (MacIntyre, *Three Rival Versions* 44,
206, 42). Or as another writer has put it, Foucault engaged in "the
impossible attempt to stand nowhere" (Taylor 99). To the degree this
commitment is observed, MacIntyre believes the genealogist's project
encounters a fundamental embarrassment. The activity of unmasking,
of emancipating, of disowning, requires "the identity and continuity
of the self that was deceived and the self that is and is to be" (*Three
Rival Versions* 214). To have no way of describing such a self or its
relationship to the past being disowned is "to be unable to find a place
for oneself as a genealogist either inside or outside the genealogical
narrative and thereby to exempt oneself from scrutiny, to make of
oneself the great exception, to be self-indulgent towards, it turns out,
something one know not what" (MacIntyre, *Three Rival Versions*
214). In fact, of course, Foucault did not (perhaps could not) consistently observe this theoretical commitment. He became, according
to MacIntyre, "a professor of professors," falling back, particularly
in his *History of Sexuality,* into an academically objective discourse
his project had called in question and, as we have seen, insisting on
the unity and integrity of his thought by repeatedly formulating and
reformulating its shape and direction (*Three Rival Versions* 53).[23] For
MacIntyre the failure is inevitable: Unless the genealogist's self is
not merely "perspectival," but "persistent and substantial" enough
to "adopt alternative perspectives," it "is dissolved to the point at
which there is no longer a continuous genealogical project" (*Three
Rival Versions* 54). What a philosophy like Foucault's must but cannot sustain is a condition of "temporariness": "dwelling too long
in one place will always threaten to confer upon such philosophy
the continuity of enquiry, so that it becomes embodied as one more
rational tradition. It turns out to be forms of tradition which present
a threat to perspectivism rather than vice versa" (MacIntyre, *Whose*

Justice? 369). What survives must, it appears, pay the price of survival. Tradition, like rereading, tends to get the last word.

We have suggested it is the awareness of discontinuity that encourages the affirmation of tradition. In *The Vindication of Tradition,* Pelikan observes that the recent past has seen both the weakening and the "rediscovery" of tradition (5). This rediscovery has been accomplished in various fields by such writers as MacIntyre, Shils, and Pelikan himself. Responding quite explicitly to the repudiation of tradition characteristic of our culture's intellectual life since the Enlightenment, they represent tradition as not only an ineradicable constituent of human life but as a conceptual category without which that life remains unintelligible. All exhibit what we may call a sense for tradition. People possess this faculty unequally. To those in whom it is strong the present appears in a far closer relation with the past than to those in whom it is weak. By those who lack this sense change is understood as a break with the past, presumed continuities are unmasked as ruptures, and "traditions" to which great age has been assigned are shown to be creations of quite recent date. To those who have this sense, the capacity for change is the sign of a still living tradition, what appear to be discontinuities are often undetected continuities, and the opponents of tradition are often adherents of a tradition they fail to acknowledge. The rediscovery of tradition observed by Pelikan is not, however, a uniquely contemporary phenomenon. Tradition is always being rediscovered, like texts reread. Pelikan cites the instance of the Italian Renaissance, for which "what was new was a sense of the old, even a new definition of the old," but adds that the Italian Renaissance was actually only the most potent of a series of historical renaissances. There is thus a "tradition . . . of rediscovering tradition," for history "is always written backwards, as, in a sense, the present moves forward into its past" (15). Tradition is in fact "rediscovered" whenever the past is reread as a precedent for the present.

Pelikan distinguishes tradition, "the living faith of the dead," from traditionalism, "the dead faith of the living," adding that "it is traditionalism that gives tradition a bad name" (65). Our inquiry has uncovered the need for a third category. Hardly traditionalists and something more than traditionists, the various figures we have considered are most adequately described as traditionizers, retrospectively mapping tradition and discerning its operations where they had not been discerned before. They may also be called inventors of tradition, but only if "invent" is taken in its original sense of "find" or "discover." In retrospect they appear to have been the actual subject of our inquiry into tradition as rereading. After all, is it not their discoveries, or their rediscoveries, that our inquiry has glanced at in the areas of constitutional history, historiography, law, theology, sociology, science, literary criticism, and philosophy? What has that inquiry uncovered but a tradition of traditionizers? We may therefore conclude by reconsidering the supposition with which we began: If tradition is a mode of rereading, it is because its most gifted students have been rereaders.

Notes

1. Probably there has been no more accomplished rereader of England's constitutional history than Edmund Burke. Pallister observes, "[Burke] regarded the English constitution at once as the product of repeated change and also as embodying a profound character of conscious persistence and conservatism, or, as he expressed it, a 'powerful pre-possession towards antiquity' which holds together the English nation. In his view, the English tradition of reverence for antiquity, which he himself shared, drew its justification not from the reputed fact that the constitution had never required or undergone change, but rather from the very different fact that the English people had always tried to preserve, through all their changes, a certain continuity of spirit and character, an organic connection between old and new" (Pallister 81). The Burke quotation is from *Reflexions* 5:76.

2. Hans-Georg Gadamer discusses the relation between theological and legal hermeneutics, but it is not specifically common law of which he is thinking (*Truth and Method* 324–41). The analogy between the function of the judge as understood by Dworkin and the function of the practicing theologian has been drawn by Linell E. Cady, but Cady's theologian enjoys so much more autonomy than I have granted to my "Catholic theologian" (or than is enjoyed by most judges) that the analogy fails at what I consider a critical point. Cady in fact acknowledges the disanalogy: "Although all theologians are affected by institutional pressures . . . they do not fulfill an institutional role analogous to that of the judge. Insofar as the theologian is not hired to loyally interpret an existing order, as is a judge, she or he has greater freedom in relationship to past precedents" ("Hermeneutics and Tradition" 459, n. 45).

3. In common law it is often necessary to infer the unexpressed intention of a precedent. Comparing legal and literary interpretation, Dworkin argues that an "insight belongs to an artist's intention . . . when it fits and illuminates his artistic purpose in a way he would recognize and endorse even though he has not already done so" (*Law's Empire* 57; Dworkin acknowledges that at this point in his argument he is indebted to Stanley Cavell's *Must We Mean What We Say?*). Lawyers are also familiar with the appropriation of older legal language to purposes for which it was not originally designed. The term "trespass," for example, has been adapted to refer to injuries involving no physical intrusion or even force.

4. The two sides of the Catholic doctrine of tradition are acknowledged in this document. The Council held that the apostolic tradition "makes progress in the Church, with the help of the Holy Spirit. There is a growth in insight into the realities and words that are being passed on" (754). It also held that the teaching authority of the church "is not superior to the Word of God, but is its servant. It teaches only what has been handed on to it" (756).

5. Congar's is the most thorough and the most informed account of the history of the Catholic theology of tradition, and I rely on it in the present essay.

6. Of earlier theologies, the two most important represented Platonic and Aristotelian readings. More recent theologies include, for example, evolutionary, phenomenological, feminist, and ecological readings.

7. "Anthropology may help to elucidate the differences, if any, between invented and old traditional practices" ("Introduction" 10).

8. For example, see the historical critique by Raymond Winch and Victor Bennett of the doctrine of the Assumption on the eve of its proclamation as a dogma: *The Assumption of Our Lady and Catholic Theology.*

9. I have not found Johnson's remark.

10. See Calinescu, *Rereading* 250–51.

11. My illustrations are taken from literary scholars because literature is the area with which I am most familiar, but analogous illustrations might be drawn from those historians of science who argue that innovators like Copernicus, Galileo, and Tycho Brahe owed more to their predecessors than is usually supposed. For an instructive discussion of the "continuity thesis" in the history of science, see Barker and Ariew, Introduction, *Revolution and Continuity* 1–19.

12. McFarland quotes Valéry: "[W]e say that an author is *original* when we cannot trace the hidden transformations that others underwent in his mind" (*Collected Works of Paul Valéry* 8: 241; qtd. in McFarland 45).

13. Popper's example—that in wearing his watch on his left wrist he is not necessarily aware he is following a tradition—is unfortunate. My left-handed friends wear their watches on their right wrists for quite

practical reasons. Unconsciously practiced traditions are not so readily uncovered.

14. For example, the Council of Nicaea (325) dealt with Arianism, the First Council of Constantinople (381) with Apollinarianism, and the Council of Ephesus (431) with Nestorianism.

15. The history of the scriptural canon furnishes an instructive analogy. A heretical canon of the books of the New Testament—that of Marcion—preceded and provoked the official or orthodox canon.

16. Conzelmann adds, "According to this self-consciousness one can draw the boundary at about A.D. 100," but matters are not so simple. As Klaus Berger observed, if "the transition from primitive Christianity had already been made when the Church started to reflect on its past, only a few writings of the New Testament would belong to primitive Christianity" ("Apostolic Church" 28). It would probably be best to regard the end of the apostolic period or, what comes to the same thing, the beginning of the postapostolic period as a conceptual rather than a historical event.

17. "No other European intellectual since Jean-Paul Sartre has been so committed to the interview as a cultural form. Foucault used it masterfully to gloss and supplement his theoretical works in an accessible and personal way and thereby assure it a central place within his *corpus*" (Kritzman, Foreword, *Politics, Philosophy, Culture* vii). Foucault's interviews will be included in the edition of his collected works to be published by Gallimard.

18. MacIntyre notes that in his "transitions Foucault made important uses of his own previous work, but also put aside certain crucial questions that had been raised by that work. So that what we have are an immensely valuable series of unfinished projects" ("Miller's Foucault" 57).

19. The Foucault tradition is not entirely uniform, but James Miller accurately characterizes one of its most conspicuous forms: "During the 1980s, a number of Americans working in a university setting enshrined Foucault as a kind of patron saint, a canonic figure whose authority they routinely invoked to legitimate in properly academic terms, their own brand of 'progressive' politics" (*The Passion of Michel Foucault* 384).

20. For such a prospective estimate, see Jonathan Arac, *After Foucault: Humanistic Knowledge, Postmodern Challenge.*

21. Didier Eribon, *Michel Foucault (1926–1984)* (1989); James Miller, *The Passion of Michel Foucault* (1993); David Macey, *The Lives of Michel Foucault* (1995).

22. One of his biographers suggests that Foucault himself contributed to this process: "The paradox of Foucault's posthumous authorship is compounded by his own wish for there to be no posthumous publication; if it continues to be respected, he will always have been the

author of completed books and not the industrious producer of draft texts which would allow him to become someone else yet again" (David Macey, *The Lives of Michel Foucault* xx).

23. Perhaps Foucault's most curious contribution to his own tradition was the article "Foucault, Michel, 1926–" that he contributed to the *Dictionnaire des philosophes* (ed. Jean Huisman [Paris: PUF, 1981], 1:942) under the name of "Maurice Florence": "If Foucault is indeed inscribed within the philosophical tradition, he is inscribed within the *critical* tradition which is that of Kant, and his undertaking might be called a *Critical history of thought.* . . ." My source is Macey, *The Lives* (xx).

Works Cited

Acta Apostolicae Sedis. Vol. 42 (1950).

Arac, Jonathan, ed. *After Foucault: Humanistic Knowledge, Postmodern Challenge.* New Brunswick: Rutgers UP, 1988.

Baker, J. H. *An Introduction to English Legal History.* London: Butterworths, 1971.

Barker, Peter, and Roger Ariew, eds. *Revolution and Continuity: Essays in the History and Philosophy of Early Modern Science.* Washington, D.C.: Catholic U of America P, 1991.

Berger, Klaus. "Apostolic Church." *Encyclopedia of Theology.* Ed. Karl Rahner. New York: Crossroad, 1984. 27–31.

Bloom, Harold. *The Anxiety of Influence.* London: Oxford UP, 1973.

Burke, Edmund. *Reflexions on the Revolution in France.* Vol. 5 of *Works.* 1808. 12 vols.

Burrow, J. W. *A Liberal Descent.* Cambridge: Cambridge UP, 1981.

Butterfield, Herbert. *Magna Carta in the Historiography of the Sixteenth and Seventeenth Centuries.* Reading: U of Reading P, 1969.

Cady, Linell E. "Hermeneutics and Tradition: The Role of the Past in Jurisprudence and Theology." *Harvard Theological Review* 79 (1986): 439–63.

Calinescu, Matei. *Rereading.* New Haven: Yale UP, 1993.

Cannadine, David. "The Context, Performance and Meaning of Ritual: The British Monarchy and the 'Invention of Tradition,' c. 1820–1977." Hobsbawm and Ranger 101–64.

Cavell, Stanley. *Must We Mean What We Say?* Cambridge: Cambridge UP, 1976.

Coleridge, Samuel Taylor. Preface to "Christabel." *Samuel Taylor Coleridge.* Ed. H. J. Jackson. Oxford: Oxford UP, 1985. 66.

Congar, Yves M.-J. *Tradition and Traditions.* Trans. Michael Naseby and Thomas Rainborough. New York: Macmillan, 1967.

Conzelmann, Hans. *History of Primitive Christianity.* Trans. John E. Steely. Nashville: Abingdon P, 1973.

Denzinger, H. J. D., ed. *The Sources of Catholic Dogma.* Trans. Roy J.
     Deferrari. St. Louis: B. Herder, 1957.
Dreyfus, Herbert L., and Paul Rabinow. *Michael Foucault: Beyond Struc-
     turalism and Hermeneutics.* 2nd ed. Chicago: U of Chicago P, 1983.
Dworkin, Ronald. *Law's Empire.* Cambridge, MA: Harvard UP, 1986.
———. *Taking Rights Seriously.* Cambridge, MA: Harvard UP, 1978.
Eliot, T. S. "Tradition and the Individual Talent." *Selected Essays.* New York:
     Harcourt, Brace, 1950.
Emerson, Ralph Waldo. *The Complete Works of Ralph Waldo Emerson.* Ed.
     E. W. Emerson. 12 vols. Boston: Houghton Mifflin, 1903–12.
———. *The Early Lectures of Ralph Waldo Emerson.* Ed. Stephen E. Whicher
     and Robert Spiller. Cambridge, MA: Harvard UP, 1966.
Eribon, Didier. *Michel Foucault (1926–1984).* Paris: Flammaron, 1989.
     Trans. Betsy Wing. Cambridge: Cambridge UP, 1991.
Foucault, Michel. *The Archaeology of Knowledge.* Trans. A. M. Sheridan
     Smith. New York: Pantheon, 1972.
———. "Sur la Sellette." With Jean-Louis Ezine. *Nouvelles littéraires* 17
     Mar. 1975: 3.
———. "Truth and Power." *Power/Knowledge: Selected Interviews and
     Other Writings 1972–1977.* Ed. Colin Gordon. New York: Pantheon,
     1980. 109–33.
———. *The Use of Power.* Trans. Robert Hurley. New York: Vintage-
     Random House, 1990.
———. "What Is an Author?" *Language, Counter-Memory, Practice.* Trans.
     Donald F. Bouchard. Ithaca: Cornell UP, 1977. 113–38.
Frye, Northrop. *Anatomy of Criticism.* New York: Atheneum, 1968.
Gadamer, Hans-Georg. *Truth and Method.* 2nd ed. Trans. Joel Weinsheimer
     and Donald G. Marshall. New York: Crossroad, 1992.
Goethe, Johann Wolfgang. *Gedenkausgabe der Werke, Briefe und Gespräche.*
     Ed. Ernst Beutler. 27 vols. Zurich: Artemis Verlag, 1948–71.
Heisenberg, Werner. "Tradition in Science." *The Nature of Scientific Dis-
     covery: A Symposium Commemorating the 500th Anniversary of the
     Birth of Nicolaus Copernicus.* Ed. Owen Gingerich. Washington, D.C.:
     Smithsonian Institution P, 1975.
Hobsbawm, Eric. "Introduction: Inventing Traditions." Hobsbawm and
     Ranger 1–14.
Hobsbawm, Eric, and Terence Ranger, eds. *The Invention of Tradition.*
     Cambridge: Cambridge UP, 1983.
Homer. *Iliad.* Trans. Richmond Lattimore. Chicago: U of Chicago P, 1951.
Hoy, David Couzens. *Foucault: A Critical Reader.* Oxford: Blackwell, 1986.
Jaenecke, Paulina. "Sum: Orientational Metaphors." *Linguist List* 7–340.
     4 Mar. 1996. (http://www.emich.edu/linguist).
Jenks, Edward. "The Myth of Magna Carta." *Independent Review* 4 (1905):
     260–72.

Keats, John. *Selected Poems and Letters.* Ed. Douglas Bush. Boston: Houghton Mifflin, 1959.

Kritzman, Lawrence D. Foreword. *Politics, Philosophy, Culture: Interviews and Other Writings 1977–1984.* By Michel Foucault. Ed. Lawrence D. Kritzman. New York: Routledge, 1988. [vii]–viii.

Lakoff, George and Mark Johnson. *Metaphors We Live By.* Chicago: U of Chicago P, 1980.

Lewis, T. Ellis. "The History of Judicial Precedent." *The Law Quarterly Review* 182 (Apr. 1930): 207–24; 183 (July 1930): 341–60; 187 (July 1931): 411–23; 190 (Apr. 1932): 230–47.

Macey, David. *The Lives of Michel Foucault.* New York: Vintage-Random House, 1995.

MacIntyre, Alasdair. "Miller's Foucault, Foucault's Foucault." *Salmagundi* 97 (Winter 1993): 54–60.

———. *Three Rival Versions of Moral Enquiry: Encyclopaedia, Genealogy, and Tradition.* Notre Dame: U of Notre Dame P, 1990.

———. *Whose Justice? Which Rationality?* Notre Dame: U of Notre Dame P, 1988.

Maine, Henry Sumner. *Ancient Law.* New York: Holt, 1885.

Mannheim, Karl. *Man and Society in an Age of Reconstruction.* New York: Harcourt, Brace, 1950.

Mayo, Robert. "The Contemporaneity of the *Lyrical Ballads.*" *PMLA* 69 (1954): 486–522.

McFarland, Thomas. *Originality and Imagination.* Baltimore: Johns Hopkins UP, 1985.

McKechnie, William Sharp. *Magna Carta.* 2nd ed. Glasgow: James Maclehose, 1914.

Miller, James. *The Passion of Michel Foucault.* New York: Simon and Schuster, 1993.

Morgan, Prys. "From a Death to a View: The Hunt for the Welsh Past in the Romantic Period." Hobsbawm and Ranger 43–100.

Newman. John Henry. "Letter to Flanagan." *The Theological Papers of John Henry Newman on Biblical Inspiration and on Infallibility.* Ed. Derek Holmes. New York: Oxford UP, 1979.

Ogburn, William Fielding. *Social Change with Respect to Culture and Original Nature.* 2nd ed. New York: Viking, 1952.

Pallister, Anne. *Magna Carta: The Heritage of Liberty.* Oxford: Clarendon P, 1971.

Pelikan, Jaroslav. *The Vindication of Tradition.* New Haven: Yale UP, 1984.

Perec, Georges. *Life: A User's Manual.* Trans. David Bellos. Boston: Godine, 1987.

Petit-Dutaillis, Ch[arles Edmond], and George Lefebvre. *Studies and Notes Supplementary to Stubbs' Constitutional History.* Manchester: Manchester UP, 1930.

Polanyi, Michael. *Science, Faith and Society.* London: Oxford UP, 1946.

Popper, Karl R. *Conjectures and Refutations.* London: Routledge and Kegan Paul, 1969.

Quint, David. *Origin and Originality in Renaissance Literature: Versions of the Source.* New Haven: Yale UP, 1983.

Rose, Mark. *Authors and Owners: The Invention of Copyright.* Cambridge, MA: Harvard UP, 1993.

Rouse, R. H., and M. A. Rouse. *"Ordinatio* and *Compilatio* Revisited." *Ad litteram.* Eds. Mark D. Jordan and Kent Emery, Jr. Notre Dame: U of Notre Dame P, 1992. 113–34.

Shils, Edward. *Tradition.* Chicago: U of Chicago P, 1981.

Taylor, Charles. "Foucault on Freedom and Truth." Hoy 69–102.

Traugott, Elizabeth Closs. "On the Expression of Spatio-Temporal Relations in Language." *Universals of Human Language.* Ed. Joseph H. Greenberg. Stanford: Stanford UP, 1978. 369–400.

Trevor-Roper, Hugh. "The Invention of Tradition: The Highland Tradition of Scotland." Hobsbawm and Ranger 15–41.

Valéry, Paul. *The Collected Works of Paul Valéry.* Ed. Jackson Mathews et al. 15 vols. Princeton: Princeton UP, 1956–75.

Vatican Council II. Ed. Austin Flannery. Northport, N.Y.: Costello, 1975.

Weber, Max. *The Theory of Social and Economic Organization.* Trans. A. M. Henderson and Talcott Parsons. Glencoe, IL: Free Press, 1947.

Winch, Raymond, and Victor Bennett. *The Assumption of Our Lady and Catholic Theology.* London: SPCK, 1950.

Young, [Edward]. *Conjectures on Original Composition.* London: A Millar and R. and J. Dodsley, 1759.

Ziman, John. *Public Knowledge: An Essay Concerning the Social Dimension of Science.* Cambridge: Cambridge UP, 1968.

Origins

5

Children's Reading, Repetition, and Rereading: Gertrude Stein, Margaret Wise Brown, and *Goodnight Moon*

Jan Susina

I intended to give up the stories, as Carol was obviously in no mood for them. However, she pleaded for The Good-night Moon [*sic*], *one of the library books we borrowed this morning, so I continued. This time she listened happily and asked for the book again in bed tonight.*
Dorothy White, *Books Before Five*

Young kids love repetition and the comfort of recurring patterns. I can't count the number of times that I read Goodnight Moon *to Chelsea or watched* The Sound of Music *with her, in a nearly catatonic state.*
Hillary Rodham Clinton, *It Takes a Village*

These observations of young children's responses recorded more than forty years apart attest to the continuing power of Margaret Wise Brown's *Goodnight Moon* (1947) as a picture book that is consistently asked to be read and reread by children. Parents have labeled it a "breakthrough book" for their children that results in demanded rereadings (Taylor and Strickland 47). In *Margaret Wise Brown: Awakened by the Moon*, Leonard S. Marcus estimated that by 1990 the total U.S. sales of the book were nearly four million copies (216). The 1994 survey of "What the Children Are Reading" conducted by the *New York Times Book Review* suggests that in the category of

picture and story books *Goodnight Moon* remains a children's favorite;
it ranks number two in sales and exceeds the popularity of such well-
known titles as Eric Carle's *The Very Hungry Caterpillar* (1969), Shel
Silverstein's *The Giving Tree* (1964) and Maurice Sendak's *Where the
Wild Things Are* (1963). The recent publication of Sean Kelly's *Boom
Baby Moon* (1993), a baby-boomer parody that begins:

> In the night-lit room
> There was a Kermit-phone
> And a Steiff raccoon
> And a hardcover copy of
> *Goodnight Moon*
> And tape cassettes (n. pag.)

suggests that, despite the increase of complex, high-tech, child-rearing
accessories, a copy of Brown's picture book remains a standard feature
in many modern, if not postmodern, nurseries. If one were to compose
a canon of nursery books, surely *Goodnight Moon* would be a part of it.

What can account for the consistent popularity of this slender, fifty-
year-old picture book written by Brown and illustrated by Clement
Hurd? Why, more than many other children's texts, is *Goodnight
Moon* frequently asked to be reread by children? *Goodnight Moon*
is a wide-ranging text that draws on traditional nursery rhymes, such
as "Hey Diddle Diddle," and fairy tales, such as "The Three Bears,"
through visual and verbal references, yet is simultaneously linked to
the stark, repetitive style of modernist experimentations of writers
such as Gertrude Stein.

Goodnight Moon was composed while Brown was the book editor
for William R. Scott, the innovative children's publisher specializing
in experimental texts for nursery-aged children and founded in 1938
by William Scott. Brown had been recommended for the position
by Lucy Mitchell Sprague, Brown's mentor and the founder of the
Bank Street College School of Education. Much of Brown's training
as a children's writer occurred during her participation in the Writers' Laboratory of Bank Street, under Sprague's guidance. Sprague's
influential educational readers—such as *Here and Now Storybook*
(1921) and *Another Here and Now Storybook* (1937)—were based
on the systematic study of children at the Bank Street nursery. In

these readers, Sprague posited that children were little empiricists living in the "here and now" who demand the sensory exploration of the immediate world, rather than the imaginary world of fairy tales (Marcus 58). Many of Brown's more than one hundred picture books reflect her adherence to Sprague's Bank Street theory of education and embody Brown's belief that to write successfully for young children one must love, "not children, but what children love" (Marcus 45).

Though Sprague was Brown's educational mentor, her literary mentor was Gertrude Stein. After graduating with a Bachelor of Arts degree in English from Hollins College in 1932, Brown arrived in New York City to attend Columbia University with the intention of becoming an "experimental writer," but dropped out of a short-story course after she felt she couldn't "think of any plots" (Marcus 38). In her children's writing, Brown remained consistently more interested in the musical nature of language and the rhythmic patterning of words rather than well developed plots; this interest links her picture books with the stream-of-consciousness style found in many modernist texts. In "Creative Writing for Very Young Children," Brown compared a good children's story to "a dream that is true for more than one child or that can suggest his own dream to him, or start him dreaming" (80). She had been strongly influenced by the work of Stein, Ezra Pound, and Virginia Woolf. Although Brown secured popular and critical recognition as the "Laureate of the Nursery," as an exceptional writer of children's picture books in a field which is dominated by illustrators (Bechtel, "Brown" 19), she aspired to be a novelist for adults.

It was Brown's suggestion that William R. Scott contact established adult writers about writing children's books, an early example of the procedure of using celebrity children's authors. Ernest Hemingway and John Steinbeck were approached, but only Gertrude Stein responded to the publisher's offer. Brown's concept resulted in the publication of Stein's best known children's book, *The World Is Round* (1939).

Stein's narrative is a mixture of poetry and prose that follows the journey of nine-year-old Rose, who must overcome her fears of the night and climb to the top of an unnamed mountain with her blue chair before she can sit down triumphantly and celebrate in song. The book's circular, typographical dedication reproduces Stein's famous phrase,

"Rose is a Rose is a Rose," which had first appeared in "Sacred Emily" (1913) and was collected in *Geography and Plays* (1922). Later in the text, Rose carves the phrase around the trunk of a tree in order to calm her fears of the forest.

Visually *World* is a stunning text, more a typographically innovative novel than a picture book. *World* blurs the distinctions between a picture book for children and one for adults. In this regard, Stein anticipated contemporary experimental children's books, such as Donald Barthelme's *The Slightly Irregular Fire Engine* (1971), Maira Kalman's *Max Makes a Million* (1990), and Jon Scieszka and Lane Smith's *The Stinky Cheeseman and Other Fairly Stupid Tales* (1992). Printed on pink paper, Rose's favorite color, with blue ink, *World* is a strikingly designed text illustrated by Clement Hurd, who had studied for two years in Paris with Fernand Léger.

More than Hurd's illustrations in *World* and *Moon* link Stein's book to Brown's. In *American Picturebooks,* Barbara Bader observes of Brown's book, "*Goodnight Moon* is probably the most abstract in form and concrete in substance, the closest to Gertrude Stein" (259). Rose's spherical world is, as Stein explained, one in which "a little girl discovers that everything is round because the world is round" (Dachy 182). The very roundness suggests the notion or circularity or return, the soft geometry of rereading. A similar poetic landscape is found in Brown's "great green room," where every object has its proper place and everything is ritualistically put to bed by the bunny child. Brown's simple and rhythmical prose parallels Stein's repetitive style. *Moon* is essentially a book of lists in which the bunny child names and says good night to the objects in the bedroom. Ellen Mahoney and Leah Wilcox note that young children desire to have the book reread so that it becomes "a part of the family's goodnight ritual" (26). Brown's listing allows preliterate children to identify the objects in Hurd's illustrations as well as in their own rooms.

Hurd's illustrations create a warm, comforting environment for the child reader. The "great green room" functions as a nurturing womb that provides a safe and secure place for the child. Brown's *Moon* allows the young reader, by its listing of the contents of the great green room, to make sense of the world. It is a children's illustrated poem that embodies William Carlos Williams's dictum in *Paterson:* "No ideas but in things" (9). For nursery-aged children, their bedrooms and the objects found there are as vast a world as the history of Paterson, New Jersey, was to Williams. The illustrations and the simple repetitive text encourage children (and often their parents) to reread the text on multiple occasions. *Moon,* like many children's picture books, is a read-aloud text, a simple poem celebrating the musical nature of verse. Its constant repetitions enable the preliterate child to participate in the reading of the text.

Stein suggested that "My poetry was children's poetry, and most of it is very good, and some of it as good as anything I have ever done" ("Interview" 183). Williams, who admired Stein's writing, observed this stylistic similarity and told her, "I hope it pleases you, but the things that children write have seemed to me so Gertrude Steinish in their repetitions. Your quality is that of being slowly and innocently first recognizing sensations and experience" (Brinnin 274). Williams's critical observation did not please Stein, who consequently informed her maid that if Williams called again, he should be told that she was not in. While Stein chose on occasion to write for children, she did not appreciate her writing style equated to that of children.

The constant repetition of the bunny child's phrase "Goodnight Moon" becomes the refrain and a stabilizing element of the text for the character and the reader, as does "Rose is a Rose is a Rose" does for *Rose* (Stein, *World* 93). The text's circular pattern, as that of Stein's epigram, is constructed as a children's text, intended to be repeated and reread. Yet despite this sense of return, so crucial to rereading, it is also, paradoxically, a lyrical book of leave-taking, a child's farewell to the world of day and entrance into the more fearful world of night and dreams. In repetition, in rereading, lies security. Arthur Applebee shows in *The Child's Concept of Story* the use of repetition in stories that children construct; this is the formula Brown borrows in *Moon,* repetitions that "provide a set of reasonable expectations to guide us in interpreting and reacting to new experience. That which has occurred before, we expect—in similar circumstances—to occur again; we rely on such constancy and consistency to gain mastery and control" (3). The parents who report their experience of rereading *Moon* to their children in Denny Taylor and Dorothy Strickland's *Family Storybook Reading* describe it as a "soothing book, a beautiful book that sets up a tremendous sense of security" (47). Listening to frequent rereadings by adults allows young children a mastery over a text, which many cannot actually read. The common phenomenon in which a young child appears to be reading is usually a recitation of the text from memory as a result of repetitive readings. Visual elements of picture books provide prompts for such prereaders. Like Brown's *Moon,* Stein's *World* is a book that Louise Seaman Bechtel declared "has to be read aloud" (128). The oral nature of the text recalls the oral nature of earlier forms of children's literature, such as nursery rhymes and folktales. The rereading is thus a performance or re-presentation.

Though *Moon* and *World* were both published as children's books, they appeal to different audiences. When the texts of *Moon* and *World* were tested with children at Bank Street, Brown found that Stein's novel resisted a specific age category, finding appreciative readers ranging from age three to thirteen (Marcus 105). Brown's picture book is aimed at the preliterate child, while Stein's illustrated novel is intended for the older child with a keen appreciation of word play. Are different forms of rereading thus required? Betchel, who praised Stein's book in her 1939 *Horn Book* review, suggested that *World* would be appreciated by "girls about twelve to fourteen" (131), a suggestion that today would make the text appropriate for middle-school readers, if not a young adult reader.

Goodnight Moon is a sequel to Brown's earlier collaboration with Hurd, *The Runaway Bunny* (1942), which centers on the contest of wills between a mother bunny and her child who imaginatively challenges the bounds of his mother's love. The illustrations of *Moon* include outtakes from *Bunny* that appear as pictures hanging on the wall of the "great green room," and an opened copy of *Bunny* is displayed on the bookcase. This element of metafiction, or more properly ekphrasis, is continued with the "quiet old lady whispering 'hush' " in *Moon,* who is simply a variation of the mother figure in *Bunny.* Hurd's illustration of the "old lady" is perhaps an homage to Stein: the mother figure in *Moon* looks somewhat like the solemn and solid Stein found in other artists' interpretations. The illustrations which repeat images from the first picture book raise the issue of what it means to "reread" visual art: do the same delights in repetition hold from text to picture, and are they processed similarly? Since visual literacy precedes verbal literacy, in *Moon* and *Bunny* these visual cues take on greater importance for the nursery-age child involved in the process of reading the picture books.

The plot for *Bunny* was borrowed and revised by Brown from a medieval Provençal love ballad, and the first edition of *Bunny* included a final "Song of the Runaway Bunny," with lyrics by Brown and arrangement by Julien Tiersot, though this was dropped in later editions. Both *Runaway Bunny* and *Goodnight Moon* are more poetry than prose, reflecting their oral nature. Brown felt that a successful picture book revealed "its musical origin" ("Stories" 166), so that the language is in "words to be read aloud; so that the sound of what you write is a part of the meaning of what you write—the rhythms, the repetitions and the sound and fury" ("Creative Writing" 77), a statement that sounds as if it could be taken from Stein's *Lectures in America* (1935). Indeed Brown attended one of the three lectures that Stein gave at the Brooklyn Academy of Music in 1934 (Marcus 41).

Picture books are composed to be read and reread to the point that a child learns the text without necessarily having the ability to read. Jim Trelease, in *The Read-Aloud Handbook,* emphasizes the importance of such rereadings as part of a child's immersion in language, despite the possibility that adults may find repeated readings boring. Trelease notes that little in the life of a young child is predictable, and repeated readings of a book enable the child to predict what will occur on the next page. Such readings allow children to become experts (71). Dorothy White, in *Books Before Five,* observes that for small children, reading a picture book may be "more satisfactory on its second and later readings"; she notes that once a child "knows the ending she can savor the suspense without *real* concern" (50). Matei Calinescu suggests in *Rereading* that one might "go so far as to say that childhood itself is essentially a 'concept' of reading" (96). I think it would be more appropriate to suggest that for the nursery-age child, this is a period of continuous rereading. The rereading process helps in the acquisition of literacy.

As examples of contemporary nursery rhymes in which patterns of words, rhythms, and repetitions are the primary features of the genre, both *Moon* and *Bunny* encourage careful reading and rereading of text and images. Writing in the *New York Times Book Review,* Ellen Lewis Buell called Stein's *World* "the most quotable book of the season" (10), and the book was recognized by Anne Carroll Moore, the influential children's librarian of the New York Public Library, as "genuine child stuff" (294). Despite its initial critical acclaim by adults, *World* has never been a popular children's text. It is rarely read by children, much less reread. William R. Scott declined to publish Stein's second children's book, "To do: A book of Alphabets and Birthdays," which she submitted to him in 1940. Even Brown, Stein's strongest advocate at the publishing house, was forced to concede that "To do" was too abstract, not a book for children (Marcus 140).

In her essay "Creative Writing for Very Young Children," Brown noted: "A book should try to accomplish something more than just to repeat a child's own experiences" (81). Brown realized that in order to write successfully for children, not only must the author use the language of children, but create that which the child reader would love. Brown explained that one of the best ways to learn how to write for young children is to listen to them tell stories and have "the experience of writing from a child's dictation," which was an exercise she learned at Writers' Laboratory at Bank Street. The best known example of such transcribed stories is the series of children's stories and sayings collected by Ruth Krauss and illustrated by Maurice Sendak, which include *A Hole is to Dig: A First Book of First Definitions* (1952), *I'll Be You and You Be Me* (1954), and *Somebody Else's Nut Tree, and Other Tales from Children* (1958).

Brown attributed her success as a children's writer to her attitude toward her material, not her daily contact with children. She recommended, "Listen to them and watch them listen to a story. Watch what interests them and what bores them, what frightens them and what comforts them and above all what delights them" ("Creative Writing" 78). Brown not only wrote like children, but she also wrote *for* children. She successfully created what Aidan Chambers has termed "the child-reader-in-the-book" (35), the distinctive implied reader that identifies a text that is intended for a child.

Yet Stein's "childlike literalness" has been frequently noted by critics (Brinnin 158). The difference between Brown and Stein's attitudes toward the child reader is made apparent in *Dear Sammy,*

Samuel Steward's memoir of Gertrude Stein, in which he records Stein reading *World* to a child. Steward describes the scene:

> Gertrude read on. It took her about forty minutes and then she put the book down. "Did you like it," she said.
> "Wonderful. You have really found your way into the mind of a child."
> "Children always seem to understand my books better than grownups," she said.
> "Oh, the adults are gradually learning," I said. (65)

While Stein may have captured the mind of the children by using their language in *World,* she failed to capture the attention of the child to whom she was reading the book. The response she elicits is that of the adult, Steward, not the child, who was ostensibly the primary audience for her reading. In Steward's memoir, the child disappears and the two adults remain to discuss the merits of *World* as a children's book. Writing like children is not the same as writing for children. The distinction separates Stein's writing for children from Brown's. In a similar fashion, William Blake's poems in *Songs of Innocence and Experience* are written about children, but not necessarily for children. At best, Stein was writing for herself as a child, or creating the sort of book she might have enjoyed as a child, more likely her concept of the idealized child reader.

Since Brown's picture books were so heavily influenced by Stein, it is through Brown's texts, rather than Stein's *World,* that Stein's theory of writing and language has been introduced to children. As the titles of the two books suggest, Stein's *The World Is Round* is the powerful force around which Brown's *Goodnight Moon* constantly circles. Brown explained in "Creative Writing for the Very Young" that children's literature is "one of the purest and freest fields for experimental writing today" (81). Jacqueline Rose has suggested that while modernism has been assimilated unevenly in various popular media, there is "the relative exclusion of modernist experimentation from children's books" (142); she has apparently not examined picture books written by Brown. *Goodnight Moon* remains a beloved text in the canon of children's literature for nursery-aged children while embodying many of the tenets of Stein's theories of writing. Dorothy

Butler suggests that " 'Read it again' will always be the highest accolade" (178) from young readers. This continual rereading cycle has been the overwhelming response of children to *Goodnight Moon* for nearly fifty years.

Works Cited

Applebee, Arthur N. *The Child's Concept of Story: Ages Two to Seventeen.* Chicago: U of Chicago P, 1978.

Bader, Barbara. *American Picturebooks from Noah's Ark to the Beast Within.* New York: Macmillan, 1976.

Bechtel, Louise Seaman. "Gertrude Stein for Children." *A Horn Book Sampler.* Ed. Norma R. Fryatt. Boston: Horn Book, 1959. 128–32.

———. "Margaret Wise Brown, 'Laureate of the Nursery.' " *Authors and Illustrators of Children's Books.* Eds. Miriam Hoffman and Eva Samuels. New York: Bowker, 1972. 19–26.

Brinnin, John Malcolm. *The Third Rose: Gertrude Stein and Her World.* Radcliffe Biography Series. Reading, MA: Addison-Wesley, 1987.

Brown, Margaret Wise. "Creative Writing for Very Young Children." *Book of Knowledge Annual* (1951): 77–81.

———. *Goodnight Moon.* Illus. Clement Hurd. 1947. New York: Harper Trophy, 1975.

———. *The Runaway Bunny.* Illus. Clement Hurd. New York: Harper, 1942.

———. "Stories to be Sung and Songs to be Told." *Book of Knowledge Annual* (1952): 166–70.

Buell, Ellen Lewis. Rev. of *The World Is Round,* by Gertrude Stein. *New York Times Book Review* 12 Nov. 1939: 10.

Butler, Dorothy. *Babies Need Books.* New York: Atheneum. 1980.

Calinescu, Matei. *Rereading.* New Haven: Yale UP, 1993.

Chambers, Aidan. "The Reader in the Book." *Booktalk: Occasional Writing on Literature and Children.* New York: Harper and Row, 1985. 34–58.

Clinton, Hillary. *It Takes a Village and Other Lessons Children Teach Us.* New York: Simon and Schuster, 1996.

Dachy, Marc. "How the World Is Written." *Gertrude Stein Advanced: An Anthology of Criticism.* Ed Richard Kostelanetz. Jefferson, NC: McFarland, 1990. 180–86.

Dusinberre, Juliet. *Alice to the Lighthouse: Children's Books and Radical Experiments in Art.* New York: St. Martin's, 1987.

Kelly, Sean. *Boom Baby Moon.* Illus. Ron Hauge. New York: Dell, 1993.

Mahoney, Ellen, and Leah Wilcox. *Ready, Set, Read: Best Books to Prepare Preschoolers.* Metuchen, NJ: Scarecrow Press, 1985.

Marcus, Leonard S. *Margaret Wise Brown: Awakened by the Moon.* Boston: Beacon, 1992.

Moore, Anne Caroll. "The Three Owls' Notebook." *Horn Book* 15 (1939): 293–95.

Rose, Jacqueline. *The Case of Peter Pan; or the Impossibility of Children's Fiction.* London: Macmillan, 1984.

Stein, Gertrude. "A Transatlantic Interview—1946." *A Primer for the Gradual Understanding of Gertrude Stein.* Ed. Robert Bartlett Haas. Los Angeles: Black Sparrow Press, 1974. 11–35.

———. *The World Is Round.* Illus. Clement Hurd. 1939. San Francisco: North Point Press, 1988.

Steward, Samuel M., ed. *Dear Sammy: Letters from Gertrude Stein and Alice B. Toklas.* Boston: Houghton Mifflin, 1977.

Taylor, Denny, and Dorothy S. Strickland. *Family Storybook Reading.* Portsmouth, NH: Heinemann, 1986.

Trelease, Jim. *The Read-Aloud Handbook.* 4th ed. New York: Penguin, 1995.

"What the Children Are Reading." *New York Times Book Review* 22 May 1994, nat'l. ed.: 20–23.

White, Dorothy. *Books Before Five.* New York: Oxford UP, 1954.

Williams, William Carlos. *Paterson.* Rev. ed. New York: New Directions, 1992.

6

Retrieving Childhood Fantasies: A Psychoanalytic Look at Why We (Re)read Popular Literature

Karen Odden

*[I]f a child has been told a nice story, he will insist on hearing it over
and over again rather than a new one; and he will remorselessly
stipulate that the repetition shall be an identical one. . . . Each fresh
repetition seems to strengthen the mastery they are in search of.*

Freud, *Beyond the Pleasure Principle*

When I think about the experience of rereading popular literature, several questions come to mind: What constitutes the difference between the way I read for my scholarly work and the way I read for pleasure? Wherein exactly lies the pleasure in rereading formula novels and mysteries, especially if I already know the ending? What psychological needs does rereading, as opposed to reading, satisfy?

Many texts have been written about the process of reading, and often these works attempt to account for the way literature influences us and the way we interact with literature. Norman Holland argues persuasively in *The Dynamics of Literary Response* that literature "does for us in an intense, encapsulated form what we must do for ourselves as we mature in life—it transforms primitive, childish [unconscious] fantasies into adult, civilized [conscious] meanings" (32). In *Lost in a Book,* Victor Nell discusses several aspects of the reading experience, and he differentiates between what he calls Type A and Type B reading: Type A reading is *"to dull consciousness.* If consciousness is unpleasant, it seems likely that reading will be used to dull it" (228). Type B reading is "*to heighten consciousness. . . .* A book . . . ceases to be primarily an instrument for shifting attention from the self to the environment in order to block out self-consciousness and becomes instead a vehicle for involvement with the characters and situations in the book" (229). J. A. Appleyard's *Becoming a Reader* maps out the progress of a reader from pre-reading infancy through adulthood, discussing reading patterns in terms of psychological development: the reader as player in early childhood; the reader as hero and heroine in later childhood; the reader as thinker in adolescence; the reader as interpreter in college; the adult reader who consciously and pragmatically chooses one of the foregoing "modes" according to his or her desire at the time.

While these texts differ in their approaches (and answers) to the question of why and how we read, they all prod at the question from a psychoanalytic perspective. Since desire for anything—love, sex, food, comfort—and the corresponding impulse to act in a way that will satisfy that desire—by communicating, making love, eating, or reading—spring from within the psyche, it seems a good place to start. None of these texts, however, fully examines how reading and rereading differ in satisfying the psyche. Rereading is a new situation, different from reading, as Matei Calinescu (among others) has so clearly pointed out.

But while *Rereading,* Calinescu has focused primarily on the experience of rereading literary works, I want to examine the experience of rereading popular literature. In this respect, my project is somewhat similar to Janice Radway's in *Reading the Romance* and Tania Modleski's in *Loving With a Vengeance.* Although these critics do not focus on the act of rereading, both use psychoanalytic theory to explore how and why women read popular formulaic romances (Silhouettes, Harlequins, and the like). However, I want to look at popular literature beyond the strictly defined genre that they discuss. This raises questions such as, how do we define popular literature? and what criteria should we use to distinguish popular literature from ("serious") literature?

These dilemmas are arguably unresolvable and certainly beyond the scope of this essay. For my purposes, I would like to define popular

literature as a type of text that differs from literature in both the
project it encourages and the experience it provides during rereading.
In rereading literature, often the intent is to discover the "hidden,
tantalizingly elusive meanings" too subtle to be caught during a
first reading, when we read for the "essential 'facts' "—answers to
questions such as, who are the characters and what are the main
events (Calinescu 3, 4)? We reread literature with the understanding
that there is more to understand than simply the characters and the
principal events; we reread literature in order to discover the subtleties
of feeling and behavior, to attend more appreciatively to the language,
to discover moments of intertextuality, and so on. In rereading most
popular fiction, however, I believe we are motivated differently—
because often there is little to discover in popular literature beyond
the "essential 'facts.' " Its very value lies in these essential facts
that transport us to a world, so to speak, beyond the text—not in
the complexity of the characters' psychology or the artistry of the
language that draws us to focus more closely, and in particular ways,
on the text itself. Put another way, popular literature provides a means
by which we may become *less* conscious of the outside world; and
while ("serious") literature may similarly allow us temporarily to
escape our world (Jane Austen's works certainly have the power
to take us back to early nineteenth-century England), literature also
provides us the opportunity to reread in order that we may discover
the multiple interpretations that refer us *more* to the outside world—
its politics, its economies, its psychology, its structures, as well as
other texts that have been written about that world. Thus, while
the experience of rereading literature allows readings of both Type
A (reading to dull consciousness) and Type B (reading to heighten
consciousness), the experience of (re)reading popular fiction tends to
be primarily Type A, which Nell labels escapist. "It . . . seems likely
that Type A readers would select highly formulaic material, which best
meets their needs for safety and predictability but which, in critical
terms, is as near to the bottom of the literary heap as prose can get"
(231). But what are we escaping, and where are we going? And why,
when we have a need for "safety and predictability," do we turn to
popular literature—"in critical terms . . . as near to the bottom of the
literary heap as prose can get"?

I believe that the desire to reread popular literature is firmly rooted in infancy and early childhood. Indeed, one of the signals that our desire for rereading popular fiction is rooted deep in our past is our tendency to talk about reading and rereading popular fiction in a way that is different from the way we talk about other genres: "I always devour that book," "I love to curl up with this book," "Rereading a book is like coming home." These phrases betray generally the way reading popular literature returns us to childhood, for they reflect our earliest experiences of comfort, nurturing, and security: oral satisfaction, the experience of being held, a secure space to which we long to return.

This essay will explore some of the specific dramas of childhood that rereading popular fiction evokes. Some of these dramas may be reenacted by reading (as opposed to rereading); others may be reenacted by rereading types of fiction other than the popular novels I will discuss here. However, by rereading popular literature we may reenact any one (or few or all) of these childhood dramas, and it is my belief that our desire to reread popular literature (sometimes even compulsively) betrays our deep longing to return to these dramas. With this discussion, I hope to begin to reveal three things: (1) the way that our emotional experience of popular literature differs upon rereading as opposed to reading, (2) the elements of popular literature that satisfy deep psychological needs, and (3) why it of all types of fiction inspires a certain kind of rereading.

I will discuss six of the dramas that occur in early childhood. There may certainly be others that are implicated in our desire to reread. However, the six I have selected all contribute to our evolving childhood sense of our own knowledge and power—the two tools that allow us to apprehend and interact with the world. These six dramas occur, for the most part, during the first two to three years, when the child is still pre-verbal: (1) learning to trust the world as a safe place, (2) symbiotic bonding through identification, (3) controlling separation anxiety, (4) shifting from absolute egocentricity to the state of being able to acknowledge the world, (5) mastering object relations, and (6) managing anxiety. These dramas are not distinct and some of them happen concurrently. Each drama may be enacted positively or negatively; often a negative enactment of a drama results in a neurosis or problematic "issue" for the individual later on. Sometimes books themselves substitute for appropriate parent-figures that we did not have to help us through these dramas. As Suzanne Juhasz points out, having an unfulfilled "need to feel recognized and loved" by parents can lead to a desire to be "reparented" and "recognized" by books (6). But many individuals read popular literature and reread it to satisfy fantasies that could not be supported no matter how appropriately nurturing the parents were.

Growing up requires that we relinquish fantasies—"romantic dreams, impossible expectations, illusions of freedom and power, [and] illusions of safety" (Viorst 2). The losses of these fantasies are enacted through the six dramas. That is, each drama, if appropriately worked through, involves relinquishing a fantasy and accepting instead a version of "real life" that, in a secure and nurturing environment, may be at first disappointing, but becomes "good enough" because it provides a means by which the child may participate with his or her loved ones, who are themselves in "real life." In environments not appropriately trustworthy or nurturing, the "real life" experience that replaces the fantastic is too frightening, and the loss of the fantasy is too traumatic. The individual represses the trauma, and with it the fantasy; but of course in lieu of remembering consciously, he repeats his fantasy unconsciously (Freud 12: 150). For example, one early fantasy is that *mother is there always, at our command, and she will never leave.* Of course, this fantasy is destroyed at some point. If the mother manages the separation anxiety appropriately, a child learns that she leaves, but she always returns. In the cases in which a mother does not respond and does not return often enough to reassure the child (or in the terrible case in which the mother dies), the grown child will often attempt to find someone who will never leave; he or she may unconsciously choose romantic partners who are "clingy," in an attempt to "refashion" the trauma and construct a different ending to the drama.

The time when children are most engaged in these dramas—working to find alternatives to the fantasies, possessing a limited number of intellectual tools, and moving from complete dependence to relative independence—is in early and later childhood (ages 0–6,

6–12). Significantly, these are the stages of life most characterized by repeating in the domain of reading. As Freud noted, youngest children often want the same story repeated over and over, without alteration; and they will often actively resist reading an unknown book. For children 6–12, repetition is achieved not only through rereading favorite books but also through serial reading, such as the Nancy Drew or the Hardy Boys mystery series (Appleyard 62). These series have an unchanging heroine or hero, an exotic or interesting setting, characters of "ideal types of good and bad persons," and an outcome that is "reassuringly familiar" (Appleyard 62). These stories have the structure of a romance—"adventure and conflict"—and provide "the simplest way of envisioning the relationship of good and evil: to acknowledge their conflict and assert the inevitable victory of good. Though children soon outgrow simpler versions of romance that put it this way, the function of romance does not change. Adults never tire of it" (Appleyard 64).

Appleyard is using the term "romance" as Northrop Frye employs it, as a structuring myth. Popular literature is nearly all romance in its most general sense—which, as Frye points out, "is nearest of all literary forms to the wish-fulfillment dream" (186; Appleyard 63). Characteristic of the romance as Frye defines it are "three main stages: the stage of the perilous journey and the preliminary minor adventures [the relative calm before the struggle]; the crucial struggle [between hero and enemy]; . . . and the exaltation of the hero; . . . and the reward of the quest usually is or includes a bride" (187, 193). The term "romance" thus encompasses detective and mystery stories (for example, Dashiell Hammett's *Red Harvest* and Robert Ludlum's *The Bourne Identity*), adventure stories (*Indiana Jones and the Philosopher's Stone* by Max McCoy), science fiction (Piers Anthony's Xanth novels and Isaac Asimov's Robot Series), Westerns (Zane Grey's *The Lone Star Ranger* and Louis L'Amour's *Jubal Sackett*), category romances (period-piece Regency Romances such as *The Bartered Bride* and the more contemporary Harlequin American Romances such as *Delta Dust*), and those that combine elements from the above (Mary Stewart's *This Rough Magic* and Victoria Holt's *Bride of Pendorric*). In a general sense, then, simply reading popular literature could be described as rereading the "romance," for every romance is a rewriting of the archetypal romance myth. As Appleyard points out, this myth has the tripartite rhythm of what Tzvetan Todorov called, in his discussion of the fairy tale *The Swangeese,* "equilibrium," "loss of equilibrium," and "re-establishment of the initial equilibrium" ("Principles" 39; Appleyard 63). This structure of most fairy tales (the childhood version of the romance) is also, of course, the tripartite structure of safety, trauma, and recovery from trauma.

I believe that if children read (or have read to them) fairy tales and other childhood romances in order to participate in a fantasy world in which they can "master" the drama of trauma and survival, the same needs drive adults to repeat their reading of popular literature (the adult romance). We adults are least like children in our thoughts, but we are most like children in our feelings (Elkind 189). Thus, when adults feel stress, we feel a need to retreat into a fantasy world (to escape the real world that is temporarily difficult) where we can reenact the dramas of childhood that felt to us at the time like dramas of trauma and survival. I believe that often we reread popular literature because it is one (socially condoned) way of recovering fantasies that we once sacrificed—as Freud points out, probably quite unwillingly (12: 145). That is, we reread popular literature in order to return to childhood dramas that may not have been acted out as we wished or that were not worked through appropriately (and therefore became traumas) in order to recover our belief in the fantasies *before they were destroyed.* Certain elements of popular literature combine to support these fantasies in ways that I will explore, but perhaps one of the most important elements is that popular literature allows us to step into a fantasy world—a world that is at once "canny" and "uncanny," to borrow Freud's terms—enough like our childhood world to allow us to reconstruct the drama and yet unlike enough to keep us from noticing that we are doing it.

I have chosen a novel by Helen MacInnes as a "model" for popular literature, not only because all her novels have been popular over decades (all were best-sellers from the 1940s through the 1980s) but also because nearly all of these novels include all six dramas (perhaps especially for women). For the most part, these tales combine a successful love story (between a man and a woman) with a mystery plot (usually international in scope); there are moments in which the hero and/or heroine are in danger of death; and the scenes are set in an exotic, strange, or beautiful location (both these latter elements are drawn from the adventure novel). In a sense, when we read any of the later Helen MacInnes novels, we are reading a formula novel, and rereading a plot we already know.

One way to observe our set of expectations is to recognize our responses when they are not met. In most of MacInnes's later novels, the hero and heroine meet, work through the mystery together, and fall in love. There is a dual resolution (often nearly simultaneous) of love plot and mystery plot at the end. However, after reading some of her later novels, I turned to her earlier ones—and I remember my shock and disappointment when at the end of *Prelude to Terror,* Avril, the beautiful agent, dies; in the final pages of *I and My True Love,* Sylvia throws herself, Anna Karenina-style, in front of a bus. I remember feeling frustrated by these endings, hoping, illogically, that in another book, these heroines might recover from their deaths. Thus, in these works, although the mystery plot had achieved a sense of pleasant closure, the love plot had not. The novels were not nearly as satisfying as those in which both the love and mystery plots were resolved. (Interestingly, all MacInnes's later novels provide closure for both plots. I wonder whether she recognized her audience's expectations and desires and worked to meet them.)

Here is the outline of MacInnes's last novel, *Ride a Pale Horse:* Beautiful Karen Cornell (blue eyes, 5'6", 120 pounds, wears Chanel-type suits for work and silk blouses with blue jeans for play), "special correspondent of the monthly *Washington Spectator,*" is in Prague, having been invited to attend the Prague Convocation for Peace and to interview the country's president. The interview is cancelled, and as the novel opens, Karen is waiting in her hotel room for the return of her notes from the censor; she is anxious about missing her flight to Vienna. A man named Josef Vasek calls her room, introduces himself as the head of press relations, and asks her to meet him downstairs. They stroll into the garden and he reveals that he is defecting and needs Karen to take some documents that will assure his authenticity to Peter Bristow of the CIA. The letters are examples of "disinformation"—

two letters that would place the blame for two political assassinations on the Americans—letters that could start the next international war. After a short but frightening adventure in Vienna, Karen returns to America, meets Peter Bristow, and, through a series of adventures abroad (including Peter saving her life once in Italy), they pool their resources to begin to solve the mystery, and they fall in love. Shortly thereafter, they return from Rome to America, to stay briefly at Peter's apartment, where there is a grand shootout in the middle of the night, during which the villains are captured and handcuffed. Peter and Karen discover that Vasek was not defecting; he was himself a disinformant, masquerading as a defector so that he could refute valid information being supplied by a true defector. Peter and Karen return to the house where they first met and declare their commitment to each other one final time before the novel ends.

In this novel, the successful intellectual quest for knowledge occurs concurrently with, and in part because of, the successful emotional quest for unity with another human being. The ending provides the assurance that through intellectual initiative and cooperation with another person, the forces of good will triumph over evil, trauma may be transcended, and the perpetrators of the trauma will be contained and removed to prevent further trauma. The drama being evoked is learning to trust the world as a safe place. The fantasies implicated in this drama, that reading novels such as these (for the first time) supports, include: *The world is eventually secure and in balance. Happy endings are usual. I will be safe and happy eventually. I will survive trauma.*

I have pointed out that reading one of the later MacInnes novels is very like rereading an already-read MacInnes novel. That is, after reading a few of her novels, a reader may guess the rhythm of the plot (indeed, the publishers and booksellers count on our ability to guess the plot and our desire to reread it). However, only with rereading (or by flipping to the end and reading the final chapter) may we be *utterly* sure of the ending. Upon rereading the novel, a deeper fantasy is recovered and sustainable: *that the world is always (as opposed to eventually) safe, even when it appears not to be.* In rereading, we may at once participate in the traumas (of Karen and Peter being menaced in various ways) and at the same time retain the feeling of assurance that these traumas are, in a sense, illusions. That is, while Karen and Peter may *seem* to be in danger, they never are. While we participate on one level with Karen and Peter's experiences, the bullets, bombs, and other threats cannot disturb our prevailing sense that Karen and Peter remain safe throughout the danger, because at the end of the novel Karen and Peter remain alive.

Naturally, in the course of childhood, we learn that the world is not always safe. What is substituted for this fantasy is that the world is "safe enough," generally speaking. But—and this point must be stressed—it does not mean that this fantasy has disappeared completely. And our desire to return to this fantasy—to believe it, to rediscover it in its unbroken state—recurs at moments when we would like to believe (because it seems otherwise) that the world is a secure environment, protective rather than threatening.

With the utter sureness that comes with rereading comes an element complicating the relationship between the heroine and the reader, involving the return to the drama of symbiotic bonding through identification. Let us consider briefly the genre that perhaps above all others evokes a strong identification between the heroine and the reader—the formulaic romance. A reader of formulaic romances feels almost sure of a happy ending for the heroine. As Modleski points out, the reader's ability to predict the happy ending—her "superior wisdom"—allows her to avoid "the heroine's confusion" and to form a "very close emotional identification" with the heroine from the very beginning (41). For example, in the first chapter of *The Bartered Bride,* Cassandra Chivers is accused of stealing "[t]hirteen an' four worth of cambric" from a shop; a cavalry officer—"the handsomest man she'd ever in her life beheld"—rescues her from this public humiliation (5, 6). If we have ever read a formulaic romance before, we are almost sure that the two will be married by the end. (They are.) Thus, little risk exists in identifying with Cassandra from the very beginning—but there is still the *little risk* that, contrary to our experience with previous romances, Cassandra might turn out to be the villain herself (and thus, for most people, not a figure of choice for identification). Indeed, Radway points out that formulaic romance readers sometimes read the endings first—precisely because the risk of a disappointing ending exists (99). However, in rereading any novel, the emotional identification may be entered into even more completely and with greater assurance because the reader knows the tale *exactly*. In achieving this heightened emotional identification, the reader returns to the drama of the primary identification, in which the infant and the mother experienced identification through their very "identical," merged, quality:

> The mother, at the beginning, by an almost 100 per cent adaptation affords the infant the opportunity for the *illusion* that her breast is part of the infant. It is, as it were, under the baby's magical control. . . . The mother's eventual task is gradually to disillusion the infant, but she has no hope of success unless at first she has been able to give sufficient opportunity for illusion. . . . Psychologically [in this primary stage] the infant takes from a breast that is part of the infant. . . . *[The] baby becom[es] the breast (or mother), in the sense that the object is the subject.* (Winnicott 11–12, 79)

A reader's desire and ability to "merge" with the heroine (or hero) allows her to slip back into this primary identification; the "subject" (the reader) becomes "the object" (the heroine). This is the psychological state of the infant before the necessary "disillusionment" in which the mother gradually effects "incomplete adaption to [the infant's] need, [which] makes objects real, that is to say hated as well as loved" (Winnicott 11). This sense of merging and reading as linked behavior begins at a very young age, for being read to evokes a feeling of being intimately connected, both physically and intellectually, with another person. Cuddled into one figure, on the parent's lap, the child experiences the same story as the parent. The sense of this symbiotic dyad between the mother and child—achieved at the moment of primary identification and then connected at a later age to the experience of reading—represents ultimate security and love. It is relinquished and never again completely recovered with another human being—and this is perhaps the most painful loss of childhood. No wonder we employ rereading to obtain it as well as we can.

However, as Modleski points out, the same "wisdom" that enables a strong emotional identification creates a split of the intellect between the heroine and the reader. This split can lead to feelings of guilt because the reader is caught in

> the double bind imposed upon women in real life: their most important achievement is supposed to be finding a husband; their greatest fault is attempting to do so. . . . [Although] the subversion of the heroine's negative reactions to the hero can appear as a process of self-discovery and growing self-awareness, not self-betrayal, . . . the reader's own guilt feelings are no doubt intensified [because of the knowledge she has from the beginning]. . . . We possess the guilty knowledge that [the heroine] must lack; we experience a split consciousness. (48, 51–53)

Formulaic romances cause this "split-consciousness" because they advance knowledge to the reader before they provide it to the heroine. (This may be said generally of all romances, including works such as Maria Edgeworth's *Belinda* and Jane Austen's *Pride and Prejudice.*) The reader knows that the man the heroine is affronted by in the first chapters will be her lover by the end; and, although the reader identifies with the heroine and participates in her (emotional) experience, the reader and heroine are divided by the difference in their (intellectual) knowledge.

In rereading a novel such as *Ride a Pale Horse,* the reader experiences the same "split-consciousness," but it is multiplied twofold because the reader knows the outcomes of both the love plot and the mystery plot in advance. Not only does the reader feel guilt (as Modleski describes it) over knowing that Karen is finding herself a husband without seeming to know she does it, but the reader is reading a different story than Karen is. As Todorov has noted, a mystery "novel contains not one but two stories: the story of the crime and the story of the investigation" (*Poetics* 44). Upon rereading, these two stories change in their relationships to us—we are no longer reading the story of the investigation; in a sense, we are "deceiving" the heroine because we know "the story of the crime" while she does not. Again, rereading places the reader in the position of being at once one with the heroine and, somewhat guiltily, superior to her.

And I would add to Modleski's idea that it is not only guilt that the reader feels but anxiety—for now the reader has both a "wisdom" and a sense of guilt that Karen does not share. This dual difference— both intellectual and emotional—threatens the reader with the loss of the relationship with Karen, *a relationship predicated solely upon identification and likeness.* Because Karen is not a separate subject and cannot acknowledge or accept the reader's difference, the reader can only manage the feelings of anxiety by repressing them and continuing to seek to identify with her in spite of them.

At first, it seems this anxiety would cause a reader not to want to reread a novel. However, although rereading threatens the identification, it offers two means of compensating for that threat. First, it is important to recognize that the feeling of duplicity creates anxiety only insofar as the reader experiences emotional involvement with the character; only because the reader is *already* emotionally involved does the duplicity feel threatening in the first place. Rereading thus becomes a means to sustain that emotional connection. Second, rereading becomes a means of retrieving a loss that has been experienced by the reader who identifies with the heroine. Upon finishing the novel, the reader may feel she has lost connection to her own emotions because she has foregone her own to experience Karen Cornell's:

> Identification with another person is a most important
> element in human relationships in general, and is also
> a condition for real and strong feelings of love. We are
> only able to disregard or to some extent sacrifice our
> own feelings and desires, and thus for a time to put
> the other person's interests and emotions first, if we
> have the capacity to identify ourselves with the loved
> person. (Klein and Riviere 66)

Identification requires that we temporarily forego (and forget) "our own feelings and desires"; in the abrupt ending of the novel, the reader may find that the withdrawal of "the other person's interests and emotions" from the dyad evokes a feeling of emotional impoverishment. Rereading becomes a means to recuperate the emotional energy invested in identification.

At the end of the novel, with the satisfactory closure of the love plot, the reader is replaced in the dyad with Karen Cornell by Peter Bristow (conversely, if a reader identified more with Peter, Karen breaks the dyad). Psychologically speaking, Karen breaks the dyad with the reader and chooses Peter; put another way, Peter steps in to break this Karen-reader dyad. This is a reenactment of the drama that Lacan calls the "Law of the Father," in which the father steps in to break "the duality of the relation between mother and child" (Rose 38). (Incidentally, I would posit that while there will be differences between the way women and men experience this loss, in part because men are less likely than women to achieve identification through "sameness," the loss is not necessarily a gendered phenomenon. When a man reads a novel with a male protagonist who falls in love, he may experience a similar feeling of loss or abandonment.) In any event, the reader is abandoned by Karen and Peter, who will go on to live happily without the reader. The tie between heroine and reader is broken not only by the final page but because the marriage between Karen and Peter excludes the reader.

One reason we reread popular fiction is that the symbiotic relationship with the heroine must be abandoned, either to the bookshelf or to marriage, on the last page—unless we immediately start a new book with the same, or a similar enough, heroine. In this way, rereading recreates the drama of learning to control separation anxiety, a phenomenon discussed by Freud, Winnicott and Klein, among others. This stage typically occurs between the ages of one and two and involves the child overcoming his or her anxiety at being abandoned. The fear is that *I am being abandoned forever;* the fantasy that must be given up is that *no one will ever leave me.* In reality, a psychologically healthy child will learn through experience that although people sometimes leave, they eventually return. The fantasy thus may be abandoned safely, for the most part. Freud describes in *Beyond the Pleasure Principle* the *"fort/da"* game that children play as they work to master their anxiety:

> The child had a wooden reel with a piece of string tied
> round it. . . . [He would] hold the reel by the string and
> very skilfully throw it over the edge of his curtained

> cot, so that it disappeared into it, at the same time
> uttering his expressive "o-o-o-o" ["fort," "gone"] He
> then pulled the reel out of the cot again by the string
> and hailed its reappearance with a joyful "*da*" ["there"].
> This, then, was the complete game—disappearance and
> return. . . . At the outset he was in a *passive* situation—
> he was overpowered by the experience; but, by repeat-
> ing it, unpleasurable though it was, as a game, he took
> on an *active* part. (18: 15–16)

When rereading any text, we are reenacting the game of *fort/da*. That is, although Karen (and Peter) may leave (and their world may leave), we can recover them at any time. Our primary object of identification, Karen, is placed in the "passive" position; we remain in the active position, with the power to control when the heroine leaves and returns simply by putting down and picking up the book. For the rereader, more than for the reader, the heroine doesn't change and doesn't leave; she remains utterly known (as far as it is possible to know her) and stable, whether we are rereading or whether the book sits on our nightstand. Similarly, her world stays stable and known, even if it is out of sight; the reread world is reassuringly unresponsive to our own. Like the ideal "facilitating environment," it does not respond in a mirroring way to our destructive emotions. If we leave, it doesn't leave too; if we are feeling frantic and upset, it remains stable and does not mirror our feeling of wanting to explode, but remains as it always is (Winnicott 141).

As infants, we must gradually learn to distinguish the world; and as we learn about the world, we gradually learn too that we are not at the center of the world. In a loving environment that remains appropriately attuned to our needs, we begin to move away from the egocentricity that characterizes infants and small children. As we gain in autonomy (at a pace appropriate to our natures), we can permit adults to shift their protective attention elsewhere, while we embrace the struggle to accomplish things on our own. In gaining our independence, however, we relinquish the (very satisfying) fantasy: *I am at the center of the (my) world, I am the most important and special object in it.* This fantasy is implicitly registered in the vast majority of popular literature simply by the placement at the center of the events of an easily identifiable single protagonist (or hero/heroine pair), with whom we are invited to identify.

In our culture, in which people are so often focused on products rather than the individuals creating them, and people are slow to praise and quick to criticize, popular literature fulfills the needs of being taken seriously, being valued, being recognized as unique or extraordinary, and being important to the world. As David Elkind points out, at moments of stress and anxiety, people become more egocentric and "self-centered" (28). It is not surprising, then, when we are depressed or feel a special need to escape the demands of our lives, that we turn to popular literature, which places one hero and/or heroine at center stage and permits us, through identification, to "do nothing more than *exist* as the center of . . . attention" (Radway 62, 97).

One of the reasons to reread *Ride a Pale Horse* is to suspend the loss of the sense of centrality, importance, and superiority that we gain through identification with the extraordinary Karen Cornell and/or Peter Bristow. This loss is related to, but distinct from, the loss of the symbiotic bond between the reader and Karen that I discussed earlier. Identification is a complex process, for it permits both the forming of a bond to another person and an appropriation (however temporary) of their traits. Thus, upon finishing the novel, the reader loses not only Karen but also the sense of superiority and esteem that this temporary appropriation of her traits engenders. As Radway points out, the superiority of the heroine or hero is of particular importance to romance readers (77–82). I believe the heroine or hero's centrality to the world, and the emotional intensity and the excitement of her or his life are other desirable elements in popular literature.

From the very beginning of *Ride a Pale Horse,* Karen Cornell is of central importance to the world around her. Vasek tells her, "My life is in your hands" (11), and the back cover of the paperback edition notes, "One false move could cost Karen her life—and throw the world into violent war." What better way to fulfill the fantasy of being important than being central to not only an important man's life but also the world's plight, instrumental in avoiding "a major upheaval—riots, wild protests, an end to the Western alliance . . . [and a] hideous war" (13)?

In rereading, the feeling of Karen's importance is increased two-fold. First, as omniscient readers, we feel an intellectual superiority and importance to the (already important) heroine. But even more important is that when rereading, we have from the first page a cumulative sense of how important Karen is throughout the entire plot. We know how important it was for her to open the sealed envelope (even though it seemed not to be a good idea upon first reading); we can appreciate her cleverness in thwarting questions from Bor because we know he is a villain; we admire her for keeping the papers from being stolen by a seemingly innocent woman named Rita, whom we later know to be a clever spy; we perceive that it is her clear narration of events that helps the CIA crack the case; we recognize that when she meets Vasek again in Rome, she provides a key bit of insight into his whereabouts and travel patterns, and so on. Thus, upon rereading, we may understand from the first page the importance of her actions and her status as central to the successful resolution of the plots, and we can enjoy it more completely because we know she will remain empowered throughout.

Her centrality and importance become a necessary result of her inherent superiority of character, intelligence, and physique. The MacInnes heroine is always beautiful, slim, elegantly dressed, attractive to men, talented, resourceful, and (at least comparatively) young. (Similarly, the heroine of Harlequin and Silhouette romances is standardized [Frenier 31–32].) To find all these traits in one person would be extraordinary, but often a heroine's unbelievable excellence (which might prohibit identification) will be rendered believable by presenting the heroine in an "ordinary" experience early in the novel. In effect, her ordinary experience masks her extraordinary character; this allows us (ordinary people) to identify with her via her situation, and from there we may appropriate her extraordinary characteristics. *Ride a Pale Horse* employs this maneuver in order to seduce the (willing) reader into an identification with Karen. At the beginning of the novel, Karen is anxious about missing a plane and disappointed at being refused an interview. These are not extraordinary emotions, and so we are (willingly) lured into identifying with this heroine who we believe is like us—and in the process, we too, become in our fantasy beautiful, slim, talented, admired, young, and always dressed in Chanel and silk.

Other elements of fantasy allowed by identification with the heroine include her exceptionally exciting, active life and her passionate emotional life. Karen Cornell's world comprises international espionage, threats of world war, handsome men, beautiful women, evil villains, and secret transatlantic plane flights in the middle of the night. Not only is the world full of drama, but the feelings are larger and more dramatic than in real life—Karen feels "mounting bewilderment, dismay, frustration, anger," (4); she finds herself "madly and truly in love" (230). Similarly, Peter's emotional experience is superlative. He feels a "swift overpowering emotion that had mastered him" (191). He speaks "savagely" (201). He kisses her "violently, a long searing kiss" (367). He considers himself "the luckiest of men" (230).

The dramatics of life and the strength of the emotion are engaging, but they may result in a feeling of loss by the last page, for the reader's daily activities will necessarily seem less fulfilling by contrast with Karen's. Even if a reader's own life is full of friends, lovers, adventure, and excitement (by normal standards), it is (usually) not of the same caliber as Karen's. In finishing the novel, the reader must relinquish racing around Prague, Vienna, and Rome with Peter and return to the couch or chair where she is sitting, alone and quiet. In itself this sitting position is an artificially inactive position and not representative of the reader's life (she does not always sit on the couch with a closed book in her hand), but even in taking up the prosaic activities of everyday life she may feel a sense of loss, or what is commonly referred to as "letdown." In addition, if the reader submerges herself into Karen Cornell's personality through identification and ascribes to Karen *all* traits of value to a high degree, the withdrawal from the novel may result in a dangerous feeling of personal devaluation for the reader. That is, if the reader temporarily posits as valuable only the traits of the heroine, the end of the novel and the relinquishing of Karen's identity may result in the reader feeling as if her traits are without value. In order to counteract these feelings of loss—of centrality, of importance, of an exciting life, of superlative physique and talent—the reader returns to the novel, or picks up another novel with the same themes and structures. After the last page of a Nancy Drew novel, I had to go back to my reality—being thirteen and slightly chubby, living an unadventurous life. Nancy went on, however, in the next novel, being eighteen, slim, with titian hair, a blue convertible, her doting father, and a host of friends who were always around to rescue her from the oncoming train. Of course I wanted to stay with her, so I went from *The Bungalow Mystery* right on to *The Mystery at Lilac Inn.*

Thus far we have examined the desire to reread as stemming in great part from losses that result from finishing a book—the loss of feelings of complete safety, symbiotic bonding, centrality, magical empowerment, and superiority. Affiliated with the infant's anxiety about losing these superlative qualities is the drama of mastering object-relations, a stage in which the infant gradually moves from an all-or-nothing world—in which superlative good and dastardly evil are distinct, easy to recognize and separate—into a world in which good and evil are mixed, people are ambivalent and conflicted, and emotions are more complex than love and hate. I quote from Klein et al. at length because this drama of exchanging fantasy for real life is complex and clearly motivated by fear:

> [In early stages of development] objects are identified with the internal conditions and so are "internalized." Then a good feeling towards an object signifies (in phantasy, creates) a good object; a bad hostile feeling a bad object. . . . Projection and introjection are employed in attempts *to keep good and bad separate,* to keep the bad out and the good in. . . . Now the full internalization of real persons as helpful loved figures necessitates abandoning this defence-method of splitting feelings and objects into good and bad. . . . It means that both good and bad feelings have to be tolerated at one and the same time. . . . *This merging of the good and bad into one*—the conflict of ambivalence—is what all previous defences have tried to avert, because it meant that the good object would vanish and be transformed into a bad one. It is only if experience has taught sufficiently that love is the stronger that the two feelings can be kept together in relation to a real person and not again be too widely separated in phantasy. But this confidence in love is severely tested . . . [by pain]. . . .

> A normal development . . . can only be attained . . . if
> the internal objects are felt to be predominantly good.
> (62–63)

The fantasy that must be relinquished in real life is that *good and bad are separate and may be easily identified so that I may prevent the good from disappearing forever into the bad.* However, most mysteries or tales of intrigue or espionage, as well as many Westerns and sci-fi adventures, support this fantasy, for the ending of the mystery insists upon reconstituting a firm distinction between "good" (often equivalent to the "group or individual who solves the mystery," usually the hero or heroine or both) and "bad" (the perpetrator of the disorder—"the villain[s]"). Often, two characters—one good, one bad—are clearly portrayed as foils for each other. For example, in *The Salzburg Connection,* one of MacInnes's most popular novels ("10 months on The New York Times Best Seller List," proclaims the front cover), the back cover tells us that Bill Mathison becomes involved with "[t]wo beautiful women . . . and one of them would betray him." In novels with mystery plots, the questions of who is bad and who is good are satisfyingly answered after many twists and turns of the plot; the novel's plot is propelled by the search to discover which characters to trust and believe; and we are compelled by our curiosity and anxiety to read until the point of resolution.

In rereading these texts, however, we know the answers to these questions from the beginning. We become complicit with the hermeneutic quest while at the same time remaining secure in our knowledge that at no time do the categories of good and bad merge; for, from the beginning, we can label without hesitation or ambivalence the good, the bad, and the ugly characters. In the fantasy world that rereading allows, there is no need to employ the more mature, and complex, way of interacting with (real) people, which would necessarily take into account their complexities, erratic or peculiar behaviors, personal quirks, emotional development over time, and perplexing moodiness. Much less effort is expended in interacting with characters who are stable and unchanging. Indeed, the world itself is more stable, less erratic, and less frightening when people can be put in categories and will behave in ways that we can predict.

This brings us to the last of the fantasies, which is perhaps the greatest drive for rereading of all. Rereading fulfills a fantasy that no first reading of any text ever can: *I am all-knowing and can avoid the negative effects of trauma by anticipating frightening events perfectly, every time.* Freud discusses this need clearly:

> We have pointed out how the living vesicle is pro-
> vided with a shield against stimuli from the exter-
> nal world. . . . We describe as "traumatic" any excita-
> tions from outside which are powerful enough to break
> through the protective shield. . . . And how shall we ex-
> pect the mind to react to this invasion? Cathectic energy
> is summoned from all sides to provide sufficiently high
> cathexes of energy in the environs of the breach. . . .
> And we still attribute importance to the element of
> fright. It is caused by lack of any preparedness for
> anxiety, including lack of hypercathexis of the systems
> that would be the first to receive the stimulus. . . . It will
> be seen, then, that preparedness for anxiety and the hy-
> percathexis of the receptive systems constitute the last
> line of defence of the shield against stimuli. . . . These
> dreams are endeavouring to master the stimulus retro-
> spectively, by developing the anxiety whose omission
> was the cause of the traumatic neurosis. (18: 28–32)

In *Beyond the Pleasure Principle,* Freud was trying to account for the trauma-dreams that World War I soldiers were having; obviously these horrifying dreams weren't "wish-fulfillments," as he had determined dreams to be in his earlier work, *The Interpretation of Dreams.* His conclusion, however, was that these trauma-dreams were an attempt to return to the trauma in order to construct retroactively an "anxiety" that would have prevented "the traumatic neurosis." It is essential to note that it is not the traumatic event itself but the "omission" of the "anxiety" that causes the "neurosis." That is, if we could all anticipate trauma correctly, hypercathect, and protect our system before the event, we could avoid the emotional trauma and neurosis. Individuals who experience too many traumas may become what is commonly known as "neurotic" or "overly-anxious," with their cathectic shield always in a state of readiness. However, no matter how anxious a person is, no one's anxiety is perfectly attuned to future traumas, and therefore no one can master them appropriately beforehand. *But this is precisely what rereading allows us to do.* In rereading we can anticipate every single trauma—for example, we know that the villain will appear on the next page and try to shoot the hero. We can successfully anticipate this attempted murder, hypercathect, and protect ourselves from the "surprise." It is the successful enactment of having anxiety and lessening the trauma that we are repeating by rereading.

This is a more complex feat than reenacting the *fort/da* game discussed earlier. Granted, in repeating the single drama of disappearance and return, we master the trauma of disappearance; however, in rereading a novel, with a series of potential traumas, we master (in our fantasy) the ability to anticipate correctly from a huge variety of possibilities the trauma that will come next. That is, at the end of chapter six, a bomb may explode, the hero may be shot, the heroine may have her purse stolen, the airplane may be late, or the villain may poison an innocent bystander. We rereaders alone can anticipate the trauma and move the "cathectic energy" to the site of "trauma" ahead of time, avoiding surprise and thereby securing some reprieve from the brutality of the trauma. Because we cannot do this in real life, we "repeat" traumas, as Freud explained; and, in great part because we can do this with rereading, we desire to reread.

It is a peculiar parallel that in rereading—repeating an act—we may reenact so much of our childhood drama. Then again, perhaps it is not so peculiar—repeating is the desire to return. We want to repeat— we have the "compulsion to repeat . . . supported by the wish . . . to conjure up what has been forgotten and repressed" (Freud 18: 32). Our rereadings represent our desire to "fulfill" or "fix" what was once wished for but unfulfilled. Perhaps, ultimately, we reread popular literature because no book manages to accomplish fully what we want it to—to take us back, before the first traumas, and allow us to mitigate their effects by having pre-trauma anxiety. What we refuse to (or cannot) remember, we are doomed to repeat: it is only through conscious remembering (reproducing as a memory) that unconscious repetition (reproducing as an action) is no longer necessary (Freud 12: 150). The problem may indeed be that the traumas that occur when we are very young (and pre-verbal) are not recoverable. They remain in the unconscious because we don't have the ability (or the language) to retrieve them. Without the ability to remember, we cannot work through them, so we repeat, again and again, rereading the familiar formula that reenacts the trauma-and-recovery pattern we unconsciously wish we had been able to enact then.

Why don't we attempt to achieve this sort of repetition with works from the other genres in Frye's cycle of myth—tragedy, irony, and comedy? Appleyard proposes that "Young children ages 7 to 12 can scarcely imagine these possibilities, which are for the most part beyond their cognitive and affective capacities. . . . So they telescope the cycle and attach the happy ending of comedy to the adventure and conflict of romance" (63–64). While Appleyard's discussion of child development and reading is for the most part wonderfully illuminating and accurate, I think he is mistaken in this point. The books children and young adults often read—fairy tales, formulaic mystery and adventure stories, and classic stories such as *Little Women* and *Treasure Island*—have not a comedic ending but a romantic one; the archetypal romance myth already ends happily and does not require an (additional) "comedic ending." I propose instead that children often select romances because, of the four, the romance structure is the one that supports the most fantasies.

Let us quickly examine the way the other three genres prohibit some childhood fantasies. The tragedy ends unhappily: sometimes the protagonist dies, or the world is proven to be too much for the individual. This obviously does not support the fantasy that the world is always safe. The ironic tale does not allow for complete identification with the protagonist (if there is one) because there are two voices speaking at once: the ostensible voice and the meaning voice. This disrupts the fantasy of the symbiotic identification that secures safety and love and the fantasy that the child is at the center of the world (because two conflicting voices cannot occupy the single center of the world). At first glance, it seems comedy ought to perform as romance does—there is a happy ending, which supports the first fantasy. However, what is missing is the element of danger, and this absence precludes the fantasy that trauma can be anticipated and its effects mitigated by anticipation (the sixth fantasy).

The romance supports the combination of fantasies that lures us to read and reread when we desire to escape to a world in which we are always loved, secure, important, powerful, and happy. Significantly, often when adults are under stress, they tend to reread popular literature more than they read new texts of any other genre. My friend Natalie told me that she read every Agatha Christie novel—"one a day, just like a pill"—the summer she had German measles. Another friend told me she rereads *Little Women* every time she is at home in bed ill. It stands to reason that at the times when we are not feeling loved, secure, important, powerful, and happy, we most need to interact with literature in such a way that will best permit us to believe we can be.

One question that this essay begs is: why do we move on to read the other genres? Why do some adults prefer fiction that is not formulaic, romantic, infinitely repetitive, and turn instead to novels without near-perfect (or readily reformable) protagonists and happy endings? My proposed answer is that some adults can enjoy reading tragedy, irony, and comedy because we have mastered some of the conflicts that motivate us to read romances and (more completely) renounced the fantasies they support because they are less necessary to us now. As adults, we have more autonomy and power over our lives than we did as children; we have more power to remove ourselves from stressful situations and unfulfilling relationships; (it is hoped) we have found the world to be a place that is "safe enough" and we are more at ease with ambivalences and changes; we have found stable relationships that we have a hand in maintaining and so we can prevent most violent separations; we have learned that overwhelming grief does not usually last forever and the world does not fall apart when we are angry or anxious. This does not mean we will never return to novels that soothe our anxieties, but perhaps we need them less because we have found other ways of managing our anxieties and because the world seems less uncontrollable now than it seemed when we were young.

Perhaps most important is that we as adults have constructed our own identities, separate from others and appreciated. We have accepted our own passions and have learned to accept and believe in our own unique subjective selves. This in and of itself provides a security in life that we do not need to find in novels. If we are relatively at ease with ourselves, and with our complex, ambiguous and sometimes uncomfortable feelings, we do not desire to identify with an ideal character in order to disown those feelings or replace our own identities. When we read we may empathize with a character, and may even set aside our "selves" in order to identify with a character temporarily; but we accomplish this without completely erasing the boundary between self and other. At some level, we remain conscious that what happens to the characters does not necessarily happen to us. And so, when we are not under stress, we may allow ourselves to give over our own point of view and still read *Anna Karenina* without needing her to pop up, miraculously alive, from the train tracks.

Works Cited

Appleyard, J. A. *Becoming a Reader: The Experience of Fiction from Child-hood to Adulthood.* Cambridge: Cambridge UP, 1990.

Calinescu, Matei. *Rereading.* New Haven: Yale UP, 1993.

Elkind, David. *The Hurried Child: Growing Up Too Fast Too Soon.* Reading, MA: Addison-Wesley, 1981.

Frenier, Mariam Darce. *Goodbye Heathcliff: Changing Heroes, Heroines, Roles and Values in Women's Category Romances.* Westport, CT: Greenwood Press, 1988.

Freud, Sigmund. *The Standard Edition of the Complete Psychological Works of Sigmund Freud.* Trans. and eds. James Strachey and Anna Freud. 24 vols. London: Hogarth Press and the Institute of Psycho-analysis, 1953–74.

Frye, Northrop. *Anatomy of Criticism.* 1957. Princeton: Princeton UP, 1990.

Holland, Norman. *The Dynamics of Literary Response.* New York: Oxford UP, 1968.

Juhasz, Suzanne. *Reading from the Heart: Women, Literature and the Search for True Love.* New York: Penguin, 1994.

Klein, Melanie, Paula Heimann, Susan Isaacs, and Joan Riviere. *Developments in Psycho-analysis.* Ed. Joan Riviere. 1952. New York: Da Capo Press, 1983.

Klein, Melanie, and Joan Riviere. *Love, Hate and Reparation.* 1937. New York: Norton, 1964.

MacInnes, Helen. *Ride a Pale Horse.* New York: Fawcett Crest, 1984.

———. *The Salzburg Connection.* Greenwich, CT: Fawcett Crest, 1968.

Mansfield, Elizabeth. *The Bartered Bride.* 1989. New York: Berkeley, 1994.

Modleski, Tania. *Loving With a Vengeance: Mass-Produced Fantasies for Women.* 1982. New York: Routledge, 1990.

Nell, Victor. *Lost in a Book: The Psychology of Reading for Pleasure.* New Haven: Yale UP, 1988.

Radway, Janice A. *Reading the Romance: Women, Patriarchy, and Popular Literature.* Chapel Hill: North Carolina UP, 1991.

Rose, Jacqueline. Introduction II. *Feminine Sexuality.* By Jacques Lacan. Ed. Juliet Mitchell and Jacqueline Rose. Trans. Jacqueline Rose. New York: Norton, 1982. 27–57.

Todorov, Tzvetan. *The Poetics of Prose.* Trans. Richard Howard. Intro. Jonathan Culler. Ithaca: Cornell UP, 1977.

———. "The Principles of Narrative." *Diacritics* 1 (1971): 37–44.

Viorst, Judith. *Necessary Losses: The Loves, Illusions, Dependencies and Impossible Expectations That All of Us Have to Give Up in Order to Grow.* New York: Fawcett Gold Medal, 1986.

Winnicott, D. W. *Playing and Reality.* 1971. New York: Routledge, 1989.

7

Taking a Second Look: The Reader's Visual Image

Ellen J. Esrock

To talk about the image in rereading is to transgress twice. The first is in considering rereading itself as a critical topic, which is to defy the longstanding presumption that the proper object of literary study is an analysis of a hypothetical, complete reading, which synthesizes knowledge from all possible readings of a text into a network of simultaneously existing semiotic pathways. To pose the question of rereading, however, is to focus specifically on sequence, on that-which-comes-after-something-else, and thus to open discussion about the sequential, temporal nature of the reading process.

The second transgression is linked to the notion of "image." Of course, attention to the image would constitute nothing out of the ordinary were we talking about the image as a linguistic figure—a combination of words that constitutes a verbal description of a perceptual object or scene. But I am choosing to discuss "image" as a mental picture of sorts formed by a reader. For such purposes, it is necessary to flesh out a notion of the reader whose actual, bodily processing of information, which can be both visual and verbal, is integral to our experience and understanding of the literary text. I call this the embodied reader.

Despite the frequent reference to the reader in contemporary theories, the embodied reader is not the commonplace object of study. Originally, the notion of the reader became significant as a response to linguistic structuralism, which conceived of the text as an atemporal, "spatialized" network of interconnected meanings. Though we have now enlarged our critical focus to include a reader or readers of this text, this addition seems to have generated a concept of the reader who is merely a text processor, a black box that translates, or mirrors, objective language-in-the-world into subjective language-in-the-mind. In effect, one posits a reader who does nothing more than exist as the repository of knowledge that one had previously ascribed to the text itself. When this reader is hypothesized to have a temporal location, race, class, and gender, as in cultural studies of audience, the reader still functions only as an interpreter of linguistic meaning.

By addressing the reader's creation of visual imagery, I am opening a discussion of how the body processes what has been called "mental contents." That literary theories have posited an exclusively linguistically oriented reader is not surprising, given the intellectual and scientific currents in our century. Although images were long believed essential to thought itself, behaviorist psychology in the early twentieth century created for Anglo-American researchers an anti-mental, particularly anti-mental-imagery, orientation. Concern for the mental crept back into psychology shortly thereafter, but the governing notion of mind became that of a language processor. The polysensory notion of the stream of consciousness, with its amalgam of visual images, sounds, touches, and vibrations that fascinated turn-of-the-century psychologist William James, was no longer a viable topic for empirical enquiry.

Along these same lines, philosophers began to valorize language as the medium of thought and the means by which we construct our worlds. By mid-century, philosophy had taken a "linguistic turn" that gave preeminence to language and dismissed the visual from its prior position of epistemological superiority. Attentive to this talk of language, literary scholars from the time of I. A. Richards onward began working with versions of linguistic and semiotic theories, in which mental imagery production was either absent, superfluous, or detrimental to the aesthetic comprehension of literary texts.

But times have changed. Scientific, philosophical, and, slowly, literary researchers are recognizing the impact of visualization on a temporally embodied mental life. The visual image when rereading is thus physically embodied and temporally processed.

To understand this visual image, however, we must not assume that it always appears in rereading—or in a first reading. Whether a reader visualizes depends on factors related to the reading context, the text, and the reader. The reading context refers to readers' understanding of the purposes served by specific acts of reading. One can read and reread for various purposes—to fulfill a class assignment, to relax on the beach, or to master a computer program—and one's motives for rereading need not coincide with those guiding a first reading. Motives are important in discussing the reading processes because the reader's choice about when to visualize will depend upon her understanding of the appropriateness of visual imagery to the purpose she wishes to accomplish (Katz 42).

The stylistic qualities of the text represent another factor that influences the reader's response. Some texts use little visually evocative imagery; they appeal, rather, to the reader's ear, as with some of Samuel Beckett's novels. By contrast, other texts are structured in ways that readily elicit visual imagery from their readers, such as Charlotte Brontë's works. Note, however, that a text that deploys visual descriptions does not necessarily craft them in a way that encourages the reader to visualize. The text may present spatially incomplete perspectives that are difficult for the reader to unify visually, or the text may shift rapidly from one view to another and thereby make it difficult for the reader to keep up with the pace of text while pausing to create visual imagery.

The skills and habits of the reader, often called "cognitive style," represent a third factor that influences reading processes. Individuals differ, not only in terms of their cognitive skills but also in terms of their styles of thinking. Some readers use visual imagery habitually in their mental life, whether they are responding to literary prose or visually mapping the directions to someone's house. Others visualize very little. Moreover, readers differ in their skills at visualizing. Alert to such individual differences, psychologists who test for imagery effects sometimes group their subjects for various experiments according to scores that identify them as either high or low imagers, categories that refer to the frequency and range of their visual imagery use. When tested using different reading strategies, readers designated as high imagers show significant cognitive benefits from imaging as compared to either the subjects also instructed to use imaging strategies but designated as low imagers or the subjects instructed simply to use some kind of imaging strategy. Differences in cognitive styles are important also to psychoanalysts, who have explored visually oriented cognitive styles because of the uses of vision in constructing the psyche. Although literary critics have paid much attention to the psychodynamics of vision in voyeuristic scopophilia, we need to explore other constructions of vision, as reflected, for instance, in psychoanalyst Otto Fenichel's description of a young reader's oral devouring of the pictures in her storybook (388).

Beyond the context, the reader, and the text as factors that influence whether a reader visualizes, the important question remains as to what might be accomplished by such visual imaging. Research indicates that the effects are both cognitive and affective. In reading and rereading, however, the effects sometimes differ.

A reader might visualize to help resolve a spatial confusion or complication. Because rereading and first readings here have different trajectories, consider initially the first reading. For example, when Dante describes Hell in canto eighteen of the *Inferno,* visualization may help us grasp the complex topography:

> Right in the middle of this evil field
> is an abyss, a broad and yawning pit,
> whose structure I shall tell in its due place.

> The belt, then, that extends between the pit
> and that hard, steep wall's base is circular;
> its bottom has been split into ten valleys. (1:18, 4–9)

The visualization of such spatial relationships has also been used as a mnemonic device. According to ancient memory systems, one could augment memory by visualizing an architectural space that would house one's memory images (Yates 1–49).

Although visual imagery can enhance a reader's cognitive grasp of spatial information, readers deploy visual imagery only if it meets their specific needs. Take a reader who wants to understand the basic narrative: his interests are cognitive. If such a reader is trying to grasp the unfolding narrative of a murder mystery, he might visualize a detailed, textual description of the spatial relationships between the mahogany chairs in the salon because they are potentially significant to the unravelling of a sinister plot. Alternatively, the reader might judge that a luxuriously rendered description of an English garden contributes more to the text's atmosphere than to its basic narrative and, thus, choose not to visualize.

Yet some readers will visualize spatial information regardless of its cognitive value. In such cases, imaging might be affectively motivated. The affect can be relatively low, recognized by the reader as such, and linked to the solution of intellectual problems, as in responding to pieces of disjointed, spatial information as if they were parts of an intriguing puzzle. Even a writer like William Gass, who objects to visualization on the grounds that it interferes with the aesthetic production of a text, admits that good readers will sometimes visualize just to figure out how something works. Imaging would here serve as a means of satisfying an intellectual curiosity (Esrock, "Inner Space" 62–63).

On the other hand, an individual's affective resonance from visual imaging can be sufficiently high and disturbing that he might be inclined to mask it under the guise of cognitive understanding. For example, Franz Kafka's short story "In the Penal Colony" provides a detailed description of a complex apparatus that inscribes words into the skin of its victim, like a farm harrow breaking the ground:

> Can you follow it? The Harrow is beginning to write; when it finishes the first draft of the inscription on the man's back, the layer of cotton wool begins to roll and slowly turns the body over, to give the Harrow fresh space for writing. Meanwhile the raw part that has been written on lies on the cotton wool, which is specially prepared to staunch the bleeding. . . . (203)

As the operation of the apparatus is quite unusual, one might need to visualize in order to understand, for cognitive purposes, how it creates the inscription. But the scene generates enormous affective power, to which one might also respond by visualizing to heighten the affect, however horrifying, or by not visualizing, in order to diminish the terror of the scene. (Esrock, *Reader's Eye* 184–85).

Because heightening one's affective horror of real life events, even relishing the horror, is generally regarded unfavorably in our culture, the reader who images from such motives may try to disguise her affective pleasure by telling herself that she is interested only in better understanding the text's spatial information.

In rereading, the uses of visualization may differ. The reader concerned with cognitive matters who has already solved the spatial puzzle that provoked her initial visualization might, upon rereading, recollect the textual information in a nonvisual form. One might simply "know" how the space is arranged without imaging it. On the other hand, the reader might again need to visualize because the textual description is complex or simply because the reader has forgotten the spatial configuration. For the reader who visualizes for affective purposes, revisualizing a spatial configuration might serve as a familiar, comforting remapping of the text. A reader might take pride in "seeing" what she has visually constructed. Where the reader's affective interests were disguised as instances of disinterested, cognitive scrutiny, in rereading one's visual imagery might serve this same function.

Visualization can also heighten the reader's sense of a cognitive and affective immersion into a fictional reality. This effect is widely sought in both rereading and first readings. The object of one's imaging might be a single, concrete object, character, or scene, or it might be a sequence of complex, changing scenes. Such visual images often set the stage for the fiction, as in traditional novels that unfold by offering detailed, visually evocative descriptions of the characters, period, and place of the narration. These descriptions are not generally hard to understand, as spatial complexities might be, and thus do not demand imaging for cognitive purposes of problem solving. Thus, when readers choose to visualize such descriptions on the first reading, the motives are likely to involve a desire to immerse themselves in the fictional reality, whether from an omniscient standpoint or from the perspective of a particular character. Readers who are deeply involved in the reality of their characters' worlds have been shown to visualize more than readers who are less involved (Hilgard 29).

When readers augment their sense of the fictional reality, their image-making might be confined closely to what the text presents—

thereby consisting of schematic or partial images—or their image-making might involve going substantially beyond the textual specifics—thus particularizing or "filling in" the textual description with knowledge of their own about the time period, costume, and character types. Margaret Atwood is a reader quite aware of her desires to set the fictional stage by filling in textual details not stated directly in the text. The kind of stageset imagery that she describes here creates an omniscient perspective:

> I am very conscious of the period in which it is set, whether it is now or at sometime in the past. I am very conscious of period costume; I've studied it. [The characters] would be dressed appropriately. I wish the room to be furnished appropriately and colored appropriately. . . . You see, I would want to know the period. I'm picky about it. I would really want to know." (qtd. in Esrock, *Reader's Eye* 192)

Imaging might also facilitate the reader's positioning within the perspective of a particular character. John Hawkes, who characterizes himself as a constant visualizer in his own reading as well as his writing, describes a character's experiences in such a way as to evoke the reader's visualization of this perspective. The following passage from *The Cannibal* conveys a boy's visual fascination with the movements of tea in his cup: "He looked into his hands, saw steaming water and watched a single star-shaped leaf turning slowly around near the bottom of the cup. He saw a pale color slowly spread, creeping up the china towards his fingers . . ." (7). To readers like Hawkes and Atwood, the initial, imagistic depiction of the fictional world provides the groundwork for entering the fictional reality.

What deserves special note is the use of imaging not simply to ease the transition into the fictional reality as a whole, as one might do at the opening of a novel, but to augment the affective power of specific textual moments. For instance, consider the scene in Julio Cortázar's "Blow-Up" when the photographer/narrator describes the disturbing encounter between a seductive woman and a young man that he spies through his camera lens: "I raised the camera. . . . The woman was getting on with the job of handcuffing the boy smoothly, stripping from him what was left of his freedom a hair at a time, in an incredibly slow and delicious torture" (108). A reader might visualize this scene as a means of identifying with the visually perceiving narrator and, thereby, heighten the affective immediacy of what the voyeuristic narrator experiences.

Readers who visualize as a means of immersing themselves in a fictional reality in order to make it more immediate, whether for purposes of cognitive understanding or affective impact, exhibit what might be called a visual epistemology for reading. According to this epistemology, the reader uses visualization as a means of knowing and, thus, entering the fictional reality and responding affectively to it. Texts like Cortázar's construct a fictional reality that operates upon principles of a visual epistemology and projects these principles upon the behavior of the reader.

When rereading, some readers will not choose to revisualize details, objects, characters, or scenes as a means of immersing themselves in a fictional reality. It will suffice simply to have stored mentally abstract representations of the information, which are invoked when one rereads, serving to make the descriptions seem familiar and thereby create the fictional reality. Although this kind of nonvisual rereading often suffices for those rereading only to gain factual information about the text, it is not likely to satisfy readers returning to a text to derive the affective pleasures gained from the first, visually oriented reading.

There are also readers who need to visualize the text upon beginning a second reading but find that the need diminishes faster than during the first reading. Such intratextual changes in deployment of visual imagery can take place also during first readings. Margaret Atwood, for instance, reports that in the first reading of a book she visualizes details less as the narrative proceeds, though her sense of immersion in the reality continues at the same level (personal interview). In some cases, the reader initially needs visualization to establish the fictional reality but fulfills this need for immersion when caught up in the plot, which does not evoke visualization as a means of absorbing the reader. In other cases, the text itself changes its stylistic direction, orienting itself less to visually oriented descriptions as the plot unfolds.

Finally, there are many readers who always need visual imagery in order to immerse themselves in a vivid, fictional reality. Such individuals visualize the text in as much detail on a repeated reading as on a first reading. When John Hawkes was asked if he forms visual images when rereading, his response was "Always. I couldn't read without forming a visual image. I've never read any fiction so abstract that you wouldn't form a visual image." Indeed, Hawkes also asserts "At any moment, really, I'm in a totally constructed visual world" (Esrock, "Inner Space" 62). As one might surmise from his own fiction, as well as from self-reports, Hawkes is the kind of reader whose cognitive and affective responses are closely integrated with visual forms of representation.

Visualization can also function formally and semantically and can operate in identical ways in both rereading and reading. Just as the formal features of a text contribute to the production of semantic meanings, as when the phonetic structures of poetry create effects with a significance at the level of poetic meaning, so too, the reader's acts of imaging can serve analogous, formal functions. Rainer Maria Rilke's "Archaic Torso of Apollo" demonstrates this point. The poem opens with the narrator's assertion that the reader lacks knowledge of the torso's lost head—"We did not know his unheard-of [unbelievable] head / wherein the eye-apples ripened"—and goes on to describe, inch by inch, what the reader does possess—the splendor of the sculpture's magnificent body. An ekphrastic description, Rilke's visually keyed words about the marble body entice the reader into visualizations. Toward the end of the poem, a sudden shift in formal and semantic structure occurs. The narrative progresses to a climactic focus on the loins of the sculpture and abruptly ceases. A narrative voice directly addresses the reader: "For here [on this torso] is no place / that does not see you. You must change your life" (146). With this direct call for personal change, the reader ceases visualizing the sculpture to register the poem's criticism and charge to the reader. In its concluding moments, the poem invites no visual imagery. This sudden shift from imaging to not imaging constitutes a formal contrast, which can be linked to the semantic meaning produced by the shift.

Similarly, imaging can create semantic meaning. Regarding the Rilke poem, the visualizing reader has experienced the formal jolt of being caught up short while imaging. Since the poem has directly addressed the reader, the reader reasonably integrates her responses into the sternly conveyed message. The poem might be understood to be dealing with two possibilities for life: One can live and know things secondhand, as an observer whose life is supplemented by the value of what is observed, and one can live and know things by doing, not watching, as an active participant whose being gives value to all it touches. To the extent that the reader's imaging of the sculpture can be likened to a form of observing what is valuable, the reader is guilty of the very thing the narrator charges. The invocation to change one's life acquires the force of a transforming revelation when the reader suddenly ceases imaging, which has acquired the semantic significance of an observational, nonvital way of being and knowing the world.

Perhaps the most complex effects of visualization occur in the domain of memory, where the temporal aspect of rereading is central. Visual imaging that affects one's memory for the text will focus the reader's expectations for future textual events and recollections of the past. Such reverberations can, in turn, influence one's basic constitution of meaning and experience of affect. Louise Rosenblatt expresses the significance of memory to reading:

> At any point, [the reader] brings a state of mind, a penumbra of "memories" of what has preceded, ready to be activated by what follows, and providing the context from which further meanings will be derived. Awareness—more or less explicit—of repetitions, echoes, resonances, repercussions, linkages, cumulative effects, contrasts, or surprises is the mnemonic matrix for the structuring of emotion, idea, situation, character, plot—in short, for the evocation of a work of art. (57–58)

Although visual imagery has been used for centuries as a memory aid, during the last few decades imagery has been proven to augment memory for verbal materials under certain conditions (Paivio, Richardson). Among recent findings are those of psychologists Marc Marschark and Reed Hunt, who found that a reader's imaging of verbal materials provides a mnemonic aid for texts that are particularly discontinuous, that is, lacking in sequential, narrative structure. One would thus expect that texts built upon associative, nonlinear structures, such as poetry and even some novels, would be affected by imaging strategies.

As Allan Paivio, the first contemporary psychologist to explore visual imagery as a distinctive component of mental processing, has suggested, imagery might also serve as a means of integrating large, upper-level portions of text. This would be consistent with the notion of the visual image as unifying discontinuous elements, except in this case the discontinuities would not exist within paragraphs but between larger, structural elements. Paivio suggests that Coleridge's albatross might serve to unify such structures (see "Mind's Eye").

Numerous examples of imagistically designed texts can be found among the works of Italo Calvino, who claims that the visual element is at the center of his fictions. In a critical essay Calvino describes the synthesis of the visual and verbal in the short-story collection *Cosmicomics:*

> In short, my procedure aims at uniting the spontaneous generation of visual images and the intentionality of discursive thought. Even when the opening gambit is played by the visual imagination, putting its own intrinsic logic to work, it finds itself sooner or later caught in a web where reasoning and verbal expression also impose their logic. Yet the visual solutions continue to be determining factors and sometimes unexpectedly come to decide situations that neither the conjectures of thought nor the resources of language would be capable of resolving. (90)

For such reasons Calvino cites "visuality" in *Six Memos for the Next Millennium* as one of the six qualities that he deems vital to preserve in our society.

The reader who visualizes when rereading a text can produce several kinds of mnemonic reverberations that differ from those produced during a first reading. This is because the reader's prior knowledge of the narrative can guide visual anticipations of the future and recollections of the past. Because this reader knows what will happen, she will have little need to correct the visual misrepresentations that occur during a first reading: She would have already eliminated the beard on the husband's clean-shaven face and reconstructed the narrative in its proper sequence. Indeed, with particularly complex works, the reader's anticipated and recollected visual imagery grows more accurate with repeated rereadings.

One should not presume, however, that rereading always augments the mnemonically guided visualizations that may have occurred during a first reading. Some readers will visualize less frequently because, after imaging during the initial reading, they have stored the basic, textual information in a nonvisual form and, for various reasons, chosen not to take the time to recreate the material visually.

In addition to rereadings driven by cognitive interests, there are readings that reverberate with affective imagery. Such imagery can structure one's experience of rereading by focusing one's anticipations affectively. For example, Carlos Fuentes describes a powerful, literary memory, which likely guides his rereading of the text:

> I think that the visual is the primary element in the poetry and the fiction of Victor Hugo, that, in effect, without the visual representation [of] the flight of Jean Valjean through the sewers of Paris, persecuted by inspector Javert—if you're not capable of translating this into visual images—it has no power. . . . I cannot for the life of me remember any word from that passage in *Les Misérables* I'm talking about. But I could not forget the visual image of that persecution through the sewers of Paris, ever. (Esrock, *Reader's Eye* 182)

From Fuentes's own description, it seems that in rereading *Les Misérables* his visual image of the flight through the Paris sewers becomes a focal point of his experience, thus shaping his specific rereading patterns so as to enhance this powerful, memorable image.

Perhaps a unique mnemonic aspect of rereading is not in the regeneration of visual images encountered on previous readings but in the interweaving of thoughts that occur between readings of the text. These are such moments as when one is idly reflecting in a crowded subway or leisurely strolling to school. The impact of these thoughts becomes pertinent when considering the temporal processing of a literary work. At such times one is not generally motivated by cognitive concerns but, rather, guided by affectively charged interests. Visual imagery produced from such interests has the value-laden character of the reverie visual images described by Gaston Bachelard in his account of the poetic visual image:

> The remembered past is not simply a past of perception. Since one is remembering, the past is already being designated in a reverie as a visual image value. From its very origin, the imagination colors the paintings it will want to see again. (105)

The pleasurable character of the imagistic reveries described by Bachelard has been noted by psychologist Michel Denis in regard to the reading process itself. Through experiments accessing the accuracy and speed of readers who were instructed to visualize and those who were not, Denis identifies what appear to be noncognitive purposes served by the production of visual imagery:

> At least a part of visual imagery activity developed during prose reading is not definitely directed toward memorization. . . . It is a matter of fact that a great deal of the visual images elicited by narratives (novels, etc.) are not "goal directed." We certainly have to bear in mind this "hedonistic" aspect of imagery in many natural situations. (544–45)

Denis's conjectures about the hedonistic aspects of imaging during a first reading seem even more applicable to the between-reading visualizations described by Bachelard, insofar as the individual's own interests, not the words on the page, guide the generation of images.

When affectively invested, between-reading visual images are evoked during the actual process of rereading, several kinds of mnemonic effects might be created. On the one hand, affectively charged visual imagery has long been thought to be recalled with more efficacy than affectively neutral information and, indeed, even nonaffective, verbal material that has been visually encoded has been shown to be recalled better over long periods of time than material that is not visually encoded (Erdelyi 74). Thus, affectively invested visual images generated between readings might enhance one's memory of the text during rereading.

The affective character of the visual information might not merely focus but distort one's memory of the text, particularly if one is sufficiently motivated to bring it into consciousness independently of the text. Although experiments have not confirmed the suggestion by Paivio that the visual format of the image makes it susceptible to synonym substitutions when the image is translated back into verbal information, this is not to deny that visual imagery can involve some unique distortions (Richardson 89). Indeed, visual images appear vulnerable to certain kind of errors. Experiments showed that students who answered questions based on their imaging of a short story were more liable than those who did not visualize to claim mistakenly that certain pieces of information were given by the text (Giesen and Peeck 87). Presumably, these readers were mistaking attributes of their own visual images for attributes given by the text. This result is consistent with the reports by F. C. Bartlett early in the century that imaging readers were more sure of their faulty recollections than those who did not visualize.

The vulnerability of the visual image to mnemonic error, however, is not necessarily an unwelcome effect for the reading of literature. To the extent that such errors reflect the operation of affect, they produce a rereading of the text more highly keyed to affective interactions than is a straight, literal memory of textual information. Such interactions might be a valuable dimension of the literary experience (Ahsen 231).

In short, the uses of visual images produced in rereading cannot be located within a single category. Even when a reader produces the same visual images as on a first reading, the visual imagery of rereading might serve quite different purposes. Whether pursuing cognitive or affective interests, the temporally embodied reader is both akin to the first reader and a new, complex entity.

Works Cited

Ahsen, Akhter. "Principles of Imagery in Art and Literature." *Journal of Mental Imagery* 6 (1982) 213–50.

Alighieri, Dante. *The Divine Comedy of Dante Alighieri.* Trans. Allen Mandelbaum. Berkeley: U of California P, 1980.

Atwood, Margaret. Personal interview. Nov. 1986.

Bachelard, Gaston. *The Poetics of Reverie: Childhood, Language, and the Cosmos.* Trans. Daniel Russell. Boston: Beacon P, 1971.

Bartlett, F. C. *Remembering: A Study in Experimental and Social Psychology.* Cambridge: Cambridge UP, 1932.

Calvino, Italo. *Six Memos for the Next Millennium: The Charles Eliot Norton Lectures, 1985–1986.* Cambridge: Harvard UP, 1988.

Cortázar, Julio. "Blow-Up." *Blow-Up and Other Stories.* Trans. Paul Blackburn. New York: Random House, 1985. 100–15.

Denis, Michel. "Imaging While Reading Text: A Study of Individual Differences." *Memory and Cognition* 10 (1982): 540–45.

Erdelyi, Matthew Hugh. *Psychoanalysis: Freud's Cognitive Psychology.* New York: W. H. Freeman, 1985.

Esrock, Ellen J. "The Inner Space of Reading: Interviews with John Hawkes, Carlos Fuentes and William Gass." *Journal of Mental Imagery* 10 (1986): 61–68.

———. *The Reader's Eye: Visual Imaging as Reader Response.* Baltimore: Johns Hopkins UP, 1994.

Fenichel, Otto. "The Scoptophilic Instinct and Identification." *The Collected Papers of Otto Fenichel.* New York: Norton, 1953. 373–97.

Giesen, C. and J. Peeck. "Effects of Imagery Instruction on Reading and Retaining a Literary Text." *Journal of Mental Imagery* 8 (1984): 79–90.

Hawkes, John. *The Cannibal.* 1949. New York: New Directions, 1962.

Hilgard, Josephine. *Personality and Hypnosis.* 2nd ed. Chicago: U of Chicago P, 1979.

Kafka, Franz. "In the Penal Colony." *The Penal Colony: Stories and Short Pieces.* Trans. Willa Muir and Edwin Muir. New York: Schocken, 1948. 191–227.

Katz, Albert N. "What Does It Mean to Be a High Imager?" *Imagery, Memory, and Cognition: Essays in Honor of Allan Paivio.* Ed. John C. Yuille. New York: Lawrence Erlbaum, 1983.

Marschark, Marc, and R. Reed Hunt. "A Reexamination of the Role of Imagery in Learning and Memory." *Journal of Experimental Psychology: Learning, Memory, and Cognition* 15 (1989): 710–20.

Paivio, Allan. *Mental Representations: A Dual Coding Approach.* New York: Oxford UP, 1986.

———. "The Mind's Eye in Arts and Science." *Poetics* 12 (1983) 1–18.

Richardson, John T. E. *Mental Imagery and Human Memory.* New York: St. Martin's, 1980.

Rilke, Rainer Maria. "The Archaic Torso of Apollo." *The Poem Itself.* Ed. Stanley Burnshaw. New York: Schocken, 1967. 146.

Rosenblatt, Louise. *The Reader, the Text, the Poem: The Transactional Theory of the Literary Work.* Carbondale: Southern Illinois UP, 1978.

Yates, Frances A. *The Art of Memory.* Chicago: U of Chicago P, 1966.

Past

8

Rereading Guillaume de Machaut's Vision of Love: Chaucer's *Book of the Duchess* as *Bricolage*

R. Barton Palmer

Rereading is not only what readers may freely choose if eager to experience again what a text contains. Rereading may also be occasioned and shaped by a particular kind of authorial rhetoric: namely, by those formal or semantic structures that allow a new work to contain or reference, in various fashions, an older one that the reader already knows. Reading a text of this kind is thus simultaneously a rereading of an absent, yet present other. This variety of rereading figures as an essential element in what Gérard Genette, following Bakhtin and Julia Kristeva, has identified as hypertextuality (not to be confused with hypertextuality in the sense of electronic text), a form of transtextuality that constructs a surprisingly common relationship between texts. For Genette, a work is a hypertext if it "derives from a previous text [its hypotext] by a simple transformation . . . or by an indirect transformation we would call 'imitation' " (14). Because hypertexts offer both reading and rereading, the hypertextual comes to border closely upon the metatextual; in other words, hypertexts implicitly comment upon, make available the possibility of a new "reading" or interpretation of the hypotexts they replace and simulta- neously contain.

The *Aeneid,* for example, both recalls and restructures Homeric epic, even as it thereby passes judgment—if never directly—on how Homer represents the experience of war, or how he thought epic materials could best be arranged. In effect, the poem offers a rereading of two previous works. That Virgil was eager for his readers to see the connection between his poem and those of Homer makes clear another general point. Hypertextual relations can either be apparent or effaced. They can be emphasized by the work's rhetorical structure, brought to light by a knowledgeable reader who responds to that rhetoric, or they can be obscured, in which case the reader may well remain oblivious of them and consider self-contained the text that in fact is tied strongly to some other(s) preceding it.

Because modern readers are situated by an explanation of the creative process and an attendant set of values that emphasize "newness" and "originality," they are not normally predisposed either to identify or consider the import of hypertextuality; nor are modern authors, formed by the same ideology of writing, likely to incorporate those relations as part of a work's rhetoric. For medieval readers, in contrast, hypo/hypertextual relations often constituted an essential element of their encounter with a text. Venerators of a tradition that was continually reinstated even as it was transformed, their experience was simultaneously the reading of something new and the rereading of the already written, an insertion into a process of textualizing without either origins or any foreseeable conclusion. As Bakhtin would have it, they viewed texts not only as answers to what had already been written, but as inviting responses in their turn.

In this essay, I will discuss a well-known medieval work, Geoffrey Chaucer's *Book of the Duchess,* that as a complex hypertext offered to its original readers the double experience of reading and rereading. The imperfect powers of literary archaeology to uncover the past in this case proved able to reconstruct, at a quite early stage in modern scholarship, the poem's hypotext: a series of narrative love visions by Chaucer's most famous French contemporary, Guillaume de Machaut. Yet Chaucerians have strongly resisted the implications of this indisputable fact. The pioneering work of turn of the century scholars George Lyman Kittredge and John Livingston Lowes did much to delineate how extensive Chaucer's recycling of Machaut was, thereby underlining what they termed the work's conventionality. Inhabitants of a post-romantic literary world, however, Kittredge and Lowes were forced to evaluate Chaucer's accomplishments in terms of genius and creativity; such values made necessary deemphasizing the hypertextuality they had labored so mightily to describe. Few Chaucerians of the last twenty-five years or so (the major exception being James I. Wimsatt) could accept that any of the poet's works, even the less valued because early *Book of the Duchess,* might be defined in powerful ways by the rewritten materials that constituted them. And yet, as we shall see, Chaucer clearly invited his readers to reread and thereby reevaluate some major works of Machaut. Modern criticism, hampered by a Leavisian focus on "the words on the page," has failed to recognize that this work depends for its effects on what is there absently present: a palimpsest that is to be reread but not as itself.

Like other literary scholars, medievalists have tended to endorse the view that style—the uniqueness inherent in a particular utterance—takes precedence over convention. This position is most importantly associated with the Karl Vossler school of linguistic thought, which has influenced modern literary studies profoundly, if often indirectly. In Bakhtin's characterization of this position, Vossler and his followers maintain that the "vital feature of every speech act does not consist in the grammatical forms, which are shared, stable, and immediately usable in all other utterances of a given language" (51). Instead, what matters is the "stylistic concretization and modification of these abstract forms, which individualize and uniquely characterize any given utterance." For Chaucerians, the poet's "stylistic concretization" of those hypotexts he has chosen to transform has meant that these works are reduced from active, competing, and harmonizing voices to an eminently plastic raw material. Given a new and single voice by the poet's shaping touch, these "sources" can thus be passed over in critical acts that attend to the splendid isolation of the artist's self-expressive creativity; hypertextual relations are consigned to literary history, become a series of facts rather than a rhetorical call to reread. My purpose here is to point out the limitations of this position, which ignores the persistent presence of the hypotext within the hypertext that revivifies it. Chaucer's poem, I suggest, should not be understood simply as a new work, one written to memorialize an

important event (though of course it is this in part). We should not
ignore what the poet also asked his original readers to do: reread
and thereby reevaluate an important series of works from the literary
tradition that was their common inheritance. *The Book of the Duchess*
even mirrors this thoroughly medieval hermeneutic, providing a figure
within the text who enacts its making, *mutatis mutandis,* and thereby
establishes the protocols according to which it should be read. These
protocols entail a doubleness: the reader is to attend to Chaucer's poem
just the same as s/he is asked to attend to the narrator's account of
his experience, as a text with an origin in itself; at the same time, the
narrator's activity as a compiler, translator, and reteller calls to mind
the absently present tradition each reader must confront and reread in
negotiating that textual newness.

A Mirror for Rereading

Chaucer's unnamed narrator in *The Book of the Duchess,* a thinly
disguised textual reflex of the poet, reminds us that "reading" involves
two distinct and sometimes complementary mental experiences: deciphering and interpretation. Wearied by a sleeplessness that is the
symptom of his profound melancholy, the narrator bids a servant bring
him a book to read, thinking that the very act of giving voice to the
words on the page might put him to sleep more expeditiously than a
game of chess or checkers. His man brings him a "romaunce," that
is, a book either written in French or full of tales told in the French
style, and the narrator peruses it, looking for something to hold his
interest in this collection of "quenes lives and of kinges" (line 58). As
he reads into his book, one tale soon catches his eye; in fact, it strikes
him as "a wonder thing" (line 61).

Reading is first of all deciphering, a translation of the silent marks
on the page into living words; in the case of a story, these words
can then be construed as a gestalt of setting, character, and event, a
second reality that can affect the reader in a number of ways, including
making him marvel. This is precisely how Chaucer's narrator at
first reads the tale he selects. Afterward, of course, determining to
transform his experiences into discourse, he reproduces that encounter
for his implied listeners, exchanging the role of passive reader for the

active one of narrator and, by implication, translator, retelling in full detail—and in English verse—the story that strikes him as so unusual. A correlative of this is that Chaucer likewise reproduces the same narrative for those who read his poem, in effect retelling the retelling, doubling the imaginary quotation marks that surround what has been borrowed from that French book.

There is a further, even more significant correspondence between the two speakers whose voices we must hear in this passage as simultaneous. Just as the narrator discovers his story to tell in a book, so did Chaucer, as many of those who constituted his initial readership and listenership must have recognized. The sad history of King Seys and Alcyone his wife had been told and retold by a number of writers when Chaucer determined to write a poem to please his patron, John of Gaunt. The same story features prominently in book eleven of Ovid's *Metamorphoses,* a work whose popularity grew tremendously in the fourteenth century; here Chaucer perhaps read it in its original Latin verse form. It is also found in the corresponding book eleven of the *Ovide moralisé,* the immense and widely read early fourteenth-century French translation of Ovid's mythological tales, where they are accompanied and explained by extensive, allegorizing moralizations. Here too is a work Chaucer may have known directly and mined in this instance for what has traditionally, if distortingly, been called "source materials."

Beyond doubt, however, the English poet encountered—and perhaps for the first and only time—the story of Seys and Alcyone while reading Guillaume de Machaut's *Dit de la fonteinne amoureuse (The Story of the Fountain of Love),* one of the most noted of the several *dits amoureux* or "love poems" by the renowned French poet that Chaucer read closely and made a part of this and several other of his early works. As it was to many in the French-speaking Ricardian court circle for whom Machaut was one of the most famous and honored poets, this much is certainly clear to modern scholars: reading his French book and struck by the marvelous story of Seys and Alcyone, Chaucer's narrator reenacts intratextually the experience of the author with his own French book, the text of Machaut's complete works that we know, for reasons to be explained later, the English poet must have had literally at hand when writing *The Book of the Duchess.*

In part, then, the narrator's reading of this story, in the elementary sense that he deciphers and construes it, constitutes a *mise-en-abyme* for the poet's exploration of literary tradition (see Calin 287). The story and its discovery is a motif within the text that precisely mirrors both the process involved in the text's composition and its resulting form. The narrator's incorporation of a well-known text through translation into his own work identifies his discourse, and by extension the poet's, as in part a revoicing of what others have written. Scavengers of the already said, both narrator and poet produce a self-proclaiming *bricolage,* a patchwork of fragments from other texts; the two also reveal— the narrator directly, the poet implicitly—the process of assemblage and adaptation by which their works have come to be. The result is a work that contains other texts but only partially controls them; these must be reread, but not as themselves.

Naturally, the poet must be understood as acting in response to motives quite different from those of his creation, who is, after all, not primarily a writer but a reader hoping to be bored asleep. Chaucer's dutiful reading of respected authorities was not only a customary act of veneration but the first step toward "invention": the identification and then putting together of suitable materials that medieval poetic theory prescribed should precede any act of composition. For the pre-romantic Chaucer, writing was less the Cartesian encounter with the absolutely blank folio than the effective marshaling of the already composed, whose form and significance would have to be altered in appropriate ways to constitute the newly emergent text.

This means that Chaucer, the writer who can succeed at his task only by first examining what others have written, would have "read" Machaut in two ways: not only acquiescing, as the narrator initially does, to a textual otherness whose dynamic can be consumed and wondered at, if not transformed; but also discovering in the flow of another's language what can with profit be repeated and refigured in one's own, in this case translated from French into English and also transferred from one textual form to another. Such reading is simultaneously an interpretation and an assessment performed with one's own writerly needs uppermost in mind.

The narrator in *The Book of the Duchess* provides an intratextual model for this more self-directed kind of reading; his actions within the diegesis constitute a detailed analogue for what must have been involved in the poem's composition, which required the poet to engage in two complementary but distinct "readings." Reading his French book receptively—that is, following its words, surrendering to their rhetorical design—does not bring on what he desires: a disengagement that would hasten the needed relief of sleep. The story the narrator chooses has proven too interesting; it has not bored him into slumber, but quickened his curiosity instead. Just as Chaucer, reading his Machaut, presumably identified the tale of Seys and Alcyone as one worthy of retelling in his own work, so the narrator singles it out for retelling in his autobiographical discourse, his record of those experiences that constitutes the diegesis of *The Book of the Duchess*. From a text chosen randomly only for the sleepiness it might induce, the story of Seys and Alcyone unexpectedly becomes intriguing because of what it has to say, for the experiential truth the narrator mistakenly thinks it expresses.

In fact, the distraught man's view of the world is drastically altered by his reading. What the narrator finds in his "romaunce" differs sharply from what he thinks he knows about life, offers a novelty he credits much too readily because he neglects the difference between the feigned, plastic world of the text and the immutable, real one he inhabits. The knowledge he thinks to have gleaned from his reading will prove useful, or so he hastens to believe, for curing the insomnia plaguing him. Just so, Chaucer himself, rereading the *Fonteinne amoureuse,* must have believed that the story of Seys and Alcyone therein contained would help him solve in part the compositional problems posed by his plans to write an occasional poem addressing the recent misfortune suffered by John of Gaunt, like Alcyone suddenly bereft of his beloved spouse. Neither narrator nor poet is proved wrong in this self-directed reading of another's story, this assertive co-optation of another's words that are then revoiced and reoriented.

Within the diegesis, the story bears only a strained and problematic relation to the use the narrator ultimately makes of it. Alcyone is overcome by grief for her husband, who has not returned from a voyage and is therefore presumed dead. She then asks Juno either to allow her to see Seys or to provide her with certain knowledge of his fate. Juno listens to her prayer and instructs Morpheus, in effect, to honor both her requests. The God of Sleep takes up the king's drowned body and conducts it to where Alcyone lies sleeping. This simulacrum of the living Seys then addresses the woman, informing her of the deadly misfortune that befell him at sea. A dead man who speaks, this Seys implicitly asks Alcyone to endorse the paradox of his unexpected appearance in her consciousness. The king's only apparently living form, animated by the emotions and voice a divine ventriloquist supplies, manifests the unmistakable signs of his own demise: "For certes, swete, I am but dede / Ye shul me never on lyve yse" (lines 204–05). Alcyone accepts the truth, but Seys's plea that God lighten the burden of her sorrow falls on deaf ears. Undone by the pain of her loss, the inconsolable woman dies of grief before three mornings come and go.

The narrator's reading of the story rejects its explicit focus on bereavement, an experience that brings two kinds of suffering: the first is the anxiety resulting from uncertainty, the sudden and unexplained absence of a loved one; the second is the pain from an irremediable loss, whose final irony is that the dead continue to live in the thoughts of those who loved them even as they have become permanently absent from the world of the living. This focus on bereavement, it turns out, is entirely appropriate to the poem's thematic concerns as these develop more clearly in its second section: the narrator's dream, whose structure and rhetoric shape the poem as an indirect memorial to the lady—Blanche, young wife of John of Gaunt—whose sudden passing provided the occasion for poetic composition. The much lamented lady figures in the dream as a thinly disguised Fair White, the beautiful woman, now dead, for whom the nobleman grieves. As rereader turned reteller, then, Chaucer has chosen more wisely and self-consciously than his intratextual reflex, picking traditional materials suited to a poem about grief.

His narrator will have none of this representation of grief; guided, or perhaps impelled, by his own concerns, he reads the tale "against the grain," as contemporary criticism would term it. For him, Alcyone's successful prayer to the goddess Juno provides the ideal solution to his psychological and physical malady. He has never heard of any gods but the single Christian one, yet he immediately becomes eager to implore for aid Morpheus and Juno, whomever will grant his wish that he be allowed to sleep a while. To this end, he offers his expected divine patrons a rich array of presents: a featherbed covered in gold cloth and satin, as well as pillows of fine linen from Rennes, and all the furnishings needed for a room, including tapestries and gold paint for the walls. The offer, he reports, must have been appealing because he immediately fell deeply asleep right on top of his book, there to dream the "swete" or pleasant vision whose narration occupies the remainder of the poem.

Chaucer is manifestly indebted to the *Fonteinne amoureuse,* not the *Metamorphoses* or the *Ovide moralisé,* for how he represents the two "rereadings" of the story of Seys and Alcyone. Following Machaut, Chaucer embeds what he borrows within a framing fiction of his own invention, assigning storytelling duties to an intratextual narrator who accurately retells the classic tale from Ovid, but then wildly misreads it, constructing a moralization or application that is idiosyncratic, quite self-serving, and, above all, stupid. Such misguided reading reveals the narrator to be both foolish and naïve, perhaps even blaspheming and only superficially Christian.

The outline for this treatment is found in Machaut, with the one important structural difference between the two versions being that the French poet doubly embeds the story, assigning its telling to a third-degree narrator. In the *Fonteinne amoureuse,* the first person narrator, once again a thinly disguised intratextual version of the poet himself, overhears the sorrowful lament—in complexly lyric verse— of a nobleman in an adjacent room. The man grieves inconsolably because he will soon be separated from the woman he loves, who unfortunately has never been made aware of his devotion to her. For the lover, true to the tradition of *fin'amors* or "refined love," is bound by the code of silence, the more or less iron rule that men should never speak their true feelings to the women they love before receiving permission to do so.

As the centerpiece of his technically sophisticated *complainte* or "complaint" (comprised of a hundred stanzas, each with a different rhyme scheme), the nobleman tells the story of Ceyx and Alchioine, which he does not identify as having a source other than his own apparently perfect knowledge of it. His version resembles closely what Chaucer's narrator finds in the French book; for example, both authors pay little attention to either the circumstances that force Ceyx to travel by ship away from Alchioine or the tragic journey itself, parts of the story treated at length in both the Latin and French Ovids. However Machaut follows these sources in one way Chaucer rejects: the French poet concludes his retelling with the metamorphosis that saves Alchioine from a miserable death and solitary eternity. Waking from her dream of Ceyx to embrace him, she grasps only air; but then the widow's endless weeping and sighing persuade Juno to reunite the couple by transforming them into birds, kingfishers who will spend eternity traversing the oceans together.

Like his English counterpart, Machaut's character ignores the explicit concern of the Ovidian tale with grief and consolation. Identifying with Alchioine's inconsolability, the lonely nobleman argues that Morpheus ought to act as his messenger. The plan is to have the God of Sleep assume the nobleman's form and appear in his lady's dreams some five or six times in order to communicate his love and distress. Because the woman he loves is such a noble creature, her natural reaction would be to pity his condition and look with favor upon his suit. Awakening, she would remember his words and manner, often meditating upon them. The nobleman thinks that because his lady would experience the same dream a number of times, she would be forced to believe it; furthermore, she would be utterly convinced by Morpheus, who knows well how to counterfeit and thus would accurately portray the suffering and affection so readily apparent in his looks and demeanor.

Machaut gently but unmistakably ridicules the nobleman's naïveté and inexperience throughout this passage (a bold move considering that this aristocrat is the obvious textual reflex of Jean, duc de Berri, the young and emotionally distraught patron for whom Machaut is writing). The young man clearly fails to recognize that the pattern of this ancient story does not precisely fit his unfortunate circumstances. For he is the one in need of a comforting vision, not the lady; after all, she knows nothing of his suffering and feels no pain herself. The nobleman can think only of his own inability to act, bound as he is by the lover's code that forbids directness and implicitly encourages scheming. If Morpheus were to speak for him, then the letter of the law would be observed since he would never beg the lady's mercy personally. In sum, he does not yet understand how he must rely on Love and not his own stratagems in order to find consolation.

The nobleman even falls victim to a more serious misunderstanding: assuming, like his obvious model in the famous *Romance of the Rose,* that the God of Love is a man, not a woman. And so he ignores the power of Venus, the dominant goddess who will later appear in his dream to correct this error and reprove his discourtesy. Though insulted, Venus manifests her liking for noblemen eager to love because they recall the Paris who awarded her the golden apple as the most beautiful of the goddesses. She brings his lady to him, that is, to the sleeping figure of himself he observes in his own dream. The lady then accepts the man's as yet unspoken request for her love, permitting him to avoid breaking the lovers' code. As a token of her affection, she bestows upon his passive form a flurry of kisses as well as a ring that, waking, he finds still on his finger, a testimony to the existential connection between dreaming and conscious experience, between idealized emotion and its worldly manifestation.

Chaucer's version of the Ovidian story of Seys and Alcyone is closely modeled on what he read in Machaut; the most important change is that he excises the closing metamorphosis. And the English poet, like his French counterpart, exploits the comic gap that opens up between the themes of the story and the misreading these receive from a somewhat foolish intratextual narrator. Because Chaucer is writing an elegy of sorts and Machaut a triumphant love story, however, the two poets make quite different use of the oft-told tale and its humorous interpretation, as we shall see later.

At the moment, I wish to emphasize one point only: unlike Machaut, Chaucer thematizes the story as a rereading—as a problematic representation of human experience contained in a written source that must be deciphered and construed. For the French poet, the tragic but finally triumphant narrative of Ceyx and Alchioine figures as a history, as an exemplum presumably chosen because its main character's sorrow and dependence upon divine intervention mirror those of the man who retells it; evidently quite learned in the tradition that Chaucer's narrator can only explore much more haphazardly in books, Machaut's nobleman gropes not without purpose or direction for the consolation he seeks, recalling an appropriate instance from ancient history. Because the story is not represented as a text, the nobleman lacks the bookishness of Chaucer's creation, who is dependent upon a problematic, somewhat slippery, but ultimately appropriate literary tradition.

Searching in his reading for one thing, Chaucer's narrator finds something quite different: a story, one of several he might have chosen, whose truth value he endorses too quickly. He thereby establishes his dependence on written authority, but shows as well his lack of sophistication in its interpretation. For he seems completely unaware of mythography, the Christian protocol of reading that demanded the divinities who figure in classical texts be understood allegorically, as representing aspects of the physical universe or human nature. He thus falls quickly, if not disastrously, into the principal danger that classical literature, so thought many intellectuals of the later Middle Ages, posed to the ill-prepared and gullible. Seduced by the possibility of an easy bargain with divine forces that his text seems to promise, the exchange of presents or sacrifices for supernatural assistance, he quickly forgets the central Christian teaching that God is one.

The narrator has not enjoyed the benefit of having his Ovid "moralized," as the anonymous cleric who produced the immense *Ovide moralisé* thought desirable, perhaps envisaging just the sort of misguided textual encounter that Chaucer's character experiences. Fortune, however, comically rewards his foolishness, or at least appears to do so, when the narrator immediately falls asleep. Chaucer's readers can appreciate the joke because they trust the poet is a more sophisticated and learned interpreter of written authority than his textual reflex, one who is not detoured so easily into intellectual error. And yet the narrator's encounter with his book, his double reading of it, mirrors within the diegesis the poet's experience with composition, for he too searches authorities, chooses what interests him there, retells stories, and exploits them for his own purposes. Machaut, in contrast, does not use the story of Ceyx and Alchioine to call attention in any way to his reading and revoicing; his text does not offer itself as *bricolage* even though later in the work the illusionism of the diegesis is comically ruptured several times, a self-reflexive move that may have given the English poet the idea for his much bolder form of textual mirroring.[1] Machaut's reader, in other words, is not asked to reread Ovid or the *Ovide moralisé* (the poet's likely source). Chaucer offers a different protocol for reading: his text incorporates others which may therein be comically misread, deliberately read against the grain, or accommodated to whatever purpose their reteller then has in mind. Such, at least, are the ways we can view the narrator's activity as a rewriter and, by implication, the poet's. The reader's task is thus no simple decipherment of the words on the page, but a simultaneous reading of what is present and rereading of what has been carried over or "translated" from one text to another.

Great Translator, Geoffrey Chaucer

Why does Chaucer thematize the act of reading and rewriting, the work of the *bricoleur* who not only makes his own texts but offers rereadings of those to which he lends renewed voice? An obvious answer, I think, is that he wished to identify the somewhat unusual nature of *The Book of the Duchess,* a poem constructed by stitching together translated lines drawn from a number of Machaut poems; these fill out a formal structure the poet assembles from motifs borrowed once again from the French master. Chaucer, in effect, asked his readers and listeners at court to understand his first major poem as a translation of both the content and form of some of Machaut's most noted works.

Even without the comic portrait that *The Book of the Duchess* offers of the narrator as a bumbling reader and rewriter, Chaucer's contemporaries perhaps understood the particular nature of his poetic project better than modern critics. Most revealing in this regard is the earliest piece of Chaucer criticism that has come down to us: a *ballade* written in 1386 by Eustache Deschamps, a French contemporary well acquainted with Chaucer because of the ongoing negotiations between England and France in which both men were involved.[2] The *ballade* is a political document in some sense, or so many modern commentators have thought. However I mention its existence here not for the light it sheds on Chaucer the career diplomat and administrator, but for what it tells us about Chaucer the poet. To Deschamps, Chaucer is a "great translator," a judgment whose importance to the understanding of the English poet's early career has not yet, I think, been properly valued.

With a style that is perhaps humorously hyperbolic, the Frenchman addresses his English counterpart as:

> Lofty eagle, who by your learning
> Shines light upon the kingdom of Aeneas,
> The isle of giants (those of *Brut*), who has there
> Sown the flowers and transplanted the rose bush
> For those ignorant of the French language,
> Great translator, noble Geoffrey Chaucer. (lines 5–10)

Here Deschamps pays Chaucer, and by extension the English court and its culture, an obviously double-edged compliment. The poet is singled out for his wise decision to introduce through translation the beauties of French books to a realm otherwise most noted, apparently, for spawning a race of physical giants. Chaucer's accomplishments, however, include not only the translation of *The Romance of the Rose,* alluded to in the passage above and identified unmistakably in the next stanza. Borrowing the most memorable metaphor of amorous experience from that monumental work, the garden of love, Deschamps refigures its meaning. Chaucer is to be commended not only for bringing the French garden to Anglian shores: as a gardener/poet himself, he has begun the construction of a new literary playscape, using the living material brought from across the channel:

> And for a long time you've been building
> A garden, for which you've requested cuttings
> From those men who write to advance themselves,
> Great translator, noble Geoffrey Chaucer. (lines
>   17–20)

A modern reader unaware of the cultural importance attached to translation in the late Middle Ages might well overemphasize the undeniable irony in Deschamps's designation of his fellow poet as a "great translator." The Frenchman, however, is doing more than according Chaucer backhanded praise, lauding him for having the wisdom to choose French poetry to translate. The effect of the poem depends on the artful deployment of a time-honored and often used topos, that of *translatio studii,* "the transfer of learning." By connecting the transfer of Trojan civilization to England with the translation of French poetry to the same country, Deschamps implies that the torch of artistic accomplishment has indeed been passed to burn brightly in a new location.

The point is that Deschamps's characterization of Chaucer as a great translator functions, like all canny diplomatic formulas, on the different, perhaps conflicting levels appropriate to the occasion, discovering a ground of mutual honor and congratulation. That Chaucer is viewed first and foremost as a translator acknowledges what no one in an England whose aristocracy was still largely French in language and culture would have thought to deny: the historical superiority of continental literary achievement. But with this formulation, Deschamps also recognizes the shifting momentum of cultural history and exchange, which fittingly retraces the archetypal pattern established by the foundational events of northern European civilization.

Translation (a physical act paralleling rereading) is no simple transference in some cases. To prepare a translation of *The Romance of the Rose* that follows the original faithfully and circulates under the same title is to create a substitute in another language. Such an act, as Deschamps recognizes, extends the cultural power of the ur-text, which, in this re-presentation, can now reach a previously unattainable readership.

However, to follow Deschamps's metaphor, it is something quite different to take cuttings from the work of those writing in a different language in order to create from them a new literary garden. This kind of translation does not extend the power of honored, if hitherto unreadable texts. Quite the contrary, it forges from them a newness authorized by a tradition that is simultaneously superseded, replaced, in a sense even destroyed. As Deschamps declares, Chaucer is creating a garden from the works of those who write to establish their own authority. Yet this English garden will not acknowledge their claims, at least directly, for, like any garden, it will be appreciated primarily as the gardener's handiwork.

The authority of French poets, including perhaps especially Machaut, will be subsumed within the greater power to compose of the Englishman who can replace their words with his own. Texts translated in this fashion do not survive under their own names. Their names are, must be, suppressed because the original texts are no longer themselves. Instead, the discarded originals continue to enjoy a kind of life only under the guise of what they are not, in the form of an otherness that denies, but cannot, indeed is not intended to, extirpate their presence. The superseded text is always present in the otherness of its reincarnation, always constitutes a ground of being for the new. In fact, its absent presence rhetorically authorizes the production of the newly created text. Most medieval authors are translators of this kind, makers of new texts from old, revisers whose activity is a continual insertion into the already written, readers who reread and thus must face the paradox that authorities are both to be honored and rejected in the act of remaking. The audience for such works hears the continuing echo of other texts whose voices have not been silenced; readers glimpse a faintly visible palimpsest beneath more recent inscriptions.

Firmly attached to the related notions of single authorship and textual unity, the modern reader cannot easily approach such texts as their authors intended. Accustomed to the idea that a text is personal property, we are inclined to deploy the term plagiarism to describe the double-voiced presence of what seems to us their unauthentic confection. But then we cannot accept that an honored author could be a plagiarist. Instead, in general we prefer to evaluate Chaucer's "translations" according to the principle of Vosslerian stylistic concretization, reducing the texts that are therein revoiced to inert, plastic, and unsignifying raw materials. In short, we valorize the poet's meaning-bestowing use by granting him ownership rights to what has been borrowed. We ignore the palimpsest, pay no heed to other voices. We read, but refuse the writer's invitation to reread as well.

An honestly historicist approach to Chaucer, however, must face squarely the difficulties of reading/rereading posed by *The Book of the Duchess*. The kind of translation that it is cannot be entirely assigned, at least in the modern sense, to either author, belongs instead to a doublespeak that emphasizes the paradox at the heart of all acts of translation: what is said again cannot be repeated, for it is not the same; yet what is said again is always already spoken, a newness that precedes itself. A corollary is that texts of this type cannot be described easily by the essentially formalist strictures of most modern literary theory. Hence the importance of Genette's work on transtextual relations. His theorizing draws our attention rightly to the various ways in which the hypo/hypertextual relation alters or transforms what kinds of meaning are generated by a given text (which must be seen in connection to some other outside its formal boundaries).

Translations of the kind I have, following Deschamps, been discussing are hypertexts that have no life, no mode of being *in themselves*. What is written on the page evokes, but can only inadequately image a complex process of affirmation and denial, a doubleness of form as well as of meaning. Such translations *are* what they also *are not*. They say what they simultaneously reduce to silence, extend the life of what must in the process fade to mere shadow. What I am advocating is that we must restore to our reading of *The Book of the Duchess* (and other Chaucerian texts as well) the category of what is not said (but which we must reread). And we can hear what is not said in this poem by abandoning post-romantic protocols of reading, for these maintain the text is simply itself, a new, discrete form of discourse. Instead, like those within his initial audience, we must read it as a translation, as the textual representation of formal and semantic absence. Reading Chaucer, we must also, like him, reread Guillaume de Machaut, paying attention to what the English poet, transforming, repeats and what he passes over in silence.

That *The Book of the Duchess* is, in essence, a translation from French originals in which the fact of translation is effaced was discovered early in modern Chaucer studies by George Lyman Kittredge.[3] Kittredge established beyond a doubt that a large number of passages and lines, including many crucial to the overall meaning of the poem, were indeed close translations or freer adaptations from a number of the narrative works of Guillaume de Machaut. A conservative accounting at the moment would list 914 or roughly two-thirds of the work's 1,334 lines as deriving directly from various French models, including works by Jean Froissart, himself heavily influenced by Machaut.[4]

Thus it would be correct to characterize *The Book of the Duchess* as a tissue or mosaic of borrowings, a *bricolage* in which what has

been scavenged from other writers has been fitted into a structure
suiting the work's occasional rhetoric. And yet the structure itself,
as we have already seen in part, is almost entirely borrowed from
Machaut as well, adapted once again not from one text, but from a
series of love vision and debate poems. What many readers recall as
the most striking features of the poem's form are in fact derivative, are
"translated" in the sense I have been discussing. These include: the
structural division between a frame dominated by a narrator who is
the poet's obvious alter ego and a dream that represents a movement
toward consolation through the revelation of higher truth; the story
of Seys and Alcyone retold but misunderstood by a main character;
the representation of a developing relationship between the low-born
narrator and the sorrowing nobleman he in some sense comes to serve;
the nobleman's idealized love for a beautiful woman he has lost, a
painful emotion for which he receives some consolation by poem's
end. The fact of translation is made somewhat occult because the
integrity of the sources is not represented in their re-presentation: the
Machaut works in question are scavenged for useful parts that are then
combined with one another in ways the French poet could hardly have
foreseen and perhaps would not have sanctioned. Like the postmodern
bricoleur, Chaucer thereby suggests the indispensable inadequacy of
these models for his project through a selective, unauthorized representation of some of their elements.

During the last fifty years, *The Book of the Duchess* has continued
to attract more traditionally minded contemporary scholars eager to
identify all its sources. Remarkably, however, there has been no further
investigation into the various questions raised by Kittredge's discoveries. Most important, how did Chaucer manage so readily to combine
passages from several Machaut works? Scholarly investigation into
the textual transmission of Machaut's poetry provides an easy answer.
Unlike most late medieval writers, Machaut was very interested that
his accomplishments, musical as well as poetic, be appreciated as a
corpus redounding to his credit. He oversaw personally, and otherwise
arranged for, the production of omnibus collections devoted entirely
to his work. With this in mind, we may easily imagine how Chaucer
composed his poem: sitting down to write with one of these omnibus
MSS. to hand, he simply flipped through the various works he had

previously and avidly read, picking out those passages appropriate for different parts of his poem. In short, we can imagine him rereading, going through his French book rather like the poem's narrator goes through his. But, unlike his textual alter ego, his choices were hardly a matter of chance. It cannot be an accident that Chaucer borrowed most heavily and significantly from three poems that enjoyed a great deal of popularity with readers (to judge from the MS. tradition) and other writers (to judge from the several imitations and adaptations in addition to Chaucer's own). Those who shared his literary culture would have recognized *The Book of the Duchess* as a work that continued, even as it superseded: *The Judgment of the King of Bohemia, The Judgment of the King of Navarre,* and *The Fountain of Love.*

Machaut, I have suggested, conceived of his narrative, lyric, and musical works as constituting an authorial whole, a body of work sanctioned by two separate calls, the first from the goddess Nature and the second from Love (such at least is the explanation for his avocation Machaut provides in the fictional *Prologue* he wrote late in his career as an introduction). Within that body of connected texts, the three poems Chaucer has chosen to translate themselves constitute a group joined by close transtextual ties (each text rewrites those preceding it in compositional order) and a shared major theme: the relative virtues and power of men and women in the game of love. Reading Machaut's textual rereading of his own productions, Chaucer appears to have been struck by the possibility of inserting himself into a series organized explicitly around rewriting (and hence offering to noble admirers their role as rereaders).

For those unacquainted with Machaut, a brief summary of this rewriting/rereading is called for.

In the *Bohemia,* an unidentified lover, about to fall asleep on a beautiful spring morning, is startled by the sudden approach of a nobleman and lady, who move toward him on separate paths that intersect. Meeting unexpectedly, the aristocratic pair discovers that each suffers the pain of a lost love. The lady's lover has died, while the man's has betrayed him with another. As the narrator listens, embarrassed in the bushes, the pair begins a heated, though polite debate over whose suffering is worse. An exploration of this love question becomes the poem's main theme. Unable to decide their own quarrel, they are led by the chagrined narrator, who reveals himself, to a nearby castle where the king of Bohemia, a fictional version of Machaut's patron at that time, decides their case. The king and his courtiers determine that the lady suffers less and will recover sooner than the knight, it being human and especially female nature to forget a lover who has died. The court rule unanimously that because the man's former beloved continues to live and enjoy the embraces of his rival, his grief will find no effective remedy.

The *Navarre* offers a complex sequel to this debate about the relative strengths of men and women in the experience of love. In this later poem, what was extratextual in the *Bohemia*—the poem's composition by Guillaume de Machaut—becomes the fictional cadre. In the *Navarre*, the main character is none other than the poet named Guillaume de Machaut who, surviving the sudden advent of the plague, rides out on a spring morning to enjoy his deliverance from death. He is so engaged in his pursuit of hares that he fails to notice his lady—a beautiful lady revealed to be an allegorical figure named Good Fortune—who is riding close by with her entourage. She complains that Guillaume has defamed women in his earlier work by implying that men are more faithful and persevering in love than women. Irritated, Guillaume vehemently denies that such a conclusion is true, and a debate ensues at the lady's castle between Guillaume and her twelve female courtiers, also allegorical figures with names such as Hope and Moderation. Guillaume, in effect, is forced to defend the truth value of his work against the charges of insulted readers; such a fictional strategy forces the reader to reread the *Bohemia*, discovering a new context for what it says about the different experiences of men and women with love. Faced with many adept female foes, who represent important aspects of human nature and experience, the embattled poet finally loses his temper and reveals a male chauvinism he had hitherto repressed. The court finds him guilty. Yet a suddenly repentant Guillaume is not harshly punished. He is condemned instead to compose three lyric poems with the correct "doctrine." One of these, the *Lai de plour* or *Lay of Weeping,* follows the *Navarre* in some manuscripts, according to what was, apparently, Machaut's original design. This lay's dramatic narrator is the bereaved lady from the *Bohemia,* who repeats more or less what she says in that earlier poem, thereby ironically "correcting" Guillaume's original judgment. For he now presents her views alone, without the male correction of either her debater's alternative opinion or the court's judgment. And yet he thereby offers no correction of his earlier opinion; he never reverses the decision reached in the *Bohemia*.

Though it is not structurally connected to the two poems in the judgment series, the *Fountain of Love* deals with the same doctrinal and authorial issues. The work opens with a clerkly narrator who, staying in the house of a nobleman, is suddenly awakened in the middle of the night by a grief-stricken voice, which, as we have discussed previously, belongs to a nobleman disappointed in love. The clerkly narrator copies down the poem he hears the man recite and, meeting him the next morning, makes him a present of the text. Made friends by their joint knowledge of the aristocrat's grief, the pair strolls into a lovely garden where, beside a beautiful fountain on which is depicted the judgment of Paris, they fall asleep and dream the same dream: Venus appears, along with the man's beloved, to offer both consolation and knowledge. She chastises the man severely for praying to the wrong gods. Even so she will comfort him. After relating the judgment of Paris in a way that emphasizes her own superiority, Venus makes the lady address the lover, preventing her from seeming cold and unresponsive. In fact, the lady bends over to kiss the sleeping form of her lover, exchanging rings with him. Upon awakening, he is consoled by his vision and the ring, thereupon departing for exile without regret. If the *Navarre* ends ambiguously, with the narrator doing compositional penance yet in effect restoring his previous work, the *Fountain of Love* demonstrates the power of Venus, to which the awe-struck narrator can only attest as he witnesses the miraculous transformation of his noble friend into a satisfied lover. All doubts about the woman's emotional strength and depth are resolved in a remarkable turnaround epitomized by the man's passive form, formerly a speaking subject, but now the object of female desire and sexual assertiveness.

Against this background, the most striking aspect of *The Book of the Duchess* is its suppression of the debate about the relative power and virtues of the two genders in the love experience. Such a debate is a central structural feature of the two judgment poems and is continued implicitly in the *Fountain of Love* (where Venus's reproof of the misguided nobleman deliberately recalls the angry accusations Good Fortune makes against Guillaume). Reading this series of texts, which were composed in the above order and so copied in the omnibus Machaut MS. Chaucer had access to, the modern reader is struck by their incremental thematizing of female power. In the *Bohemia,* the lady's sorrow is first elicited by her chance male companion, then assigned a relative place of value by him and the male-dominated court; the conclusion even suggests that this same court will do its best to heal the wounds caused by her experience. The *Navarre,* in contrast, refutes this judgment. The debate not only forces the poet to recant his views, but replaces the male authority of the first text—the king of Bohemia—with the female Good Fortune, who permits the king of Navarre no significant role beyond that of honorary judge in the proceedings. Here Guillaume must bow to the evident power of an assertive, if finally benevolent, femininity, confessing the error of his male chauvinism. His poetic penance even involves a complex transvestite performance; the *Lay of Weeping* makes us listen to two voices, that of its female dramatic monologist and that of its male author, who must demonstrate therein his changed opinion about female suffering. The *Fountain of Love* extends the power of women to the experience of love itself. Here the male god of Love—that conventionalized Cupid who appears in *The Romance of the Rose* and most other principal texts in this literary tradition—is replaced by a haughty yet gracious Venus. It is Venus, not the lover or some male divinity, who enables love to be consummated. Like Guillaume in the *Navarre,* the nobleman must eat his words and stand corrected; he must acknowledge a female power he had previously ignored.

In near total contrast, *The Book of the Duchess* offers a male-dominated experience of love. Surprisingly, Chaucer rejects the device of a Venus who offers the grief-stricken male lover the promise of deliverance (a motif eminently suitable to his theme, which is in general quite similar to that of Machaut's *Fountain of Love*). The English poet instead puts the two men in charge of the aristocrat's consolation. In the dream section of the poem, the narrator encounters a grief-stricken nobleman whom he engages in conversation in order to learn his sorrow. Either because he artfully makes him face his own grief or because he simply cannot understand his better's situation, the narrator draws his erstwhile companion into a long and comforting recounting of the love affair that finally ended tragically in the woman's death.

This reshaping of his source materials also rejects the motif from the two judgment poems of a debate between male and female versions of sorrow in which the woman can speak, and to good effect, for herself. Instead, Chaucer contrasts Alcyone, a woman who can only die from grief once released from the urge to go on living, with the dream's high-minded man in black, who masters his sorrow by narrativizing and aestheticizing it. When the narrator first encounters him, he overhears the man reciting a love lyric, a noble-minded impulse whose seriousness is never undercut. In Machaut, as we have seen, this motif is handled ironically and humorously; the nobleman's attempt both to express his grief and devise its remedy through remarkable compositional *sprezzatura* turns out to be misguided, for he must depend on Venus. In fact, he is reduced to absolute silence in the dream, becomes a figure who never wakes up, even when kissed by his beloved. Chaucer's Alcyone can neither turn her grief into a poem nor a story. However she not only lacks the intellectual and compositional powers of the man in black; unlike her model in both Ovid and Machaut, even her grief lacks the strength to effect a divinely engineered and happy metamorphosis.

Machaut's *Bohemia* offers what is judged in the later *Navarre* an antifeminist view: that women lack the same power as men to endure in love, despite suffering and loss. Chaucer's poem, in a sense, restores that rejected view through rereading, contrasting an Alcyone destroyed by misfortune to a man in black who rises above and is ennobled by his own. It is significant that from the various female characters provided by Machaut—the sorrowing noblewoman, lady Good Fortune, her allegorical courtiers, the goddess Venus, and the grieving aristocrat's willing and eager beloved—Chaucer retains the one who is the least in control of her fate. Like most of the "good women" in Chaucer's poem of the same name, in fact, his Alcyone establishes her virtue only through the ultimate act of self-negation, willing herself into death when she cannot endure the loss of her beloved. In contrast, the noble lady in Machaut's *Bohemia* survives the death of her lover, and it is agreed by all concerned that she will outlast this grief and eventually love another man. Her strength, perseverance, and remarkable gifts of self-expression are represented in *The Book of the Duchess,* but constitute the moral center of the man in black, who is often given her lines to speak.

Unlike the poems of Machaut from which it derives, Chaucer's work offers dead rather than living women; not only Alcyone, but of course Fair White, who can be evoked, who can achieve a presence in the work only through the memory of the man whose inextinguishable love for her attests primarily to his power and virtue. Fueled by the provocative readings of Carolyn Dinshaw and Sheila Delany, feminist work on Chaucer has tended to conceive the poet as a liberal in those matters we would now term gender politics, thus recuperating a favored author for contemporary readers.[5] But the way Chaucer makes us reread Machaut in his poem tells a very different story, speaks of a rewriting that is also the writing out of the female presence Machaut's texts construct as genially troublesome perhaps, yet indispensable and possessed of undeniable power.

In *Chaucer and the Fictions of Gender,* Elaine Hansen reaches a conclusion about *The Book of the Duchess* similar to my own simply by reading it "against the grain" (a contrapuntal form of rereading), not by understanding the poem as a rereading of Machaut. Her view is that the work "idealizes the historical Blanche out of existence in the battle for control over meaning and intention" (59). Thus Chaucer's text is no simple elegy, but fires another shot in that most intense of late fourteenth-century cultural struggles, the battle between the sexes. An important part of Hansen's argument is that the man in black, like many a medieval lover, is feminized by his psychological and physiological predicament. To give wider cultural resonance to this point, she makes reference to similar figures in romance, Sir Launfal in particular. But more immediate and telling transtextual relationships lie to hand. As I have suggested, most of the lines in which the man in black expresses his sorrow and grief at the loss of his beloved are taken directly from the *Bohemia,* where they are uttered by the female half of the debating pair. Unlike Machaut's, however, Chaucer's character is neither outdone by a competing version of suffering nor pitied by a paternalizing court; his objectification of grief testifies instead both to his power to express it in conventional ideal terms and to his mastery of what, for Alcyone, is an emotion leading directly to self-extinction.

Similarly, the structural changes effected by Chaucer disclose the masculinization of Machaut's representation of gender. The *Fountain of Love* offers the humorous if touching spectacle of a man in love who, failing to tell his lady how he feels, conceives a plan to win her by hiring a divine surrogate. Such cowardice, however ingenious and doctrinally correct, cannot of course succeed. Overcome by the waters of the fountain of love belonging to the goddess, the nobleman is himself instructed while asleep and then visited, in an ironic reversal, by the image of his lady love, who woos him instead. For the nobleman's self-generated image of the lady, the lady herself, with Venus's assistance, is substituted.

The Book of the Duchess radically transforms this pattern. The waking frame presents a female textual presence conjured into life by the narrator's reading. But the dream does not construct a more powerful living or "authentic" version of the feminine, one that would correct male misapprehensions about a woman's interest in love or her power to pursue the object of her desire. For Fair White is only imagined by the man in black, only given a life in the discourse whose refined emotion and expressions say more about his moral purity and emotional refinement than those of the lady love he has lost. An elegy for Blanche, but a poem written to please John of Gaunt, *The Book of the Duchess* not surprisingly centers on male experience, reducing its two women to either an intratextual presence (Alcyone) or a memory (Fair White), both of which are placed firmly under male control.

If Machaut, exploring the insufficiencies of literary tradition in a series of texts that ask the reader to reread what precedes them, clearly outlines the inadequacy of conventional male images of women (as, that is, unproblematic, passive objects of desire), Chaucer celebrates the self-sufficiency and consolatory power of these same representations. For his original audience, I believe, such a redefinition of Machaut's view that love depends upon a not inconsiderable female power would have seemed striking, perhaps shocking, especially since the French poet's very words and textual structures are recycled to sustain it. Forced to reread Machaut's works as they read Chaucer's "translation" of them, those for whom he wrote must have recognized the English poet's restoration of an older view of love, one to be found in twelfth- and thirteenth-century romance and in the first part of *The Romance of the Rose,* but not in Machaut. Undoubtedly, the meaning Chaucer's poem had for its original audience was defined to an important extent by these transformative and incorporative gestures, the creatively transtextual moves of a truly "great translator" who forces us not just to read what he has to say, but reread the tradition he both embraces and rejects.

Notes

1. See, for example, lines 1,897–98, where Venus, in the nobleman's and narrator's dream, speaks of Paris's accomplishments as an archer, but acts as if her information were derived from a written text (as the poet's knowledge of the Trojan prince certainly was).
2. I quote from the translation in Fisher's collected edition, which I have adapted somewhat. The original French is reprinted on facing pages. See Fisher 952–53.
3. The fullest discussion of these matters is found in James I. Wimsatt's *Chaucer and the French Love Poets: The Literary Background of the* Book of the Duchess.
4. See the discussion in R. Barton Palmer, ed. and trans., *The Judgment of the King of Bohemia,* for details. My account differs in some minor respects from that of Wimsatt.
5. See, especially, Carolyn Dinshaw, *Chaucer's Sexual Poetics,* and Sheila Delany, *The Naked Text: Chaucer's Legend of Good Women.*

Works Cited

Bakhtin, M. M. (as Volosinov, V. N.). *Marxism and the Philosophy of Language.* Trans. Ladislav Matejka and I. R. Titunik. Cambridge, MA: Harvard UP, 1986.

Calin, William. *The French Tradition and the Literature of Medieval England.* Toronto: U of Toronto P, 1994.

Chaucer, Geoffrey. *The Complete Poetry and Prose of Geoffrey Chaucer.* Ed. John H. Fisher. New York: Holt, Rinehart and Winston, 1977.

Delany, Sheila. *The Naked Text: Chaucer's Legend of Good Women.* Berkeley: U of California P, 1994.

Dinshaw, Carolyn. *Chaucer's Sexual Poetics.* Madison: U of Wisconsin P, 1989.

Genette, Gérard. *Palimpsestes: La Littérature au second degré.* Paris: Seuil, 1982.

Hansen, Elaine Tuttle. *Chaucer and the Fictions of Gender.* Berkeley: U of California P, 1992.

Machaut. Guillaume de. *Guillaume de Machaut: The Fountain of Love* [La Fonteinne amoureuse] *and Two Other Love Vision Poems.* Ed. and trans. R. Barton Palmer. New York: Garland, 1993.

———. *Guillaume de Machaut: The Judgment of the King of Navarre.* [Le Jugement du roy de Behaingne]. Ed. and trans. R. Barton Palmer. New York: Garland, 1988.

———. *The Judgment of the King of Bohemia* [Li Jugement dou roy de Behaingne]. Ed. and trans. R. Barton Palmer. New York: Garland, 1984.

Ovid. *L'Ovide moralisé.* Eds. Cornelis de Boer et al. Amsterdam: Müller, 1915–39.

Wimsatt, James I. *Chaucer and the French Love Poets: The Literary Background of* The Book of the Duchess. Chapel Hill: U of North Carolina P, 1968.

9

"With-hold till further triall": Spenser's Letter to Ralegh and Modes of Rereading in the 1590 *Faerie Queene*

Peter C. Herman

Rereading could be construed as an activity analogous to Milton's famous description of typology in which the reader moves "From shadowy Types to Truth" (*Paradise Lost* 12.303). That is to say, the reader progresses (and I use this term deliberately) from a "shadowy" first reading to the ever-expanding "Truth" of second, third, fourth, indeed, of infinite rereadings. According to this model, successive rereadings should lead to an increasing sense of fulfillment in the reader, who, freed from attending to mundane plot details (e.g., who does what to whom—no small matter in Spenser's epic), can now concentrate on the larger structural, or "spatial," and thematic unities. The "spatial" understanding of rereading, as Matei Calinescu writes, "enables the rereader to apprehend each part of the work within a simultaneous, 'spatial' awareness of the whole" (17). Many commentaries on *The Faerie Queene* proceed along these lines, the most compendious being James V. Nohrenberg's *Analogy of the Faerie Queene,* the "principle feature" of this work, according to the author, being "an exposition of the poem's essential unity of design." As he nicely puts it, "every plurality harbors an honorary totality" (x), and that totality manifests itself only after repeated readings, since the reader has to go back and reread in order to catch how one part of the poem echoes another.

In this essay, I want to look more closely at this issue, which is usually subsumed under the more general category of "reading."[1] Yet reading and rereading are in this text distinct activities, and I hope to show how *The Faerie Queene* not only demands rereading, but problematizes it as well. Both Calinescu and Nohrenberg assume that rereading works only one way, i.e., toward greater and greater unity. And there is much within *The Faerie Queene* that accords with this sense of rereading. Yet rereading is not exclusively an additive or a teleological process (the end point being the complete understanding of an organically unified text), but rather it is also one of continuing ambiguation. In the interests of space I shall confine myself to Book 1. More specifically, I am interested in hypothesizing the process of rereading experienced by those who made it through the entirety of the 1590 edition.

My reasons for being so precise are as follows. Spenser oversaw two editions of *The Faerie Queene:* the 1590, (Bks. 1–3, Letter to Ralegh), and the 1596 (new ending to Book 3; Bks. 4–6).[2] Contemporary editors of this poem assume that the later edition constitutes Spenser's last word on the subject, and so it is the preferred copytext. But this creates a serious editorial problem, for Spenser dropped the Letter to Ralegh from the revised *Faerie Queene,* and as a result there is little consistency in where later editors place the Letter.[3] Thomas Roche, for instance, puts the Letter to Ralegh first, proceeds to all the dedicatory sonnets (a separate problem, since Spenser cut down on them for the 1596 version), and then presents the main body of the poem. A. C. Hamilton, on the other hand, puts both the Letter and the sonnets last, i.e., after Book 6. No contemporary edition replicates the order of the 1590 edition (text of Books 1–3, Letter, commendatory sonnets), the only one in which the Letter appears with Spenser's consent. Although moving the Letter to the front makes considerable pedagogical sense, insofar as the Letter ostensibly describes what *The Faerie Queene* is about and therefore can serve as a student's guide to interpretation, doing so means we are reading this text in a version Spenser never authorized, since he put it at the end of the 1590 edition and dropped it from the 1596.[4] More, however, is at stake in the Letter's placement than the problematics of editing Renaissance texts, for restoring the original order reveals themes, in particular the need to reread, occluded by later editorial interventions (including Spenser's).[5]

The first readers of the poem would have (one hopes) plowed through until they reached the end of Book 3: "And ye faire Swayns, after your long turmoyle, / Now cease your worke, and at your pleasure play; / Now cease your worke; to morrow is an holy day" (1590 ed.; p. 589), the injunction applying as much to the reader as to Britomart and Sir Scudamore.[6] Despite the double injunction to cease working (i.e., reading), the reader might very well have turned the page and come across these words:

> Sir knowing how doubtfully all Allegories may be con-
> strued, and this booke of mine, which I have entituled
> the Faery Queene, being a continued Allegory, or darke
> conceit, I have thought good as well for avoyding of
> gealous opinions and misconstructions, as also for your
> better light in reading therof . . . to discover unto you
> the general intention & meaning [of this text]. (591)

The work, in other words, has just begun.

I

I assume that during the initial reading, the reader would have quickly realized that the poem has allegorical elements, since the main protagonist is called throughout most of Book 1 "the Redcrosse Knight," he battles such entities as Despair and the Sans brothers (Sans Joy, Foy, and Loy), and he meets Contemplation, Mercy, and Charissa, all obviously allegorical figures of considerable complexity. I further assume that the reader has been interpreting all along and has come to some conclusions about "the general intention & meaning" of the poem. But the opening of the Letter to Ralegh immediately introduces the possibility that the reader has *misunderstood* the text, and Spenser wants to provide information that will help the reader avoid the errors made by the characters in the poem. Perhaps the misinterpretation is due to "gealous opinion," yet Spenser also allows that interpretive errors may result from the difficult nature of allegory itself ("know-ing how doubtfully all Allegories may be construed"). Thus, what in contemporary editions appears as a proleptic introduction in the original, constitutes a retrospective *correction*.[7] Concomitantly, the opening statement of the Letter to Ralegh invites, perhaps even demands, that one reread with the author as one's guide, the Virgil (later Beatrice) correcting errors and guiding the reader to an enlightened interpretation of the "darke conceit."[8]

Again assuming that the reader takes up Spenser's invitation,[9] rereading demonstrates that the opening lines of the Letter put the reader into exactly the same position that Redcrosse frequently finds himself in. Generally, when Spenser's knight meets a character or comes upon a scene, he makes a judgment, and only afterward does Una or someone else give him "better light in reading therof." For example, in his first adventure, Redcrosse discovers "a hollow cave, / Amid the thickest woods" (1.I.11; p. 6). Without thinking the matter through, Redcrosse immediately gets off his horse and, perhaps even more foolishly, "to the Dwarfe a while his needlesse spere he gave" (1.I.11; p. 6). It is only *after* he cannot turn back (after he has finished reading the text for the first time and is acting upon his reading) that Una—like Spenser in the Letter—tells him where he is and what this place is:

> Yea but (quoth she) the perill of this place
> I better wot then you, though now too late
> To wish you backe returne with foule disgrace,
> Yet wisedome warnes, whilest foot is in the gate,
> To stay the steppe, ere forced to retrate.
> This is the wandring wood, this *Errours den,*
> A monster vile, whom God and man does hate:
> Therefore I read beware. Fly fly (quoth then
> The fearfull Dwarfe:) this is no place for living men.
>   (1.1.13; p. 6)

Already knowing the name and nature of this place, like Spenser already knowing the nature of his poem, Una can "read" the signs correctly. Since she has absorbed the "plot," as it were, Una can move immediately to the next stage of interpretation. So her "reading" is actually a *re*reading. And analogously to Spenser in the Letter, she "discovers" unto Redcrosse "the general intention & meaning" of this place. But if Una can "read beware," the error prone Redcrosse, like Spenser's hypothetical reader, has only a superficial first-time reading under his belt. Now Redcrosse must *reread,* i.e., go back over the "text" and correctly read the signs, this time using Una's interpretation as his guide.

Furthermore, Spenser rather clearly assumes that initial readings almost never reveal the truth of the matter, that rereading is imperative in a world where, as Una says, "The danger [is] hid, the place unknowne and wilde, / Breedes dreadfull doubts: Oft fire is without smoke, / And perill without show" (1.1.12. p. 6). One always has to reread before acting, or, again to use Una's words, "therefore your stroke / Sir knight with-hold, *till further triall made*" (1.1.12; p. 6; my emphasis). And Spenser fills his text with moments that instantiate rereading.

For example, immediately after the Errour episode, Redcrosse and Una chance to meet upon the way

> An aged Sire, in long blacke weedes yclad,
> His feete all bare, his beard all hoarie gray,
> And by his belt his booke he hanging had;
> Sober he seemde, and very sagely sad,
> And to the ground his eyes were lowly bent,
> Simple in shew, and voyde of malice bad,
> And all the way he prayed, as he went,
> And often knockt his breast, as one that did
> repent.
> (1.1.29; p. 11)

If the reader feels a little superior to Redcrosse because he or she correctly read the Errour episode before he did, both the reader and Redcrosse are now put in the same position by the narrator (a matter we will return to below). Both are reading superficially, and this mode continues in the description of the "aged Sire's" domicile:

> A little lowly Hermitage it was,
> Downe in a dale, hard by a forests side,
> Far from resort of people, that did pas
> In travell to and froe: a little wyde

> There was an holy Chappell edifyde,
> Wherein the Hermite dewly wont to say
> His holy things each morne and eventyde:
> Thereby a Christall streame did gently play,
> Which from a sacred fountaine welled forth alway.
> (1.1.34; p. 12)

The next stanza, however, changes everything completely:

> Arrived there, the little house, they fill,
> Ne looke for entertainement, where none was:
> Rest is their feast, and all things at their will;
> The noblest mind the best contentment has.
> With faire discourse the evening so they pas:
> For that old man of pleasing wordes had store,
> And well could file his tongue as smooth as glas;
> He told of Saintes and Popes, and evermore
> He strowd an *Ave-Mary* after and before. (1.1.35; p. 13)

The passage reveals the Hermit—Archimago, although he will not be named until later—as a Catholic, i.e., as evil. But it also sends the reader scuttling back to the previous passage for clues about the Hermit's true identity. And upon rereading the only clue that stands out, significantly enough, is the word "seemde." Archimago, on first reading, *appears* good, but seeming in this text is not the same as being. To understand the passage, and the passage implies that the same is necessary to understand the world, one must go back and read again to pick up the clues. The antidote to seeming, it seems, is rereading.

This lesson, however, is lost upon Redcrosse, who regularly demonstrates his deficiency at both reading and rereading. It is, in fact, Redcrosse's poor rereading skills that form the basis of Harry Berger, Jr.'s, suggestion that much of Book 1 resembles a treadmill in that even though Redcrosse is constantly confronted with the same situation, he remains unable to reread the present in terms of the past.[10] Hence he never really gets anywhere. The meeting between him and Fradubio, for instance, repeats the same process by which he and Una got lost in the Wandering Wood:

> Long time they [Redcrosse and Duessa] thus
>   together traveiled,
> Till weary of their way, they came at last
> Where grew two goodly trees, that faire did spred
> Their armes abroad, with gray mosse overcast,
> And their greene leaves trembling with every blast,
> Made a calme shadow far in compasse round:
> The fearefull Shepheard often there aghast
> Under them never sat, ne wont there sound
> His mery oaten pipe, but shund th'unlucky ground.
>
> But this good knight soone as he them can spie,
> For the coole shade him thither hastly got:
> For golden *Phoebus* now ymounted hie,
> From fiery wheeles of his faire chariot
> Hurled his beame so scorching cruell hot,
> That living creature mote it not abide;
> And his new Lady it endured not.
> There they alight, in hope themselves to hide
> From the fierce heat, and rest their weary limbs a tide.
>   (1.2.28–29; p. 27)

Having come upon this "text" for the first time, Redcrosse cannot be expected to know that shepherds shun this place. But he should recognize that the scene repeats nearly the same events that brought him to these woods in the first place. At the poem's start, Redcrosse and Una seek shelter from a storm beneath a welcoming grove of trees ("Enforst to seeke some covert nigh at hand, / A shadie grove not far away they spide, / That promist ayde the tempest to withstand" [1.1.7; p. 5]). The only difference is that now Redcrosse and his Lady seek to escape the heat. But if the reader hears the echo, goes back to the beginning of the text, rereads the latter passage in the light of the former, and comes to a larger understanding of the whole (as in Nohrenberg's and Calinescu's "spatial" model), Redcrosse does no such thing. He remains oblivious to the parallel, still caught in the world of seeming.

The passage further illustrates both the necessity of rereading and Redcrosse's inability to reread when he plucks a bough from the tree and receives Fradubio's warning to "fly, ah fly far hence away" (1.2.31;

p. 27). Significantly, Fradubio asserts that Duessa is "The *author* . . . of all my smarts" (1.2.34; p. 28; my emphasis), which in a sense makes Redcrosse a rereading of Fradubio, but, once again, Redcrosse does not see the connection. Although Fradubio describes Duessa's *modus operandi* perfectly, including "winning" her in a chivalric battle, Redcrosse does not "reread" his companion or his situation. He does not, in other words, repeat the reader's act of going back, reexamining the evidence, and making the connection between the Wandring Wood and this grove.

The most trenchant example of Redcrosse's poor rereading skills is his encounter with Despair in canto 9. Trying to induce Redcrosse to kill himself, Despair concludes with this argument:

> Why then doest thou, o man of sin, desire
> To draw thy dayes forth to their last degree?
> Is not the measure of thy sinfull hire
> High heaped up with huge iniquitie,
> Against the day of wrath, to burden thee?
> Is not enough, that to this Ladie milde
> Thou falsed hast thy faith with perjurie,
> And sold thy selfe to serve *Duessa* vilde,
> With whom in all abuse thou hast thy selfe defilde?
>
> Is not he just, that all this doth behold
> From highest heaven, and beares an equall eye?
> Shall he thy sins up in his knowledge fold,
> And guiltie be of thine impietie?
> Is not his law, Let every sinner die:
> Die shall all flesh? what then must needs be donne,
> Is it not better to doe willinglie,
> Then linger, till the glasse be all out ronne?
> Death is the end of woes: die soon, O faeries sonne.
> (1.9.46–47; p. 132)

Despair, as many critics have pointed out (e.g., Gless 142–45; King, *Spenser's Poetry* 213–16; Imbrie 146–50; and Nohrenberg 152–55), reads the Bible highly selectively. He emphasizes God's justice but completely elides all mention of God's mercy. For example, when Despair says, "Is not his law, Let every sinner die: / Die shall all flesh?", he alludes to Romans 5:12: "Wherefore, as by one man sinne entred into the world, and death by sinne, and so death went over all men: in whom all men have sinned" (Geneva trans.), but he leaves out Romans 5:15—"But yet the gift is not so, as is the offence: for if through the offence of that one, many bee dead, much more the grace of God, and the gift by grace, which is by one man Jesus Christ, hath abounded unto many," and Romans 5:17— "For if by the offence of one, death reigned through one, much more shall they which receive that abundance of grace, and of that gift of that righteousnesse, reigne in life through one, *that is,* Jesus Christ." Furthermore, Despair draws nearly all of his allusions from the Hebrew Bible, which in itself is reading highly selectively. Finally, Despair elides all mention of the doctrine of predestination, and Una forcibly reminds Redcrosse, who "was much enmoved with his speach" (1.9.53; p. 134), of both points:

> In heavenly mercies hast thou not a part?
> Why shouldst thou then despeire, that chosen art?
> Where justice growes, there grows eke greater
>   grace,
> The which doth quench the brond of hellish smart,
> And that accurst hand-writing doth deface.
> Arise, Sir knight arise, and leave this cursed place.
>   (1.9.53; p. 134)

Redcrosse's error in this passage is that he once more does not reread, that he does not submit the evidence to "further triall," as Una suggests. In place of reading Despair's evidence skeptically and testing it against the texts from which it comes, in place of checking Despair's citations, in place, in other words, of *rereading* Despair's speech, Redcrosse merely *reads* the speech and takes it at face value. Una, like Spenser in the Letter, supplies the necessary corrective by rereading Despair's evidence, rereading Scripture to find out what Despair omits, and supplies Redcrosse with this evidence. In this case, remembering overlaps significantly with rereading, since the process would probably involve recalling the passage, checking it over (rereading), and then determining what Despair leaves out. But the passage demands that the reader also go back to the Bible and reread it in order to combat Despair's marvelous rhetoric. As Imbrie notes, "Renaissance commentators recognized through the text of Matthew that the only way to counter a faulty biblical argument was with a good one" (149). But to do this, one must *find* that "good" argument, and that entails twofold rereading, i.e., to find the misused passages and then to find their antidotes.

Similarly, Spenser's first description of Duessa instigates rereading appropriate biblical passages:

> He [Sans Foy] had a faire companion of his way,
> A goodly Lady clad in scarlot red,
> Purfled with gold and pearle of rich assay,
> And like a *Persian* mitre on her hed
> She wore, with crownes and owches garnished,
> The which her lavish lovers to her gave;
> Her wanton palfrey all was overspread
> With tinsell trappings, woven like a wave,
> Whose bridle rung with golden bels and bosses brave.
>   (1.2.13; p. 22)

As John N. King has pointed out, this passage sends the reader back to a variety of texts (*Spenser's Poetry* 82), especially Revelations, and the textual genealogies accurately inform our judgment of the character. To reread, in this instance, helps avoid error.

In sum, one strand in Book 1 continuously invites the reader to become a rereader of both the text itself and of the Bible. As such, Spenser's technique in Book 1 echoes the Protestant reevaluation of individual authority in reading and rereading the Bible. Whereas the Catholic position—exemplified by Sir Thomas More—is that the individual reader needs to be guided by the "common consent of the whole holy church" and interpretations which veer from tradition are by definition in error (Tribble, "Open Text" 59), the Reformers emphasized the experience of the individual in reading the scriptures. Rather than relying upon an authority figure (like Spenser in the Letter?) to tell one what the Bible means, William Tyndale and others urged readers to experience the Bible for themselves and come to their own conclusions (within certain limits, of course). Thus in one of his prefaces, Tyndale urges the reader to:

> Cleave unto the text and playne storye and endeavaure
> thi self to serch out the meaning of all that is described
> therein and the true sense of all manner of speakyngyes
> of the scripture, of proverbs, similitudes, and borrowed
> speech, whereof I entreated in the end of the obedience,
> and beware of sotle allegoryes. And note everything
> ernestly as things partayning unto thine own herte and
> soule (qtd. in Tribble 60).

For More, however, this emphasis upon individual judgement is quite literally anathema. Toward the end of *The Confutation of Tyndale's Answer,* More compares Tyndale et al. to the sodomites struck blind by God in Genesis 19:

> so these beastly people these abominable heretikes,
> whiche nothyng so greedelye go about, as to polute
> the sanctuarye of God, and shame theyr own mother
> holy church, where as if they taryd wyth her, thei might
> bi the motherly cure and diligent helpe of her, attaine
> remedye of their other sicknesses, they runne out in
> a mad rage, and yet havynge an imagynacion of som
> truth remaining in their mad heades, that is to wytte
> that out of the churche there can non helth be had, *they
> wander about seekyng the churche eche a sundry way,
> and eche always leaving the churche upon his backe
> as they went out at several doores, the farther ever that
> eche of them gothe foreward, the farther ever eche of
> them goth from her.* (Bk. 9, 994; my emphasis)

But in the preface to his answer to a previous work by More, *The Dialogue Concerning Heresies,* Tyndale appeals to the reader's individual judgement, his individual reading of the Bible, to decide the controversy: "Judge, therefore, reader, whether the pope with his be the church; whether their authority be above the scripture; whether all they teach without scripture be equal with the scripture; whether they have erred, and not only whether they can" (*Answer* 9). Similarly, in his preface to the Pentateuch, Tyndale justifies his translation of the Gospels into English on the grounds that everyone should read the text for him and herself:

> Which thing only moved me translate the new Tes-
> tament. Because I had perceived by experience, how
> that it was impossible to establish the lay-people in
> any truth, except the scripture were plainly laid before
> their eyes in their mother-tongue, that they might see
> the process, order and meaning of the text. (394)

Consequently, the kind of rereading that Spenser regularly acti-
vates is a highly Protestant activity. Using Redcrosse as an antimodel,
Spenser keeps urging the reader to go back over his poem and endeavor
"to serch out the meaning of all that is described therein" in exactly the
same way that the Protestant tradition encouraged everyone to reread
the Bible.

II

The Letter to Ralegh, however, also instantiates another mode of
rereading. When Spenser tries to dictate the right interpretation of his
poem, judging some interpretations the result of "gealous opinions"
and giving primacy to his view of the text, he is speaking *as an
author,* i.e., from a position of considerable and growing authority.
If the postmodern era ostensibly witnessed the death of the author
(a greatly exaggerated report, to say the least), the early modern era
witnessed the creation of what Michel Foucault called the "author
function" (107), and prefatorial statements (even in the form of *en-
voi*) became one of the sites where Renaissance authors formed and
enforced their claims to authority.[11] As Annabel Patterson has noted,
"In general, late modern criticism has not paid enough attention to the
interpretive status of introductory materials in early modern texts"
(56). Yet by 1662, they were given the dubious distinction of being
considered important enough to warrant government regulation—
the Printing Act of 1662 required that all "Titles, Epistles, Prefaces,
Proems, Preambles, Introductions, Tables, Dedications" be subject to
as much scrutiny by the official censors as the main body of the text
itself (56). And the Sorbonne not only censored but tried to execute
Marot and Rabelais in the early mid-sixteenth century.[12] Certainly,
the attention paid to prefaces by seventeenth-century censors provides
some evidence for Foucault's claim that "Texts, books, and discourses

really began to have authors . . . to the extent that authors became subject to punishment, that is, to the extent that discourses could be transgressive" (108).[13]

Yet the matter is not strictly negative. Foucault also asserted that "The author's name manifests the appearance of a certain discursive set and indicates the status of this discourse within a society and a culture" (107). Almost from printing's inception, the length, numbers and sophistication of Renaissance prefaces provide evidence for the growing cultural authority of authorship.[14] Throughout the sixteenth century, the text becomes valued not only for what it contains, as would be the case for anonymous works, such as either the Homeric epics or many medieval poems, but also because of who produced it. Take, for example, the attribution of plays to "William Shakespeare," an ascription clearly intended by the publishers to increase the play-text's commercial viability even though the actual William Shakespeare often had nothing to do with the plays being sold under his name. Thus the title page of *The Yorkshire Tragedy* (1608) announces that it was "*Written by* W. Shakespeare"; the 1598 quarto of *Love's Labours Lost* says that the play is "Newly corrected and augmented *By W. Shakespere*"; and the 1608 quarto of *King Lear* loudly proclaims Shakespeare's authorship, his name emblazoned on the title-page in type substantially larger than the rest (Kastan 15–16). Similarly, the title page of Thomas Newman's edition of Sidney's *Astrophel and Stella* puts the author at the top of the page and gives the title as "His *Astrophel and Stella*," with emphasis on "*His*."

All of which is to say that when readers got to the final pages of *The Faerie Queene,* they would have been much more primed to take Spenser's comments as authoritative than perhaps we today—raised to trust the text, not the teller—would read prefatory material. The project of rereading, as suggested by the Letter's distinction between "doubtful" construings of allegory and the author's declaration of "the general intention & meaning" of his text, could thus become a matter of confirming the author's interpretation of his text, replicating the process of typology insofar as the reader's "shadowy" interpretations are replaced by the "Truth" of Spenser's. But the progress toward greater and greater certainty is significantly compromised by the manifest differences between text and gloss, as readers from the eighteenth century onward discovered and complained about.[15]

For example, in the Letter Spenser announces that Arthur is the center of his text:

> I chose the historye of King Arthure, as most fitte for the excellency of his person, being made famous by many mens former workes, and also furthest from the daunger of envy, and suspition of present time. . . . By ensample of which excellente Poets [Homer, Virgil, Ariosto, and Tasso], I labour to pourtraict in Arthure, before he was king, the image of a brave knight, perfected in the twelve private morall vertues. (592)

This description has almost nothing to do with the poem Spenser wrote. As John Hughes puts it in 1715: "Prince *Arthur* is indeed the principal Person, and has therefore a share given him in every Legend; but his Part is not considerable enough in any one of them: He appears and vanishes again like a Spirit; and we lose sight of him too soon to consider him as the Hero of the Poem" (qtd. in Bennett 25). In other words, while Spenser asserts that Arthur is the chief hero of the poem in the Letter, the text manifestly demonstrates that he is not. As for Book 2:

> The second day ther came in a Palmer bearing an Infant with bloody hands, whose Parents he complained to have bene slayn by an Enchaunteresse called Acrasia: and therfore craved of the Faery Queene, to appoint him some knight, to performe that adventure, which being assigned to Sir Guyon, he presently went forth with that same Palmer: which is the beginning of the second booke and the whole subject thereof. (595)

But as Bennett writes, "The preliminary scene does not fit the narrative of the first canto of Book II. In the poem both Guyon and the Palmer are present at the death of Amavia, and it is Guyon himself who takes up the babe with the bloody hands and carries it, not to the court of the Faery Queen, but to Medina" (32–33). As for the third book,

> there came in, a Groome who complained before the
> Faery Queene, that a vile Enchaunter called Busirane
> had in hand a most faire Lady call Amoretta, whom
> he kept in most grievous torment, because she would
> not yield him the pleasure of her body. Whereupon Sir
> Scudamour the lover of that Lady presently tooke on
> him that adventure. But being unable to performe it by
> reason of the hard Enchauntments, after long sorrow,
> in the end met with Britomartis, who succoured him,
> and reskewed his love.

Yet, to continue with Waters:

> This narrative, which Spenser describes as if it were
> the central plot of the whole book, is in fact merely
> the culminating episode, which is confined entirely to
> the last two cantos. Moreover, earlier in the letter, in
> naming the knights who are the heroes of the respec-
> tive books, he names the third "of Britomartis a Lady
> knight, in whom I picture Chastity," yet the quest is
> undertaken by Sir Scudamour. Virtue and quest have
> been separated and assigned to two different characters.
> (32–33)

There are further differences, but I assume that the above sufficiently
establishes the point.

I imagine that a reader of the first edition would have realized
with perhaps some consternation that the author's version of the
plot does not accord with what he or she has just read, and that
this person would have *gone back over* the text to compare the two,
perhaps even flipping back and forth between the Letter and the poem
several times before somehow resolving the matter. Consequently, the
troubled relation between Letter to Ralegh and *The Faerie Queene*
both occasions rereading and asks the reader to entertain the relative
value of initial readings and subsequent rereadings, between internal
versus external authority. We have already seen that Spenser asserts
the primacy of his views of the poem, but now, faced with the huge
discrepancies between text and Letter, the reader must ask if the
author's interpretation of this text is *more* valid than the reader's. Or

does the reader privilege his or her *own* views, relying upon his or her own judgment of textual evidence? Spenser, however, might consider such interpretations "doubtful" construals, at best caused by honest error (assuming, given Book 1's depiction of Error, that error can ever be honest), at worst by jealousy or malice. And as shown above, Spenser's views would have carried some weight. The contradictions lead, I would suggest, to a crossroads of sorts. Does the reader cede authority to the author, replacing the "misconstruction" with the author's construction? Or does the reader follow the Reformist doctrine of reading the text and endeavoring "thi self to serch out the meaning of all that is described therein"?

When, therefore, the discovery of the gaps between the Letter and the text sends readers back to the text, they arrive at another distinctly Protestant moment, only this time one with a less conventional outcome. Used to reading the Bible on one's own and endeavoring "to serch out the meaning of all that is described therein," readers would likely have applied these lessons to *The Faerie Queene* and *disregarded* the author's version of events. Consequently, even though Spenser tries to control the interpretation of his text in the letter, he inevitably takes on the role of precisely the external authority that Tyndale urged the English to do without. Ironically, then, Spenser's attempt to control the meaning of his poem by creating a situation in which the reader is almost obliged to reread instigates a rereading that erodes rather than increases authorial authority. Depending upon his authority as an author, Spenser asks the reader to reread and substitute the interpretation produced by the initial reading with the author's own, but Spenser instead instigates a rereading in which precisely the opposite occurs.

III

Yet the text's insistence upon rereading is even more complicated, for as much as Book 1 insists upon the necessity of rereading, Spenser problematizes rereading by using it to create uncertainty, demonstrating its limitations, and by turning Archimago into a successful rereader.

It is highly significant that Spenser begins *The Faerie Queene,* a text that concludes with a near command to reread, with a passage

that equally asks for rereading, but the result is uncertainty rather
than certainty. After Redcrosse and Una leave Gloriana's court, they
are first seen "pricking on the plaine" (1.1.1; p. 3). They enter the
Wandring Wood only because of a storm:

> Enforst to seeke some covert nigh at hand,
> A shadie grove not far away they spide,
> That promist ayde the tempest to withstand:
> Whose loftie trees yclad with sommers pride,
> Did spred so broad, that heavens light did hide,
> Not perceable with power of any starre:
> And all within were pathes and alleies wide,
> With footing worne, and leading inward farre:
> Faire harbour that them seemes; so in they entred arre.
>
> And foorth they passe, with pleasure forward led,
> Joying to heare the birdes sweete harmony,
> Which therein shrouded from the tempest dred,
> Seemd in their song to scorne the cruell sky.
> Much can they prayse the trees so straight and hy,
> The sayling Pine, the Cedar proud and tall,
> The vine-prop Elme, the Poplar never dry,
> The builder Oake, sole king of forrests all,
> The Aspine good for staves, the Cypresse funerall.
>
> The Laurell, meed of mightie Conquerours
> And Poets sage, the Firre that weepeth still,
> The Willow worne of forlorne Paramours,
> The Eugh obedient to the benders will,
> The Birch for shaftes, the Sallow for the mill,
> The Mirrhe sweete bleeding in the bitter in the bitter
>   wound,
> The warlike Beech, the Ash for nothing ill,
> The fruitfull Olive, and the Platane round,
> The carver Holme, the Maple seeldom inward sound.
>   (1.1.7–9; p. 5)

The catalogue of trees imitates, which is to say rereads, earlier
catalogues in two of Chaucer's texts (*The Parliament of Fowls* and
The Knight's Tale), Ovid's *Metamorphoses,* Statius's *Thebiad,* and

Boccaccio's *Teseida.* In the *Metamorphoses,* the catalogue is part of Ovid's retelling (rereading?) of the Orpheus legend; in the *Parliament,* the trees constitute the backdrop for the allegorical landscape, and, as the narrator says, they are "of colour fresh and greene / As emeroude, that joye was to seene" (174–75); in *The Knight's Tale,* which the sixteenth century universally considered a "noble tale," they are part of Arcite's funeral (lines 2,921 ff.).[16] My point is that the catalogue's moral genealogy is impeccable, and if the reader judges Spenser's forest by going back and rereading both his classical and his Christian sources (all of which were common knowledge for Spenser's audience), just as the text encourages the reader to judge Despair's speech by rereading his sources and Duessa by tracking down the allusions encoded in her description, then the reader will arrive at a *positive* judgment of the forest.

True, there are clues in this passage that should sound warning bells. The trees are "yclad with sommers pride," and they "Did spred so broad, that heavens light did hide," the combination of pride and hiding the light of heaven obviously not auspicious signs. Also, Redcrosse and Una are led forward by "pleasure," again not necessarily good. Yet in context, these clues are partially occluded by how the thickness of the trees will block the storm, and the pleasure arises not from rampant sensuality but from the birds' happy chirping and the beauty of the forest itself. In other words, in some instances, rereading will at worst lead to a *wrong* interpretation, at best to an equivocal one. But in this case and in others, rereading will not lead to the *right* interpretation. The forest will reveal its true nature only after it is too late to do anything about it. Furthermore, when Una finally reveals that they are in the Wandring Wood (significantly, only after Una realizes that they have reached Error's cave), the rereading of this passage creates an aporia, as Spenser is clearly using "positive" sources for a highly negative place.[17] For the reader who has noted the divergences between the Letter to Ralegh and the text, Spenser's authority has declined even more.

Spenser repeats this strategy when Archimago makes his appearance (a passage that I now want to reread from a different perspective):

> An aged Sire, in long blacke weedes yclad,
> His feete all bare, his beard all hoarie gray,

And by his belt his booke he hanging had;
Sober he seemde, and very sagely sad,
And to the ground his eyes were lowly bent,
Simple in shew, and voyde of malice bad,
And all the way he prayed, as he went,
And often knockt his breast, as one that did repent.

A little lowly Hermitage it was,
Downe in a dale, hard by a forests side,
Far from resort of people, that did pas
In travell to and froe: a little wyde
There was an holy Chappell edifyde,
Wherein the Hermite dewly wont to say
His holy things each morne and eventyde:
Thereby a Christall streame did gently play,
Which from a sacred fountaine welled forth alway.
            (1.1.29,34; pp. 11–12)

As noted earlier, almost nothing in these stanzas should set off
warning bells. True, the word "seemde" is a red flag in Spenser's
lexicon, but this is only the second time the word appears, so there
is little reason for the reader to be suspicious. But as in the forest
catalogue, rereading does not provide clues to Archimago's actual
identity. In fact, rereading actively misleads, for Spenser's description
of the Hermitage does not contain any qualifiers. The sentence "There
was an holy Chappell edifyde" gives one no reason to doubt that the
chapel is either holy or edified. Significantly, Spenser writes, "There
was" a chapel, not "There was a chapel that *seemed* holy and edified."
The past tense of the verb "to be," in other words, does not admit doubt
about the existence of its object. Similarly, Spenser underscores the
deviousness of this passage by telling the reader that at this holy,
edified chapel, the Hermit habitually said "His holy things each morne
and eventyde," which implies that the Hermit is who he appears to
be, he actually says holy things, and the omniscient narrator knows
about the Hermit's past and when exactly he says his "holy things."
Finally, Spenser concludes his description with the religiously charged
description of "a Christall streame [that] did gently play, / Which from
a sacred fountaine welled forth alway," the holiness of the stream

being further emphasized by the pun "Christ-all." Again, rereading will not lead to a correct reading, but to further error and even more erosion of the narrator's credibility, since the narrator is complicit with Archimago's deceit.[18]

Two key lines in the next stanza (35) also activate rereading: "For that old man of pleasing wordes had store / And well could file his tongue as smooth as glas." Rather than sending the reader back to the previous stanzas, these lines recall Spenser's plea to the Muses in the proem: "O helpe thou my weake wit, and sharpen my dull tong" (Pr. 2; p. 2). The request in the proem is unremarkable, but after reading Spenser's description of Archimago, rereading these lines charges them with previously unsuspected significance, for it is clear that Spenser asks for what Archimago already possesses. Rereading also contributes to greater uncertainty when Una and Archimago first spy Sans Loy, for Spenser very closely patterns his description of the villain with his description of the hero:

> They had not ridden farre, when they might see
> One pricking towards them with hastie heat,
> Full strongly armd, and on a courser free,
> That through his fiercenesse fomed all with sweat,
> And the sharpe yron did for anger eat,
> When his hot ryder spurd his chauffed side;
> His looke was sterne, and seemed still to threat
> Cruell revenge, which he in hart did hyde,
> And on his shield *Sans loy* in bloudie lines was dyde.
> (1.3.33; p. 41)

> A Gentle Knight was pricking on the plaine,
> Ycladd in mightie armes and silver shielde,
> Wherein old dints of deepe wounds did remaine,
> The cruell markes of many a bloudy fielde;
> Yet armes till that time did he never wield:
> His angry steede did chide his foming bitt,
> As much disdayning to the curbe to yield:
> Full jolly knight he seemd, and faire did sitt,
> As one for knightly giusts and fierce encounters fitt.
> (1.1.1; p. 3)

Once more, the precise verbal echo ("pricking" is not a common verb in *The Faerie Queene*) urges the reader to go back and reread the first occurrence, and, once more, rereading blurs the distinction between supposedly antithetical characters.

Interestingly, Spenser adopts a similar strategy in smudging the line separating the results (as opposed to the nature) of true and profane love. As everyone knows, Redcrosse's inability to control his passions leads to his separation from Una, and his tryst with Duessa lands him in Orgoglio's dungeon. Nothing quite so dire happens to Una, but, at the same time, Spenser demonstrates that even pure love can lead one into danger. When, for example, Una comes upon Archimago disguised as Redcrosse, she forgets her advice to always subject what you see to "further triall" and, like Redcrosse, assumes that appearance equals reality:

> Ere long he came, where *Una* traveild slow,
> And that wilde Champion wayting her besyde:
> Whom seeing such, for dread he durst not show
> Himselfe too nigh at hand, but turned wyde
> Unto an hill; from whence when she him spyde,
> By his like seeming shield, her knight by name
> She weend it was, and towards him gan ryde:
> Approching nigh, she wist it was the same,
> And with faire fearefull humblesse towards him she
>   came. (1.3.26; p. 39)

Unlike his treatment of Redcrosse, however, here Spenser explicitly diagnoses the cause of Una's inability to reread, and it is being in love:

> His lovely words her seemd due recompence
> Of all her passed paines: one loving howre
> For many yeares of sorrow can dispence:
> A dram of sweets is worth a pound of sowre:
> She has forgot, how many a wofull stowre
> For him she late endur'd; she speakes no more
> Of past: true is, that true love hath no powre
> To looken backe; his eyes be fixt before.
> Before her stands her knight, for whom she toyld so
>   sore. (1.3.30; p. 40).

If, as Spenser says, "true love hath no powre / To looken backe," then true love prevents retrospection, it prevents rereading, which in this case means going back over past events to use as guides for the present. Furthermore, like Redcrosse, Una allows her desires to determine reality. Just as Redcrosse's dreams reveal his inner sexual tension, Una's desires shape what she takes for the truth: "Approching nigh, she *wist* [i.e., knew] it was the same, / And with faire fearefull humblesse towards him she came." But of course she does not "wist"; rather, she *wishes* that the approaching figure were Redcrosse, and, like Redcrosse, she "knows" before she tests, thereby ignoring her own advice to "with-hold, till further triall made."

One cannot fault Una for being taken in when the "pilgrim"—really Archimago in disguise—tells her that Redcrosse is dead (1.6.38; p. 87). But in the next canto, she once more jumps to conclusions. After the Dwarf picks up Redcrosse's armor and shield (the knight now being enthralled to Duessa), Una takes one look at them and, without making "further triall" assumes once more that Redcrosse is no more: "when her eyes she on the Dwarfe had set, / *And saw the signes,* that deadly tydings spake, / She fell to ground for sorrowfull regret" (1.7.20; p. 95; my emphasis). Una *reads* the signs, in other words, in exactly the same way that Redcrosse initially reads Error's cave, but she does not *re*read them, and so she falls—again like Redcrosse—into error. To further compound matters, even when Una rereads, she does so erroneously. After Arthur asks her who she is and what has happened to her, her narrative splits in two. The first part concerns what happened to her parents and why she came to Gloriana's court. So far as the reader can tell, this account is accurate. The second part of her narrative, though, concerns the previous cantos of Book 1:

> It was my chance (my chance was faire and good)
> There for to find a fresh unproved knight,
> Whose manly hands imbrew'd in guiltie blood
> Had never bene, ne ever by his might
> Had throwne to ground the unregarded right:
> *Yet of his prowesse proofe he since hath made*
> *(I witnesse am) in many a cruell fight:*

> The groning ghosts of many one dismaide
> Have felt the bitter dint of his avenging blade. (1.7.47;
> p. 103; my emphasis)

One can assume that Una embellishes Redcrosse's record because she wants to make her lover look good, and that is exactly the point. Love induces her to give a version of the previous cantos that departs significantly from what the reader has just gone through. But like the Letter to Ralegh, there are gaps between the text and its recapitulation. Una has witnessed exactly one fight (with Error) before Archimago splits them, not "many a cruell fight." The passage, therefore, does two things. First, it once more encourages the reader to reread earlier passages of the text in order to compare them with Una's retelling of Book 1; second, it demonstrates that Una, like Redcrosse, is a poor rereader.

Significantly, just before Una retells her version of the story to Arthur, Spenser has the Dwarf recount the same, and the differences in accuracy are important:

> Then gan the Dwarfe the whole discourse declare,
> The subtill traines of *Archimago* old;
> The wanton loves of false *Fidessa* faire,
> Bought with the bloud of vanquisht Paynim bold:
> The wretched payre transform'd to treen mould;
> The house of Pride, and perils round about;
> The combat, which he with *Sanjoy* did hould:
> The lucklesse conflict with the Gyant stout,
> Wherein captiv'd, of life or death he stood in doubt.
>   (1.7.26; pp. 96–97).

The Dwarf gives a faithful, unembellished report; ironically, Una, who represents truth, gives an almost mendacious account. Readers concerned with the problem of epistemology in *The Faerie Queene* usually concentrate on Redcrosse's deficiencies (e.g., MacCaffrey 154–55), yet Una is clearly no more successful a rereader than the ostensible hero of Book 1. Curiously, the common denominator is the degree of personal involvement. When Una is not personally involved, as in Error's cave, then she can dispassionately read and reread, but the moment something is emotionally at stake (i.e., the reputation of her lover), she reads rather than rereads in exactly the same way that Redcrosse reads when his knightly honor is in question.

Having established that rereading has the potential for leading one not to greater understanding, but to misreading, misunderstanding, Spenser further troubles rereading by demonstrating its more than occasional futility. Significantly for the numerologically minded Spenser, he begins the mid-point of Book 1, the sixth canto, by explicitly pointing out the limitations of rereading:

> As when a ship, that flyes faire under saile,
> An hidden rocke escaped hath unwares,
> That lay in waite her wrack for to bewaile,
> The Marriner yet halfe amazed stares
> At perill past, and yet it doubt ne dares
> To joy at his foole-happie oversight. (1.6.1;
>   p.75)

Certainly, the passage implies that meaning reveals itself only *retro*actively, only upon literally reviewing, rereading the text, and as such it continues the ongoing illustration of the dangers of relying upon first readings. Yet it also demonstrates that rereading can also be like crying over spilt milk. There is no way, the passage implies, that the "Marriner" could have seen that hidden rocke even if he had stopped the ship and "reread" the path ahead for hours before charging onward. No amount of "further triall," in other words, would have helped in this instance. Analogously, there is no way that Una and Redcrosse could have seen through Archimago's disguise or understood the true nature of the forest beforehand. As much as the text demands rereading and argues for the necessity of rereading, it also illustrates that rereading is no panacea, that peril will often reveal itself only after it is past.

To make interpretation even more difficult, if Spenser provides Redcrosse and Una as examples of bad rereading, he also turns Archimago into a *good* rereader. After Archimago gulls Redcrosse and Una into staying the night, he goes to his magic books to seek "out mighty charmes, to trouble sleepy mindes" (1.1.36; p. 13). Although Spenser elsewhere insists upon the necessity of rereading, he denies the reader the opportunity to read in this instance: "Then choosing out few wordes most horrible, / (*Let none them read*) thereof did verses frame" (1.1.37; p. 13; my emphasis). By denying the chance to read, Spenser concomitantly denies the chance to reread, to put Archimago's spells into further practice, and the next passage suggests why.

Archimago's first reading, his first spell, fails, but, unlike Redcrosse, he goes back to his books, he *rereads* them—"He cast about, *and searcht his balefull bookes again*" (1.2.2; p. 19; my emphasis)— and this time comes up with a spell that is ultimately successful in parting Redcrosse and Una:

> Eftsoones he tooke that miscreated faire,
> And that false other Spright, on whom he spred
> A seeming body of the subtile aire,
> Like a young Squire, in loves and lusty-hed
> His wanton dayes that ever loosely led,
> Without regard of armes and dreaded fight:
> Those two he tooke, and in a secret bed,
> Covered with darknesse, and misdeeming night,
> Them both together laid, to joy in vaine delight. (1.2.3;
>   pp. 19–20)

Significantly, Archimago's spell obscures the differences between fiction and reality, between real and seeming, which is precisely the distinction that rereading should be able to catch but so often cannot (as in the opening description of Archimago and the catalogue of trees). And, in one of the few instances of poetic justice in Book 1, Archimago, the successful rereader, is nearly undone in the next passage because others who read and reread cannot penetrate his disguise.

Not content with having split Una and Redcrosse, "subtill *Archimago*" decides that he will take on Redcrosse's appearance:

> But now seemde best, the person to put on
> Of that good knight, his late beguiled guest:
> In mighty armes he was yclad anon:
> And silver shield, upon his coward brest
> A bloudy crosse, and on his craven crest
> A bounch of haires discolourd diuersly:

> Full jolly knight he seemde, and well addrest,
> And when he sate upon his courser free,
> *Saint George* himselfe ye would have deemed him to be.
>   (1.2.11; p. 22)

Una, as we have seen, is fooled, but so is Sans Loy, who sees "the Red-crosse, which the knight did beare" (1.3.34; p. 41), and, like Una, he assumes that reading, not rereading, is sufficient. The difference in this case is that Sans Loy nearly impales Archimago with his spear (1.3.35; p. 42).

If one strand of Book 1 argues for the necessity of rereading to avoid the Wandring Wood and error, this passage also illustrates how rereading is vulnerable, if not completely helpless, before forgery. Significantly, the text opens up at this point to include the reader, who may be the textual witness to Archimago's transformation, but otherwise would be as helpless as anyone else to penetrate the disguise. Prefiguring the "Marriner" of canto 6, at times no amount of rereading will prevent error; rather, one can learn only from retrospect what went wrong, only, in other words, when it is too late to do anything about it.

The Faerie Queene insists upon the necessity of rereading while problematizing the certainty supposedly promised by rereading. The ultimate effect is similarly complicated, for I do not think that Spenser advocates giving up entirely. Rather, by opening up gaps that invite rereading, Spenser compels the reader to participate in making sense of his text even as his text often confounds that effort. It is, I would argue, the continual process of making sense, of continually rereading, and of continually being forced to confront the limitations of rereading, that is important. Even though the New Jerusalem of interpretive certainty, freedom from the need to reread, is perpetually deferred, that does not absolve the reader from heading unto the breach one more time.[19]

Notes

1. When, for example, Isabel G. MacCaffrey writes, "But we, the poem's readers, by the very act of reading are listening all the time to our elders, and above all the poet who speaks for 'the mighty scheme of truth' devised through time by men of imagination" (135), she conflates the processes of reading and rereading.
2. The posthumous 1609 edition contains The Mutabilitie Cantos.

3. R. J. Todd puts the Letter at the start. Hugh MacLean and Anne Lake Prescott also put the Letter first in their pedagogically important Norton Critical Edition of Spenser's selected works. F. M. Padelford, on the other hand, situates it at the end of the first volume of the variorum edition, which means it comes after Book 1.

4. Paul J. Voss informs me that the prefatory material was printed last, so the fact that the signature numbers of the Letter continue those of the poem and begin with "Pp" argues that Spenser *meant* for the Letter to follow Book 3. The reordering of *The Faerie Queene* by contemporary editors also demonstrates how a text's institutional fate (e.g., this epic is read almost exclusively as part of undergraduate and graduate education) influences editorial practice. Interestingly, the Letter to Ralegh was republished separately in 1611 and 1617 (STC 23086.3 and STC 23086.7).

5. This kind of editorial interference is not unusual. For example, modern editions, student editions in particular, of Thomas More's *Utopia* do not reproduce more than one or two of the multiple letters prefacing this text. Also, the subsequent editorial treatment of *The Faerie Queene* is roughly analogous to the situation with the two texts of *King Lear,* in which the radically different folio and quarto editions, the latter perhaps being a revision of the former, have been conflated to create a text that Shakespeare may very well have never written. Curiously, the editorial desire to reproduce "true" text often means foregoing consideration of the actual book as it was published in the Renaissance, i.e., the book's organization, typography, how different editions change, and so on. As David Kastan writes, the "text never exists—that is, never exists apart from the various materializations that have made it present" (21). The result is that many analyses are based upon texts that the author never sanctioned and perhaps, as with *King Lear,* may not even recognize. I am grateful to Sherri Geller for bringing the example of More's *Utopia* to my attention.

6. All references are to the first volume of the Scolar Press edition, which reprints Books I–III of the 1596 edition, the 1590 conclusion of Book III, and the end-matter of the 1590 edition. Stanza numbers are supplied from Thomas P. Roche, Jr.'s, edition. Page numbers of Books I–III refer to the 1596 edition, and page numbers for the Letter to Ralegh refer to the 1590 edition. Also, I have silently employed the modern usage of *i/j* and *u/v.*

7. Consequently, Spenser's use of the Letter differs significantly from the "arguments" Milton provided for the second edition of *Paradise Lost.* In the latter, the author intervenes before the reader has had a chance to "err," as Stanley Fish might put it. Spenser, on the other hand, assumes that the reader will err, and he places the Letter last so that it serves almost as a chastisement. In this sense, Spenser's use of rereading significantly anticipates the "reader harassment" that Fish

found constituent of *Paradise Lost* in *Surprised by Sin,* which suggests that Milton learned more from "the sage and serious Spenser" than morality. However, whereas Fish argues that Milton's text serves to underscore doctrinal certainty, I will argue that rereading in Spenser leads to further and further uncertainty.

8. Interestingly, the illustration of St. George comes at the end of Book I, not, as one might expect, either before it or above or beside the episode it illustrates. The effect is identical in that it invites the reader to reread the book in light of this illustration. See Voss, "The Faerie Queen 1590–1596: The Case of St. George."

9. This assumption raises the problem of the differences between how the professional reader, i.e., an English professor, goes about reading texts and how the "everyday" reader might approach *The Faerie Queene.* Those with a professional investment in producing articles and books on literature necessarily assume rereading as a given, or rather, we assume that a first reading will never be sufficient. First, because our work requires that we reread the text, and second, because we hope that our reading of the text will instigate others to reread the text. Those without such an investment, though, might simply decline Spenser's invitation to go back again. On the other hand, Spenser either assumes or hopes that his reader would look upon his poem as a source of moral betterment, exactly analogous with the Bible, and such texts also assume rereading, as we are in constant need of reminders of our need to improve ourselves spiritually.

10. "The forward progress of the narrative operates in part like a treadmill: insofar as a later episode extends an earlier moment we may see him as trapped in that moment" (65). Interestingly, Berger's metaphor implies only reading, not rereading, even though the later episodes will take on further meaning through reference to the earlier episodes.

11. Clearly, the invention of printing had a major impact on the development of what Jürgen Habermas calls "the public sphere," which he defines as "the sphere of private people [coming] together as a public: they soon claimed the public sphere regulated from above against the public authorities themselves, to engage them in a debate over the general rules governing relations in the basically privatized but publicly relevant sphere of commodity exchange and social labor" (27). As Habermas points out, this public sphere is a *print* sphere in which the debates over public policy are carried on by authors, and one can see this process beginning in England much earlier than the eighteenth century (the date Habermas proposes for the beginning of this development). The English Reformation, for example, while concretized by various acts of Parliament, first crept into England by way of books, and in addition to the more physical acts of repression (i.e., imprisonment and burning), these ideas were also combatted by the publication of further books. One side effect, though, of this war by

polemical libelli was the sudden attention paid to authorship. Thus, for example, when in 1528 Cuthbert Tunstall asked Thomas More to refute Lutheranism in print, he did so by refuting as much the specific author of heretical works, William Tyndale, as the ideas themselves. Tyndale, clearly understanding the stakes, titled his rebuttal *An Answer unto Sir Thomas Mores Dialogue made by William Tindale* (1531). More called the next entry into the lists *The confutacyon of Tyndales answere made by syr Thomas More knyght lorde chauncellour of Englonde* (1532), and the next year he printed another installment in which the number of authors proliferates: *The second parte of the confutacion of Tyndals answere In whyche is also confuted the chyrche that Tyndale devyseth. And the chyrche also that frere Barns devyseth. Made by syr Thomas More knyght.* Printing, in other words, vastly increased the audience for religious and political debates, and the key to authority in this sphere is as much what Foucault terms "the author function" as much as the ideas themselves. See also Tribble (*Margins and Marginality*) for the increasing importance of authorship.

12. I am grateful to Anne Lake Prescott for pointing this out to me.

13. Patterson, for example, analyzes how Sir John Hayward's short dedicatory epistle in Latin to "the erle of Essex" became an object of interest precisely to the degree that its readers considered it treasonable.

14. See, for example, Dunn and Wall, *passim.*

15. Despite occasional quixotic attempts to rescue the Letter (e.g., Hamilton and Erickson, although also see Owen's pointed rebuttal of Hamilton's argument), Spenser clearly realized that the Letter to Ralegh confused more than it clarified since he dropped it (along with the commendatory verses and the dedicatory sonnets, except for two) from the 1596 edition, which presumably constitutes Spenser's final draft of the poem.

16. See also Wyatt's comment in "Mine own John Poyntz": "[I cannot] Praise Sir Thopas for a noble tale / And scorn the story that the knight told" (50–51). See also Curtius's description of the topos (194–95), which also outlines its positive moral valences.

17. Although the name recalls Dante's *selva oscura,* the description does not. Thus Spenser sets up a multivalent discord between the place's name and its description.

18. The same occurs when Archimago takes on the disguise of a pilgrim to gull Una and Satyrane:

> A Silly man, in simple weedes forworne,
> And soild with dust of the long dried way;
> His sandales were with toilesome travell torne,
> And face all tand with scorching sunny ray,
> As he had treveild many a sommers day,

> Through Boyling sands of *Arabie* and *Ynde;*
> And in his hand a *Jacobs* staffe, to stay
> His wearie limbes vpon: and eke behind,
> His scrip did hang, in which his needments he did bind.
> (1.6.35; p. 87)

19. I am grateful to David Galef for instigating this essay and for his support during its overlong gestation. I also thank Anne Lake Prescott for saving me from many an embarrassing error.

Works Cited

Bennett, Josephine Waters. *The Evolution of* The Faerie Queene. New York: Burt Franklin, 1960.

Berger, Harry, Jr. "Spenser's *Faerie Queene* Book I: Prelude to Interpretation." *Revisionary Play: Studies in the Spenserian Dynamics.* Intro. Louis Montrose. Berkeley: U of California P, 1988. 51–88.

Calinescu, Matei. *Rereading.* New Haven: Yale UP, 1993.

Chaucer, Geoffrey. *The Complete Poetry and Prose of Geoffrey Chaucer.* Ed. John H. Fisher. New York: Holt, Rinehart and Winston, 1977.

Curtius, Ernst Robert. *European Literature and the Latin Middle Ages.* Trans. Willard R. Trask. Bollingen Series 36. 1953. Princeton: Princeton UP, 1973.

Dunn, Kevin. *Pretexts of Authority: The Rhetoric of Authorship in the Renaissance Preface.* Stanford: Stanford UP, 1993.

Erickson, Wayne. "Spenser's Letter to Ralegh and the Literary Politics of *The Faerie Queene*'s 1590 Publication." *Spenser Studies* 10 (1989): 139–74.

Fish, Stanley E. *Surprised by Sin: The Reader in* Paradise Lost. 1967. Berkeley: U of California P, 1971.

Foucault, Michel. "What Is an Author?" Trans. Josué V. Harari. *The Foucault Reader.* Ed. Paul Rainbow. New York: Pantheon, 1984. 101–20.

Frank, Joseph. *The Widening Gyre.* New Brunswick: Rutgers UP, 1963.

Gless, Darryl J. *Interpretation and Theology in Spenser.* Cambridge: Cambridge UP, 1994.

Habermas, Jürgen. *The Structural Transformation of the Public Sphere: An Inquiry into a Category of Bourgeois Society.* Trans. Thomas Burger with Frederick Lawrence. Cambridge, MA: MIT P, 1991.

Hamilton, A. C. "Spenser's *Letter to Ralegh.*" *Modern Language Notes* 73 (1958): 481–85.

Imbrie, Ann E. " 'Playing Legerdemaine with the Scripture': Parodic Sermons in *The Faerie Queene.*" *English Literary Renaissance* 17 (1987): 142–55.

Kastan, David Scott. "Shakespeare After Theory." *Textus* 9 (1996): 357–74.

King, John N. *English Reformation Literature: The Tudor Origins of the Protestant Tradition.* Princeton: Princeton UP, 1982.

———. *Spenser's Poetry and the Reformation Tradition.* Princeton: Princeton UP, 1990.

MacCaffrey, Isabel G. *Spenser's Allegory: The Anatomy of Imagination.* Princeton: Princeton UP, 1976.

Milton, John. *The Complete Poems and Major Prose.* Ed. Merritt Y. Hughes. Indianapolis: Bobbs-Merrill, 1983.

More, Thomas. *The Confutation of Tyndale's Answer.* Ed. Louis A. Schuster et al. *The Complete Works of St. Thomas More.* Vol. 8. New Haven: Yale UP, 1973.

Nohrenberg, James V. *The Analogy of* The Faerie Queene. Princeton: Princeton UP, 1976.

Owen, W. J. B. "Spenser's Letter to Ralegh—A Reply." *Modern Language Notes* 75 (1960): 195–97.

Patterson, Annabel. *Censorship and Interpretation: The Conditions of Writing and Reading in Early Modern England.* 2nd ed. Madison: U of Wisconsin P, 1984.

Shaheen, Naseeb. *Biblical References in* The Faerie Queene. Memphis: Memphis State UP, 1973.

Sidney, Sir Philip. *Syr P.S. His Astrophel and Stella.* London: Thomas Newman, 1591.

Spenser, Edmund. *Edmund Spenser's Poetry.* Norton Critical Edition. 3rd ed. Ed. Hugh MacLean and Anne Lake Prescott. New York: Norton, 1993.

———. *The Faerie Queene.* Ed. A. C. Hamilton. London: Longman, 1977.

———. *The Faerie Queene.* Ed. Thomas P. Roche, Jr. New Haven: Yale UP, 1978.

———. *The Faerie Queene 1596.* Intro. Graham Hough. London: Scolar P, 1976.

———. *The Works of Edmund Spenser.* Ed. R. J. Judd. *The Faerie Queene.* Vol. 2. London: Rivington et al., 1805.

———. *The Works of Edmund Spenser: A Variorum Edition.* 8 vols. *The Faerie Queene.* Vol. 1. Ed. F. M. Padelford et al. 1932. Baltimore: Johns Hopkins UP, 1966.

———. *The Yale Edition of the Shorter Poems of Edmund Spenser.* Ed. William A. Oram et al. New Haven: Yale UP, 1989.

Tribble, Evelyn B. *Margins and Marginality: The Printed Page in Early Modern England.* Charlottesville: U of Virginia P, 1993.

———. "The Open Text: A Protestant Poetics of Reading and Teaching Book 1." *Approaches to Teaching Spenser's* Faerie Queene. Ed. David L. Miller and Alexander Dunlop. New York: MLA, 1994. 58–63.

Tyndale, William. *An Answer to Sir Thomas More's Dialogue.* Ed. Henry Walter. Cambridge: Parker Society, 1850.

———. "Preface to the Five Books of Moses." *Doctrinal Treatises and*

Introductions to Different Portions of the Holy Scriptures. Ed. Henry Walter. Cambridge: Parker Society, 1848. 392–97.

Voss, Paul J. "*The Faerie Queene* 1590–1596: The Case of St. George." *The Ben Jonson Journal* 3 (1996): 59–73.

Wall, Wendy. *The Imprint of Gender: Authorship and Publication in the English Renaissance.* Ithaca: Cornell UP, 1993.

Watkins, John. *The Specter of Dido: Spenser and Virgilian Epic.* New Haven: Yale UP, 1995.

Wyatt, Sir Thomas. *Thomas Wyatt: The Complete Poems.* Ed. R. A. Rebholz. New Haven: Yale UP, 1978.

10

"Surpris'd with all": Rereading Character in *Much Ado about Nothing*

David Weil Baker

"Reade him, therefore; and againe, and againe," enjoined Henry Condell and John Heminge, the supervisors of the publication of the First Folio, and this injunction to the "great Variety of Readers" contrasts with their depiction of a Shakespeare who never blotted a line and was thus presumably free from the need to reread his own work. Yet rereaders of Shakespeare's plays may find themselves in the position of the plotting Prospero as he watches Miranda and Ferdinand confirm their love according to a script that he has largely devised: "So glad of this as they I cannot be, / Who are surpris'd with all; but my rejoicing / At nothing can be more" (*The Tempest,* 3.1.93). That is, rereaders of a Shakespeare play may discover nuances and layers of meaning that delight them as nothing else, but some of the surprise is gone after their first experience of the play. Attacking what he terms the "new histrionicism," Harry Berger describes this dilemma as the conflict between "wide-eyed" playgoing and the "slit-eyed" analysis of the armchair Shakespearean, but we do not have to confine the scope of the problem to the page/stage controversy.[1] It is possible, of course, to attend performances of the same play again and again. In return for a better critical perspective on either performance or text, the "rereader" of a play would seem to lose the capacity to approach the world of the play as a completely new one and to behold it with Miranda-like innocence and wonder.[2]

The notorious instability of Shakespearean plays, however, provides some relief from the apparent dichotomy between the freshness of a first reading and the more jaded stance of the rereader.[3] For paradoxically a rereading of a Shakespeare play is often a first reading, too—at least, of some parts of the play. Restoration adaptations of Shakespeare's plays reveal this paradox at its crudest. Modern readers typically experience surprise and even outrage when they comapre Tate's adaptation (1681) of *King Lear* to the Folio text of the play or Shakespeare's *Tempest* to the Dryden-Davenant version (1667).[4] (Davenant's *The Law against Lovers* (1662) amalgamated elements from the plots of *Much Ado* and *Measure for Measure,* but the title of the adaptation does not identify it with either Shakespearean source.) However, the more recent project of "unediting" Shakespeare has shown that, such outrage notwithstanding, we are still reading adaptations of his plays. Thus, the practice, originating in the eighteenth century, of conflating the quarto and Folio texts of *King Lear* is now the object of considerable skepticism, and this kind of skepticism has led to reexaminations of the texts of other Shakespearean plays and poems, too.[5] The more carefully we reread Shakespeare, the more we seem to discover that we have yet to read him.

Character is no exception to this difficulty of fully distinguishing between Shakespeare reread and Shakespeare read for the first time. The Davenant-Dryden *Tempest,* for instance, introduces a number of new characters, and thus to move from this adaptation to the list of characters in the Folio *Tempest* is to experience a jolt. The dramatis personae, on the other hand, that accompany modern editions of Shakespeare's plays suggest that the identity of his characters is immutably fixed. They will stay the same no matter how many times they are read. Yet, as Randall McLeod has argued, Shakespeare's characters are "Poped" in most modern editions of the plays ("The Very Names of Persons" 88–96). Textual editors have imposed eighteenth-century notions of individuality and identity on these characters and rendered them more coherent than they are in seventeenth-century editions of the plays. Reread in the texts in which they first appeared, the characters of the Shakespearean quartos and the First Folio have a capacity to surprise that their counterparts in modern editions of the plays possess only faintly.

I want to examine one such potentially surprising character and her capacity to affect our rereading of *Much Ado about Nothing,* a play that, like *The Tempest,* concerns nuptials largely scripted by others besides the bride and bridegroom. Innogen, the wife of Leonato, appears in two stage directions to the Quarto of *Much adoe about Nothing* (1600) as well as the Folio version of the play, but editors, beginning with Theobald, have excised her role and relegated her to a textual note.[6] Innogen is a "ghost" character—one who is alluded to in stage directions but given no speaking part—and, as a consequence of her disappearance from the play, she has received scant attention from its critics. Michael Friedman has made a good case for the performability of Innogen's role (49–50), but to most critics of the play Innogen has represented little more than an "abandoned intention" (Wells 3–4) or at best a character who "possibly should be seen but is certainly not heard" (Smidt 399). Both of these dismissals, however, exclude the possibility of her silence being an "open" and interpretable one. As Philip McGuire and Christina Luckyj have shown, the silence of women in Renaissance plays is often meant to be heard (McGuire 1–18; Luckyj 42–48). Nor is this silence necessarily tantamount to acquiescence. Albeit a "ghost" character, Innogen may haunt the play.

Innogen, however, is "ghostly" in another way; for she has the potential to make a play that has been read again and again seem strange and unfamiliar. Indeed, Theobald's suppression of Innogen renders her appearance in the Quarto and the Folio all the more dramatic:

> I have ventured to expunge [this name]; there being no mention of her through the play, no one speech addressed to her, nor one syllable spoken to her. . . . It seems as if the poet had in his first plan designed such a character; which, on a survey of it, he found would be superfluous, and therefore left it out. (Variorum *Much Ado* 7)

Theobald's completion of what he saw as Shakespeare's intended revisions makes an implicit argument about the incompleteness of Shakespeare's own rereading of *Much Ado.* That is, Shakespeare reread the play carefully enough to know that he wanted to expunge

Innogen—i.e., blot some of his own lines—but then did not check to see whether he had remembered to do this. More important, however, Theobald's elimination of Innogen has the potential to highlight Innogen for the modern rereader of the play, who may find the presence of Innogen in the Quarto and Folio doubly intriguing precisely because Theobald deemed it superfluous. Reading backwards is, of course, a prominent feature of rereading in general: for instance, one detects an echo of an earlier scene in the fifth act of a play, and this echo leads to a rereading of the earlier scene. Yet problems of textual editing force the rereader to reverse course in a broader sense. We reread the Quarto of *Much adoe* in a historically "preposterous" manner.[7] After becoming dissatisfied or intrigued with later emendations and adaptations, rereaders return to the texts of the play that historically came first.

The opening stage direction of the play provides a key opportunity for such retrogressive rereading. In the Arden edition, this stage direction reads:

> Enter Leonato Governor of Messina, Hero his daughter,
> and Beatrice his niece, with a Messenger.

On the other hand, the Quarto reads:

> Enter Leonato governour of Messina, Innogen his wife,
> Hero his daughter, and Beatrice his neece, with a mes-
> senger.

In both cases, this opening direction presents Leonato as the center of a number of family relations and as the source of political power in Messina, but these relations change when one rereads the play in the Quarto. Preserved in a textual note to the Arden *Much Ado,* Innogen, however, prompts this rereading of the Quarto. Thus, as an example of how the play appears in modern editions, the Arden *Much Ado* shows the contradictory effect of Theobald's emendation. Innogen is not so much thoroughly expunged from the play as made into a silent provocation. She invites a historically preposterous rereading of the play in the first textual form that we have of it.

What difference, however, does Innogen's presence make to *Much Ado*? How does she enable the rereader to experience surprise? Most obviously, she necessitates a reappraisal of Leonato's family. As Claire McEachern has argued, *Much Ado* may concern the relations between fathers and daughters as much as *King Lear* (274–87), and it seems to depict a father-daughter bond as intense as those in plays such as *The Tempest* and *Lear,* which isolate the fathers and daughters from mothers. Leonato's lack of a wife intensifies the father-daughter bond of the play. On the other hand, the presence of Innogen, who in the Quarto stage direction is neatly situated between Leonato and Hero, makes the "family romance" of the play more triangular. This is not to deny the importance of the bond between Leonato and Hero but only to suggest that this bond is mediated by another character. At the very least, Innogen's appearance in the stage direction raises the possibility of evaluating Leonato as a husband and a father.

Reread in the light of Innogen's appearance in the Quarto of *Much adoe,* other relationships and exchanges between two characters become more triangular, as well. Thus, upon arriving at Messina, Don Pedro immediately identifies Hero as Leonato's daughter: Leonato's reply jokingly suggests suspicion (lines 100–05; all quotations are from the Shakespeare Quarto Facsimiles edition of the play):

> [Don] Pedro[:]   You embrace your charge too willingly: I
>   thincke this is your daughter.
> Leonato[:]   Her mother hath many times tolde me so.
> Bened. [Benedick:] Were you in doubt sir that you askt her?
> Leonato[:]   Signior Benedicke, no, for then were you a
>   child.

As far as the stage directions are concerned, Innogen is present during this male banter, where Leonato, by his very denial, conjures up the possibility of an adult Benedick impregnating Innogen. In *The Tempest* Prospero asserts in an equally dubious manner Miranda's legitimacy: "Thy mother was a piece of virtue, and / She said thou wast my daughter." But, although Prospero's wife is, as Stephen Orgel has argued, an "absent presence" in *The Tempest,* she never materializes to the point of having a stage direction devoted to her(50–51). On the other hand, the scene as we have it in the Quarto *Much adoe* contains Innogen as a silent hearer of her husband's jocular aspersions.

When included in the play rather than consigned to a textual note, Innogen instigates a rereading of other characters and their relationships. Leonato's reference to the mother of Hero is a fleeting one, but since in the Quarto she is on stage, we are more entitled to wonder about the degree to which Leonato's marriage provides the model for his treatment of Hero and vice versa. Is Leonato's joking suspicion of his own wife the reason he is so ready to believe Claudio's accusation of Hero later in the play? On the other hand, Innogen's silence offers a way of explaining Hero's submissiveness. This silence certainly reveals the effect of marriage on the only female character of the play who is a wife. Indeed, a kind of preposterous rereading obtains here, too. To be sure, one could read Innogen's silence as proleptic of Hero's actions and predicament, but a more likely model is that of returning to the opening stage direction after having read the rest of the play. It is only in the light of what comes later that this opening stage direction and Innogen's presence in the scene become significant.

A play as reread as *Much Ado* would not seem to have too many secrets left. In particular, *Much Ado* would also seem to have been sufficiently mined for literary allusions in the names of its characters. But the name Innogen offers the rereader another surprise in the form of its provenance, which is legendary British history. For Innogen was the wife of Brutus, the supposedly Trojan founder of Britain, and the daughter of a Greek king, Pandrasus, whom Brutus defeated in battle. The marriage of Brutus and Innogen was of dynastic importance because its progeny were a race of kings and queens, but this marriage also constituted a sign of revenge and conquest. As *Holinshed's Chronicles* puts it, the first article of peace between Brutus and Pandrasus was that "Pandrasus should give his daughter Innogen unto Brute in marriage, with a competent summe of gold and silver for her dowrie" (439). Like Katherine in *Henry V,* Innogen was one of the concessions yielded by her father to the young man who had overpowered him militarily. (Indeed, even before coming to Greece, Brutus had already killed his own father in a hunting accident, and this accident was the reason for his exile.) Although Brutus and his band ultimately settled in England, not Greece, Innogen still signified an older generation's transferral of its power and authority to Brutus.

As a mother—the other aspect of her role that *Holinshed's Chronicles* emphasizes—Innogen also enabled Brutus to provide for the continuation of his newfound power and rule:

> When Brutus had builded this citie, and brought the Iland fullie under his subjection, he by the advise of his nobles commanded this Ile . . . to be called Britaine; and the inhabitants Britons after his name, for a perpetuall memorie that he was the first bringer of them into the land. In the meanwhile also he had by his wife iii sonnes, the first named Locrinus or Locrine, the second Cambris. (443)

This passage is replete with names and naming, and these names all perpetuate Brutus. The name of the Britons serves as an abiding reminder of Brutus's leadership just as his son Locrinus constitutes the means of extending that leadership into the distant future. Significantly, the only unnamed figure in the passage is Innogen, who appears as "his wife." This anonymity again indicates her identity as a link between two generations of men—here, Brutus and his sons rather than Brutus and his surrogate father. Yet this anonymity is arguably only apparent when we reread Holinshed in the wake of the Quarto of *Much adoe.* That is, the Quarto renders Innogen's ghostly presence in Holinshed noticeable.

The Quarto of *Much adoe* displaces Holinshed's Innogen and provides the opportunity to reread Holinshed in the context of a Sicilian comic setting. As Northrop Frye long ago pointed out, Sicily could function in Renaissance plays and poetry as a kind of surrogate Britain, and in *Cymbeline* virtually the same set of names, Imogen and Posthumus Leonatus, reappear during a somewhat later era of British history.[8] But reread in the comic context of *Much adoe,* Holinshed's dynastic history plot acquires new emphases. Shakespeare, of course, could have named one of the characters of *Much adoe* Brutus if he had wanted to allude to Holinshed's plot in a way that retained Holinshed's emphasis on male succession. But since the name Innogen conjures up Holinshed in *Much adoe,* the focus of the male dynastic plot also shifts to the effect of this plot on wives and would-be wives. This shift is, to some degree, generic: comedy may promote patriarchy, but it does require some interaction between the sexes. Yet, the point is not only that the Innogen story reads differently in the Quarto of *Much adoe* but that it may reread differently in Holinshed after one has detected the allusion to this story in the Quarto. Indeed, there is not much of an Innogen story in Holinshed until *Much adoe* underscores her significance. Holinshed's Innogen is available preposterously, i.e., to a rereader.

The name Innogen is evocative in *Much adoe,* and it impinges upon *Much adoe* in the same allusive way that the name Claudius affects the meaning of *Hamlet.*[9] We are, of course, so used to reading again and again the identification of Hamlet's uncle as Claudius in both editions and criticism of the play that the paucity of textual evidence for this identification may seem surprising. Yet as Harold Jenkins points out, the name Claudius appears in only one speech heading and one stage direction of *Hamlet* (432–33). Elsewhere Hamlet's uncle is the king. Nevertheless, the identification of Hamlet's uncle as Claudius has become an entrenched part of criticism of the play, and interpreters have proved willing to reread *Hamlet* in relation to parallels from Roman history and vice versa.

But the evocativeness of Innogen's name provides a model for rereading other parts of Holinshed, too, and in particular the character of another wife from legendary British history. For even among Britain's first monarchs, a wife could be provoked to abandon, for a time, the role defined by Innogen. Thus, as *Holinshed's Chronicles* goes on to relate, Locrine, Innogen's son and Brutus's heir, and Guendolene, the daughter of one of Brutus's most valued allies, were married, and he aroused her ire by loving and having a child by another woman (444). Guendolene promptly defeated her husband in battle, imprisoned him, and, as Spenser puts it in *The Faerie Queene,* "first taught men a woman to obay" (2.10.20). Nevertheless, when her son came of age, Guendolene did consign her power to him. Albeit something of a Semiramis figure, Guendolene finally restored the male dynastic line from which she had briefly deviated.

The Quarto of *Much adoe* provides analogues to both the Innogen and Guendolene plots. On the one hand, Don Pedro and his band of

uprooted soldiers (they are all from different places; Claudio from
Florence, Benedick from Padua, and Don Pedro from Aragon) are
the young warriors who have established themselves in battle and
now must ratify their positions through marriage. Leonato and his
brother are the older men whose daughter(s) initially provoke enmity
but must finally signify the peace between the two generations. This
intergenerational strife is implicit in Leonato's remark that Hero must
be his daughter because Benedick was a child when she was conceived. Leonato, we may infer, is considerably older than Benedick.
But intergenerational strife becomes explicit when Leonato and his
brother challenge Claudio to a duel after the pretended death of Hero.
Thus, the Prince and Claudio joke about these threats from "two old
men without teeth" (ln. 2,207).

Innogen and Guendolene are not necessarily meant to be con-
trasted in Holinshed, but the Quarto of *Much adoe* indicates a possible
rereading of Holinshed that underscores the divide between these two
figures. For the Guendolene plot is also a part of *Much adoe* in the
form of the merry warriors, Beatrice and Benedick, who do provide
the play with a certain amount of contrast.[10] Indeed, a "jades tricke"
of inconstancy (ln. 140) may have been the initial provocation of
their merry war just as Locrine's unfaithfulness led to his battle with
his wife. But, whatever its ultimate cause, the continual "skirmish of
wit" (lns. 60–61) between Beatrice and Benedick rivals and at times
replaces the skirmishes confined to men only. Beatrice inaugurates her
first skirmish of wit with Benedick as an interruption of the male banter
over Hero: "I wonder that you will still be talking, signior Benedicke,
no body markes you" (lns. 112–13). This remark effectively highlights
herself and Benedick as combattants.

Reread in the context of Shakespeare's Sicily, the distinction
between the two female types—Innogen and Guendolyne—becomes
more pronounced. Benedick makes this distinction most explicit by
dubbing Beatrice "my Ladie Tongue" (ln. 676), and, appropriately
enough, the next and final appearance of Innogen in the play occurs
during a scene that Beatrice dominates. Thus, subsequent Quarto stage
directions read as follows: "Enter Leonato, his brother, his wife, Hero
his daughter, and Beatrice his neece, and a kinsman" (lns. 415–16).
On the other hand, modern editions of the play generally retain the

"kinsman"—who is, as Stanley Wells writes, the "shade of a shade"—
and remove Leonato's wife, whose lack of a name here suggests that
she is beginning to fade from the play.

Despite such fading, however, the silence of Leonato's wife should
provoke a rereading of those parts of the scene whose focus is speech.
For if Innogen is on stage when Leonato blames Beatrice's lack of
a husband on her shrewdness of "tongue" (ln. 433), their exchange
becomes yet another triangular one. Innogen's silence both exempli-
fies Leonato's ideal of a wife and at the same time provides a vantage
point from which Leonato's admonitions concerning the silence of
wives can be reread and critiqued. Beatrice, at least, claims to be able
to see a "church by day-light" (ln. 489), a formulation that suggests
both the necessity and difficulty of perceiving the obvious. So, too,
Innogen's silent presence as "wife" is both hard to avoid yet at the
same time something to which we must return again and again to
get. Significantly, Beatrice's reference to her own ability to see the
institution of marriage for what it is gives the cue for the maskers to
enter, and this sequence of events suggests that disguise is a recourse
of both playwrights and social groups when awkward silences become
too apparent. Nevertheless, at the same time, the attempt to hide what
is there invites renewed scrutiny. Like Theobald's suppression of
Innogen, the onslaught of the maskers has the potential to provoke
a rereading of what their arrival obscures.

Innogen's silence, however, is doubly awkward. For it invites a
rereading of the relations among the male characters of the play, too.
Such rereading reveals that, despite the apparent fixity of the dramatis
personae in modern editions of *Much Ado,* even the identities of some
of the play's primary characters are tenuous and "ghostly." Thus, the
preposterousness of rereading *Much Ado* from the perspective of a
marginal character indicates the instability of the play's center, too.
Leonato, in particular, offers some surprises to the rereader of the
play, since dramatis personae of modern editions of the play regularly
echo the opening stage direction and identify him as "governor" of
Messina. This identification then contributes to the apparent solidity
of Leonato's authority.

The play's villain, however, provides a rather surprising bridge
from Innogen to Leonato. The bastard John, dubbed "dumb John"

in one stage direction of the Quarto of *Much adoe* (ln. 494), is the character whose silence provides the most explicit parallel to that of Innogen. "I am not of many wordes," John tells Leonato in the first scene of the play (ln. 152), and this self-description (his first line) is often taken as a declaration of moroseness, or, as Hero puts it, "melancholy" (ln. 421). But John's lack of words should serve as a reminder that he, like Innogen, has been silently present during the banter over Hero's possible bastardy. Such banter does not directly allude to him, but it does highlight the stigma that sets him apart. As Jean Howard notes, women and bastards are the "natural and inevitable source of evil" in the play (175). Indeed, as a rebel who "of late stoode out" (lns. 362–63) against his brother, John is "trusted with a mussle" (ln. 372).

Given the dumbness of John, the silence of Leonato at crucial parts of the play is startling, for, unlike John, Leonato is a figure of supposedly legitimate authority. Yet a close rereading of the Quarto of *Much adoe* indicates a relative scarcity of references to Leonato's government. The opening stage direction of the play is in fact the only explicit textual basis for the designation of Leonato as governor of Messina. Neither in subsequent stage directions nor speech headings does Leonato ever reappear as "governor" of Messina. He is always Leonato. On the other hand, as the editor of the Arden *Much Ado,* A. R. Humphreys, has pointed out, other characters in the play are often identified in speech headings "by social function (Prince, Constable, Headborough) or morality trait (Bastard)" (78). Thus, for instance, one Quarto entrance reads "Enter Leonato, and the Constable, and the Headborough" (ln. 1,595), and the following entrance positions Leonato in a similar way amidst a different group of characters: "Enter Prince, Bastard, Leonato, Frier, Claudio, Benedicke, Hero, and Beatrice" (ln. 1,657). As far as textual evidence is concerned, both Dogberry's authority as constable and Don Pedro's as prince are more solid than Leonato's government of Messina.

Like the character of Innogen, Leonato's government of Messina is prominently introduced in the opening stage direction, only to be muted at crucial points of the play. As with Innogen, such muting then provides a kind of rereading of the opening stage directions. The Quarto of *Much adoe,* at least, does not so much solidly establish

Leonato's government of Messina as make it a question to be asked again and again in the light of subsequent events. Thus, on the one hand, Dogberry and his cohorts do address Leonato as "your worship" (ln. 1,614), and Leonato does discharge the Watch of its prisoners, Borachio and Conrade. But this discharge occurs after the Watch and Sexton have done all the work—that of apprehending and examining the prisoners.

Borachio and Conrade, moreover, make their confession not to Leonato but to the prince. The two henchmen of Don John are under constabulary escort when Claudio asks Don Pedro to "Hearken after their offence" (ln. 2,296), and even Borachio requests that Don Pedro attend to what he has to say: "Sweete prince, . . . do you heare me" (lns. 2,312–13). As a hearer of Borachio's confession, Don Pedro presides over the crucial and long deferred revelation of the play while Leonato is offstage. When Leonato, accompanied by the Sexton, returns to the stage, he does so more in the capacity of an aggrieved father than the governor of Messina: "Art thou the slave that with thy breath hast killd / Mine innocent child?" (lns. 2,346–47). Only after Leonato has given ample vent to his paternal outrage does he officially claim the prisoners.

Who does govern Messina? This uncertainty is particularly acute in a play where power often manifests itself as the ability to hear what one wants to hear and silence everything else by remaining deaf to it.[11] In particular, after the slandering of Hero, Leonato finds himself in the position of a suitor who cannot get an audience. "Heare you my Lords?" (ln. 2,128) Leonato asks as the prince and Claudio make haste to avoid him. An exchange follows in which Leonato and his brother challenge the two younger men to a duel but are not taken seriously. Finally, the combattants part on a note of willfull deafness:

> Leonato[:] My Lord, my Lord.
> Prince[:]   I will not heare you. (lns. 2,194–95)

The Prince effectively silences Leonato by refusing to hear what he has to say. The speech headings further reinforce the disparity between the two men. Don Pedro is speaking as prince and Leonato as subject rather than governor. Even after the deception of Conrade and Borachio is revealed, Leonato does not quite regain his governing authority as far as the prince is concerned. Thus, in his apology to Leonato, the prince claims that "to satisfie this good old man" (ln. 2,361), he will "bend under any heavy waight, / That heele enioyne me to" (lns. 2,362–63). Leonato may be able to enjoin the Prince to make amends, but such injunctions will come from "a good old man" rather than governor.

The apparent fixity of Leonato's identity as governor of Messina in modern editions of *Much Ado,* however, makes the instability of Leonato's authority in the Quarto of *Much adoe* all the more interesting and surprising. That is, just as Theobald's excision of Innogen contributes to the impact of her presence in the Quarto, so the play's undermining of Leonato's position acquires at least some of its significance preposterously—after that position has been established not only in the text of the play but its editing and reproduction as well. I am not, therefore, postulating a seventeenth-century first reading of Leonato's character that would be the same as my own rereading of it. Yet, as Margreta de Grazia puts it, once scholars begin to critique the eighteenth-century editorial assumptions about textual authenticity that mediate our understanding of Shakespeare "[i]t becomes possible to look for phenomena that have been minimized, transformed, or excluded by its preparation or 'speaking beforehand' " (13). Nevertheless, such speaking beforehand is the necessary prologue to the retrieval of excluded or minimized phenomena such as the identities of Innogen and Leonato. Innogen's exclusion from later editions of the play spotlights, for the rereader, at least, her appearance in the Quarto.

More broadly, Shakespeare cannot be "unedited"—a form of rereading—until he has been thoroughly read, digested, and reconfigured in the adaptations of textual editors. Thus, despite its critique of eighteenth-century precursors, the project of "unediting" Shakespeare can be located squarely in an eighteenth-century tradition of textual editing. As Samuel Johnson put it, the first move of any textual editor is to "demolish the fabricks which are standing"—i.e., the work of preceding editors ("Preface to Shakespeare, 1765" 99). Yet such acts of demolition are never complete, as Johnson knew only too well. To reread the Quarto of *Much adoe* is to regain the lost element of surprise, but we must acknowledge the degree to which this surprise is combined with and even a function of Prospero-like jadedness rather than a rediscovery of the role of Miranda. For the perspective of a rereader is necessarily skewed. After centuries of editing and reading, the smallest details of the play loom large to us as they may not have to a seventeenth-century audience or readership. This does not mean that seventeenth-century first reactions to the play can never be hypothesized or, to some degree, recovered. Rather, we must be wary of making the goal of unediting Shakespeare that of approaching him "free of prior interpretation," as McLeod puts it, and thus of denying our own status as rereaders.[12] For this goal is not historicism but rather the desire to recapture innocence.[13]

Notes

1. See Berger's *Imaginary Audition* 1–42. Berger is responding to Richard Levin's explicit critique of rereading Renaissance plays in *New Readings vs. Old Plays*. See Levin 1–10 and 194–207, where he links endless rereadings of Shakespeare and other Renaissance dramatists to both the New Criticism and the professionalization of literary studies as well as its attendant requirement to "publish or perish." Berger engages Levin and his followers at the level of the stage/page debate, which he implicitly evokes. Thus, Levin supports an attitude of "humility" toward the "critical tradition that has been formed by generations of viewers and readers" (201). In other words, Levin argues that the significance of Renaissance plays was relatively stable for spectators and readers until the advent of the professional journal and the New Critical "reading," which dissolved the harmony of page and stage. Another great vulnerability of Levin's attack, however, is the historical fact that the texts of Renaissance plays have never been stable and thus neither have performances of the plays. It should be noted, for instance, that my "with all" is taken from the notes to the *Tempest* in the Riverside Shakespeare, which show that the Folio reading is "with all," a reading subsequently emended by Theobald (1637).

     I will be using "rereading" to include both the activities of a viewer who sees the play more than once and the armchair Shakespearean. It is also worth noting that the two are not mutually exclusive. Thus, for instance, like numerous Shakespearean quartos, the Quarto of *Much adoe about Nothing* is advertised on its title page as the text of what "hath been sundrie times publikely acted"—a formulation that suggests the possibility of spectators buying the text of a play that they had seen on stage and liked. Despite such links, however, the play as book is undoubtedly more easily reread than the play as performance. Thus, one can see an entire performance again and again, but only a book allows for the rereading of particular scenes and lines. Even the VCR is not the technological match of the book as far as rereading goes. On the VCR it is possible to return to a particular scene or line, but the reviewer is not equidistant from all parts of the play as is the rereader of a book. With its need of being rewound, the VCR is more at the level of the scroll or *volumen* rather than the codex, much less the printed book.

2. See Desmet 8–9 for a discussion of "reading" Shakespeare that includes the plays in performance.

3. Of course, problems of textual instability accompany the editing and criticism of virtually every writer. Nevertheless, Shakespearean texts display such instability to an unusually high degree.

4. Whether Restoration audiences experienced this kind of shock, however, is debatable.

5. I take the phrase "unediting Shakespeare" from Randall McLeod's "UNEditing Shak-Speare," but, for other examples of this kind of important work, see also McLeod's "Unemending Shakespeare's Sonnet 111," and "The Marriage of Good and Bad Quartos." On the editing of *King Lear* see the essays in *The Division of Kingdoms: Shakespeare's Two Versions of King Lear,* ed. Gary Taylor and Michael Warren, eds., *The Division of Kingdoms: Shakespeare's Two Versions of* King Lear (Oxford: Clarendon Press, 1983). See also Peter Stallybrass and Margreta de Grazia, "The Materiality of the Shakespearean Text," as well as de Grazia's *Shakespeare Verbatim: The Reproduction of Authenticity and the 1790 Apparatus.*

6. For discussion of Innogen, see the Variorum *Much Ado* 7: In a long textual note, the editors of the New Folger Shakespeare suggest that Innogen should constitute a "silent presence" in the play (Mowat and Werstine 199). But the text of their edition and that of all other contemporary editions that I have seen follows Theobald. The Variorum edition of the play does include Innogen, but it contains a good deal of editorial skepticism about her. My own argument is based upon the Quarto *Much adoe,* not because I think that the Quarto is necessarily more authoritative or authorial than the Folio *Much adoe about Nothing,* but, in part, because the Quarto has traditionally served as the foundation of later editions of the play. It is worth noting, however, that Innogen was not expunged from the Folio but appears in the same places there as in the Quarto (*First Folio* 101 and 104). On the dangers of making unwarranted assumptions about the relative authority of the Folio and Quarto editions of Shakespeare's plays, see Werstine, "McKerrow's Suggestion," 157–59 and 166–68. For work on stage directions, including speech headings, see Linda McJannet's "Elizabethan Speech Prefixes: Page Design, Typography, and Mimesis" as well as Anthony Hammond's "Encounters of the Third Kind in Stage-Directions in Elizabethan and Jacobean Drama." The source for Innogen may be

Messer Lionato's unnamed wife in "La Prima Parte de le Nouvelle del
Bandello." See Geoffrey Bullough, *Narrative and Dramatic Sources of
Shakespeare* 112–34. Messer Lionato's wife is more a part of the plot
than Shakespeare's Innogen. Shakespeare seems to have been more
interested in Innogen as a name and a silent presence.

7. See Patricia Parker's "Preposterous Events" for more on the "Shakespearean preposterous." For the most part Parker is discussing events
within the plays, but she does give some indication of how preposterousness might be extended to the editing of the plays when she
critiques the "critical construction of Shakespeare as an object of study,
which . . . still reads back into the plays assumptions of stability, that
straighten out the scandal of their 'deformity,' lost earlier versions,
reassigned speeches, missing characters, or the logic of narrative or
chronological lines" (212). For more on reading Shakespeare's plays
"backwards," see Berger, *Imaginary Audition* 35–37.

8. Frye makes the point about Sicily and the repetition of names in
Cymbeline as part of a larger argument about the relation of Shakespearean comedy to romance (65). Interestingly, the issue of Imogen's
name in *Cymbeline* also depends upon the page/stage debate. Simon
Foreman's account of a contemporary performance of the play lists
Imogen as Innogen, and thus Roger Warren has recently argued that
the name Imogen in the Folio *Cymbeline* is a mistake (viii). Imogen,
however, is a richly suggestive name—a cross, perhaps, between Innogen and "image." In *Cymbeline* Imogen at times both thwarts and
encourages the implication of her name that she will be a silent image.
Thus, rejecting Cloten's advances, Imogen claims to be an unwilling
speaker: "But that you shall not say, I yield being silent, / I would
not speak." She also apologizes for forgetting a "Ladies manners"
and being "so verball" (*First Folio* 377). Here, she claims to speak
only out of necessity, but, unlike her namesake in *Much adoe,* she
does speak.

9. See Jonathon Goldberg, *Voice Terminal Echo* 68–101. Goldberg's
analysis of all that is in a Shakespearean name is one model for what
I am trying to do with the name Innogen.

10. Leonard Digges's tribute to Shakespeare, published in the 1640 *Poems*
(London: John Benson) alludes to *Much Ado* in a way that makes
Beatrice and Benedick its central attraction (Brian Vickers, ed., *Shakespeare: The Critical Heritage* 28). This allusion provides another way
of rereading the play and giving it new emphases.

11. See Harry Berger's "Against the Sink-a-Pace: Sexual and Family
Politics in *Much Ado about Nothing*" for more on hearing and its lapses
in the play.

12. See "Unemending Shakespeare's Sonnet 111" 96.

13. My thanks to David Galef and Marcia Worth-Baker for rereading this
essay many times and giving me a number of valuable suggestions.

Works Cited

Berger, Harry. "Against the Sink-a-Pace: Sexual and Family Politics in *Much Ado about Nothing.*" *Shakespeare Quarterly* 33 (1982): 302–14.

———. *Imaginary Audition: Shakespeare on Stage and Page.* Berkeley: U of California P, 1989.

Bergeron, David. *Reading and Writing in Shakespeare.* Newark: Delaware UP, 1996.

Bullough, Geoffrey. *Narrative and Dramatic Sources of Shakespeare: The Comedies, 1597–1603.* London: Routledge and Kegan Paul, 1958.

de Grazia, Margreta. *Shakespeare Verbatim: The Reproduction of Authenticity and the 1790 Apparatus.* Oxford: Clarendon Press, 1991.

Desmet, Christy. *Reading Shakespeare's Characters: Rhetoric, Ethics, and Identity.* Amherst: Massachusetts UP, 1992.

Ferguson, Margaret W., Maureen Quilligan, and Nancy J. Vickers. *Rewriting the Renaissance: The Discourses of Sexual Difference in Early Modern Europe.* Chicago: U of Chicago P, 1986.

Friedman, Michael D. "'Hush'd on purpose to grace harmony': Wives and Silence in *Much Ado about Nothing.*" *Shakespearean Criticism Yearbook 1990.* Ed. Sandra L. Williamson. Vol. 13. Detroit: Gale Research, 1990. 45–52.

Frye, Northrop. *A Natural Perspective: The Development of Shakespearean Comedy and Romance.* New York: Columbia UP, 1965.

Goldberg, Jonathan. *Voice Terminal Echo: Postmodernism and English Renaissance Texts.* New York: Methuen, 1986.

Hammond, Anthony. "Encounters of the Third Kind in Stage-Directions in Elizabethan and Jacobean Drama." *Studies in Philology* 89 (1992): 71–99.

Holinshed, Raphael. *Holinshed's Chronicles of England, Scotland, and Ireland.* London: J. Johnson, 1807.

Howard, Jean. "Renaissance Antitheatricality and the Politics of Gender and Rank in *Much Ado about Nothing.*" *Shakespeare Reproduced: The Text in History and Ideology.* Eds. Jean Howard and Marion F. O'Conner. New York: Methuen, 1987. 163–88.

Johnson, Samuel. *Johnson on Shakespeare.* Ed. Arthur Sherbo. New Haven: Yale UP, 1968.

Kastan, David Scott, and Peter Stallybrass. *Staging the Renaissance: Reinterpretations of Elizabethan and Jacobean Drama.* New York: Routledge, 1991.

Levin, Richard. *New Readings vs. Old Plays: Recent Trends in the Interpretation of Renaissance Drama.* Chicago: U of Chicago P, 1979.

Luckyj, Christina. "'A Moving Rhetoricke': Women's Silences and Renaissance Texts." *Renaissance Drama* 24 (1993): 33–57.

McEachern, Claire. "Fathering Herself: A Source Study of Shakespeare's Feminism." *Shakespeare Quarterly* 39 (1988): 269–91.

McGuire, Philip. *Speechless Dialect: Shakespeare's Open Silences.* Berkeley: U of California P, 1985.

McJannet, Linda. "Elizabethan Speech Prefixes: Page Design, Typography, and Mimesis." Bergeron 50–70.

McKerrow, R. B. "A Suggestion Regarding Shakespeare's Manuscripts." *Review of English Studies* 11 (1935): 459–65.

McLeod, Randall. "The Marriage of Good and Bad Quartos." *Shakespeare Quarterly* 33 (1982): 421–33.

———. " 'The very names of Persons': Editing and the Invention of Dramatick Character." Kastan and Stallybrass 88–96.

———. "UNEditing Shak-Speare." *Substance* 33–34. (1981): 26–56.

———. "Unemending Shakespeare's Sonnet 111." *Studies in English Literature* 21 (1981): 75–96.

Orgel, Stephen. "Prospero's Wife." Ferguson, Quilligan, and Vickers 50–64.

Parker, Patricia. "Preposterous Events." *Shakespeare Quarterly* 43 (1992): 186–214.

Shakespeare, William. *First Folio of Shakespeare.* Prepared by Charlton Hinman. New York: Norton, 1968.

———. *Hamlet.* Ed. Harold Jenkins. The Arden Shakespeare. London: Methuen, 1982.

———. *Much Ado about Nothing.* The Arden Shakespeare. Ed. A. R. Humphreys. London: Methuen, 1981.

———. *Much Ado about Nothing.* A New Variorum Edition. Ed. Horace Howard Furness. Philadelphia: Lippincott, 1899.

———. *Much adoe about Nothing* (1600). Prepared by Charlton Hinman. Shakespeare Quarto Facsimiles. Oxford: Clarendon Press, 1971.

———. *Much Ado about Nothing.* Eds. Barbara Mowat and Paul Werstine. New York: Washington Square Press, 1995.

———. *The Tempest. The Riverside Shakespeare.* Boston: Houghton Mifflin, 1974. 1,606–41.

Smidt, Kristian. "Shakespeare's Absent Characters." *English Studies* 61 (1980): 397–407.

Stallybrass, Peter, and Margreta de Grazia. "The Materiality of the Shakespearean Text." *Shakespeare Quarterly* 44 (1993): 255–83.

Vickers, Brian, ed. *Shakespeare, The Critical Heritage: 1623–1692.* Vol. 1. London: Routledge and Kegan Paul, 1974.

Warren, Michael, and Gary Taylor, eds. *The Division of Kingdoms: Shakespeare's Two Versions of King Lear.* Oxford: Clarendon Press, 1983.

Warren, Roger. *Cymbeline: Shakespeare in Performance.* Manchester: Manchester UP, 1988.

Wells, Stanley. "Editorial Treatment of Foul-Paper Texts: *Much Ado about Nothing* as Test Case." *The Review of English Studies* 31 (1980): 1–17.

Werstine, Paul. "McKerrow's Suggestion and Twentieth-Century Shakespeare Textual Criticism." *Renaissance Drama* 29 (1988): 149–73.

IV

—

Present

11

Rereading Proust: Perversion and Prolepsis in *À la recherche du temps perdu*

Elisabeth Ladenson

In *Le Plaisir du texte,* while discussing his now-famous distinction between *textes de plaisir* and *textes de jouissance,* Roland Barthes makes a parenthetical observation about what he considers to be one of the attractions of Proust's writing: "from one reading to the next, we never skip the same passages (11)."[1] Implied in this offhand remark about *À la recherche du temps perdu* are several ideas: first, that the reading of Proust's monumental novel entails an endless series of rereadings, and second, that such rereading is never entirely linear but always necessitates passing over sections of the text. Furthermore, Barthes's comment suggests that the skipping of passages in rereading Proust may indicate not so much boredom as an obscurely positive textual effect.

The acts of reading, rereading, and omission are also explored in relation to Proust's work by Jean Cocteau, who devotes some twenty pages of his published journal (1951–52) to his rereading of the *Recherche.* Cocteau, who had as a young man known Proust, rereads the entire work despite his dismayed discovery that some of it now seems to him unreadable. In the course of writing about his rereading, Cocteau relates an anecdote that gives an idea of the extent to which the act of rereading is inscribed in the very texture of Proust's work. Proust had the habit of reading his work in progress to the young Cocteau:

> He would read me what he had written the night before,
> trying out his effects, interrupting them with the hys-
> terical giggles he muffled with his gloved hand, saying
> "It's too silly! too silly!" which made it very difficult
> to follow him.
>   Sometimes he would leave out a paragraph, say-
> ing: "I'm skipping this because this passage won't be
> explained until the fifth volume." (227)

As this story illustrates, Proust wrote his novel in the full knowledge and indeed deliberate expectation that readers would initially be
mystified by certain passages, the meaning of which would only become clear retrospectively, upon their reaching subsequent volumes.
The incident Cocteau relates suggests, in fact, that Proust was much
more interested in the rereadability of his work than in its immediate
coherence. By suppressing passages in the interests of narrative flow
when reading his novel out loud to his young friend, the author was
merely acting out what is evident in the book itself: Proust neither
anticipated nor desired an immediately and entirely comprehending
public. The *Recherche* was written not so much to be read as to
be reread.

The novel has a privileged relation to the act of rereading on
several levels, in addition to the general sense of *déjà lu* that it shares
with other squarely canonical works. Not only did Proust include in
his work built-in obstacles to initial reading comprehension so as to
necessitate rereading, but the novel also suggests rereading by its very
form. Ourouboros-like, the *Recherche* ends with the spectacle of its
own inception, as the reader intrepid enough to negotiate its 3,000-
plus pages discovers that the work its narrator is finally ready to write
must presumably (if paradoxically) also be the one now drawing to a
close. We are thus sent by implication back to the point at which we
started, this time at least equipped to understand all those passages
whose meanings were not to be revealed until the fifth volume.

Writing after an interval of decades, Cocteau is obviously not
quoting Proust verbatim in the anecdote he relates, and yet his choice
of the fifth volume as the one that will clear up the mysteries presented
by the passages Proust skips over is not as arbitrary as it may at

first glance appear. The fifth volume of the *Recherche, Sodome et Gomorrhe* (translated into English as *Cities of the Plain*),[2] is indeed the one in which many purported surprises are sprung. As its title suggests, *Sodome et Gomorrhe* deals largely with homosexuality, and homosexuality is what drives a certain type of Proustian rereading encoded in the *Recherche* and which will be the central focus of this essay.

The effect that might be termed enforced rereading—that is, the inclusion in the text of passages that can fully be understood only retrospectively, in the light of later passages—is a familiar technique in literature, although Proust may have used it more systematically than most authors; he also, after all, wrote a much longer book than most authors. Proust employs variations on this device in a variety of contexts, often, for instance, relying on the irony of hindsight in social terms. Thus the contemptibly pretentious Mme Verdurin, who provides comic moments presiding over her bourgeois *salon* in the first volume, sticks around long enough to reappear with great and triumphant unlikelihood as the princesse de Guermantes at the end of the book, having achieved a sort of social apotheosis by marrying the prince de Guermantes, who would never so much as have spoken to her in the first sections. *Le Temps retrouvé,* the last volume in the *Recherche,* is full of such transformations, which serve among other things to prove that the seemingly immutable social laws set forth in the first volumes are in the end made to be violated.

Such historical ironies do not, however, really produce an effect of what I have called enforced rereading, because, no matter how incongruous the concept of Mme Verdurin as inheritor of the eminently aristocratic title princesse de Guermantes might be in the context of her initial presentation in the novel, that incongruity is dependent not on any change in the perception of her essence but rather on the vagaries of chance and ambition. The depiction of Mme Verdurin as a tiresome social climber is neither surprising nor incoherent in the light of what follows; what is disconcerting is, rather, the spectacle of her stunningly unexpected success.

A second look at Mme Verdurin's relatively humble beginnings from the vantage point of her impressive social attainments at the end of the book does not, therefore, lead to a discordant rereading in which one's initial impression of the character must undergo reassessment; one need merely congratulate Mme Verdurin in advance for her remarkable tenacity. The same is true, by and large, of all the many such rearrangements in the social hierarchy revealed in the last volume. It is, rather, in the erotic realm that the sort of phenomenon alluded to in Cocteau's anecdote tends to take place, in which a passage or element is disconcerting or even incomprehensible except with reference to later volumes. In terms of sexuality, the essence of a character's nature, and not merely his social standing (or even the nature of social standing itself), must be reexamined, and his behavior reinterpreted in the light of subsequent discoveries.

Proust's narrator both invites and performs rereading. Since *À la recherche du temps perdu* consists largely of retrospective, first-person narrative, the narrator must play an edgy game that consists in both divulging to the reader only such information as his earlier self was privy to at any given point in the story he tells, and at the same time making more or less oblique reference to later events, of which he is at the time of writing necessarily aware. (Of course, the very notion of "the time of writing" is tremendously complicated in Proust's novel, in part because of the ourouboros structure to which I have already alluded, but such concerns lie mercifully beyond the scope of the present essay.[3]) Explicit proleptic references on the order of "This episode was later, for reasons I could not imagine at the time, to play a great role in my life" are one of the ways in which Proust inscribes rereading in his text, enforcing an awareness on the part of the reader of the ignorance she shares with the narrator in his earlier incarnation at the time described in any particular passage, but not with the narrator of the story as a whole. The reader is thus implicitly enjoined to imagine an enlightened rereading of the passage in question alongside her present ignorant reading.

The hero of the *Recherche* himself spends a great deal of time and energy rereading. (In an effort to avoid numbing repetition as well as to suggest some of the text's multilayered nuances, I shall refer to the character who narrates the story as "the narrator," while terming the younger self whose thoughts and actions he describes "the hero.") The rereading of George Sand's *François le Champi,* for instance, first read to the young hero by his mother in the famous goodnight-kiss scene in the beginning of the first volume, plays an important role in the epiphanic conclusion of *Le Temps retrouvé*. But the rereading in which Proust's narrator most emphatically and repeatedly engages is that of other characters, and it is with reference to their sexuality—that is, the discovery of their homosexuality—that characters and events are most notably submitted to this process.

Rereadings along these lines fall into two categories, the same two categories alluded to in the title of the fifth volume: male and female homosexuality, or, as Proust likes to call them, Sodom and Gomorrah. His narrator's rereadings of male and female characters eventually suspected or known to indulge in same-sex eroticism differ according to gender, in several ways. Because he is at least purportedly heterosexual, the narrator's interest in male characters whom he discovers as having a sexual interest in other men is presented as purely "objective" in nature; it is research for research's sake. In the case of women, however, the narrator's desire to find out whether any given woman has such tastes stems not so much from a spirit of disinterested sociological or sexological enquiry as from his obsessive suspicions concerning the novel's chief object of desire, Albertine.

Rereadings of characters' sexualities in the *Recherche* differ according to gender in another, related but more subtle way as well. In order to demonstrate how this works, I shall focus on the characters whose sexualities the narrator devotes the most attention to rereading: the baron de Charlus and Albertine.

Charlus is initially misread and subsequently reread by the narrator in both social and sexual terms. He is one of many characters whose aristocratic identities are at first obscure to the young hero, who in the early volumes is shown in the process of learning the labyrinthine complexities of the French caste system in general and the genealogical chart of the Guermantes family in particular. With unfortunate consequences, the hero initially fails to grasp that Charlus is a Guermantes, a prominent member of the most important noble clan in Proust's cosmology. The peculiarities of aristocratic nomenclature, along with the hero's ignorance of its finer points, obscure his identity. He has, we find out, chosen the title of baron de Charlus from among the many he legitimately holds, and this proliferation of alternative entitlements anticipates the differing roles Charlus will successively play in the narrative.

We first encounter Charlus in "Combray," the opening section of the novel, when he makes a cameo appearance as the presumptive lover of Mme Swann. Swann, a friend of the hero's family, has made a bad marriage, the indignity of which is compounded in the eyes of all Combray by his wife's overt carryings-on with "her Charlus" (1:140; 1:155). The banality of this situation, the standard stuff of both soap opera and farce, is mitigated only thousands of pages later, when the hero discovers that Charlus is in fact an "invert." What had appeared to be the makings of conventional melodrama thus turns out to have been the makings of something somewhat less predictable, at least for the era in question.

Proust was aware of the dangers of playing with readers' expectations in this manner. In a letter to a critic who had expressed strong reservations about the first volume, Proust defended himself by referring to the revelations in *Sodome et Gomorrhe* that would reveal the Swann-Charlus situation to be anything but banal. Once readers had read the later volume, Proust protested, and then went back to take a look at the first scene in which Charlus appears, they would notice that the baron directs a piercing gaze at the young hero, and understand its import.[4]

The appearance of *Du Côté de chez Swann* also gave rise to moralistic criticism because of an early scene of lesbianism which seemed gratuitous to many readers, charges which Proust answered by invoking the delicate structure of the work as a whole. Responding to critic Paul Souday's objections to this passage, which the Catholic writer Francis Jammes had also begged him to remove, Proust wrote that the lesbian scene

> was, indeed, "useless" in the first volume. But its re-
> membrance is the foundation of volumes IV and V
> (through the jealousy it inspires, etc.). In suppressing
> this scene, I would not have changed very much in
> the first volume; I would have, in return, because of
> the interdependence of the parts, caused two entire
> volumes, of which this scene is the cornerstone, to fall
> down around the reader's ears. (qtd. in Rivers 24)

The essential link between homosexuality and rereading is manifest in these letters, and it is also clear from the terms in which Proust defends himself that he considers homosexuality, male and female, integral to the work not just thematically but aesthetically: architecturally necessary to the structure of the *Recherche.*

Now, of course, things have changed somewhat with respect to the representation of homosexuality, to the extent that these sorts of revelations produce neither the same sort of outrage nor the *frisson* that they did in Proust's day (*Du Côté de chez Swann* appeared in 1913, the first part of *Sodome et Gomorrhe* in 1921). In order to understand just how much—and also how little—things have changed, it is instructive to look at a somewhat analogous phenomenon of recent years. In the 1992 film *The Crying Game,* the object of desire is revealed, initial appearances to the contrary, to be not a woman but a man. This plot twist was repeatedly alluded to by the media at the time of the film's release, but its contents suppressed, with much fanfare. Times and mores have, it would seem, changed to the extent that while subverting the audience's expectations as to a character's sexual preference no longer has much of an inherent capacity to shock—for one thing, too many characters have in recent years emerged from closets—the same narrative bait-and-switch trick nonetheless still works in terms of gender identity.

And yet the revelation of Charlus as an "invert" has more in common with what transpires in *The Crying Game* than might at first appear. After all, at stake in the film's surprise plot twist is not merely one character's sex but what that gender trouble implies about Fergus, the central character who desires her—and thus, as it turns out, him—and with whom we have been set up to identify. As a result, sexual preference becomes very much the question. In addition, the issue of sexual preference is in Proust's novel concomitant with that of gender identification, so that the revelation of Charlus's taste for men, in accordance with the nineteenth-century sexological theories on which Proust bases his account of homosexuality, takes the form of a discovery that he is in some essential, although certainly not biological, sense a woman.

(Proust's account of same-sex desire follows the model established by the German sexologist, jurist, and Latinist Karl Heinrich Ulrichs and summed up in his 1868 work *Memnon* by the now-familiar formula *anima muliebris virili corpore inclusa* (the soul of a woman enclosed in the body of a man). According to this paradigm, to which Proust largely adheres in his depiction of male "inverts," a man who desires another man does so insofar as he is himself in some essential way a woman. Desire even for a member of the same biological sex is thus seen as inherently heterosexual, as it were, and it is at least in part for this reason that Proust eschews the term "homosexuality," preferring "inversion.")

The Crying Game is germane to the present discussion in another way as well. In the film, Fergus's abrupt and distressing realization that Dil, whom he had taken to be an attractive woman, is actually a man occasions an implied reassessment on his part not only of previous encounters between the two but also of the events leading up to their meeting, along with his dealings with the man responsible for bringing them together. The audience too is forced to review everything in the movie up to that point, even as the action continues.

When the film came out in 1992, much was made of the remarkable "secret" it contained, and reviewers complied with the filmmakers' wishes that the plot twist not be revealed. *The Crying Game* was treated somewhat the way detective thrillers are treated. The mere fact, however, that a film not in the mystery genre should nonetheless hinge on a mystery, combined with journalists' many coy references to gender issues, produced an effect of *déjà vu* that only the movie's earliest viewers and those least influenced by the press could have escaped.

A truly first-time viewing of *The Crying Game,* in the absence of any foreknowledge of the surprise to come, is for the most part impossible. Similarly, all but the very first readers of *À la recherche du temps perdu* are rereaders, at least where Charlus is concerned. Proust anticipated, and seems at least in part to have desired, the scandal that his representation of homosexuality in *Sodome et Gomorrhe* and the later books engendered. His letters on the subject stress, repeatedly and at length, the degree to which the public would inevitably be shocked by the place of Sodom in the second half of his novel. And indeed so it was: *Sodome et Gomorrhe* was the first "serious" book published in France to deal extensively and explicitly with the subject of same-sex love, and Proust is still known as a pioneer of what has come to figure under the rubric gay modernism. In 1921 and after, his depiction of male "inversion" was notorious, to the extent that the baron de Charlus lent his name as a shorthand code word, in literary circles, for the sexual penchant he had come to incarnate. (Indeed, the word "Proustian" itself for some time carried similar connotations, before coming to designate a flashback effect brought on by eating cakes dipped in tea).

One of the effects of the scandal surrounding Proust's Sodom has been that, with Charlus having at one time achieved the status of a brand name along the lines of Kleenex or Tampax, a great number of Proust's readers have come to his text already primed for the revelation of Charlus's sexuality and the importance of homosexuality in general in the book. The effect of initial reading is in this regard to some extent suppressed, in favor of an *a priori* rereading that may distort, but does not necessarily detract from, the integrity of Proust's project.

The revelation of Charlus as an "invert" is thus, at least for first-time readers who have come to Proust in the knowledge of his place in the canon of gay modernism, "reread" in advance into the scenes in which he appears prior to the first book of *Sodome et Gomorrhe*. Once Charlus has been unmasked as an invert, moreover, even a reader with no prior expectations as to this particular character is, having been acquainted with the theory of Sodom put forth in the opening pages of that volume, in a position to question the sexuality of various other male characters and even correctly to identify which ones will eventually be revealed as Charlus's Sodomite compatriots.

Male sexuality is thus presented in the *Recherche* largely according to a binary system in which various apparently virile men are subject to reevaluation as essentially effeminate once their "true nature" is discovered, and the reader is subsequently invited to reread, along with the narrator, their every previous word and action.

Despite the symmetry suggested by the title *Sodome et Gomorrhe,* the same is not true for the female characters whose sexual preference is put into question. Alongside and in contrast to the representation of male "inversion" in the novel, Proust depicts something that looks very much like a female "homosexuality," in the sense that the women in the novel whose exclusive or occasional sexual interest lies in other women are not "really men," as the male inverts are "really women." The binary model of sexuality displayed by Charlus and his ilk and theorized at the beginning of *Sodome et Gomorrhe* is nowhere to be found in "Gomorrah." Such women run the gamut from shy tomboys to ostentatiously feminine courtesans, and their objects of desire tend to resemble them rather than being their opposites, as Proust's theory of Sodom suggests about their male counterparts.

Female homosexuality becomes a major preoccupation in the book, as well as the occasion for extensive rereading, when the hero learns that Albertine, his central object of desire, is a close friend of two women whom the narrator knows to be a couple, thanks to the seemingly gratuitous lesbian scene in the first volume. Although the revelation of Albertine's connection with them does not occur until the end of *Sodome et Gomorrhe,* the relationship between the two women is introduced very early in the book, accompanied by an explicit announcement that this moment will become important much later on, for reasons that are for the moment withheld. As a result, this first sounding of the theme of lesbianism in the novel is imbued with proleptic rereading, with the reader forced into a contentless awareness of her own eventual, potential understanding of the scene's importance. Such moments are calculated to produce suspense, of the peculiar Proustian variety that promises the unveiling of a secret only after the reader has traversed hundreds or indeed thousands of pages dealing with many different subjects and characters, thus guaranteeing that she will have forgotten the initial riddle long before arriving at the delivery of its much delayed punch line. Consequently, Proustian suspense is predicated upon both anticipatory and linear rereading.

If all but the very first readers of the baron de Charlus are from the beginning, for reasons external to the text, rereaders, the presentation of Albertine and the other at least putatively Gomorrhean characters works differently. Charlus and other denizens of Sodom, such as his cousin the prince de Guermantes, are at first carefully portrayed as hypervirile, so that, while their excessive masculinity may eventually itself be taken as a sign of effeminacy, this is the case, in principle, only as a function of presumptive rereading. Charlus's impatience with young men whom he finds effeminate, for instance, is depicted with remarkable vehemence: "They're nothing but women," he says scornfully, leading the ostensibly credulous narrator to reflect:

> But what life would not have appeared effeminate beside that which he expected a man to lead, and never found energetic or virile enough? (He himself, when he walked across country, after long hours on the road would plunge his heated body into frozen streams.) He would not even concede that a man should wear a single ring. (2:121; 1:818)

Charlus's "obsession with virility" (*"parti pris de virilité"* [2:121; 1:818]), here presented in a manner so hyperbolic as to verge on parody, is eventually, of course, discovered to be a different sort of preoccupation than we are at first given to understand. But his apparently unimpeachable masculinity signifies just that, up until the moment when the reader understands that it actually means its opposite; that it is in the end meant to be impeached. That moment may occur before the book is opened at all, if the reader has previously encountered references to Charlus's sexuality, or it may happen that the alert reader begins on her own to comprehend that things may not be as they seem, or enlightenment may occur only, as Proust evidently intended, at the beginning of *Sodome et Gomorrhe,* along with the hero's own dawning realization. In any case, whether rereading takes place alongside initial reading or subsequently, it is both written into the pre-revelation appearances of Charlus and external to them in the sense that they are meant to be read "straight," as it were, before being accorded their full import as a performance of straightness. The text imposes a sort of double vision on the rereader, equipping her *a posteriori* with 3-D glasses.

Where Gomorrah is concerned, however, rereading is to a much greater extent internally enforced, that is, built into each successive representation. Once a woman is suspected of Sapphic inclinations, the representation of her character and actions immediately becomes double. Thus the depiction of Mlle Vinteuil, half of the lesbian couple whose association with Albertine later gives the hero cause for both dismay and rereading, is from the start, early in the first section, that of two differently gendered individuals coexisting in the same body.

Charlus, in many ways a mercurial character, in the matter of gender consistently wields his apparent virility as a shield to protect and conceal his essential femininity. Mlle Vinteuil is in contrast essentially and visibly double, as though, the narrator tells us, she contained at once an affably rough boy and his sensitive, blushing sister (1:112–13; 1:122–23). She does not need to be reread over the course of time and volumes, because her self-contradiction is simultaneous rather than successive.

Mlle Vinteuil does, however, inadvertently provide the occasion for what surely constitutes the novel's most extensive and obsessive rereading, in the form of the hero's endless and ultimately futile attempts to assign a definitive sexual valence to Albertine. Like Odette, the future Mme Swann and supposed mistress of Charlus, and unlike Mlle Vinteuil, Albertine does not appear to be double but multiple. Both she and Odette are assumed to be exclusively heterosexual until it is suggested otherwise, at which point, in each case, a dizzying cycle of rereading commences. Because Albertine is depicted as unreadable from the outset, she resists all efforts at rereading; unlike Charlus, never having been seen as any one thing, she can never be proven to be something else. Of course, the hero's readings and rereadings of Charlus and of Albertine differ greatly not only in terms of the former's eventual transparency as opposed to the latter's enduring opacity, but also by virtue of their distinct functions in the narrative that are at least in part responsible for that difference. Charlus is the paradigmatic Sodomite, and for all his idiosyncracies, representative of a taxonomic classification; Albertine, the unique and obscure object of desire.

Chiefly for this reason, the novel's "Gomorrhean" characters are portrayed in ways that differ sharply from Proust's depiction of Sodom. Unlike Charlus and his cohorts, most of the women whose tastes appear to include other women figure as objects of the hero's (or of Swann's) desire, rather than sociological enquiry. As such, they cannot yield their secrets to the voyeuristic eye—even in the early scene in which the young hero spies on Mlle Vinteuil and her friend, the shutters are closed in his face at the crucial moment (1:161; 1:178)—because desire is precisely what blocks both reading and rereading in the *Recherche*. Nor, logically, can they be revealed upon rereading as inherently masculine as Charlus is reread as inherently feminine, as that would, following the Proustian theory of inversion, imply femininity on the part of any man desiring them.

The affair between Swann and Odette detailed in "Un Amour de Swann," the second section of *Du Côté de chez Swann,* serves as a template for the hero's subsequent adventures with Albertine, and Odette prefigures her successor in various particulars, including that of putatively ambiguous sexuality. This is one of the many ways in which Proust inscribes rereading into his text: much of what occurs in the later volumes necessarily reads as an expanded variation on themes already lengthily outlined in the first sections of the book.

Even before he encounters Albertine, moreover, the hero rehearses for what occurs between them by staging an adolescent version of the Swann-Odette story with himself in the title role and the daughter of their union, Gilberte Swann, assuming the function her mother had previously filled. (To cap it all off, at the very end of the novel, after many years have passed, the duc de Guermantes has conceived a passion for one Mme de Forcheville that recalls the hero's for Albertine just as the latter repeated Swann's for Odette; all this would be unremarkable enough were Mme de Forcheville not Odette herself, having now been widowed and remarried and surely no spring chicken [see 4.593; 3.1,068–69]). Indeed the rather anomalous insertion into the first volume of "Un Amour de Swann," which breaks with narrative chronology in order to give an account of events that occurred years before the hero's birth, serves chiefly to suffuse the later volumes with a flavor of predetermination. It is as though the entire rest of the book were a vast rereading of "Un Amour de Swann," and Proust had set out to illustrate in fictional form Nietzsche's theory of eternal recurrence.

While Odette anticipates Albertine, and while both are suspected of extracurricular Sapphism, the depiction of Albertine blocks rereading, and her character remains opaque; Odette's does not. This is in part because Swann eventually falls out of love with Odette (although he does not escape marrying her), whereas Albertine dies while the hero is still obsessed with her, so that the cycle of rereading might continue in futile perpetuity were he not in the end to achieve deliverance in the writing of his book. The difference between the relative transparency—the translucence—of Odette's desires and Albertine's continued, indeed posthumous, capacity to elude erotic definition is also, though, to a great extent concomitant with the difference between first- and third-person narration. "Un Amour de Swann" is anomalous not only in its violation of narrative continuity, but also in that it reads like a small, nineteenth-century novel implanted in the middle of the first volume. Using a Proustian version of Flaubert's free indirect style, the narrator almost entirely effaces himself in presenting what occurs. As per Flaubertian method, events are seen chiefly from the point of view of the central character, Swann, with occasional excursions into the minds of others, notably Odette.

Leaving aside the question of how the narrator can possibly (that is, verisimilarly) relate conversations, much less thoughts, that occurred before his own birth, we should note that the third-person, semi-omniscient narrative used in this section accounts to a large extent for Odette's greater (re)readability than Albertine's. Because he is relating not his own but someone else's love story, however many parallels the reader is eventually invited to draw between the two, and because he borrows for the occasion the device of free indirect style, Proust's narrator is able in "Un Amour de Swann" to have, and to afford the reader, access to Odette's interiority in a way that is necessarily impossible in terms of Albertine. This impossibility is a function both of narrative convention—as a first-person narrator of his own story he cannot after all display an omniscient knowledge of the thoughts and motivations of others, though he often does just that when dealing with peripheral characters—and of the laws of Proustian desire. Ultimately Albertine resists both reading and reread-ing, despite all the hero's efforts, specifically because she represents what he most wants to comprehend, the text he most urgently needs to decipher.

Or so he thinks, and so he leads us to believe. At the end of the novel, however, we are invited to reread Albertine once again, this time definitively. She is finally presented as having been a mere lure, a temptation rather along the lines of what befalls St. Anthony in the desert, and the hero's obsessive desire for her as an erotic and epistemological way station on the road to his eventual salvation in art and transformation into the narrator of the book we are reading and which he is finally prepared to write.

One of the elements of his epiphanic realization at the end of *Le Temps retrouvé* involves, as I have mentioned, the rereading of *François le Champi,* the book the hero's mother had originally read to him in one of the novel's first and most famous scenes. Rather than an actual rereading, though, what takes place is the hero's coming across a copy of George Sand's novel in the prince de Guermantes's library. In the initial "goodnight-kiss" scene, the hero's mother reads *François le Champi* aloud in an effort to lull him to sleep. This marks the hero's first encounter with a "real novel" (1:41; 1:44). The strangeness of the experience is heightened by the fact that his mother expurgates the narrative, leaving out the love scenes. Several aspects of this bear further scrutiny. First, *François le Champi* tells the story of the love that develops between an orphaned boy and his adoptive mother, a relation that begins as innocent familial passion and ends in marriage between the two characters. Therefore, as many commentators have pointed out, this book acts as a *mise-en-abyme* representation of the oedipal desire that quite clearly drives the hero in "Combray" and motivates the insomnia that leads to its reading during the night in question. Sand's novel, moreover, which disclaims its incestuous theme, contains no love scenes to speak of, certainly nothing before its very ending that could be deemed worthy of censorship by the most vigilant reader. *François le Champi* skirts the suggestion of immorality and thus may be considered suitable for reading to a child, precisely by avoiding the very sort of scene attributed to it in the *Recherche.* Proust, or his narrator, has invented the steamy passages of oedipal love that the mother is obliged to censor.

Because of his mother's scrupulous rereading that becomes a mis-reading, the hero does not quite understand what *François le Champi* is all about, and this produces in him a sense of "profound mystery" (1:41; 1:44–45). The book's incestuous overtones are never discussed; in question is simply its comprehensibility. We never actually witness the hero's own corrective rereading of Sand's novel, only his initial wonderment at the mysteries it seems to hold as a result of his mother's bowdlerization (again, of nonexistent scenes).

In the passage cited at the beginning of this essay, Jean Cocteau rereads the *Recherche* and describes his experience of having been read to from the work-in-progress. Proust "made it very difficult to follow him," Cocteau reports, by interrupting his own reading with hysterical self-deprecating laughter and cries of "It's too silly!" The author further, it will be remembered, skipped passages, elements that wouldn't be explained until *Sodome et Gomorrhe* and thus that contained *in ovo* stories of same-sex love. The anecdote Cocteau relates places him in the position of Proust's young hero being read to by his mother, receiving a strangely adulterated, pre-reread version of the text. Both are forced to "reread" in advance the passages that render the plot incomprehensible, real or imagined love scenes that by their very suppression inevitably conjure up images of a seduction that is mirrored, and indeed reenacted, in the act of suppressing them.

The passage in which the mother reads *François le Champi* to the young hero has pride of place in the *Recherche,* and it is crucial to any understanding of the book as a whole. By the same token, however, this first scene of being read to calls into question the very notion of "the book as a whole." The integrity of the *Recherche,* as Cocteau's anecdote illustrates, paradoxically depends on the partial incomprehensibility of any first reading. The book does not become a whole until it is reread, and indeed, as Roland Barthes notes, it yields a different text upon each subsequent rereading. The withholding of textual information—whether in the form of missing passages or incoherently supplementary ones—operates as seduction, enticing the rereader to active participation in the production of the text. In this respect Proust's novel bridges Barthes's categories of *texte de plaisir* and *texte de jouissance,* offering us a textual pleasure that leads to endless consummation in the act of rereading.

Notes

1. Although Barthes uses these terms in slippery ways, and rigid definitions are difficult to establish, the distinction is roughly as follows:
   the *texte de plaisir* or readerly text corresponds approximately to
   the nineteenth-century model of reader-friendly, plot-driven narrative
   characterized by closure and coherence, as opposed to the *texte de
   jouissance* or writerly text, an impossible ideal that impedes passive
   reception, forcing the reader to collaborate in the production of meaning.
2. Subsequent citations of this work are accompanied by volume and page
   references to the French and English editions respectively.

3. Many studies have been undertaken on the problems of time and Proustian narration. See, for example, Gérard Genette's essays on Proust in *Figures I* and *Figures III.*

4. See Proust's letter to Henri Ghéon in Proust, *Correspondance* 13:25–26.

Works Cited

Barthes, Roland. *The Pleasure of the Text.* Trans. Richard Miller. New York: Farrar, Straus and Giroux, 1975.

Cocteau, Jean. *Past Tense: The Cocteau Diaries.* Trans. Richard Howard. Vol. 1. New York: Harcourt Brace Jovanovich, 1987.

Genette, Gérard. *Figures I.* Paris: Seuil, 1966.

———. *Figures III.* Paris: Seuil, 1972.

Proust, Marcel. À la recherche du temps perdu. 4 vols. Paris: Gallimard, 1987–89.

———. *Correspondance.* 19 vols. Ed. Philip Kolb. Paris: Plon, 1970–91.

———. *Remembrance of Things Past.* 3 vols. Trans. C. K. Scott Moncrieff and Terence Kilmartin. New York: Random House, 1981.

Rivers, J. E. *Proust and the Art of Love.* New York: Columbia UP, 1980.

12

Gertrude Stein and Disjunctive (Re)reading

Juliana Spahr

Those who like to read books over and over get continuously this
sensation of the excitement as if it were a pleasant distant thunder that
rolls and rolls and the more it rolls well the further it rolls the
pleasanter until it does not roll any more.
Gertrude Stein, *Lectures in America*

Gertrude Stein wrote "Rose is a rose is a rose is a rose" and it is, despite her productivity, perhaps the line by which her work is best remembered (*Geography and Plays* 187).[1] Stein and Toklas openly admit to a behind-the-scenes orchestration of the phrase. They put it on plates, on stationery, on the cover of *The Autobiography of Alice B. Toklas,* and, it is rumored, even painted it above their bed.[2] In Stein's time this phrase was popular enough that the *New Yorker* ran a cartoon that has a beleaguered customs official deciphering Stein's customs form. The punch line: "It begins like this: 'gertrude says four hats is a hat is a hat.' What the hell can you make out of a declaration like that, chief?"[3]

Undeniably, the phrase has the catchiness and repetition of a pop song's refrain. And undeniably this is partially responsible for the way it has slowly seeped into popular consciousness. Quality Paperback Books based a campaign around this phrase a few years ago that used the phrase "a book is a book is a book" to illustrate their "three books for three dollars" deal. Even now, newspapers love the phrase. It is not unusual to read something like "evidence is evidence is evidence" in the coverage of a court trial (only in these uses its meaning is often contrary to Stein's intent, and the phrase is used to speak of how the evidence will convict the criminal rather than of the multiplicity of evidence). I saw it once in an English-language newspaper in South Korea as "rose is a rose is chaos," which has an inescapable and wonderful truth to it.

Despite this, little attention has been paid critically to the why and the how of this phrase. It is not that nobody discusses it, just that few linger on it. It often gets the cursory notice as to how the repetition of the word "rose" forces readers to read the word as verb, subject, and proper name, to attend the puns "Eros," "arose," "arrows," "rows," and other meanings.[4] And there is something to those who point to the phrase's mobility of meaning for some of its popular appeal. But there is, I want to suggest, something in this phrase beyond its mere catchiness. What often gets missed in all this libidinal play with meaning is how the phrase gains its mobility of meaning only as the "rose" is read again and again and then again. The power of this phrase is that it forces its readers immediately into rereading and demonstrates the necessary closeness between reading and rereading.

Although I use Stein's work as the terrain on which this article travels, my interest here is with the larger concern of rereading. More specifically, I examine how rereading can reevaluate or redirect the way we think about how humans interact with written words and how this interaction is manifested in literary works. Reading by itself is a wonderfully complex act. The reader must consistently translate and make the mark on the paper into the phonetic sound, connect it to other sounds to form a word, a sentence, a paragraph, a thought. It is fraught with interruption: thoughts cannot help but intrude from outside, connect, leave; a dog might bark down the street; the television from the next room might intrude. This makes reading more resemble a John Ashbery poem than the tight linear line we associate with narrative's conventions. In this vein, Michael Taussig notes that reading is an act bound up with "excesses of interpretation" (x). It is these very excesses of interpretation which excite me, and I am further interested in what happens when rereading is added to these excesses, for it is rereading that devotedly pursues diversionary ways of reading, its meta-awareness, its rambling and gathering.

My interest in rereading is not without motivation. For when I consider the question of what we need from reading, my answer tends to utopian ideals of conversation, shifts of thinking's conventions, exchanges of ideas. Reading has a complex social role. It is one of the most important ways humans take in knowledge, learn, and go about the business of what Stein could call, with her fondness for gerunds, being human. Without a reading that pursues ideals, all this is at risk. Without pursuing reading's renewal through acts like rereading, we hazard no longer thinking of ourselves as doers, as shifters of thought patterns. My insistence on utopianism here is willfully naïve. But also realize that when I use the word *naïve* here I am not urging an end to complexities of thought; rather I am urging that we begin our thinking with a faith that utopia is possible and that this faith is a necessity to begin thinking complexly about reading. In an academic and cultural moment that is unwilling to consider utopias or idealizations of any sort, it is only by taking on this naïveté that we can begin to even talk about the possibility of a reading adequate to or complicated enough for the intricate times in which we live.

Much of the work by Stein that I examine in this article is disjunctive.[5] Stein uses a range of disjunctive techniques to challenge patterns of syntax: repetition, puns or nonsense, excessive line breaks or long convoluted sentences, fractured or joined or repeated words. The intent here is reconnection; a desire for freshness.[6] The insistence that readers reread is, unlike a Dadaist destructive aesthetic, to startle readers out of the conventional flows of meaning and to show other possibilities. Stein's work shifts emphasis away from the single, inherent meaning and toward the choices and possibilities of meaning that, to some extent, are encountered by any rereader of her works. Her works are built around moments where readers take active roles in their relationship with the work. These works do not emphasize community but rather that which makes community work: communication. It is in this continual return to words (rather than an avant-garde breaking off) that the transgressive possibilities of rereading are evident. Disjunctive works allow readers to connect with multiple meanings and thus to recognize multiple strategies of response.

In this context, the disjunctive work provides a middle ground between the well-worn theories of resistance (which come out of cultural studies, where readers are active responders to works) or reification (which come out of the Frankfurt school, where readers' responses are appropriated by larger cultural powers). We need to consider both the work and the ways it constrains or empowers readers as much as the liberties readers take with works. My desire here is not to abandon formalism's attention to textual structure (at the expense of readers) nor to abandon post-structuralism's attention to the role of readers (at the expense of the text). I want instead textuality complicated by readers and readers complicated by textuality. I like to think of Stein's works as using rereading to encourage a sort of anarchy—not the sort the Sex Pistols called for where all the rules be abandoned in the name of chaos—but rather one where the work allows the reader self-governance and autonomy, where the reading act is given as much authority as the authoring act. The reference here is to a form of self-governing that resembles Peter Kropotkin's territorial and functional decentralization.

In proposing this sort of anti-authoritarian, nonconformist reader, I have drawn on Matei Calinescu's theories of (re)reading. In *Rereading,* Calinescu proposes to switch attention from reading to rereading, or, as he writes, he occasionally uses "what might look like an ortho-graphic oddity or mannerist affection: the word (re)reading" (xi). A theory of (re)reading has within it the possibility of explaining both the attraction of and the necessity for disjunctive works. Although Ca-linescu does not spend much time on disjunctive works in *Rereading,* his turn to (re)reading and his examination of its "vertical or circular, intratextual and intertextual" methods provide a way to approach works written so as to challenge certain norms or assumptions of readability (12). (Re)reading contains within it a self-aware flaunting of the way any act of reading invokes the act of repetition, the way any work contains within it residue from other works, the way any work requires some sort of rethinking of our previous experience. This interconnection, the basis of studies of intertextuality, is no new news. Calinescu's turn to (re)reading, however, is useful in that it presents a model for nonlinear, hypertextual, reformative ways of reading and thinking. As he writes: "Like the notion of first reading, that of rereading is in large part a theoretical construct, a hypothetical model meant to help us get a better grasp of certain experiences with which we are familiar (we actually reread much more often than we suspect) but of which we are usually unself-conscious" (8). As such, it provides a provocative way of thinking about the way certain types of writing exacerbate (re)reading and deny the possibility of an innocent, first reading.

Stein pulls a lot of tricks out of her bag in pursuit of disjunction. As such her work is an ideal place to examine the intrusions of and on (re)reading. Her work is constructed so as to be extreme: extremely repetitive ("Business in Baltimore"), extremely fractured (*Tender Buttons*), and extremely lengthy (*The Making of Americans*). And, as her rose phrase shows, her works are built so as to encourage the repeated exposure of (re)reading. Stein herself gives a pragmatic explanation of the experiential nature of (re)reading. In *The Geographical History of America,* she tells of getting her hair cut one afternoon and having to take her glasses off, despite the fact that she is reading. In this passage, Stein writes of reading as something that becomes pleasurable when one has one's glasses off and uses them as a magnifying glass to enlarge and distort each individual word:

> reading word by word makes the writing that is not anything be something.
> Very regrettable but very true.
> So that shows to you that a whole thing is not interesting because as a whole well as a whole there has to be remembering and forgetting, but one at a time, oh one at a time is something oh yes definitely something. (115)

When Stein speaks of reading "one at a time" she speaks not only of her interest in the distorted detail and the disjunctive connections between words, but also in (re)reading. The relationship between "one at a time" and (re)reading is literalized in "An Instant Answer or a Hundred Prominent Men," where Stein writes:

> I tell their names because in this way I know that one and

one and one and one and one and one and one and one
and one and one and one and one and one and one and
one and one and one and one and one and one and one
and one and one and one and one and one and one and
one and one and one and one and one and one and one
and one and one and one and one and one and one and
one and one and one and one and one and one and one
and one and one and one and one and one and one and
one and one and one and one and one and one and one
and one and one and one and one and one and one and
one and one and one and one and one and one and one
and one and one and one and one and one and one and
one and one make a hundred. (150–51)

Stein uses several other similar metaphors throughout her writing that make the connection between "one at a time" and (re)reading a little clearer. In *The Autobiography of Alice B. Toklas,* Stein (in Toklas's voice) compares the act of reading to that of proofreading or dusting: "I always say that you cannot tell what a picture really is or what an object really is until you dust it every day and you cannot tell what a book is until you type it or proof-read it" (130). Reading as a duster or a typist similarly means reading one word or letter at a time and also illustrates Stein's interest in (re)reading's necessary repetition. Reading for the detail without the whole is, like the glasses, a refiguring of the gaze. As Stein is well aware, reading is an act complicated by the gaze of the eye on the book. In modern western cultures, the eye is always interrupted as it arrives at the end of a line, then quickly must turn back to the left to begin reading again. Her writing continually pursues this fractured gaze of reading as it sets up obstacles to distance readers from the easy conventions of reading. Her work also is in many ways constructed so as to challenge the conventions of what is "readable," all the while demanding that it be read. What Stein's work adds to theories of reading is a glorification of all those moments of (re)reading that many theorists filter out as irrelevant or uncommon or mistaken. The question here shifts from one that asks what the world looks like and how it should be represented by the author to one that requires the work to ask readers to be engaged in the question of how to represent it and to bring in their own engagements. I like to see Stein's theories here as not simply registering the difference of her writing but as a concern for how others experience it and a cultivation of their differences. And I also think it is important not to overlook who Stein's "ideal" readers are here: dusters, typists; women basically. Her feminism, always a subject of some controversy and doubt, resonates in this passage not as essentialism but rather as a revision of women's domestic space and the repetitive task. The metaphor is interesting here, for it clarifies reading's consequences, its potential to overlook a detail, to go too quickly. It is reading that misses the fragility of the ornament or cannot see the error but it is (re)reading that allows sight. What is provocative here is that while Stein's work is in many ways an aesthetic of brashness, of knocking you over the head with obviousness, to understand it requires caresses of consciousness.

Some (re)readings:

Different compositional strategies produce different sorts of reading practices. The rich mixed-genre collage of Robert Duncan's "Poem Beginning With a Line By Pindar" takes readers to a different place than the sleek minimalist economy of Robert Creeley's homage to Duncan in "The Door." Readers of works inlaid with symbol and metaphor travel to different worlds than those reading a confessional rhetoric of subjectivity and honesty. Consequently the techniques of disjunctive writing take one more easily to (re)reading than what is considered conventional.

Stein uses many different formal techniques of disjunction to provoke (re)reading, and I want to give examples of a few here. The one that she pursues most is repetition. She uses it with a dedication not previously seen in the Western literary tradition. Her use of repetition is clearly not the domesticated and controlled repetition of traditional forms such as the repetition of rhyme in the sonnet, the repetition of the last word in the sestina, the repetition and slight variation of a line in the rondeau. In contrast, Stein creates a barrage of repetitive text, at times so extreme that whole pages of patterns of repetition with very slight variation appear.

An example of Stein's interest in repetition as a compositional technique is her 1927 "Patriarchal Poetry." While undeniably one of Stein's major works, it has had a difficult reception.[7] But it has been even more common for critics to ignore the piece altogether. While its title might make it the place to begin a feminist reading of Stein, its repetitive form has made it difficult to fit within feminist interpretative frames. The sentences, despite the suggestive title, refuse theoretical templates. What "Patriarchal Poetry" suggests instead is the message of an interpretative freedom, or, as Stein repeats over and over: "Let her be to be to be to be let her be to be to be let her to be let her to be let her be to be" (*Bee Time Vine* 268).[8]

As what is mastery and what is authority are no longer clear when questions of a reader come into play, what is "patriarchal" in Stein's "Patriarchal Poetry" is similarly not clear. "Patriarchal Poetry" radically challenges the politics of canonicity as it raises a series of difficult questions for its readers. Is this work, for instance, a mimicry of the patriarchal poetic tradition, which is full of repetition, of repeated forms, metaphors, similes; or is it an escape from the poetry of patriarchy, a space where words play freely with each other; or is it both, a parody in which Stein wants to treat the words of patriarchy as she does nouns, to "refuse them by using them"? These questions haunt much of Stein's work in one form or another. Stein uses moments of heavily repetitive diction not to induce meaninglessness but rather to expose the workings of meaning. As a compositional strategy, repetition forces the reader to be constantly (re)reading and thus aware of and examining how language works and walks hand in hand with power. As the rose phrase also makes clear, repetition in Stein's work is about letting go, a denial that mastery or authority are even possible as readers become aware of changing meanings each time the word reappears.

Yet whether "Patriarchal Poetry" is mimicry, escape, or a mutant both, the poem never, in Marianne DeKoven's words, "defies reading" (128). Rather, it becomes all the more readable for its extremes. The refusal, the inapplicability of critical frameworks to construct a narrative, is the freedom of this work. What is required, however, to read a work like "Patriarchal Poetry" is to move from reading, often an act of clarification, to (re)reading, an act that gives readers a series of meaning choices.

By reformulating what might be considered linear, nonrepetitive narratives, this work pursues a multiple displacement of authorities.

The authority of gender narratives, for example, is twisted in this excerpt from a section called "A Sonnet":

> To the wife of my bosom
> All happiness from everything
> And her husband.
> May he be good and considerate
> Gay and cheerful and restful.
> And make her the best wife
> In the world
> The happiest and the most content
> With reason. (272)

In this passage, what starts out as a poem directed to a wife by an assumed husband turns into a poem which wishes the wife either distance from or happiness from her husband. The poem pursues gender ambiguity by not being clear about whether to read it as one which wishes that the husband make her "the best wife" or not. More important, this ambiguity is obvious only when one (re)reads or reads the piece in more than one way. To just read here is very literally to misread. What I like about this sonnet is that it appears in the middle of a piece that is so relentless that it almost forces one to call it only, and without subtlety of reading, disjunctive. But the sonnet throws readers out of that mode and shows Stein's poetic intelligence, the strategies of her refusals. It trips readers with its sudden coherence, its easy charm. It also points to how both the disjunctive and the not-so-disjunctive have something to say about (re)reading.

Many of Stein's other techniques similarly use disjunction to provoke (re)reading. Often words are cut, fractured into parts and left for the reader to pick up the pieces. As has often been noted, Stein is constantly fracturing Toklas's name into syllables like "Ada," "a less," "alas," or "alias." Similarly, in a piece called "Carry," she spaces out or reduces the word to its letters to direct attention to the parts of words:

> Fed in an f e d this makes a color sure.
> Fed in fed makes a pleasant shoulder with it.
> Cup back, cup back the swing, cup back in swing. To
> rent. To makes u. To makes u so glass. Rest. less.

> Rest less, rest less in stephens regular hand book, rest
> less that makes a curve a curve has v, v is c that is to
> say rest has not t, not in tea, not in t. Rest has in s s.
> (*Bee Time Vine* 41)

Like the fractured words of "Carry," in "In" words are split in half or
sections are added on to words:

> (I) Was. Cream
> Pear——ery.
> Cut——ery
> Slice ear——ie
> A creamerie. (44)

In these two passages, the reader is left with the question of how to
read. There is no indication of what, if anything, should be created
out of the words. One can, for instance, add an "l" to "Cut——ery" to
make "cutlery" and create the knife that would cut the word. But the
reference the fractured word makes is multiple.

Unconventional line breaks, which insert a pause or a silence after
each word to draw attention away from the flow of reading, are another
sort of disjunctive device, one popularly used by modernists such as
E. E. Cummings and James Joyce. Here is a passage from "No":

> Left.
> Left.
> Pretty.
> I
> had
> pretty
> a
> good
> pretty
> like if
> room
> pretty
> all
> and
> I fire

> chairs
> pretty
> silver
> good
> left. (*As Fine as Melanctha* 35)

The disruptive nature of the passage is further enhanced by the context of the piece, in which a military marching song ("I had a good wife and she left, right, left," which itself uses a disruptive technique by doubling the meaning of "left") is very literally torn apart.

At other times, readers are encouraged to construct their own reading by combining words. In this passage from *Tender Buttons,* Stein mocks the act of creation in a series of puns that the reader creates:

> Pain soup, suppose it is question, suppose it is butter, real is, real is only, only excreate, only excreate a no since.
>
> A no, a no since, a no since when, a no since when since, a no since when since a no since when since, a no since, a no since when since, a no since, a no, a no since a no since, a no since, a no since. (58)

Here the possibilities and necessities of (re)reading are especially evident. A word like "excreate" appears to be only bordering on sense, but upon (re)reading the obvious puns of "excretion" and "creation" (and a possible negative of something like x-creation) become clear. "A no since" similarly makes little sense unless (re)read for the nuances of "nonsense" and "innocence."

Similarly, punning is another often used disjunctive device. In this passage, from one of Stein's books for children, a first reader, the puns are numerous:

> So, now sew and so, so is so and sew is not so, you see to know whether sew is so or so is sew how necessary it is so that is to read is so necessary so it is. And read just think of read if red is read, and read is read, you see when all is said, just now read just then read, do you see even if a little boy or a little girl is very well

> fed if they do not read how can they know whether red
> is read and read is red. How can they know, oh no how
> can they know. (*First Reader and Three Plays* 11)

Here the sight-centered pun registers the irregularity of Stein's verse: "read" (present tense) and "read" (the past tense) and "red"; "sew" and "so"; "no," "know," and "now." (I am especially delighted by Stein, who was a champion of child rights, calling this a "first reader.") When reading this passage the reader sees reading as a variable process. Through these visual puns, the meanings of words become mobile and mutating as the reader must stop, adjust content and context of the surrounding words, separate from any easy moment of reading, to (re)read to figure out the sound the word "read" makes.

My own readings here are indebted to and informed by critics of Stein who concentrate more on the formal construction of her work than on its symbolic coding. See, for example, Charles Bernstein's essay "Professing Stein/Stein Professing" and his and Bruce Andrews's edited collection of different statement readings in *The L=A=N=G=U=A=G=E Book* (195–207); Harriet Scott Chessman's emphasis on the dialogic possibilities and enactments in Stein's works; both Ulla Dydo's textual scholarship on the manuscripts and her attention to Stein's often forgotten works (see especially her *A Stein Reader* and "Landscape Is Not Grammar: Gertrude Stein in 1928"); Marjorie Perloff's reading of Stein's "poetics of indeterminacy" in poems like "Susie Asado" (*A Poetics of Indeterminacy: Rimbaud to Cage*); and Neil Schmitz's wandering, associative readings in *Of Huck and Alice: Humorous Writing in American Literature*. These critics have managed to avoid the trap of assigning too limited a meaning to Stein's work by beginning with the assumption that while Stein's work is at times difficult, it is a difficulty that is radically and, to use a Steinian adverb, lively engaged with a rethinking of language.

In direct contrast to these critics are those who feel that the blatancy, the extremes, of Stein's work makes it "difficult" or "unique" (or worse). To those who do so, my interest in the anarchic and utopian potential of Stein's work is somewhat counterintuitive.[9] But there is also an undeniably willful simplicity to her writing in the way the words in her work tend to be resolutely common, never obscure or archaic. As Perloff has noted, "Stein's fabled obscurity is, ironically enough, a function of what we might call her hyperrealism" (51). While this does not necessarily make her work completely clear for all readers, it does suggest an intent different from how much high modernist work is read. A useful comparison, for example, is how Stein uses the word "rose" to demonstrate her linguistic pyrotechnics, while James Joyce uses the word "bababadalgharaghtakamminarronnkonnbronntonner-ronntuonnthunntrovarrhounawnskawntoohoohoordenenthurnuk" to demonstrate his. I am choosing a deliberately extreme example, but as I point out to students when teaching Stein's work, it is always useful to remember that what makes Stein's work sound strange is not vocabulary. Her words are intentionally common, never esoteric. Instead it is the shift from reading to (re)reading that is necessary to make sense of much of Stein's work. I have had amazing experiences teaching Stein to students in introductory level composition courses. While the students' first response is often laughter, I have also found that, when encouraged and after the laughter dies down, they could produce fascinating, if at times bizarre, readings of Stein's work. It is necessary, however, to encourage them to (re)read, to bring their own concerns to the work. In one class I once had a reading of "Glazed Glitter"[10] (a section of *Tender Buttons*) arguing that it was about counterfeiting and the falseness of money (centered around the phase "[n]ickel, what is nickel" that begins the passage [9]); another that argued that it was about racial categories in twentieth-century America (this one reading "There can be no breakages in Japanese. That is no programme. That is no color. It was chosen yesterday . . ." [9] as a critique of racial constructions); another that it was a critique of cleanliness (this one reading " . . . very charming is that clean and cleansing. Certainly glittering is handsome and convincing" [9] as speaking to the superficial values of cleanliness). This is an exceptional range of readings for an introductory writing class, but it does illustrate what readers can do once they are encouraged to brush past their initial resistance.

These students' readings reflect the way Stein's work plays with the concepts of authoring and authority. Throughout her work, she challenges the definitional closeness between the words "author" and

"authority." For instance, she places the author behind the door in
Tender Buttons: "The author of all that is in there behind the door
and that is entering in the morning" (64). This same work urges the
translation of authority so as to show a choice: "Dance a clean dream
and an extravagant turn up, secure the steady rights and translate
more than translate the authority, show the choice and make no more
mistakes than yesterday" (76). At other moments she self-reflexively
explains how to escape this authority: "Largely additional and then
completely exploding is one way to deny authorisation" (*A Long Gay
Book* 98). In this play with the word "authority" Stein abandons her
own authorship and turns it over to readers, who when (re)reading
the work actively participate by constructing their own readings.
Her work does not deny authority but instead advocates its dispersal
(decentralization), a dispersal that occurs as readers (re)read. "Any
and every one is an authority," she writes in "A Little Novel" (*A
Novel of Thank You* 262). For Stein, the author is an actor: an agent or
facilitator. While the author cannot help but be a creator, the author
is just one of many—and also the one who remains behind the door
when the work leaves and becomes read. *The Autobiography of Alice
B. Toklas* is the literalization of this. Stein writes the work but it leaves
as Toklas's. Similarly, in *Everybody's Autobiography,* Stein hands the
autobiography over to everybody.

What Stein's work adds to the discussion of (re)reading is a
demonstration of what happens when the unself-conscious experience
of (re)reading is made blatantly conscious through intense repetition,
stuttering line breaks, fragmented words, and provocative punning.
Through disjunction her language is as open to those otherly cultured
or those who resist the normative cliché of acculturation as to those
dominantly cultured. It is not *unique,* but it is disjunctive. This disjunction is crucial. As Peter Quartermain has observed, Stein's language is
democratic, available to "any speaker or reader of English no matter
how 'alien' she or he may be, no matter how ignorant of cultural
matters and conventions" (142).[11] And this very commonness of the
(re)reading required by Stein's work makes her work provocative.
The sort of (re)reading required by her work is different from the sort
of rereading that Michael Riffaterre proposes in *Semiotics of Poetry.*
Riffaterre's theory is in many ways useful for its emphasis on how

"poetry expresses concepts and things by indirection" (1). He is a rare theorist of reading who is not scared of disjunction (the term he tends to use is "ungrammatical"). But he ends up arguing that such moments actually make reading even more restrictive: "The reader's freedom of interpretation is further limited because of the poem's saturation by the semantic and formal features of its matrix: in other words, continuity and unity, that is, the fact that the semiotic unit is the text itself, forbid the attention to wander, deny the opportunities for hermeneutic deviance that the multiple facets of mimesis offer" (165). In Riffaterre's model, readers are conservative forces who reassert the unity of the work as they continually seek relief "by getting away from the dubious words, back to safe reality (or to a social consensus as to reality)" (165). This safe reality is always to Riffaterre unstable, and readers end up seesawing between mimesis and distortion. What Stein's theories of reading do, in contrast, is deny the need or desire to seesaw, because in her work mimesis and distortion are so wonderfully mixed. (Re)reading, as she formulates it, is, after all, tied up with those most ordinary of acts: cutting one's hair, dusting, proofreading. . . . For this theory, what might be seen as extraordinary (Stein's disjunctive works) instead becomes the forms of (re)reading that are familiar and everyday.

The statements Stein makes about her writing in works like *Lectures in America* are often so down-to-earth they sound more like truisms than profound thinking. "Of course knowledge is what you know," she writes in "Plays" (*Lectures in America* 94), for example.[12] But this statement, which makes the most obvious of claims, also indicates Stein's anti-authoritarian approach to knowledge and to writing. This deceptively simple statement, with its profoundly anti-elitist theory of knowledge, is representative of much of Stein's work. Throughout her writing she refigures creation from an act that requires authority to an act that can be done by anybody or everybody or somebody (to use those all encompassing pronouns that Stein uses so often in her own writing). She writes, for example, of how: "Nouns are the name of anything and anything is named, that is what Adam and Eve did and if you like it is what anybody does" (*Lectures in America* 229). Here it is not merely, as it is in Genesis, that Adam names, but Eve joins him, and even she is not alone, as they are both pointedly joined by the nongendered "anybody," a common person, the reader. And her rhetoric, instead of being concerned with inventing new or preserving archaic words, presents, as she puns, the "intellectual recreation" of the work, meaning the possibilities for re/creating meaning anew while inspiring thought provoking play. She writes:

> Language is a real thing it is not imitation either of sounds or colors or emotions it is an intellectual recreation and there is no possible doubt about it and it is going to go on being that as long as humanity is anything. So everyone must stay with the language their language that has come to be spoken and written and which has in it all the history of its intellectual recreation. (238)

To stay with the language is not to make new but to call for revision, (re)reading's complement.

As Stein's argument with Robert Maynard Hutchins of the University of Chicago (told by Stein in *Everybody's Autobiography*) demonstrates, knowledge to Stein is something that one knows by one's self, something outside a "great books" curriculum.[13] After teaching Mortimer Alder's class, she tells Hutchins that the reason "they [the students] talk to me is that I am like them I do not know the answer" (213). In this argument Stein also sums up what I think is crucial about her work and about (re)reading in general: that it requires one to not know the answer but allows a number of answers, allows readers to bring their own answers, as they need them, to the work.

I realize that some might say there is good reason to avoid these moments; in fact, some might say that reading has gotten a little too free because of an unprecedented range of possible reading practices available to a critic in the mid-1990s. While I'm not oblivious to this and to some extent remain befuddled myself before the wealth of critical options before me, I don't see the turn to (re)reading and the works that provoke it as a battle between close reading and theory. Instead it seems that while disjunctive works require a theory of reading that is at once more anarchic, hypertextual, and nonlinear than most, they do not require the sacrifice of either textual meaning or readerly freedom.

While one of the major lessons of post-structuralism has been that meanings and texts are constructed by the reader, this construction does not take place on a blank slate. There can be a middle ground between New Criticism and post-structuralism: a text-based theory of reading with an attention to the individual reader's agency and resistances. While reader-oriented theory has been of undeniable influence to both my work and my teaching, I have found its distrust of readers's potential for anarchic rebellion and its lack of attention to (re)reading of limited applicability to disjunctive works such as Stein's. This fear of anarchy has led a number of critics, the very critics most concerned with resisting readerly restrictions, to conceive of the reader as one of them, a literary critic who categorizes and follows reading's conventions.[14] Through these models, the New Critical restrained and domesticated text is replaced with a restrained and domesticated reader: one who does not misread, does not read disruptively, and rarely (re)reads. This reader reads mainly narrative works (as earlier discussed, even though his work is not directly applicable to Stein's work, Riffaterre is an important exception here). Such a tendency is evident in the canon of works, for example, that theorists of reading have relied upon to illustrate their work, such as Roland Barthes's reading of Balzac's Sarrasine in *S/Z*,[15] Stanley Fish's reading of Milton's *Paradise Lost* in *Is There a Text in This Class?* or in *Surprised by Sin,* Paul de Man's reading of Proust's *Remembrance of Things Past* in *Allegories of Reading,* and Wolfgang Iser's readings of prose fiction in *The Implied Reader.* Devices such as narrative, and also plot, archaic reference, or symbolism can often require a conquering or restrictive attention, because they assume a nondisrupted relation between reader and work. The drug of narrative, for instance, works around the presumption that it is smooth, easy for a reader to slip into, control, and identify with.

While the character of the model readers that these critics present often varies, and requires more attention than I dedicate here, Fish's turn to a community-oriented model of reading provides a succinct example of the potential repressive possibilities of such models. When he asks the question "Is there a text in this class?" and answers no, there are only readers, he must, since he also fears the anarchy that could happen when there are only readers, propose readers who will not misbehave. Fish's introduction to *Is There a Text in This Class?* presents him wrestling constantly with the question of a reader's potential anarchy (which he calls "subjectivity") and continually sidestepping the issue until he reconceives "the reader in such a way as to eliminate the category of 'the subjective' altogether"(10). Instead of seeing reading's difficult relation to subjectivity as a crucial part of reading's power, he establishes the kinder, gentler authority of community. Readers may create the work, but not individually, only through their input into the interpretive community. While undeniably a community-oriented plurality, his model assumes the members of this community to be critics. This community, as Elizabeth Meese notes, establishes "a gender-based literary tribalism, that comes into play as a means of control"(7).

The issue here might be a larger one of convention or pedagogy than of obtuseness. While few might argue that the linear, narrative form is either literally linear or narrative, it is still hard to maintain that Stein's work is not difficult, even for her fans. This is, I think, because we are taught to read by a Dick and Jane narrative. Then we are taught to value what mimics this narrative; taught to ignore or filter out all those other moments of perceptual disjunction as confusing; taught not to think back, not to (re)read. But the crippling insistence that disjunction is difficult damages our ability to take advantage of (re)reading's possibility, its anarchic autonomy. Disjunctive work inverts literary tribalism, insists on crossed and mixed communities. Part of (re)reading, Stein's work makes clear, is a cutting away of convention, an abandoning of the Dick and Jane story that taught us to read, and an embracing of reading as something that transforms the everyday.

The common complaints about disjunctive works—that they are fragmented, that they lack a coherent position or theory or subjectivity—are also their strengths. These qualities are precisely what allow these works to challenge multiple relations of linguistic power. For instance, Bruce Andrews provides a tantalizing beginning of this conversation, "the writing (as reading) can account for the system & help put the social self in question. . . . And so the reading might solicit a different future: by getting distance on the sign & getting distance

on identity, on how they're produced: by rereading the reading that
a social status quo puts us through" (27). Through (re)reading, the
activity of reading—an activity often seen as secondary to writing or as
writing's first step—becomes a crucial turf, a place where one's vision
of the world and its relation to response is developed. What Stein does
is shift language's conventions and thus shift readers' understanding
of the world as they become themselves authors. This shift has within
it the possibility of seeing existing structures of linguistic power while
allowing one to imagine a response from somewhere else.

Disjunctive techniques are not only interruptive of received meaning. They also interrupt the hierarchies of grammar. Western languages
support and are supported by the mercantile tendencies of society, that
valorize whatever can be counted: the grammatical subject/object. The
subject of the sentence is always an object—a person, place, or thing—
and is given hierarchical priority. Subserviently, the verb gives action
to this subject. Its conjugation is dependent on the subject/object's
numerical quality, and the adjective bestows qualities on this subject.
These objects are represented in grammar as fixed, locatable, count-
able. Even uncountable subjects, abstract nouns such as "freedom"
or "love," appear to be quantitatively manageable in the sentence.
But, through disjunction, Stein's writing challenges the forces of
grammatical hierarchy. There is something here, Stein insists, as she
repeats to force (re)reading the small words, the connecting words of
language, into the excess of "Patriarchal Poetry":

> Never which when where to be sent to be sent to be sent
> to be never which when where never to be sent to be
> sent to be sent never which when where to be sent never
> to be sent never to be sent never which when where to
> be sent never to be sent never to be sent which when
> where never to be sent which when where never which
> when where never which to be sent never which when
> where to be sent never which when where to be sent
> which when where to be sent never to be sent never
> which when where to be sent never which when which
> when where to be sent never which when where never
> which when where which when where never to be sent
> which when where. (122)

This is a list of qualifiers—relative pronouns, adverbs, future passive verbs—all words that provide grammatical support and that function as slaves in a sentence's hierarchy. But in Stein's writing they become the stuff of the sentence, not its support.

When I speak of decentralized reading practices and of readers as authors I am talking about a form of response that resembles what has come to be called "resistance." "Resistance" and "subversion"[16] became catch phrases of literary studies in the late 1980s and early 1990s. In the current critical situation that surrounds the academy, these are difficult words. On the one hand much of the criticism that is called cultural studies fetishizes resistance by locating it in all sorts of acts, from nose rings to such direct political actions as the black power movement. On the other hand, there are those who deny resistance and point to large structures of power that co-opt any move toward independent response. Both positions have their seductions and their problems. The resistance school, despite its egalitarian pursuits, leans at moments toward what Meaghan Morris has called "banality" (3), reducing all action to resistance (and thus reducing resistance's value). The recuperation school, despite its necessary attention to structures of power, leans toward a vision of an equally banal world which allows no room for agency. And too many arguments end with the mere observation that something has been resisted or subverted, thus sidestepping the responsibility for assessing the politics and dynamics of these acts in a larger arena. A work can, after all, encourage the most minor of subversive acts from its readers only to keep them better in line.

Despite the relentless overuse of the word "resistance" in contemporary theoretical discussions, I am unwilling to abandon questions of agency and resistance in the encounter between reader and work. The commonsense response to such a critical dilemma is to realize that both sides are true in some ways, both false in others. Acknowledging an inherently active role for readers, one in which readers bring to the work their skills as (re)readers, requires a reevaluation, a complication, in the way we think about resistance. Looking to (re)reading, to make yet another argument about resistance, may be seen as just another example of the possible banality of cultural studies. But I want to argue that (re)reading is a place where we can learn to see outward. Disjunctive works have much to tell about the patterns, the limitations, and also the possibilities of thinking. (Re)reading is in some ways a terrifying invasion of reading's more engaging moments, those moments where one reads to escape the unpaid bills, the long, conversational excesses. This is what T. S. Eliot must have meant when he said that Stein's work "is precisely ominous" and "not good for one's mind" (595). And in our particular political moment there is the peril of being faced with too many choices, not too few. It is easy to understand why we would not want more, much less not value more. It is probably in response to the too-many-choices feeling that the business of literary criticism argues constantly for the superiority of one form of reading over another and rarely wants to examine works that leave the choices open for readers (themselves). But when something is declared not good for one's mind it is always worth thinking about what this might mean. Further, if feminist criticism has taught us anything with its relentless attention to Virginia Woolf's *A Room of One's Own,* it is that what is read matters. If, as Annette Kolodny (in her pivotal "Dancing through the Minefield" essay) has noted, *"as we are taught to read, what we engage are not texts but paradigms,"* then we need to revise our paradigms of reading so as to include these works which challenge the limitations of originality and form (10). So it is crucial to take the risks these works propose, risks that complicate and interest.

What we learn from Stein that we do not learn from many other writers is that for there to be a political art form that has relevance in today's culture of multiplicity, a culture defined by the media onslaught of mass cultural products of political ambiguity (the "Save the Earth" bumper sticker on cars that perpetuate the earth's death by exhaust; the politically vetted *Star Trek* and Bill Cosby shows; the intrusion of advertisement into traditionally nonmarket zones), this form must be one that is willing to give authority to readers. Works that encourage and enable (re)reading have a faith in the maligned and underrepresented diversions of intelligent readers, ones intelligent enough to deserve freedom. While it is perhaps naïvely utopian, it is also a radical and necessary politics. The cultivation of readerly resistance in Stein's works requires us to question what changes in perception, knowledge, and thinking occur through moments of textual encounter. What the disjunctive work crucially does for readers is shift the terms of the struggle and provide the ability to see (re)reading, to realize its position within existing structures, and to provide an example of a response from somewhere else. It is in this very space of loss of absolutes that the act of (re)reading distinguishes itself from the potential reification inherent within a first reading. And when reading Stein, one cannot avoid the responsibility of creating. The extreme exposure of the reading act combined with the insistence that readers do the difficult work of (re)reading adds a resolute questioning of authorial authority to the discussion of resistance.

The question then is whether this agency can be transformed into some other, more socially reformative mode of agency. I cannot answer this. I can provide no empirical, statistical evidence of a concrete social change stemming from the reading of a disjunctive work. Disjunctive works have also tended to be marginalized, seen (unfairly) as too difficult for our educational systems, too disruptive for relaxation, thus further complicating this issue. But I'm not willing to take W. H. Auden's "poetry makes nothing happen" as the end-all of this discussion (197). Instead, I want to put against this the ending of Charles Bernstein's *The Artifice of Absorption:*

> As writers—
> & everyone inscribes
> in the sense
> I mean here—
> we can
> try to intensify
> our relationships by considering
> how they work: are we putting
> each other to sleep
> or waking each other up;
> & what do we wake to? Does our writing stun
> or sting? We can try to
> bring our relationship with readers to
> fruition,
> that the site of reading become a fact of value. (65)

Notes

1. "Sacred Emily" in *Geography and Plays* is accepted as its first reference. The phrase does appear, however, in many works.
2. Stein, in Toklas's voice, writes: "It was he [Carl Van Vechten] who in one of his early books printed as a motto the device on Gertrude Stein's note-paper, a rose is a rose is a rose is a rose. Just recently she has had made for him by our local potter at the foot of the hill at Belley some plates in the yellow clay of the countryside and around the border is a rose is a rose is a rose is a rose and in the centre is to Carl" (*The Autobiography of Alice B. Toklas* 169). Edward Burns writes, "It was Toklas who selected the line as a motto to appear on Stein's stationery. Toklas also embroidered it on place mats, napkins, and handkerchiefs. The motto appears in a circular design, both with and without a rose in the center, and different colors—silver, blue, and red—were used in printing the motto" (24, n. 1). Stein also wrote this phrase into other works such as "Objects Lie on a Table," "As Fine as Melanctha," and *The World Is Round.* Rose is also a character in "Melanctha," in *The World Is Round,* and in "The Autobiography of Rose." See Mossberg for more discussion.
3. This is reproduced in Alice B. Toklas's *What is Remembered* 127.
4. Among those critics who have lingered on it are Harriet Scott Chessman, Barbara Clarke Mossberg, and Bob Perelman. In Chessman's reading: "What is important in this formulation is not the capacity of "rose" to represent, but the relationship between the author and the word. The noun becomes a palpable entity, invited and participating in a relationship of love" (81). Mossberg is less optimistic: "The sentence is a linguistic spider web in which the rose is not only the spider but the helpless, paralyzed fly; the intransitive verb cannot release the trapped 'rose' but only can confirm her fate—that is, her identity" (200). Bob Perelman argues that the phrase's popularity is indicative of how no one can read Stein. To him it indicates a legitimate lack of interest in what Stein's work is *actually* doing. In his telling, Stein has conned her readers into thinking there is something worthwhile about her work, yet all that remains is the trace of a popular usage of the rose phrase.
5. This is a term I've taken from Peter Quartermain's *Disjunctive Poetics.* He uses this term to group together Stein, Louis Zukofsky, Basil Bunting, Ezra Pound, Charles Reznikoff, Robert Creeley, Robert Duncan, Guy Davenport, and Susan Howe.
6. According to Thorton Wilder, Stein said: "Now listen! I'm no fool. I know that in daily life we don't go around saying 'is a . . . is a . . . is a. . . .' Yes, I'm no fool; but I think that in that line the rose is red for the first time in English poetry for a hundred years" (vi).
7. The intense repetition, evasion of easy meaning, and length of this poem have provoked critical ire such as Marianne DeKoven's remark

    that "[m]ost of 'Patriarchal Poetry' not only defies interpretation, it defies reading. In fact, Wendy Steiner's pejorative phrase 'militantly unintelligible' is an apt epithet for this extreme example of experimental writing as destruction of literature" (128).

8. David Galef briefly touches on this. He writes, "Some texts, moreover, enact re-reading within themselves. Gertrude Stein's repetitive syntax, in an attempt to disrupt the linear, chronological progression of narrative, has such an effect that the reader is re-reading even on first perusal. In a work such as 'Patriarchal Poetry,' for instance, the line 'Never to be what he said' occurs four times in succession (121). The thought-provoking process of repetition here forces us to re-examine the syntax, question the meaning, and search out nuances much in the way we do when re-reading" (40).

9. Bob Perelman's *The Trouble with Genius* presents the most recent and perhaps best argued elucidation of this position. He writes: "Despite her insistence that the meaning of her work was as obvious and immediate as the words of her explanations, her writing was obviously unusual and obscure" (150). My major problem with Perelman's argument is that he spends much more time complaining about Stein's interest and belief in the idea of genius (which might at times be ironic, it is hard to tell) than actually looking at Stein's work. *The Trouble with Genius* is more about how ideas get marketed and sold in the academy. A lot of Perelman's evidence of how readers cannot relate to Stein's or other authors' work tends towards assertion (and is rarely even backed up by anecdote from others' or his own reading experience).

10. "Glazed Glitter" in its entirety reads:

> Nickel, what is nickel, it is originally rid of a cover.
> The change in that is that red weakens an hour. The change has come. There is no search. But there is, there is that hope and that interpretation and sometime, surely any is unwelcome, sometime there is breath and there will be a sinecure and charming very charming is that clean and cleansing. Certainly glittering is handsome and convincing.
> There is no gratitude in mercy and in medicine. There can be no breakages in Japanese. That is no programme. That is no color chosen. It was chosen yesterday, that showed spitting and perhaps washing and polishing. It certainly showed no obligation and perhaps if borrowing is not natural there is some use in giving. (9)

11. Quartermain argues that Stein's unique linguistic techniques might be a result of an alienation from English during her childhood (her parents were German immigrants, and she herself lived in Germany in her early years, probably learning some German before she learned English).

He points to often ignored cultural concerns that inform experimental writing practices, such as the influence of immigration on American English and its alternative representations. He argues that "those millions of immigrants who crossed the Atlantic in the last quarter of the nineteenth century (and before) fled from Europe to escape what Americans had learned to define as its 'feudal' society in order to start again. With a new beginning came a new language, and a new but more often than not an intensely localised culture" (42). This argument provides a useful frame for any discussion of the political ramifications of an experimental American poetics. The alternative modernist line—which he locates in Stein, William Carlos Williams, Charles Reznikoff, and Louis Zukofsky—rather than preserving Western culture or language, reflects the increasingly diverse linguistic construction of American society because these writers either "learned English as their second (or third) language or grew up bilingual" (10). The important consequence of Quartermain's argument is his recognition that the literature that these writers produce opposes hierarchies of ordering. While I agree with Quartermain's observation that Stein's writing "demands very little acculturation of its readers," I do not think, as he continues, that "Stein deliberately excludes such cultural apparatus" or that her writing "is notoriously devoid of immediately identifiable reference" (41, 41, 8). Her work in *Three Lives* indicates this clearly. This argument is too close for comfort to complaints that Stein's work has no meaning. There is in Stein's work an engagement with language that is at times extreme and always one that recognizes language as active. Further, what is most interesting about Stein's linguistically extreme works is how clearly they demonstrate the impossibility of ever excluding the immensity of the "cultural apparatus." As Stein is well aware, a reader cannot help but bring whatever cultural knowledge s/he possesses into the reading of the poem. The genius of Stein's work is the way she embraces the allusive nature of the word in an attempt to free the word. Related to this is Charles Bernstein's recent work, such as "Poetics of the Americas," where he argues a connection between the alternative language practices of avant-garde or experimental poetries and that of ethnically inflected dialogic writing.

12. She must also be parodying and modifying Socrates' claim that he knows nothing except that he knows nothing.

13. For Stein's complaints about Chicago's "great books" program, see her discussion of an argument she had with Robert Maynard Hutchins, the president of the University of Chicago, and Mortimer Adler in *Everybody's Autobiography* (206).

14. Umberto Eco's "model reader," Wolfgang Iser's "implied reader," Michael Riffaterre's "super reader," Jonathan Culler's "ideal reader," and Stanley Fish's "community of readers" are all examples of this sleight of hand. See also Jane P. Tompkins's collection *Reader-*

Response Criticism: From Formalism to Post-Structuralism and Robert C. Holub's *Reception Theory: A Critical Introduction.*

15. An obvious and important complication of Barthes's theories in *S/Z* is his *The Pleasure of the Text,* where "Text means Tissue" and reading turns away from conquering and toward words like "pleasure" and "bliss" (64). Barthes's theories, despite his personal lack of interest in much alternative contemporary writing, have proven useful for many Stein critics, including Neil Schmitz and Harriet Scott Chessman, and they have certainly informed my own readings. But my work here is also in some ways opposed to the domestication of textual multiplicity that occurs in *The Pleasure of the Text.* Barthes, for example, writes of how "the text is never a 'dialogue': no risk of feint, of aggression, of blackmail, no rivalry of idiolects—the text establishes a sort of islet with the human—the common-relation" (16). My thesis is that Stein's work is important precisely because it is resolutely dialogic, full of aggression and the rivalry of idiolects.

16. The word "subversion" has been especially open to use when it comes to Stein's work. For instance, two critics who take very different critical positions use this word freely. Marianne DeKoven describes "the intentional subversiveness of Stein's experimental writing" in her reading of Stein's language as pre-symbolic (xxiv); Lisa Ruddick, who decodes *Tender Buttons* with a gnostic frame, writes of how "Stein's gnosticism, on the other hand, recreates from the Bible a subversive message about and for women" (10).

Works Cited

Andrews, Bruce. "Poetry as Explanation, Poetry as Praxis." *The Politics of Poetic Form: Poetry and Public Policy.* New York: Roof, 1990. 23–32.

Andrews, Bruce, and Charles Bernstein. *The L=A=N=G=U=A=G=E Book.* Carbondale: Southern Illinois UP, 1984.

Auden, W. H. "In Memory of W. B. Yeats." *Collected Poems.* Ed. Edward Mendelson. New York: Random House, 1976. 197–98.

Barthes, Roland. *The Pleasure of the Text.* Trans. Richard Miller. New York: Noonday Press, 1975.

Bernstein, Charles. *Artifice of Absorption.* Philadelphia: Paper Air, 1987.

———. "Poetics of the Americas." *Modernism/Modernity* 3.3 (1996): 1–23.

———. "Professing Stein/Stein Professing." *A Poetics.* Cambridge, MA: Harvard UP, 1992. 142–49.

Burns, Edward, ed. *The Letters of Gertrude Stein and Carl Van Vechten: Volume 1, 1913–1935.* New York: Columbia UP, 1986.

Calinescu, Matei. *Rereading.* New Haven: Yale UP, 1993.

Chessman, Harriet Scott. *"The Public Is Invited to Dance": Representation, the Body, and Dialogue in Gertrude Stein.* Stanford: Stanford UP, 1989.

Culler, Jonathan. *On Deconstruction: Theory and Criticism in the 1970's.* Ithaca: Cornell UP, 1982.

Davidson, Michael. "On Reading Stein." *The L=A=N=G=U=A=G=E Book.* Carbondale: Southern Illinois UP, 1984. 196–98.

DeKoven, Marianne. *A Different Language: Gertrude Stein's Experimental Writing.* Madison: U of Wisconsin P, 1983.

De Man, Paul. *Allegories of Reading: Figural Language in Rousseau, Nietzsche, Rilke, and Proust.* New Haven: Yale UP, 1979.

Dydo, Ulla. "Landscape is Not Grammar: Gertrude Stein in 1928." *Raritan* 7 (1987): 97–113.

———. *A Stein Reader.* Evanston: Northwestern UP, 1993.

Eco, Umberto. *The Role of the Reader: Explorations in the Semiotics of Texts.* Bloomington: Indiana UP, 1979.

Eliot, T. S. "Charleston, Hey! Hey!" *Nation and Athenaeum* 40 (29 Jan. 1927): 595.

Fish, Stanley Eugene. *Is There a Text in This Class?: The Authority of Interpretive Communities.* Cambridge, MA: Harvard UP, 1980.

———. *Surprised by Sin: The Reader in Paradise Lost.* Berkeley: U of California P, 1971.

Galef, David. "Second Thoughts: A Prolegomenon to Re-reading." *Reader* 31 (Spring 1994): 29–46.

Gilbert, Sandra M., and Susan Gubar. *No Man's Land: The Place of the Woman Writer in the Twentieth Century.* Vol. 2. New Haven: Yale UP, 1989.

Holub, Robert C. *Reception Theory: A Critical Introduction.* New York: Methuen, 1984.

Ingarden, Roman. *The Cognition of the Literary Work of Art.* Trans. Ruth Ann Crowley and Kenneth R. Olson. Evanston: Northwestern UP, 1973.

Iser, Wolfgang. *The Act of Reading: A Theory of Aesthetic Response.* Baltimore: Johns Hopkins UP, 1978.

———. *The Implied Reader: Patterns of Communication in Prose Fiction from Bunyan to Beckett.* Baltimore: Johns Hopkins UP, 1980.

Kolodny, Annette. "Dancing Through the Minefield: Some Observations on the Theory, Practice and Politics of a Feminist Literary Criticism." *Feminist Studies* 6 (1980): 1–25.

Long, Elizabeth. "Textual Interpretation as Collective Action." *The Ethnography of Reading.* Berkeley: U of California P, 1993. 180–211.

Meese, Elizabeth A. *Crossing the Double-Cross: the Practice of Feminist Criticism.* Chapel Hill: U of North Carolina P, 1986.

Morris, Meaghan. "Banality in Cultural Studies." *Discourse* 10.2 (1988). 3–29.

Mossberg, Barbara Clarke. "A Rose in Context: The Daughter Construct." *Historical Studies and Literary Criticism.* Madison: U of Wisconsin P, 1985. 199–225.

Perelman, Bob. *The Trouble with Genius: Reading Pound, Joyce, Stein, and Zukofsky.* Berkeley: U of California P, 1994.

Perloff, Marjorie. *A Poetics of Indeterminacy: Rimbaud to Cage.* Princeton: Princeton UP, 1981.

———. " 'Grammar in Use': Wittgenstein/Gertrude Stein/Marinetti." *South Central Review* 13 (1996): 35–62.

Quartermain, Peter. *Disjunctive Poetics: From Gertrude Stein and Louis Zukofsky to Susan Howe.* New York: Cambridge UP, 1992.

Riffaterre, Michael. *Semiotics of Poetry.* Bloomington: Indiana UP, 1978.

Ruddick, Lisa Cole. *Reading Gertrude Stein: Body, Text, Gnosis.* Ithaca: Cornell UP, 1990.

Schmitz, Neil. *Of Huck and Alice: Humorous Writing in American Literature.* Minneapolis: U of Minnesota P, 1983.

Stein, Gertrude. *As Fine as Melanctha.* New Haven: Yale UP, 1954.

———. *The Autobiography of Alice B. Toklas.* New York: Harcourt Brace, 1933.

———. *Bee Time Vine And Other Pieces* [1917–1927]. New Haven: Yale UP, 1953.

———. *Everybody's Autobiography.* New York: Random House, 1937.

———. *First Reader and Three Plays.* Dublin: Maurice Fridberg, 1946.

———. *The Geographical History of America; or, The Relation of Human Nature to the Human Mind.* New York: Random House, 1936.

———. "An Instant Answer or A Hundred Prominent Men." *Useful Knowledge.* Barrytown: Station Hill P, 1988. 144–61.

———. *Lectures in America.* Boston: Beacon Press, 1985.

———. "A Long Gay Book." *GMP: Matisse Picasso and Gertrude Stein with Two Shorter Stories.* Barton: Something Else Press, 1972. 13–116.

———. *A Novel of Thank You.* New Haven: Yale UP, 1958.

———. *Tender Buttons.* Los Angeles: Sun & Moon, 1990.

Stimpson, Catharine R. "Gertrude Stein and the Transposition of Gender." *The Poetics of Gender.* Ed. Nancy K. Miller. New York: Columbia UP, 1986. 1–18.

———. "The Mind, the Body, and Gertrude Stein." *Gertrude Stein: Modern Critical Views.* Ed. Harold Bloom. New York: Chelsea House, 1986. 131–44.

Taussig, Michael. *Mimesis and Alterity: A Particular History of the Senses.* New York: Routledge, 1993.

Toklas, Alice B. *What Is Remembered.* San Francisco: North Point Press, 1963.

Tompkins, Jane P., ed. *Reader-Response Criticism: From Formalism to Post-Structuralism.* Baltimore: Johns Hopkins UP, 1980.

Wilder, Thorton. "Introduction." *Four In America.* New Haven: Yale UP, 1947. v–xxvii.

13

Two Modes of Rereading in the Twentieth-Century Novel

Gregary J. Racz

Declaring the modernist novel written to be reread has been a critical commonplace for nearly a century, yet little scholarship exists linking modernist narrative techniques to the actual second-time reading process. This reluctance is simple to comprehend, since introducing the nebulous phenomenological categories and speculative conclusions inherent in subsequent acts of reading almost always serves to complicate the formalist niceties of other more "empirical" paradigms. In fact, the idea of an infinite series of rereadings exposes the prevailing tension within the conflicting definitions of modernist prose; i.e., whether, in their self-proclaimed status as artistic constructions and orderly substitutes for the transience and anomie of lived experience, modernist novels promulgate a text-centered poetics of literary meaning through a well wrought stylistic and structural design that nevertheless insists upon the inclusion of extratextual factors for interpretation. Put another way, the modernist novel's use of embedded structures of reiteration pleads for the reader's return to the text as the ultimate repository of literary signification that its formal features and often nonreferential language belie in their otherwise elitist "religio-aesthetic withdrawal from existential time into the eternal simultaneity of essential art" (William V. Spanos, qtd. in Wilde 19).

Modernist fiction, in its frequent reliance on spatial forms that both produce and are the products of linguistic redundancy, compensates in part for its attack on the unifiable totality of representation by integration through reflexive reference. These textual operations in the reader's mind take as their prompt repetitive features of the work that seem to unify the novel as a concrete verbal entity, while other notable aspects of content argue for the impossibility of a totalized textual recuperation. These topoi constitute by now a familiar taxonomy: limited, biased, or deficient point of view; gaps in chronology and story line; evident contradiction or semantic negation; "metalingual comment" and the like (Fokkema 17). Modernism's double movement is thus both duplicitous and paradoxical: while appearing to declare its aesthetic autonomy in the face of an increasingly disorderly reality, modernism simultaneously flaunts the irresolutions inherent in its fragmentary nature, stressing the importance of extratextual consider-ations in determining truth in narrative worlds. This dualism provides modernist novels with a singular textuality, confounding the surety of absolute interpretation while inviting readers to return continually to the text to bring about successive levels of interpretation.

The constant retroactive restructuring required by this kind of novel, prompted by the narrative redundancy that is partly a function of, as well as a counterpoise to, the limited perspectivism modernism exploits, inevitably leads to a version of first-time rereading that entices readers into believing they are rereading portions of narrative even during an initial perusal. This phenomenon reinforces the impres-sion that the modernist work's indeterminacy nevertheless constitutes a stable grid of signification to which readers may return at all times to check, reinforce, or revise the conclusions of earlier, provisional stages of interpretation. The modernist novel, therefore, simultaneously ar-gues against its status as a self-contained, text-centered entity, while ensuring the ultimate futility of a full comprehension.

André Gide's use of block repetition in *Les faux-monnayeurs* (1925, trans. *The Counterfeiters,* 1927) provides a clear example of modernism's double movement, since the repetition-as-rereading design the novel employs is at odds with its attempts at representing a unified fictional world. The imbrication in the novel not only gives the reader a sense of having reread substantial portions of the text on a first perusal, but also leaves the impression of spatial signification through the tangibility this redundancy supplies—one to which the reader may have endless recourse upon subsequent rereadings. *Les faux-*

monnayeurs recounts the visit of the novelist Édouard to his nephew Olivier Molinier, whose older brother Vincent wishes to break off his relationship with Laura Douviers, a married woman who believed she was dying when they met in a sanatorium. Not only does Édouard's diary pick up the story line of the preceding chapter with only a slight overlap, but the novel presents a block reiteration of this "micro-episode" (Bennett 406) in which Vincent jilts the pregnant Laura. That this incident is only one of many with this special forefronting serves to underscore the crucial relevance to the novel's structure that this technique entails. For the reader learns little that is new or integral to the plot in the subsequent page-long iterations of the lamentable situation of Laura Douviers, a character almost always presented embedded in the language or writings of other characters. Still, no fewer than three versions of Laura's abandonment appear in the work, the first from the perspective of Olivier as eavesdropper:

> —*Elle lui disait: "Vincent, mon amant, mon amour, ah! ne me quittez pas!"*
> —*Elle lui disait vous?*
> —*Oui. N'est-ce pas que c'est curieux?*
> —*Raconte encore.*
> —*"Vous n'avez plus le droit de m'abandonner à présent. Que voulez-vous que je devienne? Où voulez-vous que j'aille? Dites-moi quelque chose. Oh! parlez-moi." Et elle l'appelait de nouveau par son nom et répétait: "Mon amant, mon amant", d'une voix de plus en plus triste et de plus en plus basse. Et puis j'ai entendu un bruit (ils devaient être sur les marches)— un bruit comme de quelque chose qui tombe. Je pense qu'elle s'est jetée à genoux.*
> —*Et lui, il ne répondait rien?*
> —*Il a dû monter les dernières marches; j'ai entendu la porte de l'appartement qui se refermait. Et ensuite elle est restée longtemps, tout près, presque contre ma porte. Je l'entendais sangloter.*

> "She kept saying: 'Vincent, my love—my lover . . . Oh, don't leave me!'"
> "Did she say *you* to him and not *thou*?"

"Yes; isn't it odd?"

"Tell us some more."

" 'You have no right to desert me now. What is to become of me? Where am I to go? Say something to me! Oh, speak to me!' . . . And she called him again by his name, and went on repeating: 'My lover! My lover!' And her voice became sadder and sadder and lower and lower. And then I heard a noise (they must have been standing on the stairs), a noise like something falling. I think she must have flung herself on her knees."

"And didn't he answer anything? Nothing at all?"

"He must have gone up the last steps; I heard the door of the flat shut. And after that, she stayed a long time quite near—almost up against my door. I heard her sobbing." (36, trans. 30, 31)

A few pages later, the episode reappears from a position of narrative omniscience, and then a third time in Laura's letter imploring Édouard for his help, a letter that Bernard Profitendieu (Olivier's friend and interlocutor in the initial telling) surreptitiously acquires along with Édouard's papers. The second of these instances does fill in some missing details from Olivier's highly subjective account, supplying a fuller, more "objective" picture of the abandoned Laura. For example, the reader learns of Vincent's gambling losses, his prior correspondence with his lover, and his abrupt departure at the first sign of her insistence that he do more to help her. The third achieves a similarly meager expansion. Normally, as James R. Bennett claims, an "almost whole action is repeated for thematic modification, the enigma of the action only partially solved, the problem kept open for examination through recurrence" (407). In these passages, though, no enigma exists beyond the more or less conventional circumstances leading up to the illicit liaison, nor any great thematic revalorization of Laura's tragedy. This kind of "textual memory," by which later portions of the work recall what has transpired earlier, conveys the sense that *Les faux-monnayeurs* is a text that is rereading itself, or at least proffering to the reader the sensation of rereading portions of the text the first time through. Admittedly, part of this phenomenon is owed to the peculiar phenomenology outlined in Joseph Frank's theory of spatial form, in which a reader retroactively restructures portions of the narrative through the return to prior segments of the work. However, the textuality of *Les faux-monnayeurs* and novels like it takes spatial-form operations one step further, where, through inscribed devices such as Édouard's journal, the reader is pursuing first-order rereading before finishing the novel. This phenomenon is realized to a great extent through the frequent repetition of narrative, which in turn reinforces the illusion of a textually based signification.

At the same time, *Les faux-monnayeurs* relies heavily on a multiplicity of perspectives and temporal gaps, thereby indicating its failure to depict a stable whole, while suggesting that absolute linguistic referentiality is impossible. In a journal entry concerning his novel in progress (which mirrors *en abime* the larger workings of the frame), Édouard reveals the "sujet profond" (deep-lying subject [201, trans. 205]) of his book: "*la rivalité du monde réel et de la réprésentation que nous nous en faisons*" (the rivalry between the real world and the representation of it which we make to ourselves [201, trans. 205]). Elsewhere, Mme Sophroniska remarks on the inadequacy of psychoanalytic terminology: "*Les mots nous trahissent*" (Words betray one's meaning [177, trans. 179]), while the troubled Boris repeats "*GAZ. TELEPHONE. CENT MILLES ROUBLES*" "(GAS . . . TELEPHONE . . . ONE HUNDRED THOUSAND ROUBLES [202, trans. 207]) as a masturbatory mantra, emptying language of its referential force and so bringing about dire consequences for his own life. A short while later, in a rite of initiation into a schoolboy society, Boris shoots himself in the head with a revolver which he believed was not loaded. Similarly, in a chapter titled "*L'auteur juge ses personnages*" (The Author Reviews His Characters [215, trans. 219]) that concludes the first part of the novel, Gide himself becomes a character in his own work, taking time out to speculate on its future course and to expand on his earlier observation that writers "*devraient laisser chaque lecteur se réprésenter chacun [des personnages] comme il lui plaît*" (ought to allow each individual to picture their personages to himself according to his own fancy [75, trans. 73]). This use of language to frustrate and, ultimately, confound its own referential capabilities is at odds with the mechanics of modernist fiction that cause a first-time rereading effect, and thus provides the ambiguity that leads to the paradox of modernist textuality.

These same dual tendencies can also be found in Faulkner's *Absalom, Absalom!* (1936), which, from its redundant title forward, employs retelling as a trope for the structural rereading that informs the narrative and thus represents another variation of the repetition as rereading that marks modernist fiction. The novel exhibits qualities of the modernist paradox in counterpoising the text-centering effects of structural redundancy—the formal analogue to the eddying narration of events which is Faulkner's novel—with an implicit reliance on the reader's extratextual ordering activities as a requisite for comprehension. *Absalom, Absalom!*'s unending rehearsal of plot incidents and character nuances, some of which can never be objectively verified, has led Eric S. Rabkin to speak of the work as "a series of concentric circles" (98) that nonetheless relies on a more or less chronological progression. "The form," he states, "which is the experience of the movement of the reader's consciousness, is a dialectic between spatial structures as they are created and more closely come to resemble the circle of stories, and the plot moves rather more simply in and out" (99). This double movement of the novel's design is in evidence in Quentin's response to Shreve's urging that he continue his story of Sutpen's children:

> "Yes," Quentin said. "The two children" thinking *Yes. Maybe we are both father. Maybe nothing ever happens once and is finished. Maybe happen is never once but like ripples maybe on water after the pebble sinks, the ripples moving on, spreading, the pool attached by a narrow umbilical water-cord to the next pool which the first pool feeds, has fed, did feed, let this second pool contain a different temperature of water, a different molecularity of having seen, felt, remembered, reflect in a different tone the infinite unchanging sky, it doesn't matter: that pebble's watery echo whose fall it did not even see moves across its surface too at the original ripple-space, to the old ineradicable rhythm* thinking *Yes, we are both Father. Or maybe Father and I are both Shreve, maybe it took father and me both to make*

> *Shreve or Shreve and me both to make Father or maybe*
> *Thomas Sutpen to make all of us.* (261–62)

As is typical with modernist texts, the language of *Absalom, Absalom!* succeeds in undermining the first-time rereading effect proffered by its own structural redundancy. Incident, theme, and psychology all recur systematically, with the story itself ultimately biased, incomplete, and, in parts, even wholly imagined. Multiple narrational perspectives tinged with subjective motivation, limits to omniscience, and the fading of memory compel the reader to reconstruct parts of the story chronologically, but with frequent gaps and indeterminacies, even allowing for Shreve's outright fabrication of certain unrecuperable portions of the narrative. "Let me play a while now" (280), he requests before he and Quentin are described as "both thinking as one, the voice which happened to be speaking the thought only the thinking become audible, vocal; the two of them creating between them" (303). The central, unbridgeable gap in *Absalom, Absalom!*— the cause of the virulent encounter between Thomas Sutpen and his son about Charles Bon's plans to marry Sutpen's daughter Judith— is hopelessly clouded by the surfeit of speculation surrounding the event. Does Sutpen know or ascertain during a fact-finding trip to New Orleans that his would-be son-in-law already has an octoroon wife? Will Judith's marriage to Bon repeat Sutpen's own "error" of marrying a Haitian plantation owner's daughter who he later learns has black blood? Or is Sutpen's concern actually due to the fact that Bon is his own son, and thus on the verge of committing both miscegenation and incest? Seldom objective, never entirely self-sufficient, *Absalom, Absalom!* at one and the same time provides its reader with more information than is required, yet with never quite enough to ensure its credibility as a self-contained textual and spatial object.

Similar instances of structural redundancy that lead to the repetition-as-rereading effect can, of course, be found throughout the canon of modernist novels. In Joyce's *Ulysses* (1922), the frequent near-miss encounters of Stephen Dedalus and Leopold Bloom during their daylong wanderings through Dublin prompt this first-time rereading effect, as does the musical motif of the "Sirens" episode. The lyrical evocations of the Ganges River at the start of the "Mosque" and

"Caves" sections of Forster's *A Passage to India* (1924), which collapse the intervening chapter in the reader's mind, also confer a provisional unity of spatial form onto this portion of the novel. The repetition of Dr. Aziz's line, "Then you are an Oriental," serves as a summation of the novel's action and themes, appearing near the beginning and end of the work, and thus emphasizing this process of repatterning before closure: "[Dr. Aziz] unclasped as he spoke, with a little shudder. Those words—he had said them to Mrs. Moore in the mosque in the beginning of the cycle, from which, after so much suffering, he had got free. Never be friends with the English! Mosque, caves, mosque, caves. And here he was starting again" (311). Pointing out how the verbal gymnastics in Joyce offset the grounding of literary significance on the textual level (which is partially occasioned by these patterns of structural redundancy) would require more space than this essay could allow. In Forster, a brief reminder of the Marabar Caves' flattening of semantic difference into the hollowed nonsense of a monotonous echo, or of Mr. Fielding's *faux-naïf* flaunting of linguistic ambiguity, or of Mrs. Moore's metaphoric apotheosis into the Hindu goddess Esmiss Esmoor, suffices to signal the strong countercurrent to textual authority at play in these (and other) modernist novels. That the discovery of the tensions inherent in this central paradox of modernism remains largely the product of the recent, intensified focus on the role of subsequent readings in the production of literary meaning merits stressing here, since the largely end-stopped assumptions of structuralist, post-structuralist, and reader-response models of interpretation explore this concept of textual infinity only tangentially, and from distinct angles.

By mid-century, Beckett's *Mercier et Camier* (1946, trans. *Mercier and Camier,* 1974) had come to herald the end of structural redundancy as the preeminent organizational method underlying modernist narrative technique. Exposing through broad parody the repetition-as-rereading design as a cumbersome and hackneyed manifestation of the latent holistic patterns of spatial form, *Mercier et Camier* announces postmodernist literature's need for compelling, innovative techniques of self-duplication and inexhaustibility after the decline in modernist artistic ascendancy. The novel's self-conscious reliance on the heavy-handed and immediate repetition of versions of the same trivial, narrated events proclaims a shifting away from the genre's total dependence on textual significance, and suggests that alternative strategies for textual infinity lie in as yet unexplored avenues of aesthetic self-multiplication. As with most Beckettian texts, little of great consequence "happens" in *Mercier et Camier.* The novel recounts the ploddingly episodic, if picaresque, journeys of the titular protagonists, but is unique within its genre for employing a peculiar twelve-chapter structure in which every third "chapter" comprises merely a cryptic summational listing of the events recounted in the previous two, each time under the heading: *"Résumé des deux chapitres précédents"* (Summary of Two Preceding Chapters.) Instead of faithfully subsuming earlier events, though, these lists display a special flair for confounding the easy integration of prior action, postponing (even preventing) provisional interpretive closure of the spatial-form variety. The relation between these summational chapters and the narration proper in *Mercier et Camier* suggests little textual concern with unity, as well as a sustained flaunting of nonrepresentational fiction's ability to weave ontological uncertainty into language.

To begin with, many of these *résumés* tend to be inexact summaries of the preceding action, and thus fall short in various ways of "duplicating" elements of plot or character, particularly in a repetition-as-rereading fashion. The major problem with any repetition, of course, is that no two entities, even if apparently exact, can claim absolute equivalence, due to the corresponding change in context. The conventions of fictional mimesis, however, often seemingly offset this phenomenon of difference, causing the reader to believe that textual redundancy leads to a version of first-time rereading through the work's illusion of spatial signification. The *résumés* in *Mercier et Camier,* though, are far from matching the events which their presence putatively heralds. The items relating to the laboriously recounted rendezvous of Beckett's heroes, for instance, are simply these: *"Mise en marche"* (Outset [46, trans. 35]) and *"Rencontre difficile de Mercier et Camier"* (Meeting of Mercier and Camier [46, trans. 35]), hardly apt echoes of the wordy, drawn out action preceding them. The list continues, as do all the *résumé* chapters, with a haphazard recollection of previously narrated material that exhibits a blatant disregard both for order and priorities of inclusion. In some cases, significant aspects of the novel's story line are slighted, while other less important elements merit disproportion-ate emphasis. All of Chapter X, for example, is subsumed wryly in five self-consciously cryptic phrases that ensure subjective gapping, rather than straightforward correspondence. Conversely, entire sections of Chapter IV go ignored and unmentioned, in particular an opening monologue by an unidentified speaker and pages of incoherent ram-blings by an elderly man on a train, whose existence is intricately tied to his incessant jabbering. The lists are also confusing in their occasional interpolation of both nonnarrative events and conclusions, as well as in their tendency to act as self-contained units featuring a series of "refrains"—identical, reappearing entries that refer as much to themselves as to their formerly narrated counterparts.

The ultimate effect of these pseudo-summaries, therefore, is one of parodic distancing, which invites the reader to consider these patterns of repetition not so much as parts of a now unified whole—some of which have been reread several times upon a first perusal—but as techniques flouting the linguistic-structural confines of the modernist novel. *Mercier et Camier*'s self-aware, gnomic commentary on its borrowed compositional design, "*Que cela pue l'artifice*" (What stink of artifice [10, trans. 9]), lays bare modernism's reliance on structural redundancy's assumed ability to make fictional texts cohere, and paves the way for the genre to reinvent models of rereading that can sustain in other ways an inexhaustibility of aesthetic meaning. The novel exploits the reader's impulse (fostered by conventional modernist reading habits) to take each *résumé* at face value as a literal attempt to summarize the contents of the preceding chapters, and flouts the facile assumption that each summation ought to function as a tool to enhance meaning. *Mercier et Camier*'s most important function—arising from a structure without parallel in novelistic history—is to signal the end of the text-centered model of repetition as rereading in modernism. Through its revolt against spatial modes of effecting provisional closure at various points in the text, *Mercier et Camier* issues a rejection of the desirability, even the possibility, of first-time rereading. The work thus sets the stage for the second mode of rereading to appear on the novel's horizon, in which not even an unlimited number of rereadings could be said to constitute one complete textual processing.

Reacting to the resonant aesthetic transcendence of its elitist, high-art forebear, postmodernism pushes modernist fragmentation to its radical extreme, transforming spatial properties into randomly contingent structures that refute the reader's attempt at unification. By outrightly rejecting the possibility of encapsulation under any one cohesive rubric, postmodernist novels defy the interpreter's endeavor to ascertain stable, verifiable truths or systems of knowledge at work in their fictional worlds, in some cases going so far as to foster a reckless incomprehensibility through their chaotic structures and ludic styles. Postmodernism thus substitutes a preoccupation with the poetics of "immanence" (Hassan 268)—capturing the elusive rules of the narrative game—for modernism's ploy of positing the text as the repository of a meaning ultimately unknowable and incomplete. The postmodernist novel's concern with the ontological status of text, world, literary meaning, and the blurry interstices between these elements in the complex act of reading, occasions the continual placement in doubt of the text's ability to signify in logical, consistent, rational, or empirically determinable fashion, thus emptying language of its representational capacities and proffering a textuality that tends in many cases toward silence.

The reader's sense that the postmodernist novel's locus of meaning is extratextual manifests itself most clearly in the workings of the multiple or "schizoid" narrative (McHale 190), which boasts no fixed sequentiality and aspires to break free of its material confines as a two-dimensional intentional object. With these works, as with postmodernist fiction as a whole, the reader has little impulse to return to the text's lexical field to rediscover narrative components not in evidence on a first reading, since the conventions of this artistic movement discourage conceiving of literary signification as stable, recuperable, or in any sense text-bound. These novels are distinguished by becoming many novels in one through a break in the sequentiality of reading they encourage, sanction and, indeed, rely upon. While modernist novels are imbued with a sense of their own mythopoetic aestheticism, inculcating in the reader a learned habit of returning to the body of a work to review or supplement aspects of meaning not captured through earlier perusals, these works explode the confines of textual space by defying the book's rigid linearity and announcing that they are multiple versions of their own selves latent simultaneously in the book's "diptych" construction (Michel Butor in Kestner 122). While modernist texts assume a text-centered autonomy of literary signification, this second class of novels attests to the genre's increasing movement toward the ephemeralization of meaning, beginning with language's flight away from a grounding in the immutable order of language on the page.

Until recently in the novel's history, these variations rarely surfaced in critical concepts of genre. Indeed, the representational assumptions of such movements as romanticism, realism, and modernism have relied to a large extent on precisely this invariability of the material structuring of the printed book and page. Modernism in particular makes extensive use of the book's "strongly spatial power of reversibility," and acquires its seemingly contradictory qualities from the sustained ability to make its readers take for granted the side effect of "making looking back easy" (Kestner 122). Thus, the structural redundancies of modernism that provide the illusion of a work rereading itself, coupled with the extreme gapping that leads a reader naturally to reperuse portions of a text, conspire to ground this aesthetic's potential for meaning in the language of the work itself. So, whereas novels of the first half of the twentieth century remain "a congeries of so many close, spatial, formally organized works: a series of self-sustaining organic constructs distantly proclaiming their inherent superiority to the messiness of life" (Wilde 19), at least one branch of the genre begins an exploration of its artistic potential by opening up the single text into various competing versions of itself, mostly through offering an implicit or explicit choice of reading sequences, such that, it might be argued, one work could be reread an infinite number of times without ever being reread in the same order twice. Accompanying this new textual model, of course, is the added phenomenon of the reader's own physical manipulation of the text/book, a sometimes agile handling of twists, turns, flips and the like that introduces a radical new element into the reader/text interaction. The reader's repeated breaking off from the work's page-bound linearity in search of a continuation in the narrative or of other connections contributes to a postmodernist sense of meaning that is extratextually based, due not only to the text's own lack of fixed sequence, but to the manual maneuvering of the work at various points throughout the reading process. The very back-and-forth movement newly adduced to the reading act highlights the notion of the text's intangible significance—one that cannot be directly pinpointed or fully grasped during reading—and lays bare the ephemeral, ontic quality of multiple novels through these frequent jagged interruptions.

Vladimir Nabokov's *Pale Fire* (1962) pushes to the limit the potential for textual (in)comprehension by testing the boundaries between structural fixity and untried strategies of reading. Though the four sections composing the novel appear tightly formal and self-contained, the language remains forever mutable because of the unending variation of sequences in which it can be read. Nabokov's work is putatively an academic edition of the final poem of one John Shade, replete with the weighty, incongruous (though transparently parodic) scholarly apparatus of an introduction, notes and index supplied by his fawning colleague Charles Kinbote. The novel playfully suggests the latter may also be the deposed ruler Charles the Beloved of Zembla, or the Russian émigré professor Botkin, who has conjured up this former king's precarious existence in exile. *Pale Fire*'s structural design demands that its reader impose a new and provisional order on the work each time it is read, thereby guaranteeing that no two rereadings will ever be identical. For instance, are the cross-references that appear on nearly every page of the novel to be taken as mere suggestions for further reading or as implicit commands to flip forward or backward to another part of the text? Directions to skip to other portions of the narrative are present even before the poem itself appears, in the novel's foreword. If followed, they serve only to send the reader precipitously to still other sections of the work. The novel's improvisational structure thus redefines textual infinity by formally transmuting into a different text during each subsequent perusal. *Pale Fire*'s nonlinear sequence refutes modernism's promise of the continued unfurling of a text-bound signification, and presents its readers with a challenging new model for postmodernist rereading. Since the novel "offers itself for (nonsequential) rereading from the outset," Matei Calinescu explains, "[i]ts implied reader, who is supposed to solve a large number of correlated onomastic, verbal and intertextual literary puzzles, is actually a rereader" (124).

What's more, the cross-referencing that permeates the work some-times proves futile, leading the reader in circles, as with the entry for "*Word golf*" in the novel's index. The citation of Shade's favorite word game involving the substitution of one letter in a starter word in order to proceed to an ultimate target word, is cross-referenced to "Lass," which in turn yields "Mass," which then provides "*Mass, Mars, Mare, see Male,*" the last entry of which sends the reader back to "*Word golf.*" The delusional Kinbote's own suggestions for reading *Pale Fire* sound counterintuitive as well, typically tinged as they are with self-importance and schemes of financial gain. Whether Kinbote is a reliable source of either poetic or biographical information depends firmly upon limiting the far ranging *Pale Fire* to one determinate ver-sion of events, an undertaking the novel purposely makes impossible in favor of the kind of unstable textuality which all the rereadings in the world could not hope to clarify. *Pale Fire*'s ability to keep a series of core events knowable and authoritative, while maintaining competing stories within the same narrative, undercuts the novel's semantic force and overloads its referential capacity. Coterminous interpretations cancel each other out where textual impasses or ironies arise, leaving gaps of signification at frequent intervals in a novel otherwise seemingly rigid in its clear-cut structural divisions. So, while Richard Pearce's contention that an assessment of Kinbote's rationality is crucial to our reading of the novel (79), it is hardly a necessary determinant of reading order, the responsibility for which lies almost exclusively with the reader's ambitious pursuit of the work's pervasive cross-referencing, not with an aesthetic judgment of either Shade's poem or the poem's explicator.

In addition, *Pale Fire*'s projection of its material being into the production of meaning shifts literary signification from the text as such to an intangible, interstitial realm, as it were, between the words, which suggests a movement toward verbal and semantic ephemeralization. The "ontological cut" (McHale 180) dividing the book as text and book as object, compounded by the layered images of genres that make up *Pale Fire*, foregrounds the novel's departure from a textually based aesthetic toward an extratextual space somewhere between work and reader. Pearce's description of Nabokov's seemingly static, four-part structure emphasizes the specifically physical quality of the reader/text interaction. "The hole between the poem and the commentary opens a rudimentary physical problem: Which way does the book go?" (77), he asks.

> Whichever choice we make, we will continually return to an experience of the book as a physical object divided in two parts, and we will inevitably find ourselves reading in two directions. The empty space divides the poem absolutely from the commentary and compels us to turn back and forth between them. . . . We discover that the book is designed to frustrate our sense of center—or that the only center we can know is the empty space that secures our forefinger as we flip between poem and commentary. (78)

Pearce's conception of the spaces between the novel's four sections as "black holes" suggests a slippage that cannot be accounted for by structure or phenomenology alone, but by the peculiar nature of the reading transaction (which itself remains elusive as the ultimate subjective experience of readers). He pinpoints the crux of the interplay between the formal features of text and preconceived manners of reading that leads to the quality of intangibility that marks *Pale Fire.* Absence becomes ephemeral presence over the course of the reading process:

> On first reading, of course, we hardly see the blank pages; we expect these clear demarcations in such a text. But by the time we finish *Pale Fire,* we discover that they mark not rational divisions but complete separations, the central separation governing the two. If we now think about the text as a whole, we may describe these separations, empty spaces, holes, as presences in our reading experience. (78)

Pale Fire thus exhibits qualities of postmodernism in tending toward silence and an absence of signification. Ihab Hassan characterizes this dominant topos of late twentieth-century novelistic discourse as follows: "Disjunctive forms turn into disruptive forms, and the latter renounce their aristocratic commands, setting the audience free of the author's control. . . . Forms define themselves by their absence, their felt omissions" (10). The black holes of Nabokov's novel are thus never satisfactorily bridged, putting into play the empty space of the material book that announces a further ontological cut between word and world. *Pale Fire*'s elaborate textual apparatus supporting the evasive shading of meaning in a work that can never be forced to gel into one cohesive unit cancels out competing semantic and structural possibilities, resulting in an increased sense of the work's intangibility during rereading: "Words appear in either case on the page only to declare themselves invalid. . . . Postmodernist literature moves, in nihilistic play or mystic transcendence, toward the vanishing point," Hassan remarks (23). And so the ephemeralization of meaning comes to the fore in postmodernist narrative.

To be sure, the thematic and metaphorical devices employed throughout the novel also reveal *Pale Fire*'s tendency toward insubstantiality on a level quite different from that of the manipulation of the book as object. The constant references to shades of meaning, from the self-conscious source of the novel's title in Shakespeare's *Timon of Athens* to Shade's burning of his own manuscript "in the pale fire of the incinerator" (3), are just two examples. The double movement of rescuing and destroying the possibilities for meaning (Shade salvages some note cards, but destroys his drafts "the moment he cease[s] to need them" [3]), reflects the novel's larger design, and is personified by the shadowy hint in the poet's name, as well as in his eventual assassin's, Gradus, which in the novel's fictional world means "tree" in Zemblan (3). That Kinbote reads Shade's "Pale Fire" as a linguistic trace of another narrative system, including discovering Gradus's name in such unlikely signs as "Tana*gra dus*t" (155, my italics), guarantees the continued instability of reference that pervades the novel, and is another example of the work's self-conscious literariness. Nowhere is this more in evidence than in the traditional definition of "gradus" as a dictionary of prosody once used by poets who (Kinbote-like?) hoped to achieved a lasting fame by emulating their classical forebears.

In contrast to the shading of meaning but in accordance with a similar principle flouting direct reference are the many mentions of mirroring and reflection in *Pale Fire*. Kinbote's obvious misreading of this motif in Shade's poem underscores the importance of the concept to an understanding of verbal operations in the novel, as he comments: "the poem is the only 'shadow' that remains, we cannot help reading into these lines something more than mirrorplay and mirage shimmer" (89), referring to Gradus's murder-bent schemes while at the same time signaling the reader to take special notice of the rules of the textual game. *Pale Fire* further contributes to the deconstruction of meaning in being a text literally and figuratively haunted by ghosts. The decidedly metaphysical, even paranormal, character to Shade's poem in its search for significance and surety beyond the grave entwines with the remembrance of a "barn ghost" whom Shade's daughter Hazel attempts to contact, an endeavor which results in a recorded manuscript of apparent nonsense. Kinbote, too, reinforces the novel's shaky realism by referring rather offhandedly to his magical powers, as when he casually remarks on his telekinetic ability to force Shade's wife, Sybil, into reenacting the apparently puzzling motion of answering the telephone.

Another "schizoid" novel, Julio Cortázar's *Rayuela* (1963, trans. *Hopscotch,* 1966), in contrast to *Pale Fire,* consciously flouts determinate narrative order by presenting itself *explicitly* as a work which may be read in any number of sequences, clearly demarcating these options for rereading in the novel's "table of instructions." This unique *tablero de dirección* starts off by declaring *Rayuela* to be many books in one: "*A su manera este libro es muchos libros, pero sobre todo es dos libros*" (In its own way, this book consists of many books, but two books above all [5, trans. I]). The first of these books, the reader learns, is the more conventional modern narrative, following the lives and loves of Oliveira and his bohemian circle of fellow expatriates in France, before their return to Argentina. Proceeding in perfect sequence from chapters 1 to 56, this book foregoes the remaining ninety-nine "*capítulos prescindibles*" that make up the remainder of the volume. These, the novel suggests, are to be incorporated into the "second" book, which is *Rayuela,* a hopscotch construction that jumps from chapter to chapter in a nonetheless strict order prescribed in the table of instructions, one which interweaves the ninety-nine "expendable" chapters among the first fifty-six. Although the novel boasts that it is many books in one, only two scripted sequences for reading are provided here, leaving the reader to conclude either that these limited schemata must also take into account some general notion of the infinite plurality of signification at play in the work's claim to polyvalence, or that the novel is assuming the reader will improvise orders of reading not expressly set forth. While it is true that the experience of the first book differs radically from the schizoid construction of the second, the complex grid of the novel's infinite combinatorial design takes full shape only in the course of book two, which encompasses the novel's entire lexical range (with one maddening exception), including an inscribed authorial counterpart, Morelli, whose views on the anti-novel closely parallel Cortázar's experiment with *Rayuela.*

Rayuela, much like *Pale Fire,* is solidly divided into three main sections or blocks of text, which taken together give rise to unbridgeable gaps in the narrative. Recalling Iser's designation of these textual spaces as "blanks," Santiago Juan-Navarro equates the "*organización general del texto*" (text's general organization) with "*la aparición de 'espacios en blanco'*" (the appearance of blank spaces [237, my trans.]). In some cases, the prescribed reading order of the second book entails no other disjunction besides the required page flipping, and so generally respects the sequential logic of the narrative. But this is more the exception than the rule. In one instance, an extended string of chapters from the third section of the novel seems to marginalize important segments of story line, most curiously Oliveira's affair with the dying Pola, with whom he takes up after ending his detrimental relationship with La Maga. This apparently important, but structurally slighted, plot development is just one of many reasons why the reader must consider the designation of these final chapters as "expendable" to be highly ironic, another obviously being the cache of avant-garde pronouncements on the novel by Oliveira's favorite author, Morelli, which is contained exclusively therein. By means of contrast, the rapid movement from the first two portions of *Rayuela* to these final ninety-nine chapters can also serve as metaphoric commentary on the novel's main action, as when La Maga's description of her rape as a young girl is followed immediately by a chapter in which ants devour a worm, or the death of her infant son yields to an admonition on the perils of boys catching their genitals in pants' zippers. For the most part, though, the relation between contiguous chapters is often associational at best, and sometimes completely incongruous, so that it is left to the consecutive chapters of book one to maintain the work's narrative progression in spite of the intrusions and disruptions of the so-called expendable chapters.

Few critics would consider the reading of the first book that is *Rayuela* (chapters 1–56) to be a thorough first grasp of the novel. The improbable consecutive reading of book two immediately after book one also fails to constitute what most would consider a rereading proper, since these two fixed versions of the novel differ enormously with respect to textual inclusivity. While no conventional reader would begin *Rayuela* in the random, hopscotch fashion it may eventually entice a reader to undertake, this sort of haphazard reading, too, would not qualify as rereading justly considered. The one guarantor of disparity between the first and all subsequent readings of *Rayuela* turns out to be the gap in sequence introduced by the elaborate hopscotch order of the second book, the "maddening exception" mentioned previously. For if a straight reading of chapters 1–56 ultimately remains an incomplete rendering of the work, so, too, does the sequence provided for the second book, which ludically omits chapter 55 in its directions and repeats chapter 131 as the "final" installment, thus placing the reader in a loop *ad infinitum*. No readers who believe they have fully read *Rayuela* can have done so without first improvising a sequence not explicitly delineated in the novel, and so must take the initiative in creating a reading order that encompasses the text's every word. If the second book aspires ironically to be a fuller rereading of *Rayuela,* a sort of "padded" first reading no one ever experiences as such, the omission of chapter 55 ensures that the novel *"pertenece al género de obras que exigen nuevas relecturas, que nunca se manifiestan como iguales ni definitivas"* (belongs to the genre of works that demand new rereadings, that never declare themselves to be equal or definitive [Juan-Navarro 240, my trans.]).

In these various ways, *Rayuela* announces its status as an "open" novel, the many books in one which it claims to be in the *tablero de dirección.* Its text a potentially orderless grid inviting an infinite series of rereadings, even partial ones, *Rayuela* undercuts the mimesis of any one social world by heralding its self-referential status as provisional verbal artifact. As Anthony Percival explains:

> In the more conventional novel, gaps at the level of sentence, paragraph or chapter tend to result from cutting, withholding of information and deception. This type of gap is naturally discernible in *Rayuela,* but, more spectacularly, gaps in the novel are of a spatial order. Whereas in the standard kind of novel, as one reads, the eye scarcely ever has to leave the page, except in that split second when the page is turned over, in *Rayuela* locating the first page of a new chapter can take several seconds, during which time mind and imagination can play on what has just been read in the previous chapter. When the eye turns away from the page, the mind is freed from the printed word and, theoretically, the "reader's share" is increased. (245)

Though clearly divided into three discrete sections, *Rayuela,* like *Pale Fire,* confutes the conventional expectations of closure through the unique requirements of its textuality, and even plays further with this finite/open tension by ending its three sections with verbs of closure: "*acabaría por*" (would end up [251, trans. 216]), "*se acabó*" (the end [399, trans. 349]) and "*termine*" (finish [634, trans. 564]).

The figure of the experimental novelist Morelli, in addition, reinforces the theoretical concerns and schizoid postmodernist mechanics of the frame-novel. Morelli's disagreement with traditional novelistic discourse centers first and foremost on what he considers undue authorial insistence on controlling interpretation through narrative that appears self-contained and, therefore, closed to contingencies. "*Parecería que la novela usual malogra la búsqueda al limitar al lector a su ámbito definido cuanto mejor sea el novelista*" (It would seem that the usual novel misses its mark because it limits the reader to its own ambit; the better defined it is, the better the novelist is thought to be [447, trans. 396]), he declares. Though the genre as a rule "*se contenta con un orden cerrado*" (is content in a closed order [447, trans. 396]), Morelli's suggestions for ways to open the form reflect some of the more conservative strategies employed in *Rayuela,* including "*la ironía, la autocrítica incesante, la incongruencia, la imaginación al servicio de nadie*" (irony, ceaseless self-criticism, incongruity, imagination in the service of no one [447, trans. 396]). Less common are his views on narrative fragmentation and sequence, which constitute the principal basis for the absurdly partisan support he receives from Oliveira's circle of exiles. Étienne's championing of Morelli's writings on the novel, for example, is based on the aesthetic appeal of a text's radical dissolution into fragments that never quite coalesce into a whole. Speaking to Oliveira of Morelli's avant-garde tendencies, Étienne explains that

> *le revienta la novela rollo chino. El libro que se lee del principio al final como un niño bueno. Ya te habrás fijado que cada vez le preocupa menos la ligazón de las partes, aquello de que una palabra trae la otra . . . Cuando leo a Morelli tengo la impresión de que busca una interacción menos mecánica, menos causal de los elementos que maneja; se siente que lo ya escrito condiciona apenas lo que está escribiendo, sobre todo que el viejo, después de centenares de páginas, ya ni se acuerda de mucho de lo que ha hecho.*

> the Chinese-scroll novel makes him explode. The book read from beginning to end like a good child. You've probably noticed already that he gets less and less worried about joining the parts together, that business of one word's leading to another . . . When I read Morelli I have the impression he's looking for a less mechanical interaction, one less caused by the elements he works with; he feels that what has already been written just barely conditions what is being written, especially since the old man, after hundreds of pages, doesn't even have a clear memory of what he's done. (501, trans. 443)

Oliveira, too, comes away from a Morelli novel with a similar impression, believing at times that Morelli himself "*había esperado que la acumulación de fragmentos cristalizara bruscamente en una realidad total*" (had hoped that the accumulation of fragments would quickly crystallize into a total reality [532, trans. 469]). But of all his projected innovations for the novel genre, none is more surprising than the contention that his own work may be read in any order— that it is, in fact, written with rereading in mind. *"Mi libro se puede leer como a uno le dé la gana"* (You can read my book any way you want to [626, trans. 556]), he tells Oliveira. *"Lo más que hago es ponerlo como a mí me gustaría releerlo"* (The most I do is set it up the way I would like to reread it [626, trans. 556]). It is this hopscotch construction bordering on complete contingency that nearly prompts Morelli to title his complete works the "Almanac," and which provides an apt analogue of the mode of rereading prevalent in the postmodernist novel.

While literary critics await the full-fledged emergence of a successor to postmodernist aesthetics, striking parallels exist between the ephemeral and extratextual qualities of postmodernism and the uses of literary language in cyberspace. Robert Coover's succinct description of the linguistic and structural operations of computer novels or "hyperfiction" recalls postmodernism's attempts to break with conventional strategies of narrative progression by neutralizing the rigidity of paginal and linear sequentiality, as he declares these pioneering works in their new medium to be the artistic heirs of such novels as *Pale Fire* and *Rayuela*. He writes that

> unlike print text, hypertext provides multiple paths between text segments, now often called "lexias" in a borrowing from the pre-hypertextual but prescient Roland Barthes. With its webs of linked lexias, its networks of alternative routes (as opposed to print's fixed unidirectional page-turning) hypertext presents a radically divergent technology, interactive and polyvocal, favoring a plurality of discourses over definitive utterances and freeing the reader from domination by the author. Hypertext reader and writer are said to become co-learners or co-writers, as it were, fellow-travelers in the mapping and remapping of textual (and visual, kinetic and aural) components, not all of which are provided by what used to be called the author. ("End" 23)

A true hypertext is thus the narrative the fragmented novel aspires to be. Of the intangibility of literary meaning in cyberspace, Coover elsewhere remarks of hyperfictional textuality: "there is no 'thing,' just light" ("Hyperfiction" 8), and confesses that he is "always astonished to discover how much of the reading occurs in the interstices and trajectories *between* text fragments" ("End" 24).

Of course, it will be some time before readers can know whether the novel in cyberspace will contribute lasting changes to the print novel's aesthetic dimensions. What seems clear, though, is that narrative's continuing quest to renew the forms of the past and guarantee increased rereadability through techniques that bring added degrees to the text has not slowed in recent years. Writers such as Italo Calvino, William Gass, Georges Perec and Walter Abish have all created ever more innovative variations on the exclusively linear work, picking up where Alain Robbe-Grillet and Jorge Luis Borges, whom Calinescu refers to as "compulsively rereadable" (3), left off. Whether semantic ephemerality must remain a feature of these future texts is uncertain, though signification that resists a textual grounding seems destined to imperil conventional referentiality. Novelists of the twenty-first century will undoubtedly exploit this lexical propensity by composing works that redefine novelistic textuality as we know it, and thus reinvent not only notions of what it means to read, but to reread as well.

Works Cited

Beckett, Samuel. *Mercier et Camier.* Paris: Éditions de Minuit, 1970.
———. *Mercier and Camier.* Trans. Samuel Beckett. New York: Grove, 1974.
Bennett, James R. "Plot Repetition: Thematic Variation of Narrative Macro-Episodes." *Papers on Language and Literature* 17 (1981): 405–20.
Calinescu, Matei. *Rereading.* New Haven: Yale UP, 1993.
Coover, Robert. "The End of Books." *New York Times* 21 June 1992: 7: 1+.
———. "Hyperfiction: Novels for the Computer." *New York Times* 29 Aug. 1993, sec. 7: 1+.
Cortázar, Julio. *Hopscotch.* Trans. Gregory Rabassa. New York: Random House, 1966.
———. *Rayuela.* 1963. Barcelona: Bruguera, 1984.
Faulkner, William. *Absalom, Absalom!* 1936. New York: Vintage-Random House, 1972.

Fokkema, Douwe. *Literary History, Modernism, Postmodernism: The Harvard University Erasmus Lectures,* Spring 1983. Philadelphia: John Benjamins, 1984.

Forster, E. M. *A Passage to India.* 1924. New York: Harcourt, Brace, Jovanovich, 1984.

Frank, Joseph. *The Widening Gyre: Crisis and Mastery in Modern Literature.* New Brunswick: Rutgers UP, 1963.

Gide, André. 1925. The Counterfeiters, *with Journal of* The Counterfeiters. Trans. Dorothy Bussy and Justin O'Brien. New York: Random House, 1927, 1973.

———. *Les faux-monnayeurs.* Paris: Gallimard, 1985.

Hassan, Ihab. *The Dismemberment of Orpheus: Toward a Postmodern Literature.* Madison: U of Wisconsin P, 1982.

Joyce, James. *Ulysses.* 1922. New York: Vintage-Random House, 1986.

Juan-Navarro, Santiago. "*Un tal Morelli: Teoría y práctica de la lectura en* Rayuela, *de Julio Cortázar.*" *Revista Canadiense de Estudios Hispánicos* 16 (1992): 225–52.

Kestner, Joseph. "Secondary Illusion: The Novel and the Spatial Arts." *Spatial Form in Narrative.* Ed. Jeffrey R. Smitten and Ann Daghistany. Ithaca: Cornell UP, 1981. 100–28.

McHale, Brian. *Postmodernist Fiction.* New York: Methuen, 1987.

Nabokov, Vladimir. *Pale Fire.* New York: G. P. Putnam's Sons, 1962.

Pearce, Richard. *The Novel in Motion: An Approach to Modern Fiction.* Columbus: Ohio State UP, 1983.

Percival, Anthony. "Reader and *Rayuela.*" *Revista Canadiense de Estudios Hispánicos* 6 (1982): 239–55.

Rabkin, Eric S. "Spatial Form and Plot." *Spatial Form in Narrative.* Ed. Jeffrey R. Smitten and Ann Daghistany. Ithaca: Cornell UP, 1981. 79–99.

Wilde, Alan. *Horizons of Assent: Modernism, Postmodernism, and the Ironic Imagination.* Philadelphia: U of Pennsylvania P, 1987.

V

Musings
and Beyond

14

Nonce Upon Some Times: Rereading Hypertext Fiction

Michael Joyce

That which is reread is that which is not read. The writer rereads and unreads in the same scan, sometimes looking for the place which needs attention, other times seeking surprising instances of unnoticed eloquence which her attention now confirms in a process of authorship. Most often she looks for the thicket, the paragraph or phrase which relinks a vision or reforms it, a vision which she put aside or lost, which dwindled or lapsed, which exhausted her or she exhausted. In the process of reading for what she has not written (or written well) she often does not read what she has written well (or not written).

For over eight years now in workshops with writers exploring hypertext fiction I have posed a question about rereading and held my breath fearing an obvious question in return.

Suppose at this point your reader, before going on, has to reread one part of what comes before, I ask.

No one asks why. There are reasons.

For the writer rereading, the question seems to be one of ends. "What happens at the end of a text?" asks Hélène Cixous, "the author is in the book as we are in the dream's boat. We always have the belief and the illusion that we are the ones writing, that we are the ones dreaming. Clearly this isn't true" (98). While Cixous is not thinking explicitly of hypertext here but rather the novels of Thomas Bernhardt, she nonetheless evokes the reader's experience of hypertext. Hypertext only more consciously than other texts implicates the reader in writing at least its sequences by her choices. Hypertext more clearly than other texts seems to escape us before we have it formed into an understanding we might call a reading. It beckons us as it escapes. The writer reading (or the reader as writer) thinks toward ending but more often looks for transport and escape, a way out which is after all another way in. It is as Cixous says:

> We are not having the dream, the dream has us, carries us, and, at a given moment, it drops us, even if the dream is in the author in the way the text is assumed to be. What we call texts escape us as the dream escapes us on waking, or the dream evades us in dreams. We follow it, things go at top speed, and we are constantly— what a giddy and delicious sensation!—surprised. In the dream as in the text, we go from one amazement to another. I imagine many texts are written completely differently, but I am only interested in the texts that escape. (98)

Start again.

Hypertext is the confirmation of the visual kinetic of rereading. This is not a good first definition of the form or art but rather one made possible by a kind of prospective rereading which, given a world in which ketchup bottles have Web sites listed with their ingredients, assumes the reader has at least a muddled sense of hypertext from the World Wide Web. Hypertext is a representation of the text which escapes and surprises by turns.

The traditional definitions of hypertext begin with nonlinearity, which, however, is not a good place to start given the overwhelming force of our mortality in the face of our metaphors. Either our lives seem a line in which our reading has ever circled, or our lives seem to circle on themselves and our reading sustains us in its directness and comforts us in its linearity. My own amended definition of hypertext acknowledged the mortality and turned the metaphor to drama while unfortunately adding an element of the metaphysical: "hypertext is reading and writing in an order you choose where your choices change the nature of what you read" (177).

Our choices change the nature of what we read. Rereading in any medium is a conscious set of such choices, a sloughing off of one nature for another. The computer is always reread, an unseen beam of light behind the electronic screen replacing itself with itself at thirty cycles a second. Print stays itself—I have said often and elsewhere— electronic text replaces itself. What hypertext does is to confirm this replacement, whether in the most trivial sense in which we as readers sustain the text before us by merely foregoing the jittery shift of mouse button or PageDown key, or in the deeper sense, itself shared with rereading in any medium, where we linger or shift back intentionally upon a text, making each recurrence or traversal its own new or renewed text, the exploration of a dark seam of meaning which mere choice seems to illuminate and (we hesitate to suggest) create for us.

Each iteration "breathes life into a narrative of possibilities," as Jane Yellowlees Douglas says of hypertext fiction, so that in the "third or fourth encounter with the same place, the immediate encounter remains the same as the first, [but] what changes is [our] understanding" (118).

Start again.

The workshop exercise with which I began this essay seeks to isolate a set of primitive choices which both prompt the visual kinetic of rereading in hypertext and at the same time isolate the elements of what Douglas calls a narrative of possibilities. The attempt is to move from the nonce upon some times, not so much telling an old story with new twists, as twisting story into something new in the kinetic alternation of ricorso, flashback, renewal. The great advantage of this exercise is that it immediately confronts writers who are often quite skeptical about hypertext fiction with literary and artistic questions about linking rather than technical ones about software. It engages working writers with aesthetic and readerly questions about linking rather than encouraging a choose-your-own-adventure sort of drearily branching fiction.

What I do is to ask the writers to write four parts of something, keeping the notion of parts and something intentionally fuzzy but making it clear we are talking narrative. I ask them to use the hypertext

system (in this case, Storyspace, created by Jay Bolter and myself
with John Smith) to create four spaces (boxes) for the four parts. I
encourage them to do this very quickly and not to worry about how
extensive or finished the writing is.

Once this is done, I first have them recreate linearity, i.e., link the
four parts, not merely to teach the simple hypertextual skill but also
to reinforce that in hypertext even the linear is a choice. Then I ask
the question with which I began this essay: Suppose at this point your
reader, before going on, has to reread one part of what comes before,
which would it be?

No one asks why. There are reasons.

Not the least of which is that writers in my experience contemplate
a reader in motion across the space of a text like someone inhabiting
a map not as a map but as the rereading of a map which we enact
and test in motion. That is, writers imagine readers reading as they
read when they reread and rewrite. To try to see this let us consider a
simple story, it is in fact the example I use in presenting this exercise
to writers, a sweet, old and endlessly compelling story in which each
part is a single sentence: Two people meet. They fall in love. They
quarrel and part. They reconcile.

Suppose at this point the reader of this story, before going on, has
to reread one part of what comes before, which would it be?

A writer may decide that having read this story and reached its
reconciliation, her reader should reread the second section in which
the two characters fall in love. Obviously a variant of this strategy
(not necessarily requiring that the exact text be reread) is of course
what constitutes flashback. With Storyspace this link involves a visual
stitch, in the case of this example a line between the fourth and second
boxes on the screen. For a later reader this stitch will offer a way back
into the sequence of the text and beyond.

Once the writer has linked back into the sequence at whatever
point, she is confronted with the following analytical situation: We
can agree, I suggest, that we always have at least a theoretical fifth
space in mind at the point where we intervene in the text to require a
rereading. This fifth might have been a virtual closure, an understood
(if uninscribed) gesture toward an end or 'The End.' This end space
I call the metanode. Or in fact the fifth space may be a "next" step

(a genuine fifth part to the four parts) which the creating mind automatically or instinctively generates despite the exercise's requirement that there be only four parts. However, it may also be that the very act of rereading and thus reentering the text has suggested another direction for the narrative, something which not only recapitulates the story but somehow begins another one newly discovered there or at least disclosed in the repetition. "To come back to the only thing that is different is what is seen when it seems to be being seen," Gertrude Stein suggests, "in other words, composition and time-sense" (514).

Once there is a general understanding of these possibilities, I am also prepared to suggest that for the writer only three possible kinds of links exist from the place where we have linked back into the story (in my example only three possible outcomes from our retrospective look at reconciled lovers first falling in love).

If after rereading we go from two to three again (or in fact any part of the four-part sequence), the link is a recursus (or cycle), often a stratagem of modernist/absurdist fictions. This ricorso (the nonce: to begin again) takes the modernist turn around the track, where the mind loops, by commodius vicus of recirculation ever across the space of the same text, with an implicit promise that there is more to be seen in the turning and that we are not (or are, it is the same thing) looped like Yeats in the loops of brown hair.

If we leap from two across three and four to the uninscribed fifth space held in mind, then the link is a flashback. That is, the story resumes its intended course (or ends) refreshed by this new look at previous thematic material. Flashback (the next: a leap to the metanode, onward or ending) is an old friend, alternately refreshing or confirming our sense and indeed the experience of a previously viewed episode. It is the woven etymon, text as textus.

If we go from two to a new space, not an imagined fifth but escaping inward and outward simultaneously, then the link is a renewal. Linking itself—rereading itself—has discovered and opened a story dimension. Renewal is not textus but narrative origami, where what opens and renews is not the inscription but the narrative of possible inscriptions. This space in which the visual kinetic of rereading unfolds is one which the computer offers, a medium for which it is uniquely, though not exclusively, suited.

To be frank: the workshop is always both a fascinating and a mildly disappointing exercise, a bit of formalist conjuring in which all the ballet of three-card monte is lost in the mere shine of the face cards. That there are three link primitives does not speak to their myriad types of course. Of recursus, there is hallucination, déjà vu, compulsion, riff, ripple, canon, isobar, daydream, theme and variation, to name a few. Of flashback there is the death of Mrs. Ramsay and the near disintegration of a house, the chastened resumption of the Good Soldier, Leopold Bloom on a walk, and a man who wants to say he may have seen his son die. Of the renewal there is every story not listed previously, the unrecollected whisper of your mother, and the barely discerned talk of lovers overheard at the next table as they eat potstickers and drink bad Chinese beer.

The real task of the workshop is thus for the writer to reread the inner folds of sequence and possibility and to fashion what follows from her decision to reopen the text, especially if she has not decided upon the cycle, but rather the metanode or even more compellingly the renewal.

> Not "Revelation"—'tis—that waits,
> But our unfurnished eyes—
>
> —Emily Dickinson

At this point, most writers see that once the text has been revisited and either the new space or the delayed closure of the metanode has been created, the second space now cries for some way to shape its reading for different readers. We want the reader newly come into this simple story to proceed briskly through its inevitable narrative, pause at the reentry, and then leap, without orbiting endlessly unless that is our intention. In any text there are ways to do this: by inference, suggestion, rule, music or seduction. To these hypertext adds memory and resistance. Storyspace and other complex hypertext systems let a writer set conditions which shape the reading according to simple rules which match the reader's experience of the text against the possibilities it opens to her. In a richly linked hypertext these rules (in Storyspace they are called "guard fields") can compound. While a local reading may be as severely shaped as a sestina or a fugue, the permeability of the hypertext makes even a rigorous sequence contingent. You can link in and from any point. A reader may have sailed to this first star from another constellation for which this one forms the third part of a cluster so thick it seems itself a single star and this first star of ours a mere bright spot on its surface. A hypertext fiction spawns galaxies where such constellations link and spin, where other lovers meet and quarrel and part or live forever according to other local rules. This whole dance of complication finally folds in on itself, not in a black hole but a shower of possibilities.

The leap to the new introduces the paradox of hypertextual rereading. Hypertext fiction in some fundamental sense depends upon rereading (or the impossibility of ever truly doing so) for its effects. Yet in a sufficiently complex and richly contingent hypertext it is impossible to reread even a substantial portion of the possible sequences. Indeed for any but a reader who has consciously blazed her way through the thicket (breadcrumbs, in fact, has become a technical term for computer tools designed to keep track of the reading of hypertexts), it is unlikely that successive readings by a single reader will be in any significant way alike. Even in less vigorous hypertext systems such as current instantiations of the World Wide Web, bereft of the systematic memory which shapes possible readings, the linked surfaces of possibility themselves compound. Despite the most earnest efforts of so-called human factors specialists, and despite the earnest accumulation of lists, breadcrumbs and bookmarks and other virtual aides de memoir within the interfaces of Web browsers, the narrative of possibilities unfolds. Even the flattest list of visited Web pages is thick with possibilities and mixed sequences, as suits and meld are folded within a deck of cards dealt out upon a table.

The reader's task in hypertexts becomes a constant rereading of intentions against the rereading of elusive or irrecoverable sequences. We see and lose our hopes for the text by turns in the shifting screens. Again this experience is not exclusive to electronic texts but rather one for which the computer is uniquely suited and within which the inevitable exchange between our intentions and our recognition of the text's possibilities becomes more transparent. "Genuine books are always like that," says Cixous, "the site, the bed, the hope of another

book. The whole time you were expecting to read the book, you were
reading another book. The book in place of the book" (100).

That which is reread is that which is not read. To read the book in
place of the book is not to read the book placed (by whom?) in the scope
of our expectations. As is her practice, Cixous seamlessly moves from
reading to writing, seeing in the exchange between them a recognition
of mortality, which is to say the body. "What is the book written while
you are preparing to write a book? There is no appointment with
writing other than the one we go to wondering what we're doing here
and where we're going. Meanwhile, our whole life passes through
us and suddenly we're outside" (100). It is we who place ourselves
retrospectively within the scope of our expectations. Retrospective
expectation is fundamental to the experience of rereading in any
medium. Outside, our lives passed through us, we are nostalgic for a
complex tense in which what was can be again what will have been
other than what it is. Like hypertext, the tense disappears in the parsing,
we both cannot and must reread the what was which will have been
otherwise.

Yet it isn't difficult to do the impossible. We relive our lives in
reverie aware that we cannot embody dreams. We reread any text
in humility, not only aware that we cannot recapitulate our original
experience of it but also that the experience itself was originally
unsubstantiated, its evidences lost not merely to history and memory
but to even surface recognition. *Où sont les mêmes d'hier?*

Start again.

It isn't difficult to do the impossible. It seems merely literary
stratagem, the artifice of the avant garde, to claim that the experience
of a new textuality is somehow not reproducible in the old. Innovation
(whether literary or rhetorical) reads and is read by what it extends,
alters, ignores or supplants. With enough rereadings it isn't clear that
anything has really changed. In Milan some years ago an exhibit
of Rodchenko seemed staid and even conventional to eyes used to
computer graphics and morphing fonts; the Constructivist project
seemed a matter of the organic quality of pre-offset inks, the geometry
of hand-ruled typographical elements, the counterplay of red and
green inks against yellowing papers. We reread the prospect of change

from the vantage of change and find it wanting, its fulfillment robbing it of its possibility.

Yet this is not simply an aside about the place of hypertext as a literary experiment, but rather an attempt to isolate a distinctive quality of the experience of rereading in hypertext. The claim that hypertext fiction depends upon rereading (or the impossibility of ever truly doing so) for its effects is likewise a claim that the experience of this new textuality is somehow not reproducible in the old. The question at hand is not whether print textuality anticipated or can accommodate innovations of electronic textuality (it did and often can) but rather whether distinctive differences in reading, and thus rereading, characterize each of them.

To see differences, however, it is not necessary, or even helpful, to argue for or against succession (this is why an avant garde always dissipates: it means to become what it wishes to end). Instead it may be useful, and surely is symptomatic of our age, to argue for parallelism and multiplicity. Differences show as differences are allowed. As Mireille Rosello notes, "the delay in the emergence of new knowledge may also be the condition of its future growth. Rather than imagining our period of transition to hypertext as a point where something old is replacing something new, I would be content to see it described as a time when two ways of reading and writing, and two ways of using maps, are plausible at the same time" (151).

This is to see change as something different (the self-referentiality here intended), as if Rodchenko created computer graphics at the same time that he and other Constructivists pushed the limits of print. Richard Lanham argues as much for the Futurists. Or for the matter at hand, this is to say that an independent system of reading exists in parallel with the current system of reading in hypertext; that they do not so much confuse each other as enhance each other; and that they do not promise the extinction of one or the co-opting of the other but rather the permeation of each other. More important (or closer at hand), the system of reading hypertextually is intimately related to what is called rereading in the parallel system of reading print.

There is of course another argument I want to make here, or have been making though not overtly, and it is that reading in hypertext means to recreate the writer's experience of rereading in the process of composing printed works. In fact many hypertext rhetoricians, critics and theorists assert this claim with greater or lesser elegance and subtlety. Many commentators append the initial of the writer in the inelegant formulation of "wreader" to characterize the new system and its roots. My own notions of exploratory and constructive hypertext are only slightly more subtle. In the sentence before those quoted above, Rosello makes a distinction between screening and reading texts: "For a long time, I suspect, the activity of reading hypertexts (rather than screening them) will be considered acceptable and normal."

In her term "screening," Rosello wants to recover something like the seamless move between reading and writing which I have suggested Cixous sees in our embodied mortality. It likewise means to evoke (and in fact is probably the source of my sense of) how the reader in motion across the space of a text inhabits a map not as a map but as the rereading of a map which we enact in (and as) our bodies. Yet there is a trap in the seam in the seamless, and the map infects the body which enacts it. Rosello speculates whether "a new geometry of space is needed in order to invent communities that will have little to do with proximity and context," and it is a speculation which spills, as light through a screen, on the image of the writer rereading seen as the reader writing. We are not the writer because we are reading, we are not the reader because we are writing; the questions at hand are ones of proximity and context. "While the noun *screen* connotes an outer, visible layer, the verb *to screen* means to hide," writes Alice Fulton:

> The opposing definitions of screen remind me of stellar
> pairs, binary stars in close proximity to one another,
> orbiting about a common center of mass. Astronomers
> have noticed a feature common to all binaries: the
> closer the two members lie to one another, the more
> rapidly they swing about in their orbit. So screen oscil-
> lates under consideration. (111)

Start again a last time (at last?).

I know when I confuse, at least when I confuse myself. I reread Rosello and Fulton desperately seeking the thread I saw there, not in them but in an argument as yet unwritten. I reread them for my intentions but then worry that I have misread their intentions. I intend to read them and yet leave unread what I mean to see there. Knowing my confusion is often as much as I can hope for in my rereadings.

In the confusion of reader and writer inevitably lies the confusion of characters in a fiction, the confusion of episodes in its sequences, the confusion of voices in what we attribute to ourselves as a dialogue. It is not a literary stratagem but a matter of fact that the particular experience of the new, albeit parallel, textuality of reading hypertexts is somehow not reproducible in the old. I said that differently, in inverse, before above. You can reread and find out as much, or perhaps you kept it in mind long enough to notice as soon as it occurred.

This is not entirely possible in hypertext. You can neither always go back above, or in fact count upon the existence of the same "above" from reading to reading. What follows from this, of course, is that you cannot always count upon the applicability of what you keep in mind to what follows upon the choices you make based upon that mindfulness. Mary Kim Arnold's hypertext fiction "Lust" is not much longer than a poem (although it starts with one, it is not one), something short of eighteen hundred words in thirty-seven screens (or spaces), fugal, multiple, confusing (even for some readers, my students especially, maddening), haunting, irreproducible here although I could easily (with permission) include all its episodes.

In the story, a woman has hurt a man or the man her, there is a knife and blood and gravel and a rug, they have a child or she thinks him one or he does her or they each or both imagine or desire or recall when they were one, he abuses her or she him or we imagine as much, they make love or do not, they sleep or do not, she runs off or he brings her back, they may or may not drink orange juice. There are men named Dave, John, Jeffrey and Michael; the woman is unnamed, always called "she." It is possible to read all thirty-seven screens in a single reading and possible to read for a very long time without seeing one or a substantial number of the screens. Sometimes the same screens appear in the same order but interrupted by different sequences between them. There are one hundred and forty-one links among the thirty-eight spaces, thirty-six of which begin with the individual words of the following poem which is the entire text of the first screen:

Nearly naked
this summer night
sweet and heavy,
he comes to her.

This night, she follows him,
sweat between them.

They speak of the child
and the summer sun
with words that yield
to the touch.
('Prologue')

Let us concentrate for a moment on a single, simple, screen entitled 'He and the Child' (note that screen names are indicated here by single quotes since hypertexts are, largely, unpaginated). 'He and the Child' engages us with one of the less controversial, seemingly more easily apprehended plot elements. "He is gentle with the child. Speaking softly, deliberately, muscled arms embracing soft naked flesh." This is the text of the screen in its entirety. It happens that there are five screens which can lead a reader to this one (although to know this, you have to radically reread or unread the text, in fact dissect it within the Storyspace program in which it was created). The first leads directly from the word "that" in the second last line of the Prologue poem; a click on that word will change the screen to the text of 'He and the Child.' A reader can also reach this screen coming from a screen called 'He expects,' but only if the reader has previously read a screen called 'Touching,' which has four links leading to it, including one directly from the word "sweat" in the sixth line of the Prologue poem (not from the word "touch" in the last line, which instead leads to a screen called 'Penis') but which itself does not lead directly to the screen called 'He expects.'

A third link to the screen 'He and the Child' comes from a screen entitled 'Innocent,' which has also four links into it (one from the Prologue) and two other links from it, including one (to a screen called 'In noce') which is followed if the reader has already encountered the screen called 'He and the Child.'

And so on.

No one reads this way, of course, except the hacker or the literary critic. Or perhaps the writer. Although no one writes this way, to read this way while writing is to reread as a prospective reader and in the process unread the text in favor of what is not normally read within it.

The combined text of one sequence of the screens mentioned above would read (does read) as follows:

> He touches her. He touches the child. The child
> screams.
> She touches the blade of the knife to him, cold,
> smooth. He does not speak.
> He screams. The child does not speak. The child picks
> up the knife. There is no blood.
> There is no child.
> There is only morning.
> ('Touching')
> He was nearly naked, except for the baseball cap. He
> does not speak to her.
> He expects her to come to him.
> ('He expects')

No one reads this way, of course. First, in this sequence the text is always bracketed, in the case of the sequence described above by screens 'Prologue' and 'He and the Child,' which I have not quoted again in this text since they have already been seen. The sequence is also bracketed by the act of the mouse click or keypress and the flicker and shift of screens which confirm the intention of the reader to go on. Pages likewise settle and sigh though we no longer account their confirmation.

Second, no one (or only one in thirty-six readers making the same choice at the Prologue) comes upon this sequence in this order unless by chance, while any number of readers can come into this sequence at the point past the Prologue (through another path to 'Touching'), and some readers can come to 'He and the Child' (or 'Touching') having already seen either of them in another sequence, which, unlike the one from 'Innocent,' for instance, makes no account for a reader who has already encountered the screen called 'He and the Child.'

The hypertext sometimes recalls what the reader has read and sometimes not, but obviously only in a systematic (we might almost say mechanical, were it not a silicon-based slab of light) way. That is, if such an inconsistent if not contradictory recalling can be called systematic. Hypertext builds a systematic level of the literal upon the experience of rereading, with words like "recall" and "recollect" taking on (reassuming the name, rereading the sign) their literal meaning: When a text is recalled by the system, the recollection remains within the reader.

"Assembling these patched words in an electronic space, I feel half-blind," Shelley Jackson writes in her hypertext novel *Patchwork Girl or A Modern Monster,* a work attributed to Mary/Shelley and Herself. It is part of a long section—multiply and contingently linked in much the same manner that "Lust" is—called "body of text." Most hypertext fictions include these self-reflexive passages. The section seems to oscillate in its voices among these three attributed authors and at least once engages in a dialogue with (a text of) Derrida. Despite this, I think these passages are something more than a postmodernist token for the pinball game of blur and blink; and, to the extent that my own work can be seen as wellspring, they do not, I think, merely mark the fledgling stream (a flow is hardly a tradition) of a passing form in an uncertain medium. Instead, or more accurately concurrently, these passages are also a gesture toward a parallel system of reading which invites the reader to read as the writer does rereading. It is, says Jackson,

> as if the entire text is within reach, but because of some
> myopic condition I am only familiar with from dreams,
> I can see only that part most immediately before me,
> and have no sense of how that part relates to the rest.
> When I open a book I know where I am, which is restful.
> My reading is spatial and even volumetric. I tell myself,
> I am a third of the way down through a rectangular
> solid, I am a quarter of the way down the page, I am
> here on the page, here on this line, here, here, here. But
> where am I now? I am in a here and a present moment
> that has no history and no expectations for the future.
> ('This writing')

No expectations except motion, sequences bracketed by the act of mouse-click or key-press, the kinetic of rereading. "Or rather," Jackson continues, "history is only a haphazard hopscotch through other present moments. How I got from one to the other is unclear. Though I could list my past moments, they would remain discrete (and recombinant in potential if not in fact), hence without shape, without end, without story. Or with as many stories as I care to put together" ('This writing'). If no one reads hypertext by dissection (although Jackson's story from time to time literally dissects, both Mary Shelley's monster and Frank Baum's girl cut and repatched), how does the reader mark this hopscotch of history, the kinetic text? In a voice which anticipates (or participates in the same swirl which engenders) Alice Fulton's, and which likewise recalls (or recollects?) my own suggestion above of the renewal link as narrative origami, and which finally marks the commonplace poetry and virtuality of the sewing pattern, Jackson's tripartite narrator suggests that we read along the dotted line:

> The dotted line is the best line:
>> It indicates a difference without cleaving apart for good what it distinguishes.
>> It is a permeable membrane: some substance necessary to both can pass from one side to the other.
>> It is a potential line, an indication of the way out of two dimensions (fold along dotted line). In three dimensions what is separate can be brought together without ripping apart what is already joined, the two sides of a page flow moebiusly into one another. Pages become tunnels or towers, hats or airplanes, cranes, frogs, balloons, or nested boxes.
>> Because it is a potential line, it folds/unfolds the imagination in one move. It suggests action (fold here), a chance at change; it also acknowledges the viewer's freedom to do nothing but imagine. ('Dotted Line')

What we read is suggested action, one way out of the two dimensions, a gesture toward Rosello's "new geometry of space" beyond proximity and context. It is this gesture which Jackson marks in the only link from the space 'Dotted Line,' a link which discloses the dots in its lack of gap, the directness of its bracketed action for the reader: "I hop from stone to stone and an electronic river washes out my scent in the intervals. I am a discontinuous trace, a dotted line" ('Hop').

Poet, hypertext theorist and computer scientist Jim Rosenberg, in his poetic sequences *Intergrams* and *The Barrier Frames,* has created new poetic textuality which is quite literally not reproducible in this older one. His poems flicker and focus from a dark sea of blurred and overprinted language as the mouse-track moves over their surfaces, clearing suddenly into discernible patches, like the backs of golden carp rising briefly to sunlight in a dark pool or floating into focus like the fortune cookie scraps of text of the old prognostic Eightballs. No sooner do they snap into clarity than with the least movement they are lost again and again as soon as they are gained. His is, he says, a hypertext of "relations rather than links" (*Barrier* 22), and it is no wonder that, when he comes to propose a hypertext poetic, it is one which attends to action. His paper "The Structure of Hypertext Activity" argues that "readers discover structure through activities provided by the hypertext" and offers a three-level taxonomy of the activities of reading from acteme to episode to session, starting with his coinage "acteme is an extremely low-level unit of activity, like following a link" (22).

Or rereading, which in hypertext rhetoric becomes dissected (along dotted lines) into varieties of "backtracking": "One may revisit a lexia simply to read it again," says Rosenberg, simply throwing the baby of this current essay out with the golden carp's dark bathwater, "or it may be a genuine 'undo,' perhaps the reader didn't mean to follow that link at all." His immediate, low-level interest here is in how to represent the meaningfulness of an action for the reader. "These [backtrackings] are arguably different actemes," he says, "though typically not distinguished by the hypertext user interface" (22).

His higher-level interests, however (or are they the Chomskyan deeper structures? or perhaps instead—simultaneously—the topsy-turvy, each-side-up, permeable membrane of body or screen?) are in episodes and sessions where "the episode itself *emerges* from reading activity" (26) and where, in place of closure, the reader may at the end of a session "obtain a sense of completion about the gatherings; i.e., the reader's sense of completion is exactly a writer's sense of completion: the gathered result 'works' artistically as is, now is a good time to stop" (28).

Under such conditions, rereading and unreading are alive in contention, and vie like subjects of a fugue. "Whether an instance of backtracking is really an 'undo' may be rephrased," says Rosenberg:

> Does backtracking *revoke* membership of actemes in an episode? It depends on the circumstances both of the hypertext and the reader's frame of mind. The reader might revisit a previous lexia to read it again— perhaps for sheerly "musical" repetition, or to reread a prior lexia based on some resonance or reference in the present lexia. Here one might argue that all the backtracking history is part of the episode. Or, the reader may be backtracking to undo having arrived at the current lexia by mistake—backtracking to *remove* from the episode the acteme that caused arrival at the current lexia. The episode is thus a combination of history through the hypertext, the reader's intention, and the reader's impression of what "hangs together." (24)

Emerging meaning gathers in episodes which combine in sessions of reading and rereading and sometimes seem (to the reader) to mean on their own. "There is a kind of thinking without thinkers," says Jackson: "Matter thinks. Language thinks. When we have business with language, we are possessed by its dreams and demons, we grow intimate with monsters. We become hybrids, chimeras, centaurs ourselves" ('it thinks'). Such a thinking without thinkers occasions Rosello's notion of screening as well. She speculates about "what kind of context is being created as the result of experimenting with apparently arbitrary connections . . . not . . . the kind of arbitrariness that comes from conventional forms and discourses, but rather a deliberate incursion into the messy realms of chance, random connections and meaninglessness" (134).

Traditional definitions of hypertext begin with nonlinearity, which, however, is not a good place to end, given the overwhelming force of our mortality in the face of our metaphors. "I align myself as I read with the flow of blood," says Shelly Jackson's triple narrator:

that as it cycles keeps moist and living what without it
stiffens into a fibrous cell. What happens to the cells
I don't visit? I think maybe they harden over time
without the blood visitation, enclosures of wrought
letters fused together with rust, iron cages like ancient
elevators with no functioning parts. Whereas the read
words are lubricated and mobile, rub familiarly against
one another in the buttery medium of my regard, rearrange themselves in my peripheral vision to suggest
alternatives. If I should linger in a spot, the blood
pools; an appealing heaviness comes over my limbs
and oxygen-rich malleability my thoughts. The letters
come alive like tiny antelopes and run in packs and
patterns; the furniture softens and molds itself to me.

(I do not know what metaphor to stick to; I am a
mixed metaphor myself, consistency is one thing you
cannot really expect of me.)

What I leave alone is skeletal and dry. ('Blood')

Screeners and gatherers, we do not know which metaphors to stick
to, although the body is our type for stick-to-itiveness. And so, as
autumnal readers we wait for the leaves to fall. What we leave, alone,
is skeletal.

Start again (backwards, back words).

"We live," says Shelly Jackson,

in the expectation of traditional narrative progression;
we read the first chapters and begin to figure out whether
our lives are romantic comedy or high tragedy, a mystery or an adventure story; we have certain hopes for
our heroine, whose good looks can be expected to
generate convoluted formations among the supporting
characters and indicate the probable nature of her happy
ending; with great effort we can perhaps lean sideways
and veer into a different section of the library, but
most of us do our best to adhere to the conventions
of the genre and a kind of vertigo besets us when we
witness plot developments that had no foreshadowing
in the previous chapters; we protest bad writing. (We

are nearly all of us bad or disorderly writers; despite ourselves we are redundant, looped, entangled; our transitions are awkward, our conclusions unsubstantiated.) ('Lives')

In the process of reading for what she has not written (or written well), she often does not read what she has written well (or not written). Most often she looks for the thicket, the paragraph or phrase which relinks a vision or reforms it, a vision which she put aside or lost, which dwindled or lapsed, which exhausted her or she exhausted. The writer rereads and unreads in the same scan, sometimes looking for the place which needs attention, other times seeking surprising instances of unnoticed eloquence which her attention now confirms in a process of authorship. That which is reread is that which is not read.

Works Cited

Arnold, Mary Kim. *Lust.* Diskette. *Eastgate Review of Hypertext* 1.2 (1993).

Cixous, Hélène. *Three Steps on the Ladder of Writing.* Trans. Sarah Cornell and Susan Summers. New York: Columbia UP, 1993.

Douglas, Jane Yellowlees. "The Act of Reading: The WOE Beginners' Guide to Dissection." *Writing on the Edge* 2.2 (June 1991): 112–25.

Fulton, Alice. "Screens: An Alchemical Scrapbook." *Tolstoy's Dictaphone: Machines and the Muse at the Millennium.* Graywolf Forum I. Ed. Sven Birkerts. St. Paul: Graywolf P, 1996. 102–19.

Jackson, Shelley. *Patchwork Girl or A Modern Monster.* Diskette. Watertown, MA: Eastgate Systems, 1995.

Joyce, Michael. *Of Two Minds: Hypertext Pedagogy and Poetics.* Ann Arbor: U of Michigan P, 1995.

Lanham, Richard. "The Electronic Word: Literary Study and the Digital Revolution." *New Literary History* 20.2 (1989): 265–90.

Rosello, Mireille. "The Screener's Maps: Michel de Certeau's 'Wandersmänner' and Paul Auster's Hypertextual Detective." *Hyper/Text/Theory.* Ed. George Landow. Baltimore: Johns Hopkins UP, 1994.

Rosenberg, Jim. *The Barrier Frames.* Diskette. Watertown, MA: Eastgate Systems, 1996.

———. "Intergrams." Diskette. *Eastgate Review of Hypertext* 1.1 (1993).

———. "The Structure of Hypertext Activity." *Hypertext '96.* New York: ACM Proceedings, 1996. 22–30.

Stein, Gertrude. "Composition as Explanation." 1926. *Selected Writings.* Ed. Carl Van Vechten. New York: Vintage-Random House, 1990. 511–24.

15

Some Thoughts on Rereading

Sven Birkerts

Not long after I'd agreed to pull together some thoughts about rereading, I came upon this quotation from Nabokov: "Curiously enough, one cannot *read* a book; one can only reread it." Never one to ignore the beck of serendipity, I scribbled the words down; I trusted that they would magnetize the particles needed for a little *feuilleton*. But as that formulation began to radiate its spokes of energy, I found myself more irritated than intrigued. I had the same chafing sensation I'd had in grade school when the wag in the next seat passed me a note that read, "This sentence is false."

I knew what Nabokov meant, of course—that there is no real appreciation without closer focus, that literature does not kiss on the first date, and so on. But I had other problems with his declaration. One was strictly logical: how can we use the word "rereading" unless "reading" already means something? Whether or not we understand a work of literature the first time through, we are nonetheless doing something by moving our eyes back and forth. That's obvious, though, and I'm sure Nabokov knew quite well he was being provocative. The other difficulty, a more serious one, has to do with the implications of the idea. For what he is saying is that there is no living, only remembering. That may have been true for Nabokov (read his *Speak, Memory*), but I don't believe it's binding on the rest of us. I would sooner hold, with Heraclitus, that it's always a different river and always a different I stepping into it. In which case, clearly, the proposition would be reversed: you cannot reread a novel, you can only read it.

I can think of a number of reasons for going back to a novel. If it was difficult to get through the first time—as with *Ulysses* or *Molloy*—

we may return with a desire for mastery. If, on the other hand, our first experience was one of delight, or discovery, we may try to recoup some of those same sensations. Often we recall not so much the contents of a novel as our reactions to it. "I really loved that book," we might say in all honesty and yet be unable to tell our interlocutor the first thing about it. Then, invariably, there are the select novels we consider our own. We pride ourselves on knowing them well; when we pick them up again, it's for self-confirmation. They are where we store our fantasies and ambitions; we have dreamed our secret lives into them. Opening to the first page is like biting into a honeycomb.

That may be wishful thinking on my part. I know that going back to a novel, even a favorite, can be like running into an old lover on the street: the flat plane of the present gets a hole punched through it. Indeed, the book can be even more disconcerting than the lover. For we know that flesh succumbs to gravity, and we can deflect the true horror of time's passing with a simple reversal: "How you've changed. . . ." But words are supposed to stand still. Were these the people we read about, suffered with? Or did some archfiend come in the night and rearrange the scenes? Soon enough we have to admit it: we have changed.

What a perplexing thing! The same letters, the same words and sentences, but everything means differently. When I read *The Great Gatsby* in high school, for instance, I enclosed Jay Gatsby in a soft mist. His love for Daisy Buchanan was noble and rare, and it redeemed any character flaws he might have had. Yet when I reread the book a few years back, I was shocked to see what a pathetically deluded creature he was. Naturally, I prided myself on having picked up a thing or two about human nature. At the same time, though, I found I missed the fellow I had known. Both of them, in fact—Gatsby with his dream of love, and myself in all my susceptible innocence.

As we pass our eyes over rows and rows of words, the situations and sensations that they denote arouse in us a persuasive phantom reality. This mysterious semblance is only in part the author's creation. He marshals his sentences to create one particular world; we elicit from them quite another. We modify landscapes with images from our own experience; we thrust tics and attributes upon characters in order to pull them into the desired shape. When we return to a book, we encounter more than just the author's words—we simultaneously tour the picturesque ruins of our former selves.

We discover, too, how fickle and selective is our gaze. Rushing along to discover whether Alphonse would marry Giselle, we took no notice of Cedric's remarkable yellow waistcoat. The second time through, however, when we know damned well that the lovers will triumph, we find ourselves blinking with delight at the canary brightness of the cloth. Background and foreground are determined only in part by the author, whatever his skills; our own attention pattern decides the rest. Neither can we control what we notice and what we slight. We read and reread with the same irreproducible singularity with which we live and remember. To paraphrase Wallace Stevens: two people talking about one book are two people talking about two books. . . .

Memory compresses impressions, at times to the verge of invisibility. When we finish a novel, we don't retain the whole sequence in our minds. We fold the events and the resolution together into a kind of magician's handkerchief. A conversation or recollection may prompt us to unfold a particular episode for reinspection. But it is not the episode that we originally read, even if we are gifted with perfect recall. For hindsight—our knowledge of how it all came out—has already played its tricks with the passage. Looking back on a novel, or rereading it, is, in this sense, analogous to looking back on events from our own past. With this difference: in the novel the facts are all in and only interpretations remain; in our own lives, however, future events may yet rearrange the past. Closure comes for us, if at all, with the last exhalation.

The subtlest and most potent pleasures of rereading derive from this strange correspondence between written narrative and the narrative that we fashion of our own lives. When we read a novel for the first time, we are paralleling—though in a very compressed way—our own processing of experience. We expect, to be sure, that the novel will have a dramatically satisfying shape. But do we finally hope for anything less with regard to our own lives? Events, unforeseen combinations, and decisions stream toward us out of the diminishing sheaves of type, as if out of the obscurity of our future. We recognize this; we hypostatize the unread pages so that they become, in effect, the future. We could, it's true, skip, skip quickly forward to find out how everything works out. But unless we are perverse, we resist the temptation. It is far more interesting to savor the coming events under the illusory aspect of free choice. Maybe the doomed lovers will find happiness; maybe Gatsby will win Daisy. We pit ourselves against the already determined unknown, and the tension of our will imparts to the words a special electricity.

But then what about rereading? Wouldn't we have to say that reading—finding out—discharges the electricity once and for all? With the ordinary narrative (a run-of-the-mill mystery novel, say), it clearly does. With any novel substantial enough to support a rereading, however, the tension just manifests itself differently.

Reading takes place in the order of free choice, rereading in the order of destiny. As we would probably act differently if we could relive certain parts of our lives, so do we read differently when we know the fates of the characters. The second time around, our desires are set into play against our knowing. The sensations are entirely different: I can still hope that Gatsby will get Daisy, but now I suffer his every move with the certainty that he will not. He becomes another man. In my original reading I felt congruous with him—at least in the sense that I knew no more of the future than he did. Now, of necessity, I am in the superior position. I can only pity his illusion of free choice. He can do nothing that will not lead him to the pistol and the swimming pool. Rereading flatters me by allowing me the vantage of a god, or at least of an author.

Looking at my own shelves, I see only two kinds of novels: those that I mean to read and those I mean to reread. Future and past, you might say. But that wouldn't be quite right. In his essay "Writers and Daydreaming," Freud wrote that the memory of an experience in which a wish was fulfilled "creates a situation relating to the future which represents the fulfillment of the wish." To me that means that when I look at the books I've read and kept—kept because they have in some way fulfilled a desire—I am in fact projecting myself into the future.

I was going to end by saying: tell me what you reread and I'll tell you who you are. Then I changed it to: tell me what you reread and I'll tell you who you'd like to be. But now I'm wondering whether the two are so different. Couldn't we say: you are what you'd like to be? Or is the logic of that simply too Nabokovian?

16

The Poem on the Wall: A Rereading

Alan Michael Parker

One

On a hot and windy day in July of 1990, alone in a rented trailer in Dungannon, Ontario, I dumped fifty-three of my poems on an orange couch, stepped back, and stared at the mess. Somehow I was going to organize these poems into my first book; somehow these fifty-three poems would have to be reduced, boiled down from seventy-nine pages to a manageable sixty-four. More important, somehow, I would need to reconsider, with an eye on my own aesthetic: to discern, shape and posit an idea of my poetry representative of the previous five years of my writing; to reread.

To do this, as is my wont, I self-cannibalized. I went back to my notebooks (again ceremoniously dumped) to see what I had been thinking about, or thinking around, when I had first written the poems; to locate my reading, my jots and marginalia. I found Bishop, Giacometti, Heidegger, Parra, and lots of Calvino. I found James Gleick's *Chaos* and Richard Rhodes's *The Making of the Atomic Bomb*. I found Max Frisch's *Man in the Holocene*. I began to make little piles of my poems.

Nicknamed by my wife "The Baked Potato," the trailer had a tendency to heat up: sheeted with what looked to be aluminum foil, the walls almost glowed come high noon. Our bedroom, down the hall, faced east and a field of feed corn. The building's lone air conditioner, mounted in the bedroom far wall, chugged along like some dying Briggs and Stratton lawn mower, rattling the flatware in its drawer—a drawer lodged in a kitchen wall, all the way down the hall at the other end, the west end, of the trailer. The knives banged together, the spoons banged together, the forks banged together. And the air conditioner's compressor steadily wheezed its way toward scrap metal.

I had to get some air. I was sweating all over my poems, even with the AC cranked. So I threw open all the windows, then wedged them open with odd bits of molding and cracked kindling, whatever we had found near the woodpile, where most of a dead cherry tree had been stacked forever. The kitchen windows. The dining porch. The living area. The bathroom, spare room, and bedroom. Of course, what ensued was a strong westerly storm wind from Lake Huron—and caught in an updraft, my poems began to fly. The wind felt good: I stood in the middle of my swirling poems like a snowman in a paperweight, in the midst of what I had made as it had remade me.

What could I have been thinking? I thought, as the wind died down. (A poem landed on my shoulder.) Piles of poems? With epigraphs from my notebooks? Epitaphs seemed more precise, a manuscript divided into little deaths, each with a quotation by another writer, condemning myself to comparison. (One poem lay atop another on the kitchen counter, where they both soaked up a condensation ring.) Then I thought again about the Frisch novel.

Man in the Holocene had been important to me for some time, a book I had read and reread. In the novel's opening "scene," a man builds a pagoda of crispbread:

> It is always with the fourth floor that the wobbling
> begins; a trembling hand as the next piece of crispbread
> is put in place, a cough when the gable is already
> standing, and the whole thing lies in ruins—(3)

To be sure, even though the protagonist's cough ultimately decimates the pagoda, the relationship between his physical body and the crispbread building seems analogous rather than causal, as the structure's collapse foreshadows the character's demise. Death prefigured, we think, and we are not wrong. But we are also not right. For Frisch's novel is primarily a meditation on the nature of mind, of the novel as a "novel," and a reimagining of itself; as such, the body proves mostly a distraction, and death a means, rather than an end unto ourselves.

An austere and disjunctive rendering of an elderly widower's progressive incapacitation from a series of mini-strokes, *Man in the Holocene* also recapitulates geologic history: as the protagonist Herr Geiser deteriorates, he cuts a variety of reference books to bits, scotch-taping excised pages to the walls of his house. (These excerpts are reproduced within the novel, including pictures of dinosaurs, amphibia, and homo sapiens.) As a result of his efforts, Geiser's house becomes his mind, in a way, a manifestation or a reification of his memory—until the moment when apoplexy overwhelms, when Geiser's daughter arrives to find her father near death:

> There would still be many things to stick to the wall if
> there were any point in it; the Magic Tape is useless; a
> puff of air as Corinne opens the shutters and the slips
> of paper are lying on the floor, a confused heap that
> makes no sense. (106)

This is the physical demise of Geiser, the scattering of his thoughts. It is also, though, the rebirth of "Man," and of a much larger idea worthy of another essay, another day.

At the end of the book, we learn through a brilliant, discursive manipulation of point of view that the Man of the novel is not dead. Man, in fact, emerges from novelistic convention, and if we follow the book's German title, *Der Mensch erscheint im Holozän,* more strictly, Man emerges within the present geologic age. Time winds back through the final pages, until "All in all, a green valley, wooded as in the Stone Age" (111). Geiser's mind has become the novel; the world has become a way of reading. The house stands in the valley, still. The novel ends as time starts again.

Thinking about Frisch's novel had given me an idea. I turned back to my scattered poems—as time started again in the Dungannon trailer, over which the sky had begun to darken. I pushed the furniture to the center of the living room. If a drop cloth had been available, I would have covered the sofa and love seat, as though in expectation of paint-fall and splatter. (Or to enshroud the referential world as I prepared to revisit my poems? Perhaps.) As is, armed with an industrial-sized roll of masking tape, I began to stick my poems on the room's three walls, enraptured as I was—quite literally—by and in the incipient text. Then

I rummaged in my wife's boxes, found a Flair pen amongst the well-worn brushes and squeezed-flat tubes of Old Holland oil paints, and began to number the poems on the wall, left to right; east, south, west.

Two

A truism: we reconsider as we read. All new information gained from a text progressively complicates prior experience with the text, as a reader recapitulates the known. Quite clearly, Frisch's novel works this way, for what we learn of Herr Geiser informs our earlier knowledge of him, and calls to mind (over the short term) our own impressions, which become a part of reading. Not incidentally, though, the fragmentary and illusory rendering of the novel's narrative forces us further into reconsideration, insofar as we attempt to conjure a plot from among the apparently disparate discourses.

I looked at my poems on the walls. My textual concerns were necessarily different from Max Frisch's, as the genre dictated. I wasn't building a novel, postmodern or otherwise, but a book of poems. For my reader to reconsider the known—whether or not the reader flipped through and back, "surfing" the text, or proceeded in order, cover to cover, poem after poem—seemed almost a given. (One assumes that the nature of reading fairly dense poetic language would probably spark reconsideration.) What I realized, then, was that beyond my ambitions for the individual poems, I wanted to construct a text a reader would reread. And that was an entirely different act, epistemologically.

Rereading a book of poems involves and invokes an experience of the poems beyond their singular achievements. Since I know the ending of Keats's "Ode to a Nightingale," I anticipate (with dread) the restitution of "my sole self" at the end of the poem, once the bird and inspiration flee. This anticipation has deepened my regard for the sorrow of the poem's opening lines: "My heart aches, and a drowsy numbness pains / my sense" (279). Sorrow, I understand from having read the poem before, is a waking into the mundane. What I understand about Keats's poem has taken years to grasp; moreover, I know what I know as a result of rereading all of the Odes as separate poems *against each other,* which means not as Helen Vendler reads Keats. (In fact, I have reread the Odes so often, I have a tendency to hear them elsewhere, as a kind of textual hum underlying unrelated experience.) As a result, the dread with which I now reread the opening of "Nightingale"—informed by my knowledge of the poem's ending—is the same dread which colors my encounter with "No, no, go not to Lethe . . . ," the opening of Keats's "Ode on Melancholy" (283). These poems, in my experience, exist inseparably within a field of values, where they reread each other, as it were, with each rereading.

My poems have long existed similarly, in my consciousness. I know them all "by heart," well enough to recite each. ("Epistemology, and all the afternoon / clouds perform their dying," I said to myself, aloud in my head.) Nonetheless, when "reading" publicly, I refer to the page every three or four lines, to avert the sudden onslaught of performance anxiety. Some of my poems answer others; many enter into a dialogue with failed, unpublishable poems long since condemned to recycling. Most of my poems have been inspired by my reading of other poets: at times, allusive vestiges of this reading linger in a finished text, at other times not. Often, too, my favorite poem is the one I'm currently writing.

Before bed, if I have been fortunate enough to write that day— which usually means if my life has allowed me to do so, circum- stantially, and which usually happens at least a few times a week—I reread my work. In the morning, before writing, I'll reread again; a session that includes other poets, and other poems of mine. I'll flip back in my notebook, riffle pages. I'll count lines. I'll scan something. Then, often, I'll begin the day's session by revising an older poem, even if I am aware that a new work waits. As my memory and schedule allow, I find myself occupied daily with my poems; I hear iambs in conversation, read the line breaks and enjambments on the advertisements for Spring Break in Ft. Lauderdale. Mostly, though, I tell myself again the poem in progress, revising in my head, and try to concentrate if I'm behind the wheel.

Which is to say, all told, that I have a relationship to my work that constitutes a constant state of rereading.

Which is to say that a poet is always her or his own ideal reader.

Which is to say that to collect my poems in such a way that inspires rereading would necessarily entail an amnesia, of sorts, so that I forget some of what I know about my own work. A disremembering.

But the model I had adopted for this disremembering, as I stood in the Dungannon trailer, was Herr Geiser's cutting-and-pasting, the desperate mnemonic act of a dying character in a work of fiction.

Three

Increasingly over the past few years, I have begun to work with the iamb, as well as with apparently recognizable stanzaic patterns. The former comes from reading and teaching poetry, from lines memorized and aesthetics historicized. The latter may be attributed more specifically to a remark I encountered of Wallace Stevens regarding "typographical queerness" (326), i.e., the visual hijinks of modernist poets such as Mina Loy. For my purposes, of late, a poem need not look typographically queer to be radical; as is, given that so many of my rhetorical gestures within the poem have the semblance of associative logic, the external appearance of form offers the reader a sense of familiarity, a historical touchstone.

For example, a poem of mine entitled "The Ticket" begins "Pulled over, parked, indicted by the high / beams flashing in her rear-view mirror, pure / as loss." What I hope is that the poem's iambs lull the reader, as they make recognizable "poetry" sounds, but that the enjambments—frictive, religious transitions—prefigure a sudden and dramatic move to interior monologue, and to the speaker's realization: "Oh god, I just can't make myself slow down. . . ." In a sense, what I hope is that the first impression seduces as it asserts a known, consensual universe—which frees me, the poet, to scribble all over the realism. And of course, because it is my own work of which I speak, I can only hope that this proves true for the reader.

But what about the second impression? or the third? Although not a Confessional poet, I perpetually fear that much of my work could only matter to me. How could I facilitate my readers' rereading, if this insecurity proved. . . .

The thought was getting in the way.

Looking at the poems on the wall, I realized that much of what Frisch achieves in his central image results from counterpoint, from movement within the text against the natural momentum of reading, i.e., linearity, despite the turning of pages one at a time, approaching an end. (And if my use here of "natural" inspires a nature/nurture argument, I won't complain.) The natural movement of the rereader's mind, however, is never exclusively forward—for if it were, as the reader encountered a work for the first time, the act of reconsideration, and the arc of thought back over the linear text, would never be possible.

For example: the passage of geologic time documented by Herr Geiser's cut-outs works against the narrative. As *Man in the Holocene* proceeds, and the protagonist deteriorates, time reels itself in, moving back toward the Stone Age. Herr Geiser's walls are steadily covered with encyclopedic scholia and geologic history; and slowly an affirmation of existence forms, which resolves into an ethical construct despite the protagonist's physical deterioration. Nonetheless, it takes a nifty bit of writing over the final few pages to connect these notions, as though Frisch and the reader were suddenly on a tandem bike together, riding backwards.

Still, this is reconsideration. Rereading *Man in the Holocene* means that the ethical construct is known from the outset: our questions no longer concern how or when Geiser will die, but what varieties of time does a novel embody. (In effect, with the "plot" revealed, the idea of the novel emerges in the Holocene, again in counterpoint to the progress of the narrative.) Plus, knowing already that the walls will be covered with Geiser's cut-outs—cf. Matisse, Picasso's work with newsprint, even Barbara Kruger—allows us to contextualize Frisch's exploration of the form, to see the cut-outs as collages, or even bursts of visual poetry.

I realized, though, that to adapt Frisch's architectonics, and create this kind of movement in my book, would require at least the semblance of a narrative, if only to offer the reader something to reread against. But was it possible to fashion a narrative, even an implied narrative, out of my forty-five or so lyric poems and short odes? If so, then the collection would take the form of another form, so to speak.

Bursts of poetry? A book of poems as an implied narrative? Is rereading an act of genre-bending?

Maybe I had come to something. In a sense, rereading *Man in the Holocene,* once plot and suspense were effectively compromised, leveled the field of regard. (As I reread, I could play passages of the text against other passages, much as I would play one Keats ode against another.) In a sense, then, rereading the novel made the text not a novel, given that the trappings of genre had been stripped away. What was left? The demands of subtext and discourse, which the writer always hopes a reader will engage, on some level. Or maybe, once the trappings of genre had been stripped away, the novel became even more of a novel, as I gained access to subtext and discourse.

Hypothetically, then, my book of poems needed either to masquerade as a narrative or be disguised as a narrative. But what was so good about that, especially since writers such as Frisch had spent books exploring the inadequacies of narrative, implied or otherwise? Unto itself, nothing. And yet, to induce a rereading. . . . If I organized my collection of poems in such a way as to imply a narrative, then once that narrative revealed itself, the individual poems might ask to be reread against each other, as a colloquy of subtext and discourse.

I felt as though I had stumbled upon a dirty secret.

Four

Well and good, subtext and discourse. The wind picked up, and the walls seemed to flutter as though in a dovecote, the white wings of the poems affixed there, going nowhere. It was time to act.

First, in the making of my book certain facile connections had to be preempted. Two poems in a row about kids, for example, seemed too pat—or the too-quick repetition of similes invoking snow. These were easy enough to identify, and to move to different walls. I began to order the poems, untaping and retaping until poetic poles were established: these poems removed from those, these poems between, these poems as "bridges," these poems out of place. I winnowed. Three poems dropped. I shaved. Does this poem achieve what that poem tries? Another poem fell.

In no short time I had almost reached my goal of sixty-four pages (built to publish, since book production depends upon signatures, preferably in multiples of eight.) I also had arrived at what seemed to be a balance of forms, if only by accident: there was a call-and-response kind of counterpoint at work, between the first ten poems and the final ten, which had created an aesthetic argument. Chronologically, poems in received forms yielded to poems in numbered sections, which then yielded to free verse; aesthetically, the more metaphoric entered into a dialogue with the metonymic, as the collection progressed.

I stepped back: I had created a reconsideration.

But would it be an implied narrative?

And would it be rereadable? I asked myself, creating an ugly word.

Five

Clearly, in rereading a poem, certain aspects of the initial reading are rendered moot. The surprise of the language, for example— the New—is made known by prior acquaintance. Closure, too, is somewhat altered: one knows when to expect the ending, and this expectation alters the experience of the next line, the next, and then . . . no more. (Of course, in the initial reading, unless the page break graciously divides the penultimate from the ultimate lines, the eye often "cheats," and glancing below, approximates the ending.) But what was lost when one reread? What were the differences between reading a single poem once or twice? In a sense, one might say that Fate plays no part in rereading, for the future has been revealed. In a sense, too, any lyric poem rooted in the epiphanic has to endure the reader's foreknowledge of the poem's epiphany, in order to withstand the scrutiny of a rereading.

I turned around, slowly pivoted: the poems on the walls, if reread against one another, might unearth subtext and discourse, as I had hoped. Nonetheless, within the individual works, the loss of the New and the sacrifice of the epiphanic would necessarily change the reader's regard for the effects of the poem. Or, and this was a big Or, maybe the "effects of the poem" were exactly what I wanted to undermine, so that the poem's technical achievements wouldn't overwhelm all else. I picked up my notebook and reread: *rereading the novel made the text not a novel, given that the trappings of genre had been stripped away.* I looked up at my poems; the wind had begun to pick up again, the storm had arrived. Time to close the windows.

I ran barefoot from room to room, un-wedging wedges (a block of wood pulled from every sill), disremembering the previous hour.

Had it been an hour? I sat on the orange love seat, *whump,* picked up my notebook, and, slightly out of breath, began to read aloud: *On a hot and windy day in July of 1990, alone in a rented trailer in Dungannon, Ontario, I dumped fifty-three of my poems on an orange couch, stepped back, and stared at the mess.* Wait a minute . . . when had this been written? And when had it happened? All of a sudden, with the emphasis on the *sudden,* I realized what I was up against.

One effect of rereading is the collapse of time, in which an experience of Poem A underscores the next experience of Poem A, and the next, and so on. However, and most significantly, with each rereading—like a pile of overlays, the newest not quite aligned—we begin to create a multivalent text which contains all readings and rereadings.

Six

With the windows closed, the Baked Potato started to cook, despite the perceptible coolness of the incipient storm. On the kitchen wall, the mercury in the brass barometer began to fall. A high met a low; in a television studio somewhere, an isobar mapped the disappearance of cumulonimbi—just as the gray-white clouds to the east fled my window. Somewhere a weather forecaster was practicing backwards penmanship, a Dry Erase marker smudged between three fingers.

Standing in the midst of my poems, the notebook open to a blank page, the newly scrawled table of contents set atop an ugly varnished cedar stump, I was struck by the redundancy of my actions. Windows open. Windows shut. AC off, on, off. Reading, rereading. Copying a moment, revising a circumstance, renewing an emotion, revisiting the future. A poem forgotten, half-remembered, put away, reconstituted in tranquility. I picked up my copy of *The Norton Anthology of Poetry,* third edition.

Section seven of Keats's "Ode to a Nightingale" ends with the phrase "in faery lands forlorn"; section eight begins "Forlorn! the very word is like a bell / To toll me back from thee to my sole self!" (662). Mimesis proves a clarion: "my sole self," in the purity of its aloneness, is sounded. The internal rhyme of "toll" and "sole" resounds in its homonym, in the soul, where the singularity of existence echoes.

I tore the poem from the book, pages 660–62, then taped the pages on top of the first poem in my manuscript (on the east wall, upper left corner.) I stepped back. Of course! Keats was rereading Spenser.

I tore pages 110–34 from the *Norton,* then taped them across the wall, from Keats to the window, *The Faerie Queene:* Book 3, cantos 9 and 10, Book 5, canto 2, stanzas 29–50. I read aloud:

> His battred ballances in peeces lay,
> His timbered bones all broken rudely rumbled,
> So was the high aspyring with huge ruine humbled.
>   (134)

The fall, quite rightly, began to resonate—and the rhyme made me think of Pope.

There's a certain violence to Pope's handling of sin, particularly in relationships between people and the angels. I turned to "An Essay on Man":

> Let earth unbalanced from her orbit fly,
> Planets and suns run lawless through the sky,
> Let ruling angels from their spheres be hurled,
> Being on being wrecked, and world on world. (429)

In the *Norton,* a footnote provided a gloss on the word "spheres": "Of the Ptolemaic universe, the images of which were still available to poetry" (429). I took a pen, circled the footnote, and ripped pages 424–30 from the book. These I taped on the west wall of my trailer, just because.

What next? Auden's Icarus. I tore pages 1,100–01 from the book, taped them to the right of Pope, changed my mind, moved them to Pope's left. To be read before "An Essay on Man." I semi-chanted as I worked, a kind of poet's whistling: "About suffering they were never wrong, / the Old Masters. . . . About suffering they were never wrong, / the Old Masters. . . . About suffering they were never wrong, / the Old Masters . . ." (1,100).

Then Bishop's "The Fish," pages 1,136–37.

Then Wilbur's "The Death of a Toad," page 1,221.

Then Thomas Traherne's "Shadows in the Water," pages 379–80.

Then H. D.'s "Wine Bowl," pages 980–81.

Then Emily Dickinson's "I felt a Funeral, in my Brain," pages 806–07, and "The Soul selects her own Society—," pages 807–08. (I didn't want to include the poem anthologized between these two, "A Clock stopped—" [807], but I couldn't bring myself to cross it out.)

These six poems I taped between the Spenser and the Auden, all along the south wall of the trailer, atop my poems, until the room read Keats, Spenser, Bishop, Wilbur, Traherne, H. D., Dickinson, Dickinson, Auden, Pope.

A rereading room.

I filled in "Sir Patrick Spens" and Gwendolyn Brooks's "The Bean Eaters" after Spenser, Gascoigne's "Lullaby" between Wilbur and Traherne, "Lycidas" after Dickinson, "Dejection: An Ode," after Auden, "Diving into the Wreck" after Coleridge. (Two pages to go.) Then Robert Hass's "Meditation at Lagunitas" and Sylvia Plath's "Ariel" after Brooks. I was done.

Each of my poems was covered with another person's poem. In a sense I had turned my allusive textuality inside out, a historicized gloss obscuring the "original." I had also made quick work of the *Norton,* a volume which had never been quick.

But what had I done actually, in my pre-storm frenzy, aside from violating a book?

I think that in my inspired lunacy, something had finally clicked. (A trigger? Perhaps.)

No poem is ever better than its worst line, no book is ever better than its worst poem. The storm had arrived, and with it my hopes of making a text were washed away. Unless I was somehow capable of recombinant text design, *à la* Cortázar, my poems would always be reread within their historicized moment, allusive and contextualized, framed by formal and aesthetic ideas.

For every poem rereads itself and history. Each storm comments on the nature of rain.

To hell with it!, I said aloud, as the metal roof thundered, and water ribboned from a clogged gutter, pounding the daisies next to the front stoop, pounding the dandelions on the scorched lawn, equally.

And I opened a kitchen window.

Seven

I had once heard a physics professor comment on the chance of winning the *Reader's Digest* Sweepstakes as akin to, statistically, the chance of all the air suddenly leaving a 10' x 10' room. Something about atmospheric conditions and freak pressure systems. I had also read fairly recently—or has this been more recent? I'm not sure—of scientific research which had debunked the idea of the pure vacuum, in nature or otherwise. It wasn't supposed to happen.

What did happen was this: I think that I opened the window at the exact moment the fronts met, beneath the exact juncture of their meeting. A sudden, violent vacuum ensued; I felt as though I were in a wind tunnel—yes, the aerodynamics on the orange sofa need some work, yes, I'll see to it in the morning—as the air rushed by me. Poems flew from the walls. (Cheap tape.) And just as quickly, the kitchen curtains reversed their happy dance and rain poured into the trailer.

Or what happened was this: a rereading.

Or what happened was this: I threw out the rest of the *Norton,* amused myself briefly with the correspondences between my poems and the poems I had taped on my poems, shucked some corn, watched the Jays on the tube. The first game of a twilight double-header, Dave Stieb on the mound.

Or I sat down with my table of contents and reread my poems in order, in what constituted a manuscript.

Then I went to bed early, to reread *Man in the Holocene.*

Works Cited

Allison, Alexander W., et al., eds. *The Norton Anthology of Poetry.* 3rd ed. New York: Norton, 1983.

Frisch, Max. *Man in the Holocene.* Trans. Geoffrey Skelton. New York: Harcourt Brace Jovanovich, 1980.

Keats, John. *Complete Poems.* Cambridge: Belknap-Harvard UP, 1982.

Stevens, Wallace. *Letters of Wallace Stevens.* Ed. Holly Stevens. New York: Knopf, 1972.

17

Doing Time, or How to Reread on a Desert Island

Thomas Easterling

Growing up, I refused to see anything redeeming about my hometown. I climbed to the top bleachers of the high school football stadium and saw a cultural wasteland unfolding beneath me. To comfort myself, I prayed for escape. What if I could travel to a desert island? But then what would I bring to read? I tried to establish fair rules to the game. Tried to make it realistic: limit myself to five books, which was how many I could fit in my book bag and still have room for a change of clothes and dental floss. I was insufferable, not to mention wrong— what good is it to leave a cultural wasteland for a desert island? Nor was I the first unhappy adolescent to dream of recreating the world through a bizarre arithmetic of the imagination plus books. Yet the sum of the exercise, making list after list, was a healthy diversion. If I had copies of the list now, I could see the growth of my mind as surely as I can see the growth of my body notched vertically into the kitchen doorjamb.

Returning to the desert island scenario I set for myself years ago illustrates nicely the importance of books that lend themselves to multiple readings instead of books that take a long time to read once. And once rereading emerges as the criterion for evaluating books, questions about rereading itself become more relevant: At what point in rereading might a book offer diminishing returns for the time invested? Are certain genres better than others for rereading? Would rereading improve attentiveness to the text, or attest to changes endured by the island inmate? Can literature offer society enough, or must solitude result in solipsism? Answers to such questions suggest limits for using rereadability as an aesthetic criterion, and offer insight into the kinds of books I'd bring.

Since there have been frontiers, the prospect of being stranded has offered no shortage of fodder for the imagination, and therefore, for reading. Ulysses spent ten years returning to Ithaca. Shakespeare, before writing *The Tempest,* no doubt knew of George Somers's party being stuck in the Bermudas. In pre-Revolutionary North America, one of the earliest popular narratives was *Ashton's Memorial,* the story of Philip Ashton's strange and providential rescue first from a disreputable ship, then from being left ashore in Central America. At about the same time, Defoe's *Robinson Crusoe* was a hit on the other side of the Atlantic. But the desert isle itself is becoming increasingly difficult to imagine. In the most literal sense, there are fewer isolated geographic locales than there were for Homer or the Bard. The communications age has also made it hard to escape radio, television, the Internet, beepers, and brokers contacting us through our cellular phones. My island must be uninhabited because the prospect of turning it into a laboratory for rereading entices me. Otherwise the drama of rereading will give way to the dramas of living with others. Science fiction has its versions of the desert isle; contemporary psychologists are fond of the notion of "biosphere" experiments; *Gilligan's Island* still entertains. But the difference between these scenarios and the desert isle conundrum—as I see it, anyway—is that they involve human company. Ulysses has Calypso, Prospero has Miranda, and, though nobody has Ginger, it's not inconceivable that the Professor, or anyone else, will try.

Certain amenities must be granted: For instance, the isle must resemble paradise if I am to have any hope of surviving. Any number of the 520 known arboviruses might lurk in the insects of a tropical isle. Native waters could be teeming with giardia, hepatitis A, and dysentery. The catalogue of dangers is longer than a pockmarked arm even before I mention that, thanks to long years of comfortable suburban living, I cannot rely upon myself to craft habitable shelter, to find or grow edible crops, or to purify native water that might otherwise bring on dysentery or typhus. Unless I find perfect conditions, I'd need a library of instruction manuals in carpentry and field biology merely to live. I would prefer to resolve my desert island conundrums, what to read and how to reread it, through principle rather than necessity. Oh, and one thing more: I demand to be rescued after five or ten years. If the purpose of going to the desert isle is to learn about rereading, I'd like to be able to share my discoveries.

Those of us who indulge in the fantasy of creating a desert island library almost always do so with a romantic's faith in the beneficence of nature. *Rereading,* Matei Calinescu's aptly named book, contemplates at length the aesthetics of rereading for the first time since Roland Barthes published *The Pleasure of the Text* in 1973. When Calinescu reports André Gide's adolescent diversion of naming the twenty books he'd like to have on a desert isle, no mention is made of practical considerations. Rather than rereading to learn, Gide and most others reread for pleasure alone:

> It is obvious that the criterion of selection used in Gide's game is one of rereadability as distinct from, and even opposed to, mere readability. In an imaginary wilderness, with a theoretically inexhaustible supply of spare time but severely limited reading material (this being the main rule of the game), one would of course select rereadable books, reusable and all-purpose classics for all seasons. (*Rereading* 61)

No known "wilderness" offers an "inexhaustible supply of spare time." And if one did, we'd probably go mad without repetitive, form-giving work. Rereading should be one of many such tasks. If it's the sole activity, then we'd have to restructure radically our understanding of the relationship between time and existence. Accordingly, for my experiment in rereading to be useful, there's got to be trouble in paradise. There's got to be work, anyway, or what I learn from rereading will have no relevance to myself—or to anyone else, should I be rescued, or should future voyagers stumble across my scrawled thoughts. Even the most routine and mundane task, from making a bed to washing clothes, helps us structure time profitably. Milton thought so, too. He wasn't shy about having all the characters in *Paradise Lost* work. Adam and Eve "come forth to their daily labors"

in Book Five, and throughout, angels are "servants" of God. When
the stakes are high, the kind of work we do at least adds meaning
to life; it's conceivable that work would become the meaning of life.
Without learning to forage and farm, for example, existence on a desert
isle would be absurd, meaningless, and brief. Work also informs the
way we read literature. It's no accident that twentieth-century readers,
thanks to their experience in service economies, can appreciate Willy
Loman's frustrations with his job because they have some of their
own. Once our economies change, our literature does, too. So my
island can't be paradise, even though I need it to be close to that.

Merely reading all day and sleeping all night, though it sounds
heavenly at first and is not really all that different from what many editors and researchers do now, would deprive us of watershed moments:
first love, first child, first creation. I don't mean to sound hopelessly
vague about such firsts, but they are universal enough for all of us
to recall particulars: I can picture the first time I kissed a girl in a
car, the first time I got mad at a bully and did something about it, the
first time I saw my name in a byline. Such events help me to find my
literary heroes and villains. The former help me see myself as I'd like
to be, the latter draw my attention to traits I hate to find in myself or
in others. The limits of our experiences parallel the limits of the art
we love. It's why the agrarians were horrified by their vision of an
industrialized America. It's why we can read about making love, yet
must admit there is no substitute for the real thing. Reading shows us
the promised land, but cannot take us there.

It follows that each rereading gives us a different perspective of
the promised land. However, what we want promised shifts as well.
The eighteen-year-old who hates his hometown thinks he empathizes
with the protagonist of *The Stranger.* The same man at thirty has a
mortgage and misses his youth; he picks up *The Stranger* seeking
fire and finds flat melodrama. But what about the man on the desert
island? Without the mortgage or the car payment or any of the other
worldly tugs that would change him from reading to reading, will his
take on the text remain the same? On the indolent island imagined
by most people, because reading resources would be so limited and
rereading so constant, there would be no new materials that could
inform revisions of the text. Would even the finest books become

stale? Arguably, yes. Should the amount of time we have to read become "inexhaustible," there's no indication that our desire to read could possibly increase. The mathematical result is the attenuation of our longing for the text. Aesthetically, the result is a new, and no doubt insufficient, apprehension of technique: At some point our minds would completely leave the text in favor of the metatext, which we would compose mentally to compensate for the loss of appetite for the written word. Without realizing it, we would become writers instead of readers. My vision of Quentin Compson might be different from anyone else's right now, but it would be unrecognizably so after too much isolation.

About the only thing that could save us from watching our island friends, our books, pass away, would be applying ourselves to necessary tasks around the island. Like most good friends, ours would encourage us to do things we shouldn't: Should I weed my sweet potato patch, or finish this chapter—and the next and the next—of the book in my hands? Reading literature would become more decadent and more meaningful simultaneously. It's something that wouldn't be absolutely necessary for survival, yet it would immeasurably enrich life. There's no better way to measure the value of rereading than to see how it affects our lives away from the text. We put a good book down only when it becomes less compelling than the world around us.

At this point, devising a desert island library clearly amounts to picking your own poison. Chinua Achebe and arsenic? H. D. and hemlock? Wallace Stevens and strychnine? As I've noted, bringing only impractical "literary" works is a step on the short road to death. I cannot hope to survive the physical trials of solitude on an island without instructions. Thus, out of the five books I'll permit myself to bring, one will be some sort of survival manual and another will be a field guide. But my remaining choices are the ones that generate the most anxiety. I am certain to bring books I already love rather than risk the damnation of bringing highly recommended books I might dislike. But should I find representatives of three separate genres? Select the three books dearest to me? Should my books offer moral seriousness or should I tap into veins of humor for consolation?

Initially, I must distinguish between what I enjoy reading and what I enjoy rereading. From April until October, there's nothing I love more than reading weekly rags about baseball. It gratifies me to see how certain teams and players change throughout the season. But such a publication would clearly be a poor choice for a desert island library. Even contemporary accounts of the Braves 1995 World Series victory, or their more exciting 1991 defeat, would grow tiresome quickly. The same holds true for just about any periodical. We read them primarily to find out what's going on around us, not to inspire us. Once we consider ourselves informed, we throw the paper away and wait to find out what will happen tomorrow. Other genres and types of publications could also easily be jettisoned. Mysteries, propelled by plot more than anything else, would hold little entertainment value after the first read. Thrillers, too, would cease to thrill. Knowing the conclusions of such works can prompt me to wonder on subsequent readings when I should first have suspected, but not much more than that. Nor would there be much use in selecting books of world records, magazine annuals, screenplays, and sheet music. It's easier to say what I don't want than it is to give a title an affirmative nod. But as my ship nears my future home, I discern three values bobbing to the surface as measures of rereadability, and a book attached to each one.

First is the notion that books worth rereading seduce us into loving them. This principle has two parts: the romance of the text, which reveals itself in relationships between characters and sometimes between the writer and the characters; and the romance between us and the text, which can be physical, intellectual, and emotional. Roland Barthes, in *The Pleasure of the Text,* likens these two loves to an orgasm:

> Two edges are created: an obedient, conformist, pla-
> giarizing edge (the language is to be copied in its
> canonical state, as it has been established by school-
> ing, good usage, literature, culture), and *another edge,*
> mobile, blank (ready to assume any contours), which
> is never anything but the site of its effect: the place
> where the death of language is glimpsed. These two
> edges, *the compromise they bring about,* are necessary.
> Neither culture nor its destruction is erotic; it is the

> seam between them, the fault, the flaw, which becomes
> so. The pleasure of the text is like that untenable,
> impossible, purely *novelistic* instant so cherished by
> Sade's libertine when he manages to be hanged and
> then to cut the rope at the very moment of his orgasm,
> his bliss. (7)

Barthes's idea works, at least metaphorically and possibly literally.
It's tempting to think of the relationship between the text and me
in physical, pornographic terms. Years of solitude might transform
obscene pictures and words into the closest significant approximations
of human touch. Sailors have thought this for centuries. Whether
they were preparing themselves for eternity in Davy Jones's locker or
for a desert isle—or for shore leave—their penchant for pinup girls,
and now pinup boys, is legendary. My grandfather, a surgeon on a
troop ship in World War II, is to this day amazed by Marines' mental
capacity for base thoughts, and at their footlocker capacity for Bibles
and dirty books.

But pornography is not something I'd take with me to the island. At
first glance, it does not seem that porn would lend itself to rereading.
Such an assessment is wrong. Pornography touches a button in our
brains, not to mention our bodies, that permits us to return repeatedly
to our favorite fantasies. We giggle, but the velvet tips, monstrous
machines, and weapons of pleasure in *Fanny Hill* stay sexier than they
are ludicrous. Pornography has enough staying power to have inspired
combat from generations of moral purists. I do not align myself with
them, yet in the end I would not take a dirty book with me to the
desert island. I'm afraid I'd find myself vulgar for buying into the
"pleasure of the text" so literally. The romance I want for my desert
island library will appeal to heart and mind, not to mention my sense
of style. There are loads of runners-up: Duras's *The Lover,* Chopin's
The Awakening, Flaubert's *Madame Bovary.* But the winner, for what
it's worth, is *Anna Karenina.* I've read it twice already. Once I was in
the Yucatan, and I read it for hours a day while sitting in the shadow
of a seventeenth-century cathedral. I thought I was in love, and as
toothless Mayan women tried to sell me hammocks, or just plain beg,
my mind would flit back and forth from my girlfriend to the first time

Anna saw Vronsky. The second time I read it I was falling out of love, and it struck me as perfect that Vronsky breaks the back of his racing mare. What's important, ultimately, is that *Anna Karenina,* as well as my runners-up, conflate the romance of the text and the romance of the reader.

Another crucial function of rereading is the sense of ritual it imparts. I've mentioned that rereading alone provides an insufficient structure for life. But when rereading complements, rather than defines, our everyday lives, it offers soulful sustenance and rewards. Again from Barthes:

> Repetition itself creates bliss. There are many ethnographic examples: obsessive rhythms, incantatory music, litanies, rites, and Buddhist nembutsu, etc.: to repeat excessively is to enter into loss, into the zero of the signified. But: in order for repetition to be erotic, it must be formal, literal, and in our culture this flaunted (excessive) repetition reverts to eccentricity, thrust toward various marginal regions of music. The bastard form of mass culture is humiliated repetition. (41–42)

I don't doubt that I'm confusing the sense of ritual that comes from rereading anything with an appreciation of ritual itself. A cereal box would conceivably become the Bible on a desert island. Yet I'm allowing myself indulgences, so I'll choose the real thing—or something not far off. Barthes might find me shallow to cling to such old beliefs, but the book I've read more times than any other is the 1979 *Book of Common Prayer* for the Episcopal church. With my lack of knowledge of carpentry and medicine, divine intervention is a particular necessity for my survival. *The Book of Common Prayer* includes prayers for agriculture and for those who live alone, two of the most important bases to cover. It also features all of the Psalter, a respite from the prose that would otherwise dominate my reading on the island.

Solitude and rereading lead to introspection. No wonder books of moral seriousness, such as the Bible and *The Sound and the Fury* and *Paradise Lost,* are those reread most often. Defoe places spiritual books in Robinson Crusoe's care, including "three very good Bibles which came to me in my cargo from England, and which I had packed up among my things; some Portugueze prayer books also, and among them two or three popish prayer-books" (82). But Crusoe doesn't crack the good book open for the better part of his first year alone, from September through July. Keeping his journal is his only literary activity until then—he turns to it to ameliorate his despair. Writing has been glorified as the sport of the forlorn. Especially since Wordsworth's declaration that the poet is more sensitive than the ordinary person, we tend to see in every writer an extraordinary unhappiness. There's some truth to the stereotype, but what morbid bibliophiles overlook is that the pen opens an escape from suffering. Larry Brown, who has drawn critical acclaim and a wide audience for the novels *Dirty Work* and *Joe,* was a member of the Oxford, Mississippi, Fire Department for twenty years before he decided that he could make his living writing. As we learn from *On Fire,* a collection of essays and memoirs, he had to do something to live with the horror of the burned bodies he pulled from houses and cars. Other firemen turned to cable television for enough sex and violence to attenuate the force of the real thing. Brown began writing, a wholly different realm of imaginative satisfaction, if not, in his case, a prayer for life itself.

Accordingly, the last book I'll choose is yet unpublished: it is the journal I will keep during my time away. Of all the work that I must do on the island, writing is the most relevant to my reason for being there in the first place: to reread. Each rereading will create a new interpretation, which is the externalization of what I take in. Reviewing and contemplating differences between Tolstoy's creations and the ones he might inspire will require a written record. Books demand to be shared, to be written about. The joy of reading involves devouring the words on the page, but that's only half the story. For the joy to be complete, tangible, we must put it into writing, or at least try. This essay is proof. I'll also be able to make my own artifacts, testaments to the will required to shape life rather than living passively.

It's tempting to claim that spending several years with two literary works will confirm or repudiate their place in the canon. After all, there is no better measure for what belongs on our list of great works than some sort of calculation of how rereadable it is. But the canon is a slave to culture. It must change like everything else. A young man in the 1940s might select *Look Homeward, Angel* as part of his desert island library. Wolfe's best book finished second in Pulitzer balloting, and Wolfe's work was treated with high regard until Mark Schorer lambasted him in 1948 in "Technique as Discovery" for being too autobiographical, and too loose with narrative structure. Some notables, like Pat Conroy and Allen Gurganis, still list Wolfe as an influence. But the young man from the 1950s, rescued, say, in 1980, would find his favorite nearly forgotten. For better or worse, his world was lost the moment he left it. His rereading, unless it miraculously paralleled the changes in American society, would be an exercise in affection.

Thus, as a laboratory for rereading, the desert island initially functions as a sophisticated time capsule. It tells us what we want to have with us for posterity's sake. But the greater truth is that the conundrum forces us to inquire why we reread. It's for that reason I selected *Anna Karenina, The Book of Common Prayer,* and a journal—for romance, for ritual, and for reflection. They are the greatest comforts I draw from literature.

Works Cited

Barthes, Roland. *The Pleasure of the Text.* Trans. Richard Miller. New York: Farrar, Straus and Giroux, 1975.

Calinescu, Matei. *Rereading.* New Haven: Yale UP, 1993.

Defoe, Daniel. *The Life and Adventures of Robinson Crusoe.* New York: Penguin, 1965.

Index